in

Theory and Practice

Democratic Peace in Theory and Practice

EDITED BY
STEVEN W. HOOK

THE KENT STATE UNIVERSITY PRESS
KENT, OHIO

© 2010 by The Kent State University Press, Kent, Ohio 44242
ALL RIGHTS RESERVED
Library of Congress Catalog Card Number 2009047066
ISBN 978-1-60635-031-7
Manufactured in the United States of America

"Kant, Liberal Legacies, and Foreign Affairs," Parts 1 and 2 by Michael W. Doyle were originally published under the same title in the journal *Philosophy and Public Affairs*, V.12, 3 (pp. 205–235) and 4 (pp. 323–353), 1983. Copyright © 1983 Princeton University Press. Published by Blackwell Publishing. Reprinted with permission.

Library of Congress Cataloging-in-Publication Data
Democratic peace in theory and practice / edited by Steven W. Hook.
p.   cm. — (Symposia on democracy series.)
Includes bibliographical references and index.
ISBN 978-1-60635-031-7 (pbk. : alk. paper) ∞
1. Democracy. 2. Peace. 3. Democratizaion—Government policy—United States.
4. United States—Foreign relations—1989– 5. United States—Foreign relations—Philosophy.
I. Hook, Steven W., 1959–
JC423.D3813565 2010
303.6'6—dc22   2009047066

British Library Cataloging-in-Publication data are available.

14 13 12 11 10   5 4 3 2 1

Contents

Preface and Acknowledgments ... vii
Introduction: Democratic Peace Theory
    STEVEN W. HOOK AND TODD NELSON ... 1

PART ONE: DEMOCRATIC PEACE IN THEORY

1 Kant, Liberal Legacies, and Foreign Affairs
    MICHAEL W. DOYLE ... 17
2 Faulty Correlation, Foolish Consistency, Fatal Consequence
    JOHN MUELLER ... 45
3 The Common Origins of Democracy and Peace
    ERIK GARTZKE ... 61
4 Democracy, the State, and Global Capitalism
    DANIEL EGAN ... 79
5 Poverty and Democratic Consolidation in Sub-Saharan Africa
    ABDULAHI A. OSMAN ... 96

PART TWO: DEMOCRATIC PEACE IN PRACTICE

6 Kant, Liberal Legacies, and Foreign Affairs, Part 2
    MICHAEL W. DOYLE ... 115
7 Competing Values in U.S. Democratization Policy
    R. WILLIAM AYRES ... 142
8 The Forgotten Element of Democratization: Bringing the Citizen Back In
    ANDREA KATHRYN TALENTINO ... 160

9   Sanctioning for Democracy
       A. COOPER DRURY AND DURSUN PEKSEN   184
10 Washington in the Mideast: A Doctrine, a Dilemma, and
    Durable Despotism
       SEAN L. YOM   198
11 Promoting Democracy by Example
       LOCH K. JOHNSON   222
12 Democracy and Counterterrorism: Multiple Issues, Varied Effects
       PAUL R. PILLAR   243
13 Encouraging Democracy or Terrorism?
       BARBARA ANN J. RIEFFER-FLANAGAN   262

    References   277
    Contributors   301
    Index   303

Preface and Acknowledgments

The deadly violence that occurred at Kent State University in the spring of 1970 shocked a statewide, national, and global audience. At home, the shooting deaths of four students by members of the Ohio National Guard shattered the university community. Coming to grips with this traumatic episode, and its larger context in the social upheavals of the Vietnam War period, has been a challenge ever since for our faculty, students, and alumni. Honoring the victims' memory in a meaningful way—one that channels the lessons of the past toward greater understanding in the future—has become an ongoing mission of Kent State and the foundational inspiration of this book.

The calamity of May 4, 1970, brought the troubling divisions between American citizens and their government into stark relief. The escalating war in Vietnam, which coincided with heightened racial conflict in many urban areas, raised concerns that went far beyond the policies of the Nixon administration. The very nature of American democracy came into question during this period as many citizens felt excluded from the political process, unable to affect change in a government that seemed increasingly dominated by special interests and the "military-industrial complex." Overseas, the United States routinely violated its own democratic principles by supporting military dictatorships across Latin America, in the Middle East, and elsewhere around the world. Its conduct of the Vietnam War, whose victims included millions of civilians, frequently ran counter to the accepted principles of "just war."

Subsequent research on American politics and foreign policy reflected this disillusionment with the U.S. government, which was widely revealed to be neither democratic nor peaceful on a regular basis. Political scientists such as Theodore Lowi (1969) identified institutional barriers to popular sovereignty that threatened the end of liberalism in the United States. Revisionist historians chronicled the moral lapses in U.S. foreign policy previously neglected by mainstream scholars, and political economists highlighted the gaps in global development that left countries in the Southern Hemisphere dependent on the industrialized North. More recently, linguists and sociologists have called attention to the "constructed" nature of political life that renders traditional American values and cultural identities problematic.

These national self-doubts, which persisted long after the Vietnam War, led Kent State University in 2000 to initiate an annual Symposium on Democracy. Since then leading scholars have come to campus each year to share their knowledge on the relationship between democracy and religion, globalization, homeland security, the arts, and other topics. This volume comes out of the eighth annual symposium, held in May 2007 and entitled "Democracy and Peace: Historic Links and Implications for World Order."

As organizer of the conference, I believed the time had come to revisit the theory of democratic peace, which claims that governments that respect the political liberties of their citizens, while frequently warlike in their relations with repressive or authoritarian regimes, observe a "separate peace" with one another. This empirical link between democracy and peace is widely considered to be a virtual law of international relations, and the theory maintains a normative appeal for its emphasis on political reform and human rights. To take part in this venture, I sought out leading scholars from a wide range of theoretical and methodological traditions who were active in the discourse on democratic peace.

Taking stock of the theory seemed especially appropriate given the turbulence of the early twenty-first century. While the preventive U.S. invasion of Iraq in March 2003 did not violate the assumptions of democratic peace theory, since the target was a repressive state, the actions taken by the United States revived many of the questions raised in the backlash against the Vietnam War. Was this a war of necessity or choice? What national interests were at stake that compelled U.S. military intervention, and how compelling was the evidence used to justify the use of force? How honest were the nation's leaders as they sought public support for the war, and how open were they to contrary evidence and dissenting views? Finally, how has the conduct of this war, which continues today, along with the conflict in Afghanistan, reflected the moral principles that justified U.S. military intervention?

The authors of the chapters in this volume consider these and other questions in probing the many facets of democratic peace theory. The book is divided into two sections. The first explores the underlying logic and validity of the theory. The second section examines the ways in which governments, particularly the United States during President George W. Bush's "global war on terror," have explicitly or implicitly relied on the theory to justify the promotion of democracy overseas by a variety of measures, including the use of military force.

A point of departure for our symposium, and for this book, is the two-part study authored by Michael Doyle in 1983 that reignited scholarly research and debate about the theory and practice of democratic peace. Both parts of the study, organized along the same lines as this project, are reprinted verbatim at the opening of each section of this book. Readers are urged to use Doyle's seminal analysis as a guide to the current chapters that assess our subsequent understanding of the theory. The authors were chosen for their diversity of personal backgrounds, research methods, and theoretical perspectives, creating for the symposium and the book a microcosm of the democratic peace research community.

It has often been noted that democratic governments, while maintaining peaceful relations with one another, are not only war-prone toward repressive governments but are often poorly equipped to prepare for and fight wars. As Quincy Wright, whose *Study of War* (1942: 842) informed a generation of security studies, observed, "Democracies normally require that important decisions be made only after wide participation of the public and deliberate procedures which assure respect for the law and freedom of criticism before and after the decision is made. They are, therefore, ill adapted to the successful use of threats and violence as instruments of foreign policy. . . . Consequently, in the game of power diplomacy, democracies pitted against autocracies are at a disadvantage."

Wright's observation is vital to our inquiry into the democratic peace, as it calls attention to domestic factors that influence the war policies of states, whose strategies have grown more complex as civil wars have become more common than cross-national conflicts and as nonstate actors, such as ethnic groups and terrorist organizations, have become actively engaged in militarized conflicts. The calculations of foreign policymakers have been further complicated by changing norms in world politics regarding national sovereignty, human rights, and the utility of global governance in filling gaps in the "anarchic" interstate system. As the scope of the democratic peace has steadily widened since World War II along with the growing number of liberal states, the war policies of these states are increasingly driven by transnational concerns that are vaguely linked to "national interests." Still, the impediments to sound decision making in liberal states persist, making the coercive application of democratic peace theory especially difficult.

The authors in this volume share a common concern for a greater understanding of this critical phenomenon in world politics. Their chapters challenge many of the theory's underlying assumptions while generally accepting the historic association of democracy and peace. In some chapters other factors such as economic openness and globalization are considered, alongside regime type, as agents of interstate cooperation. Many of the chapters are critical of the foreign policies of the United States, whose unipolar stature in the post–cold war balance of power has provided its leaders with unprecedented leverage in foreign policy. In keeping with the spirit of the Kent State Symposium on Democracy, however, the authors' main goal is to identify lessons from this past experience that can guide scholars, policymakers, and others toward a more democratic and peaceful future.

This project would not have been possible without the commitment of resources by Kent State University. President Carol Cartwright consistently supported the annual symposium, and her successor, Lester Lefton, honored this commitment by hosting the eighth annual event in May of 2007. His assistant, Charlene Reed, ensured that the symposium, which drew a record audience and featured a keynote by political activist Tom Hayden, lived up to its promise.

Since then the editors of the Kent State University Press have carefully, and patiently, shepherded the manuscript through a rigorous external review process and subsequent refinement of the chapters. I am grateful to the Press's director, Will Underwood, and to his team of editors, including Joyce Harrison, Mary D. Young, and Joanna Hildebrand Craig. I also received invaluable assistance from doctoral students Todd Nelson and Frank Lebo. None of their efforts, however, could have produced a volume of this quality without the commitment and passion of our authors, whose collective expertise on the democratic peace is clearly reflected in their chapters.

Introduction
Democratic Peace Theory
Roots and Branches

Steven W. Hook and Todd Nelson

The global scope of democratic governance has reached unprecedented levels. More than three million people live in "free" countries—nearly one-half of the world's population, and more than twice the number recorded just two decades ago (Freedom House 2009).

This trend toward democratic rule is hardly universal and is by no means guaranteed to persist. Most countries in the Middle East maintain repressive control, a fact Freedom House, a prominent research organization devoted to human rights, attributed to the numerous military regimes in the region and to the hold on power retained by monarchs with little interest in sharing their immense power and wealth. Elsewhere, democratic transitions have stalled or are moribund. Russia's Vladimir Putin maintained his sweeping powers as prime minister even after elections in 2008 brought Dmitry Medvedev to the presidency. China's government, despite its burgeoning economy, continues to suppress political rights for fear their exercise would spark challenges to the Chinese Communist Party's longstanding monopoly on power.[1] Even the United States, the world's most powerful state and a forceful advocate of democratic reform, remains widely distrusted overseas as the result of abuses of prisoners and attacks on civilians during the Bush administration's "global war on terror."

The most brutal suppression of political rights and civil liberties continues to occur in developing countries. Sudan's Arab government persists in a campaign of genocide against black Africans in the Darfur region; Somalia remains a failed state incapable of keeping order, let alone protecting human rights; and military dictators in the Central African Republic, Libya, Myanmar, North Korea, and Turkmenistan continue to crush political dissidents and reform movements on a daily basis. Afghanistan, the first target of President George W. Bush's 9/11 counteroffensive, succumbed in 2008 to rampant lawlessness and government corruption.

The uncertainties surrounding these regimes raise ongoing questions about the relationship between democratic governance and world peace. According to democratic peace theory, governments that uphold political freedoms and empower their civil societies are more likely to cooperate with one another politically and to establish more productive trade relations. While these democracies are not so peacefully inclined toward authoritarian regimes, a fact clearly reflected in U.S. diplomatic history, "the idea that democracies almost never go to war with each other is now commonplace. The skeptics are in retreat and the proposition has acquired nearly law-like status" (Levy 1994, 452).

The prospect of a stable order among the rapidly growing majority of liberal democracies, therefore, makes the question of democratic peace vital to world politics. This volume builds on a generation of rigorous scholarship on the theory and practice of democratic peace. A diverse range of scholars confronts the theory from several perspectives and offers new insights for students and practitioners of foreign policy. Their essays focus on the intrinsic validity as well as practical applications of the theory in foreign policies, with particular emphasis on the United States. While their findings do not put to rest the chronic ambiguities and contradictory policy implications of the theory, the authors hope to advance the dialogue in light of the turbulent international developments since the dawn of the twenty-first century.

FOUNDATIONS OF THE THEORY

The theory of democratic peace as known today originated in the Enlightenment era and thus is hardly a newcomer to scholarly debates. Even so, greater attention has been paid to the theory as the pace of political reform has accelerated during the past several decades. Sociologist Dean Babst (1964) was among the first scholars to apply the theory to the post–World War II international system. Soon afterward quantitative analysts in political science (e.g., Small & Singer 1976) exposed the theory to empirical scrutiny, with mixed results. Michael Doyle's (1983a, 1983b) two-part essay on democratic peace, reprinted in this volume, fully revived the theory during the waning years of the cold war.

Doyle revisited the three "definitive articles" of Immanuel Kant's theory of democratic peace—constitutional, international, and cosmopolitan laws—and placed them in contemporary perspective in the forms of republican representation, normative commitment to fundamental human rights, and transnational interdependence, respectively (see also Doyle 2005, 1986). He thus adopted Kant's causal claim and his tripartite division of causal variables, though in modified terms.[2] Influential research by Bruce Russett (1993, 1990) solidified the theory's credibility, and subsequent work by Russett and Oneal (2001, 9) produced a familiar empirical claim: "the chance that any two countries will get into a serious military dispute can be estimated if one knows what kinds of governments they have, how economically interdependent they are, and how well connected they are by a web of international organizations."

In his pioneering treatise *Perpetual Peace,* Kant (1932) asserted that liberal states must be democratic since the right of citizens to voice their opinions is the fundamental mechanism by which a resort to military conflict may be avoided. The collective will of a democratic republic would rally against war. In such a system, the constitutional deference to the wishes of the citizenry should thus restrain any war-making impulses that might otherwise sway the executive or other representatives of the people. As Kant (1932, 13, 14) argued:

> To decree war would be, to the citizens, to decree against themselves all the calamities of war, such as fighting in person, furnishing from their own means toward the experience of war; painfully to repair the devastations it occasions; and, to fill up the measure of evils, load upon themselves the weight of a national debt, that would embitter even peace itself, and which, on account of constant new wars, can never be liquidated. They will certainly beware of plunging into an enterprise so hazardous.

The second and third of Kant's definitive articles relate more broadly to a transnational order in which liberal values are embraced and would presumably lead to the natural aggregation of liberal states into what Kant called a "pacific federation." From this foundation, liberal republics would follow an unwritten international law that would bind them together, not only normatively but also instrumentally, through political institutions. While Kant was cautious regarding the universality of his model, contemporary theorists have identified an emerging "constitutional" world order (Ikenberry 2001), amenable to great and weak powers alike, that is today highly regulated through an ad hoc system of global governance.

The international system has changed in significant ways since Doyle shed new light on democratic peace theory. Liberal reforms swept across Eastern Europe in 1989, transforming the geopolitical landscape along with the strategic underpinnings of U.S. foreign policy. No longer was realism the sole lens through which policy objectives were to be viewed; President George H. W. Bush's proclaimed "new world order" would be characterized by a stronger United Nations, the acceleration of world trade, and the consolidation of political reforms in the former Communist bloc as well as by authoritarian regimes that were previously sustained by strategic ties to the United States. The prospect of a constitutional world order challenged realist assumptions regarding the "anarchic" interstate system that had been dominant throughout the cold war years. While realists continued to emphasize state action as based on the imperatives of national interests and self-help, liberals recognized the heightened regulation of global affairs through a widening array of international institutions and agreements.

Doyle's study inspired a wave of research after the cold war that reinforced the theory while adding meaningful caveats and conditional variants (see, e.g., Starr 1997; Chan 1997; Ray 1996; Levy 1994; Owen 1994; and Dixon 1993). Mansfield and Snyder (1995), for example, found that "mature" democracies indeed maintain a separate peace with their peers, but new or "transitional" democracies are likely to be even more warlike. More recently, Lektzian and Souva (2009) identified open flows of information as a crucial factor in restraining militarism, and Leeson and Dean (2009) revealed a "democratic domino effect" among neighboring countries. Henderson (2008) challenged the model's universality by demonstrating that "politically open" African countries have experienced *more* rather than less political violence toward like-minded regimes.

Not surprisingly, the theory gained traction as a rationale for proactive democratization, particularly in the United States. Indeed, as Owen (2005, 122) observed, few presidents prior to George W. Bush had "tied their foreign policies more explicitly to the work of social science." Security concerns returned to the forefront of U.S. foreign policy after the 9/11 terrorist attacks and the onset of Bush's war on terror. At the same time, the attacks provided new impetus for coercive democratization, as in the cases of regime change in Afghanistan and Iraq. The administration's "National Security Strategy" (White House 2002) embraced U.S. primacy as the linchpin of a unipolar balance of power that "favors human freedom" and identified democracy as a "single sustainable model" of government with universal application to all rational states and societies. The document's assertion of preemptive war as an acceptable means to counter threats from "rogue" states raised familiar fears of "democratic imperialism" underscored by Doyle (1983b) and other theorists.

TWO SCHOLARLY DEBATES: THEORY AND PRACTICE

As the previous discussion suggests, widespread consensus regarding the tendency of liberal governments to engage peacefully with one another has not precluded scholarly debates about the phenomenon. These debates fall into two general categories: the theoretical validity of the claim, including its empirical veracity (Doyle 1983a); and the applications to which the theory may be applied in foreign policies (Doyle 1983b), particularly those of the United States. As we will find, the theory's most basic concepts—including *democracy* and *peace*—are open to widely varying definitions and interpretations; and the theory's causal claims, which posit mirroring liberal regime type as the primary independent variable, are also open to question. Similarly, theorists (and policymakers) are hardly of one mind regarding the ends to which the leaders of democratic states have applied the theory to their foreign and security policies. Given the empirical hold of the theory, do these leaders have a moral obligation to promote democratic transitions elsewhere, coercively or otherwise, for the sake of a peaceful world? Such a position, espoused by the utilitarian theorist John Stuart Mill in the nineteenth century, runs firmly against Kant's deontological view that state efforts to "change" history, however well intentioned, must be avoided. These concurrent debates, highlighted in each of the Doyle essays, comprise the structure of this volume.

THEORETICAL VALIDITY

The first area of scholarly debate concerns the validity and empirical veracity of the theory. Much of this debate is semantic in nature. On the one hand, how does one define *democracy* or, for that matter, *peace*? Is democracy defined by constitutional rights, by institutional designs, or by the recurrent holding of free elections? On the other hand, what is the defining characteristic of *war*—a formal declaration, the number of casualties, or something else altogether? Such unanswered questions have resulted in the absence of a universal standard for assessing these concepts.

Ongoing conceptual and even semantic debates abound in the scholarly literature (see e.g., Rosato 2003; Elman 1997; Maoz 1997), making it unlikely that a consensus will emerge anytime soon. Indeed, there are seemingly as many definitions of the key terms related to the theory as there are scholars trying to understand it. Waltz (2002, 34), for example, observes that democracy is in the eyes of the beholder, noting that "a liberal democracy at war with another country is unlikely to call it a liberal democracy." Similarly, Oren (1996, 270) bases his argument against the democratic peace theory on the assertion that *perceptions* of democracy are just as important as objective measures. He notes that research on the democratic peace has repeatedly used definitions of *democracy* that are uniquely "American" in nature and that even these subjective definitions have changed over time. Critics such as Layne (1994, 40) have charged that "it is only intellectual suppleness—the continual tinkering with definitions and categories—that allows democratic peace theorists to deny that democratic states have fought each other." Similarly, Spiro (1994, 55) claims that liberal proponents of the democratic peace "ignore their own arguments, and [they] selectively adopt definitions of key variables so that data analysis yields the results they seek."

These questions of validity are at the heart of the empirical debate. Even the theory's prominent advocate, Bruce Russett (1993, 15), acknowledges in his study of ancient Greece that "democracy did not mean quite the same thing to [them] as it does to people of the late twentieth century." The often restrictive definitions of *democracy* that scholars have used to justify the exclusion of such conflicts as the War of 1812 have led to lively debate between proponents and critics of the theory (see Russett et al., 1995). In this conflict, neither Great Britain nor the United States at the time was viewed as a fully formed democracy. Layne (1994) asserts that in World War I Germany was as democratic as France and Britain, although none of them fell under the definition of a liberal republic offered by Doyle.[3] In a detailed study of the German case, Oren (1996, 270) points out the subjective nature of the theory's core concepts and observes how perceptions of Wilhelmine Germany have changed over time, noting that "the 're-coding' of Imperial Germany cannot be attributed to the discovery of new facts regarding the nature of the political system.... The disagreement between the current coders and their predecessors is rather about the *selection* of the facts."[4]

With regard to the second piece of this semantic puzzle—What is *war?*—Finland's stance vis-à-vis the Allied powers during World War II is a contentious case. Seeking to avoid annexation by the Soviet Union, and having fought a war with the Soviets to avoid exactly that, Finland allied itself with Nazi Germany and the Axis powers (Elman 1997). Thus, democratic Finland was technically at war with a handful of liberal states from 1941 to 1944 (Spiro 1994). Again, the semantics of *democracy* and *peace* became central to resolving an apparent contradiction. Ray (1993), for example, called attention to the absence of any direct military conflict between these countries. Russett (1993, 12) noted that because the conflict did not produce more than 1,000 combat deaths (commonly used by scholars in defining warfare), the case fit with his definition of war as "large-scale, institutionally organized lethal violence" and thus could not be applied to the theory. (For other perspectives on this debate, see Doyle 1995.)

Recent constructivist studies raise additional questions. Fiala (2009, 80), for example, identified a history of "mythological idealism" that privileges such terms as "civilization" and "modernity," leading to a dubious claim that "war is a just and noble endeavor that creates progressive historical change." Ish-Shalom (2008), meanwhile, found that the "rhetorical capital" of Israeli leaders provided them cover for policies that precluded a two-state solution with the Palestinian Authority in 2002. Both scholars emphasized the discursive roots of policy behavior that extended beyond political leaders to more general sets of embedded relations among social actors.

Still other scholars have focused on nonmilitarized but coercive state actions that bear on democratic peace theory's validity, such as covert operations by intelligence services undertaken to destabilize undesirable democratic regimes. The U.S. Central Intelligence Agency's involvement in Chile in the early 1970s is a widely cited example of this phenomenon (see Rosato 2003; Waltz 2002). Russett (1993, 121) justifies excluding these cases on the grounds that the countries where these operations took place, including Iran (1953) and Guatemala (1954), were not "fully democratic." Once again, such interventions rarely reached the common threshold of interstate war and were commonly dismissed as a result. Layne (1994), taking another tack, asserts that "near misses"—narrowly averted wars between democracies—should be explained by the democratic peace theory if the theory is indeed valid, because the features of liberal democracies that allow them to avert war with one another should not have allowed even these near-misses to occur. It is easy to see that there is no shortage of cases to which the label of "exception" to the democratic peace may be applied.

To some critics, there arguably have been instances of warfare among democracies that, if true, would rebut the theory's central empirical claim and related causal inferences. The previously mentioned findings of Mansfield and Snyder (1995) on "transitional" democracies, and of Henderson (2008) on African states raise such doubts. Also in recent scholarship, Hellmann and Herborth (2008) identified several low-level militarized disputes between electoral democracies involving fishing rights. Others advanced statistical support for the linkage between democracy and peace but find the causal arrows pointing from the latter to the former, or in both directions at once (see Green, Kim, & Yoon 2001; Beck, Katz, & Tucker 1998).

These contrary findings are also evident in studies that have found statistical linkages to factors other than regime type, including the balance of power, nuclear deterrence, and bilateral trade ties. A common claim in this debate involves levels of economic development, which some studies have linked more closely to dyadic peace than regime type (see Mousseau, Hegre, & Oneal 2003). Similarly, Mousseau (2009) found that "contract-intensive" economies, whose material interests depend on transparent and highly regulated commercial exchanges, have a shared interest in stable intergovernmental relations. Economic development, in this view, may serve as a mediating or "conditioning" variable. The shift in the global balance of power after the collapse of the Soviet Union is another such variable. Further refining the theory's boundary conditions, Choi and James (2008) found that such societal factors as civil-military structures and political communications strengthened the link between democracy and peace. (See also Ferejohn & Rosenbluth 2008 for another recent analysis of societal factors.[5])

These attempts to modify the theory raised a variety of methodological issues. Among the unsettled questions is how far back one should begin examining the validity of democratic peace. Doyle (1983a) began his analysis at the beginning of the nineteenth century, insisting that no liberal states went to war with one another from 1816 on. Other studies have gone further back in the historical record, although the lack of cross-national data from those periods renders validity claims suspect. Nonetheless, all of the debates noted above have failed to undermine the central theoretical argument regarding the separate peace that exists among liberal states.

Applications of the Theory

The second set of critiques involves the potential policy implications of democratic peace theory. Doyle (1983b) warned of the temptation to impose liberal political systems on countries, especially by intervention or other forceful means. While this is a critique of the *applications* of the theory, rather than of its validity, recent developments in world politics, particularly the U.S.-led ventures in regime change in Afghanistan and Iraq, make these questions highly relevant. As noted above, theorists of democratic peace are generally skeptical of the "liberal imperialism" that stems from such aspirations (Doyle 1983b). To Russett (2005, 405), "As a general principle, democratization by force is full of practical and moral dangers, depending on many highly unpredictable contingencies, and not to be undertaken as the purpose in a war of choice." Neorealists (e.g., Waltz 2002, 37) have shared liberal apprehensions that coercive democratization "will be taken up by the American military with some enthusiasm."

American foreign policy has always been viewed as "exceptional" given its presumed basis in moral as well as strategic imperatives. Early diplomatic statements, including George Washington's farewell address and the Monroe Doctrine, drew a connection between autocratic regimes, militarism, and expansionist foreign policy behavior. Yet the United States often brutally pursued its own rapid course of continental expansion, a policy explainable by realists despite its explicit and implicit justifications regarding America's "manifest destiny." As the United States emerged as a global power after World War I, Woodrow Wilson sought to capture the moral high ground by framing the war as one fought to make the world "safe for democracy" and by designing a system of collective security that would prevent further wars of this scale.[6]

Franklin Roosevelt similarly emphasized "four freedoms" that he expected to prevail after World War II, although both the structure of the newly created United Nations and the conduct of U.S. foreign policy during the cold war fulfilled realist more often than liberal expectations.[7] The U.S. occupations of Germany and Japan after World War II are still regarded as the most successful state-building enterprises to date. The United States built new governments in these countries virtually from scratch, writing constitutions that separated powers, produced independent judiciaries, and protected the freedoms of speech, press, and religion. Foreign aid funds were then used for the construction of government buildings and the training of civil servants, military and police officers, journalists, and trade unionists. The German and Japanese efforts became models for subsequent state-building missions, although none would compare in scope until after the cold war.

The collapse of the Soviet Union completed the transition of the global balance of power from bipolar to hegemonic, with the United States enjoying the status of the "lone superpower." It was thus during the Clinton administration that the democratic peace theory began to be actively cited as justification for U.S. military interventions. Domestic politics, however, restrained Clinton's national security strategy of "engagement and enlargement," as a Republican majority in Congress began a unilateral turn in U.S. foreign policy that continued into the new millennium. The retreat of the United States from multilateral cooperation and global governance had already rendered the United States a "rogue nation" overseas by the time George W. Bush came to power in 2001 (Prestowitz 2003).

Bush initially espoused a "modest" foreign policy based on realist principles, but he abandoned this model in the aftermath of the al-Qaeda terrorist attacks. As foreign policy advisers, Bush's team of neoconservatives, or "Vulcans," sought a return to Ronald Reagan's vision of benevolent U.S. hegemony (see Mann 2004). These advisers quickly used the attacks to justify a "muscular" security policy that became known as the Bush Doctrine. The invasion of Iraq in 2003 was the most obvious example of the promotion of democracy by force based on the belief that increasing the number of democracies (especially in the Islamic states of North Africa and the Middle East) would lead to greater security for the region and Western democracies. Bush, however, had previously subordinated this goal to the primary casus belli of Saddam Hussein's purported weapons of mass destruction (WMD), and the United States also lacked the legitimacy it would have gained from an endorsement of the Iraq campaign of regime change by the UN Security Council.

The credibility of the United States in Iraq was further damaged by the unanticipated rise of insurgent and sectarian violence, by the Abu Ghraib prisoner abuse scandal in 2004, and by subsequent revelations of mistreatment of prisoners at the U.S. detention center at Guantanamo Bay, Cuba. Bush's denial of habeas corpus rights to war prisoners, along with his administration's rendition of other suspected terrorists to secret prisons overseas, fueled charges of U.S. hypocrisy as a champion of the rule of law. The White House also came under attack for mismanaging the war effort against Iraq (see Ricks 2006; Woodward 2006). Critics also identified U.S. double standards in its cooperation with "strategically vital" autocracies such as Egypt, Pakistan, and Saudi Arabia and in its close economic relations with the one-party People's Republic of China. With Iraq unable to resolve its internal conflicts among Kurds and Sunni and Shia Muslims, and with Afghanistan under siege by Taliban and al-Qaeda insurgents, Bush left office early in 2009 with his agenda for democratic peace in tatters.

American leaders, therefore, seem driven to impose "democracy by force" (von Hippel 2000). The longevity of the United States's own democratic system, however strained by internal contradictions and double standards, provides a powerful basis and temptation for the "export" of its system. In this respect, Afghanistan and Iraq were only the latest in a long-term and ongoing project of state building (see Fukuyama 2004b). President Barack Obama pledged to renew U.S. prestige in the international community by restoring engagement as a diplomatic priority. Beyond this shift, Obama did not renounce the imperative of the United States to serve as a catalyst for democratic transitions across the world.

In this context, it should be recalled that the United States traditionally maintains a conception of human rights that differs from that adopted by most other countries. To the U.S. government, human rights apply primarily to political and civil rights. Of primary concern in the United States is that government power must be tightly constrained for individuals to enjoy the "inalienable" freedoms of "life, liberty, and the pursuit of happiness." The more widely accepted view of human rights is broader, encompassing economic, social, and cultural rights as well as political freedoms. From this perspective, citizens cannot be truly free if many of them suffer from deep economic inequalities and the societal disadvantages that stem from gaps in material welfare and disparate treatment based on cultural identity.

While the U.S. conception of human rights focuses on liberty, that favored by most other governments emphasizes equality as well as liberty. This more inclusive perspective was written into the Universal Declaration of Human Rights adopted by UN members in 1948. Distancing itself from the language of the UN declaration during the cold war, the United States seized on communism, in both its Soviet and Chinese forms, as a primary threat to human rights. Communist leaders claimed that their system better protected their citizens' human rights by ensuring them jobs, housing, education, and medical care, if not the political freedoms of utmost value to Americans. Most European governments, as well as developing countries, adopted the broader conception of human rights, leaving the United States virtually alone in the UN General Assembly.

Even though the collapse of Soviet Communism represented a moral as well as a geopolitical victory for the United States, the nation remains vastly outnumbered by foreign countries that oppose its narrow conception of human rights. If anything, the focus on socioeconomic equality is strengthening as globalization pressures spark new tensions between the world's rich and poor. Bush, remaining true to the traditional stance of the United States, replaced "human rights" in his speeches with "human dignity," a term that emphasized individual freedoms *from* state interference rather than an obligation *by* the state to provide for the material welfare of its citizens. This fundamental difference, left unaddressed in Obama's first year in office, continues to cloud U.S. efforts to promote democratic reforms, especially at a time when "soft authoritarian" regimes in China and other areas have maintained public support by improving living standards in the absence of democratic freedoms.

OUTLINE OF THE BOOK

All these controversies regarding the theory and practice of democratic peace suggest that further reflection is in order. This volume responds to this need, which is perhaps more urgent than ever given the extent to which the presumed linkage between democracy and peace remains central to the foreign policy of the world's predominant power, the United States.

To John Mueller, democracy itself is widely misunderstood as a "superior gimmick" that aggregates societal preferences. Inflated conceptions of democracy, including a sense that it also *creates* public preferences, are reflected in the enthusiasm expressed by advocates of the democratic peace theory. War aversion, he argues, represents a historical trend that emerged long after the first wave of democratization and has a discernible life of its own. "In this view," Mueller argues, "the rise of democracy not only is associated with the rise of war aversion but also with the decline of slavery, religion, and capital punishment and with the growing acceptance of capitalism, scientific methodology, women's rights, environmentalism, abortion, and rock music."

The next two chapters of the volume further question the causal relationship between democracy and peace. Erik Gartzke suggests that each may be a product of common underlying forces, primarily economic development. Modern modes of production, which provide for greater material welfare and societal stability, "change the interests of developed countries so that they prefer commerce to conquest." Daniel Egan adopts a neo-Marxist critique in rejecting "capitalist globalization that maximizes market liberalization at the expense of democracy." In Egan's view, there can be no democratic peace when the parties involved have abandoned economic equality as a fundamental tenet of democracy.

This ambiguity regarding the nature of democracy is a central concern to Obdulahi Osman, who recounts the disappointing "second wave" of democratization in sub-Saharan Africa during the 1990s. In many countries, he notes, African citizens remain plagued by poverty, disease, and political violence. While troubling, he argues that the halting pace of democratic transitions reflects Western conceptions of democracy that are not readily applicable to the African context. "Democratic regimes," he suggests, "neither exist uniformly nor function effectively in all cases."

Part Two confronts the question of democratic peace "in practice," or the ways in which governments, particularly that of the United States, have attempted to promote democracy in other countries in part to enhance the prospects for peaceful relations. The authors in this section approach this question from a variety of perspectives, often critical, and reinforce the warnings of Michael Doyle and other democratic peace theorists regarding the limitations of "exporting democracy" by force.

The first of these critiques, by R. William Ayres, examines democracy promotion as a central objective of U.S. foreign policy throughout its history. Ayres explores the distinctive values underlying American democracy as articulated by the nation's early leaders. In particular, he identifies individual liberty as a central element of the U.S. political system, and he questions whether the protection of liberty at home is compatible with a foreign policy of democracy promotion. To Ayres, the United States is internally conflicted over the meaning of its own system of government and the coercive promotion of democracy, which may at once advance and contradict the nation's domestic political values.

While in this book and in public discourse the United States is most often the target of criticism regarding the "export" of democracy, one must recall that the international community as a whole, including states and nongovernmental organizations, is actively engaged in democratic state building. The process by which these reforms are elicited is addressed by Andrea Talentino, who argues that citizens in reforming states, the presumed beneficiaries of democratic transitions, are often excluded from the process. The top-down nature of democratization, with its mechanical emphasis on legal and institutional restructuring, is regrettable. The process, she believes, must be more broadly construed as *nation building,* or the winning of the peoples' "hearts and minds." When citizens are empowered in the reform process, she finds, they are more likely to respect democratic norms in the future, including not just an aversion to military conflict with other democracies but a greater concern for human rights at home. Similarly, A. Cooper Drury and Dursun Peksen are skeptical of the use of economic sanctions as a tool of reform and demonstrate that the objects of such coercion are more likely to become less rather than more democratic throughout the course of the externally imposed sanctions.

The discussion then returns to the U.S. government's recent efforts to promote democracy through coercive means, including regime change. Loch Johnson shares Ayres's concern that the United States has pursued this policy at the cost of its own democratic principles and practices at home. Recent intelligence scandals, together with the widening scope of domestic surveillance, are reminiscent of the government's conduct of the Vietnam War, argues Johnson, who served on the Church Committee that investigated these practices more than three decades ago. Sean Yom explores a "devastating self-contradiction" in U.S. democracy promotion efforts in the Middle East, where he believes successful electoral reforms "would likely bring into power Islamist groups that evoke fierce hostility toward Washington's vital strategic interests." Indeed, Yom concludes from his examination of the Jordanian case that U.S. officials recognize this contradiction and often place security self-interests above the pursuit of democracy despite the latter's emphasis in government rhetoric.

Paul Pillar echoes this critique, highlighting the "tacit bargains" struck by Washington and oil-exporting states in the Middle East. To preserve access to oil supplies, an explicit U.S. strategic interest for half a century, the U.S. government has pledged to their suppliers to avoid "interference in, or even criticism of, their backward and authoritarian internal structures." And while stepped-up domestic security measures have compromised U.S. democratic values, history demonstrates that the repression of domestic freedoms neither produces enhanced security nor reduces the threat of terrorism in the long term. Pillar concurs with Talentino that democracies not only avoid militarized conflicts with one another; they have beneficial effects on the "temperament and habits of the ruled themselves."

In the concluding chapter, Barbara Ann J. Rieffer-Flanagan also argues that democracies embrace "norms of toleration and respect for their fellow citizens" that have spillover effects on interstate relations. Her finding leads her to explore the prospects for democracy promotion as a means to moderate the behavior of terrorist groups. In a comparative study of these groups, Rieffer-Flanagan concludes that these prospects are closely linked to the groups' objectives. Whereas groups seeking political rights themselves or that are pursuing territorial concessions may be amenable to reform pressures, those determined to wage religious wars or to secure regional dominance have little to gain from democratic reforms.

This insight, like those of the other authors in this volume, suggests lessons for policy practitioners as well as scholars. We hope our collective effort provides pathways for understanding the "global war on terror," which will certainly be a central element of world politics long into the future. Readers will form their own opinions about the validity, policy implications, and applications of democratic peace theory. The authors will be pleased to the extent that this anthology informs, in some measure, ongoing scholarly debates as well as the fateful decisions of political and military leaders.

NOTES

1. China's government in 2008 ruled 60 percent of the people living in countries considered "not free" by Freedom House (2009), a fact that sustains global pressure on the Chinese Communist Party to reform its political system.
2. Some contemporary theorists (e.g., Aksu 2008; Baum 2008) argue that the utilitarian theorist Jeremy Bentham, who contended that "perpetual peace" is only possible if great powers renounce colonization and greatly restrict their military forces, provided a superior ethical basis for democratic peace theory than that devised by Kant.
3. In a footnote, Doyle (1983a, 217) accepts that Germany had some features of a liberal state but maintains that control over the conduct of foreign affairs by the emperor and the military made it "a state divorced from the control of its citizens in foreign affairs."
4. Reflecting on the scholarly impasse over these concepts, Maoz (1997, 182, 183) argues that "the democratic peace proposition is not about political scientists refraining from fighting each other: it is about democratic states not fighting each other."

5. Rasler and Thompson (2005) adopt a systemic perspective in identifying geographical factors that have shaped the economic relations and related security policies of states.
6. It remains a compelling mystery as to whether the system would have served its purpose had the United States itself joined the League of Nations.
7. The four freedoms were freedom of speech and expression, freedom of religion, freedom from want, and freedom from fear.
8. The creation of a "national security state" in Washington, D.C., is usefully described by Douglas T. Stuart (2008), who argues that the National Security Act of 1947 paved the way for the military adventurism consistently pursued by U.S. presidents since World War II.

Part One

Democratic Peace in Theory

1

Kant, Liberal Legacies, and Foreign Affairs

MICHAEL W. DOYLE

I

What difference do liberal principles and institutions make to the conduct of the foreign affairs of liberal states? A thicket of conflicting judgments suggests that the legacies of liberalism have not been clearly appreciated. For many citizens of liberal states, liberal principles and institutions have so fully absorbed domestic politics that their influence on foreign affairs tends to be either overlooked altogether or, when perceived, exaggerated. Liberalism becomes either unself-consciously patriotic or inherently "peace-loving." For many scholars and diplomats, the relations among independent states appear to differ so significantly from domestic politics that influences of liberal principles and domestic liberal institutions are denied or denigrated. They judge that international relations are governed by perceptions of national security and the balance of power; liberal principles and institutions, when they do intrude, confuse and disrupt the pursuit of balance-of-power politics.[1]

Although liberalism is misinterpreted from both these points of view, a crucial aspect of the liberal legacy is captured by each. Liberalism is a distinct ideology and set of institutions that has shaped the perceptions of and capacities for foreign relations of political societies that range from social welfare or social democratic to laissez faire. It defines much of the content of the liberal patriot's nationalism. Liberalism does appear to disrupt the pursuit of balance-of-power politics. Thus its foreign relations cannot be adequately explained (or prescribed) by a sole reliance on the balance of power. But liberalism is not inherently "peace-loving"; nor is it consistently restrained or peaceful in intent. Furthermore, liberal practice may reduce the probability that states will successfully exercise the consistent restraint and peaceful intentions that a world peace may well require in the nuclear age. Yet the peaceful intent and restraint that liberalism does manifest in limited aspects of its foreign affairs announces the possibility of a world peace this side of the grave or of world conquest. It has strengthened the prospects for a world peace established by the steady expansion of a separate peace among liberal societies.

Putting together these apparently contradictory (but, in fact, compatible) pieces of the liberal legacy begins with a discussion of the range of liberal principle and practice. This article highlights the differences between liberal practice toward other liberal societies and liberal practice toward nonliberal societies. It argues that liberalism has achieved extraordinary success in the first and has contributed to exceptional confusion in the second. Appreciating these liberal legacies calls for another look at one of the greatest of liberal philosophers, Immanuel Kant, for he is a source of insight, policy, and hope.

II

Liberalism has been identified with an essential principle—the importance of the freedom of the individual. Above all, this is a belief in the importance of moral freedom, of the right to be treated and a duty to treat others as ethical subjects, and not as objects or means only. This principle has generated rights and institutions.

A commitment to a threefold set of rights forms the foundation of liberalism. Liberalism calls for freedom from arbitrary authority, often called "negative freedom," which includes freedom of conscience, a free press and free speech, equality under the law, and the right to hold, and therefore to exchange, property without fear of arbitrary seizure. Liberalism also calls for those rights necessary to protect and promote the capacity and opportunity for freedom, the "positive freedoms." Such social and economic rights as equality of opportunity in education and rights to health care and employment, necessary for effective self-expression and participation, are thus among liberal rights. A third liberal right, democratic participation or representation, is necessary to guarantee the other two. To ensure that morally autonomous individuals remain free in those areas of social action where public authority is needed, public legislation has to express the will of the citizens making laws for their own community.

These three sets of rights, taken together, seem to meet the challenge that Kant identified:

> To organize a group of rational beings who demand general laws for their survival, but of whom each inclines toward exempting himself, and to establish their constitution in such a way that, in spite of the fact their private attitudes are opposed, these private attitudes mutually impede each other

in such a manner that [their] public behavior is the same as if they did not have such evil attitudes.²

But the dilemma within liberalism is how to reconcile the three sets of liberal rights. The right to private property, for example, can conflict with equality of opportunity and both rights can be violated by democratic legislation. During the 180 years since Kant wrote, the liberal tradition has evolved two high roads to individual freedom and social order; one is laissez-faire or "conservative" liberalism and the other is social welfare, or social democratic, or "liberal" liberalism. Both reconcile these conflicting rights (though in differing ways) by successfully organizing free individuals into a political order.

The political order of laissez-faire and social welfare liberals is marked by a shared commitment to four essential institutions. First, citizens possess juridical equality and other fundamental civic rights such as freedom of religion and the press. Second, the effective sovereigns of the state are representative legislatures deriving their authority from the consent of the electorate and exercising their authority free from all restraint apart from the requirement that basic civic rights be preserved.³ Most pertinently for the impact of liberalism on foreign affairs, the state is subject to neither the external authority of other states nor to the internal authority of special prerogatives held, for example, by monarchs or military castes over foreign policy. Third, the economy rests on a recognition of the rights of private property, including the ownership of means of production. Property is justified by individual acquisition (for example, by labor) or by social agreement or social utility. This excludes state socialism or state capitalism, but it need not exclude market socialism or various forms of the mixed economy. Fourth, economic decisions are predominantly shaped by the forces of supply and demand, domestically and internationally, and are free from strict control by bureaucracies.

In order to protect the opportunity of the citizen to exercise freedom, laissez-faire liberalism has leaned toward a highly constrained role for the state and a much wider role for private property and the market. In order to promote the opportunity of the citizen to exercise freedom, welfare liberalism has expanded the role of the state and constricted the role of the market.⁴ Both, nevertheless, accept these four institutional requirements and contrast markedly with the colonies, monarchical regimes, military dictatorships, and communist party dictatorships with which they have shared the political governance of the modern world.

The domestic successes of liberalism have never been more apparent. Never have so many people been included in, and accepted the domestic hegemony of, the liberal order; never have so many of the world's leading states been liberal, whether as republics or as constitutional monarchies. Indeed, the success of liberalism as an answer to the problem of masterless men in modern society is reflected in the growth in the number of liberal regimes from the three that existed when Kant wrote to the more than forty that exist today. But we should not be complacent about the domestic affairs of liberal states. Significant practical problems endure: among them are enhancing citizen participation in large democracies, distributing "positional goods" (for example, prestigious jobs), controlling bureaucracy, reducing unemployment, paying for a growing demand for social services, reducing inflation, and achieving large scale restructuring of industries in response to growing foreign competition.[5] Nonetheless, these domestic problems have been widely explored though they are by no means solved. Liberalism's foreign record is more obscure and warrants more consideration.

Table 1

Period	Liberal Regimes and the Pacific Union (By date "liberal")[a]	Total Number
18th century	Swiss Cantons[b]	3
	French Republic 1790–1795	
	the United States[b] 1776–	
1800–1850	Swiss Confederation, the United States	8
	France 1830–1849	
	Belgium 1830–	
	Great Britain 1832–	
	Netherlands 1848–	
	Piedmont 1848–	
	Denmark 1849–	
1850–1900	Switzerland, the United States, Belgium, Great Britain, Netherlands	13
	Piedmont—1861, Italy 1861–	
	Denmark—1866	
	Sweden 1864–	
	Greece 1864–	
	Canada 1867–	
	France 1871–	
	Argentina 1880–	
	Chile 1891–	
1900–1945	Switzerland, the United States, Great Britain, Sweden, Canada	29
	Greece—1911, 1928–1936	
	Italy—1922	
	Belgium—1940;	
	Netherlands—1940;	
	Argentina—1943	
	France—1940	

Period	Liberal Regimes and the Pacific Union (By date "liberal")[a]	Total Number
	Chile—1924, 1932	
	Australia 1901–	
	Norway 1905–1940	
	New Zealand 1907–	
	Colombia 1910–1949	
	Denmark 1914–1940	
	Poland 1917–1935	
	Latvia 1922–1934	
	Germany 1918–1932	
	Austria 1918–1934	
	Estonia 1919–1934	
	Finland 1919–	
	Uruguay 1919–	
	Costa Rica 1919–	
	Czechoslovakia 1920–1939	
	Ireland 1920–	
	Mexico 1928–	
	Lebanon 1944–	
1945[c]–	Switzerland, the United States, Great Britain, Sweden, Canada, Australia, New Zealand, Finland, Ireland, Mexico	49
	Uruguay—1973;	
	Chile—1973;	
	Lebanon—1975	
	Costa Rica—1948, 1953–	
	Iceland 1944–	
	France 1945–	
	Denmark 1945–	
	Norway 1945–	
	Austria 1945–	
	Brazil 1945–1954, 1955–1964	
	Belgium 1946–	
	Luxemburg 1946–	
	Netherlands 1946–	
	Italy 1946–	
	Philippines 1946–1972	
	India 1947–1975, 1977–	
	Sri Lanka 1948–1961, 1963–1977, 1978–	
	Ecuador 1948–1963, 1979–	
	Israel 1949–	
	West Germany 1949–	
	Peru 1950–1962, 1963–1968, 1980–	

Period	Liberal Regimes and the Pacific Union (By date "liberal")[a]	Total Number
	El Salvador 1950–1961	
	Turkey 1950–1960, 1966–1971	
	Japan 1951–	
	Bolivia 1956–1969	
	Colombia 1958–	
	Venezuela 1959–	
	Nigeria 1961–1964, 1979–	
	Jamaica 1962	
	Trinidad 1962–	
	Senegal 1963–	
	Malaysia 1963–	
	South Korea 1963–1972	
	Botswana 1966–	
	Singapore 1965–	
	Greece 1975–	
	Portugal 1976–	
	Spain 1978–	
	Dominican Republic 1978–	

a. I have drawn up this approximate list of "Liberal Regimes" according to the four institutions described as essential: market and private property economies; polities that are externally sovereign; citizens who possess juridical rights; and "republican" (whether republican or monarchical), representative, government. This latter includes the requirement that the legislative branch have an effective role in public policy and be formally and competitively, either potentially or actually, elected. Furthermore, I have taken into account whether male suffrage is wide (that is, 30 percent) or open to "achievement" by inhabitants (for example, to poll-tax payers or householders) of the national or metropolitan territory. Female suffrage is granted within a generation of its being demanded; and representative government is internally sovereign (for example, including and especially over military and foreign affairs) as well as stable (in existence for at least three years).

Sources: Arthur Banks and W. Overstreet, eds., *The Political Handbook of the World, 1980* (New York: McGraw-Hill, 1980); Foreign and Commonwealth Office, *A Year Book of the Commonwealth 1980* (London: HMSO, 1980); *Europa Yearbook, 1981* (London: Europa, 1981); W. L. Langer, *An Encyclopedia of World History* (Boston: Houghton-Mifflin, 1968); Department of State, *Country Reports on Human Rights Practices* (Washington, D.C.: Government Printing Office, 1981); and *Freedom at Issue*, no. 54 (Jan.–Feb. 1980).

b. There are domestic variations within these liberal regimes. For example, Switzerland was liberal only in certain cantons; the United States was liberal only north of the Mason-Dixon line until 1865, when it became liberal throughout. These lists also exclude ancient "republics," since none appear to fit Kant's criteria. See Stephen Holmes, "Aristippus in and out of Athens," *American Political Science Review* 73, no. 1 (Mar. 1979).

c. Selected list, excludes liberal regimes with populations less than one million.

III

In foreign affairs liberalism has shown, as it has in the domestic realm, serious weaknesses. But unlike liberalism's domestic realm, its foreign affairs have experienced startling but less than fully appreciated successes. Together they shape an unrecognized dilemma, for both these successes and weaknesses in large part spring from the same cause: the international implications of liberal principles and institutions.

The basic postulate of liberal international theory holds that states have the right to be free from foreign intervention. Since morally autonomous citizens hold rights to liberty, the states that democratically represent them have the right to exercise political independence. Mutual respect for these rights then becomes the touchstone of international liberal theory.[6] When states respect each other's rights, individuals are free to establish private international ties without state interference. Profitable exchanges between merchants and educational exchanges among scholars then create a web of mutual advantages and commitments that bolsters sentiments of public respect.

These conventions of mutual respect have formed a cooperative foundation for relations among liberal democracies of a remarkably effective kind. *Even though liberal states have become involved in numerous wars with nonliberal states, constitutionally secure liberal states have yet to engage in war with one another.*[7] No one should argue that such wars are impossible; but preliminary evidence does appear to indicate that there exists a significant predisposition against warfare between liberal states. Indeed, threats of war also have been regarded as illegitimate. A liberal zone of peace, a pacific union, has been maintained and has expanded despite numerous particular conflicts of economic and strategic interest.

During the nineteenth century the United States and Britain negotiated the northern frontier of the United States. During the American Civil War the commercial linkages between the Lancashire cotton economy and the American South and the sentimental links between the British aristocracy and the Southern plantocracy (together with numerous disputes over the rights of British shipping against the Northern blockade) brought Great Britain and the Northern states to the brink of war, but they never passed over that brink. Despite an intense Anglo-French colonial rivalry, crises such as Fashoda in 1898 were resolved without going to war. Despite their colonial rivalries, liberal France and Britain formed an entente before World War I against illiberal Germany (whose foreign relations were controlled by the Kaiser and the Army). During 1914–15 Italy, the liberal member of the Triple Alliance with illiberal Germany and Austria, chose not to fulfill its obligations under the Triple Alliance to either support its allies or remain neutral. Instead, Italy, a liberal regime, joined the alliance with France and Britain that would prevent it from having to fight other liberal states, and declared war on Austria and Germany,

Table 2
International Wars Listed Chronologically*

British-Maharattan (1817–1818)
Greek (1821–1828)
Franco-Spanish (1823)
First Anglo-Burmese (1823–1826)
Javanese (1825–1830)
Russo-Persian (1826–1828)
Russo-Turkish (1828–1829)
First Polish (1831)
First Syrian (1831–1832)
Texan (1835–1836)
First British-Afghan (1838–1842)
Second Syrian (1839–1840)
Franco-Algerian (1839–1847)
Peruvian-Bolivian (1841)
First British-Sikh (1845–1846)
Mexican-American (1846–1848)
Austro-Sardinian (1848–1849)
First Schleswig-Holstein (1848–1849)
Hungarian (1848–1849)
Second British-Sikh (1848–1849)
Roman Republic (1849)
La Plata (1851–1852)
First Turco-Montenegran (1852–1853)
Crimean (1853–1856)
Anglo-Persian (1856–1857)
Sepoy (1857–1859)
Second Turco-Montenegran (1858–1859)
Italian Unification (1859)
Spanish-Moroccan (1859–1860)
Italo-Roman (1860)
Italo-Sicilian (1860–1861)
Franco-Mexican (1862–1867)
Ecuadorian-Colombian (1863)
Second Polish (1863–1864)
Spanish-Santo Dominican (1863–1865)
Second Schleswig-Holstein (1864)
Lopez (1864–1870)
Spanish-Chilean (1865–1866)
Seven Weeks (1866)
Ten Years (1868–1878)
Franco-Prussian (1870–1871)
Dutch-Achinese (1873–1878)

Balkan (1875–1877)
Russo-Turkish (1877–1878)
Bosnian (1878)
Second British-Afghan (1878–1880)
Pacific (1879–1880)
British-Zulu (1879)
Franco-Indochinese (1882–1884)
Mahdist (1882–1885)
Sino-French (1884–1885)
Central American (1885)
Serbo-Bulgarian (1885)
Sino-Japanese (1894–1895)
Franco-Madagascan (1894–1895)
Cuban (1895–1898)
Italo-Ethiopian (1895–1896)
First Philippine (1896–1898)
Greco-Turkish (1897)
Spanish-American (1898)
Second Philippine (1899–1902)
Boer (1899–1902)
Boxer Rebellion (1900)
Ilinden (1903)
Russo-Japanese (1904–1905)
Central American (1906)
Central American (1907)
Spanish-Moroccan (1909–1910)
Italo-Turkish (1911–1912)
First Balkan (1912–1913)
Second Balkan (1913)
World War I (1914–1918)
Russian Nationalities (1917–1921)
Russo-Polish (1919–1920)
Hungarian-Allies (1919)
Greco-Turkish (1919–1922)
Riffian (1921–1926)
Druze (1925–1927)
Sino-Soviet (1929)
Manchurian (1931–1933)
Chaco (1932–1935)
Halo-Ethiopian (1935–1936)
Sino-Japanese (1937–1941)
Changkufeng (1938)

International Wars Listed Chronologically*

Nomohan (1939)	Second Kashmir (1965)
World War II (1939–1945)	Six Day (1967)
Russo-Finnish (1939–1940)	Israeli-Egyptian (1969–1970)
Franco-Thai (1940–1941)	Football (1969)
Indonesian (1945–1946)	Bangladesh (1971)
Indochinese (1945–1954)	Philippine-MNLF (1972–)
Madagascan (1947–1948)	Yom Kippur (1973)
First Kashmir (1947–1949)	Turco-Cypriot (1974)
Palestine (1948–1949)	Ethiopian-Eritrean (1974–)
Hyderabad (1948)	Vietnamese-Cambodian (1975–)
Korean (1950–1953)	Timor (1975–)
Algerian (1954–1962)	Saharan (1975–)
Russo-Hungarian (1956)	Ogaden (1976–)
Sinai (1956)	Ugandan-Tanzanian (1978–1979)
Tibetan (1956–1959)	Sino-Vietnamese (1979)
Sino-Indian (1962)	Russo-Afghan (1979–)
Vietnamese (1965–1975)	Irani-Iraqi (1980–)

*The table is reprinted by permission from Melvin Small and J. David Singer from *Resort to Arms* (Beverly Hills, CA: Sage Publications, 1982), pp. 79–80. This is a partial list of international wars fought between 1816 and 1980. In Appendices A and B of *Resort to Arms,* Small and Singer identify a total of 575 wars in this period; but approximately 159 of them appear to be largely domestic, or civil wars.

This definition of war excludes covert interventions, some of which have been directed by liberal regimes against other liberal regimes. One example is the United States' effort to destabilize the Chilean election and Allende's government. Nonetheless, it is significant (as will be apparent below) that such interventions are not pursued publicly as acknowledged policy. The covert destabilization campaign against Chile is recounted in U.S. Congress, Senate, Select Committee to Study Governmental Operations with Respect to Intelligence Activities, *Covert Action in Chile, 1963–73,* 94th Congress, 1st Session (Washington, DC: U.S. Government Printing Office, 1975).

The argument of this article (and this list) also excludes civil wars. Civil wars differ from international wars not in the ferocity of combat but in the issues that engender them. Two nations that could abide one another as independent neighbors separated by a border might well be the fiercest of enemies if forced to live together in one state, jointly deciding how to raise and spend taxes, choose leaders, and legislate fundamental questions of value. Notwithstanding these differences, no civil wars that I recall upset the argument of liberal pacification.

its former allies. And despite generations of Anglo-American tension and British restrictions on American trade, the United States leaned toward Britain and France from 1914 to 1917. Nowhere was this special peace among liberal states more clearly proclaimed than in President Woodrow Wilson's "War Message" of 2 April 1917: "Our object now, as then, is to vindicate the principles of peace and justice in the life of the world as against selfish and autocratic power and to set up amongst the really free and self-governed peoples of the world such a concert of purpose and of action as will henceforth ensure the observance of those principles."[8]

Statistically, war between any two states (in any single year or other short period of time) is a low probability event. War between any two adjacent states, considered over a long period of time, may be somewhat more probable. The apparent absence of war among the more clearly liberal states, whether adjacent or not, for almost two hundred years thus has some significance. Politically more significant, perhaps, is that, when states are forced to decide, by the pressure of an impinging world war, on which side of a world contest they will fight, liberal states wind up all on the same side, despite the real complexity of the historical, economic and political factors that affect their foreign policies. And historically, we should recall that medieval and early modern Europe were the warring cockpits of states, wherein France and England and the Low Countries engaged in near constant strife. Then in the late eighteenth century there began to emerge liberal regimes. At first hesitant and confused, and later clear and confident as liberal regimes gained deeper domestic foundations and longer international experience, a pacific union of these liberal states became established.

The Realist model of international relations, which provides a plausible explanation of the general insecurity of states, offers little guidance in explaining the pacification of the liberal world. Realism, in its classical formulation, holds that the state is and should be formally sovereign, effectively unbounded by individual rights nationally and thus capable of determining its own scope of authority. (This determination can be made democratically, oligarchically, or autocratically.) Internationally, the sovereign state exists in an anarchical society in which it is radically independent; neither bounded nor protected by international "law" or treaties or duties, and hence, insecure. Hobbes, one of the seventeenth-century founders of the Realist approach drew the international implications of Realism when he argued that the existence of international anarchy, the very independence of states, best accounts for the competition, the fear, and the temptation toward preventive war that characterize international relations. Politics among nations is not a continuous combat, but it is in this view a "state of war . . . a tract of time, wherein the will to contend by battle is sufficiently known."[9]

In international relations theory, three "games" explain the fear that Hobbes saw as a root of conflict in the state of war. First, even when states share an interest in a common good that could be attained by cooperation, the absence of a source of global law and order means that no one state can count upon the cooperative behavior of the others. Each state therefore has a rational incentive to defect from the cooperative enterprise even if only to pursue a good whose value is less than the share that would have been obtained from the successful accomplishment of the cooperative enterprise (this is Rousseau's "stag dilemma"). Second, even though each state knows that security is relative to the armaments level of potential adversaries and even though each state seeks to minimize its arms expenditure, it also knows that, having no global guarantee of security, being caught unarmed by a surprise attack is worse than bearing the costs of armament. Each therefore arms; all are worse off (this is the "security dilemma," a variant of the "prisoner's dilemma"). Third, heavily armed states rely upon their prestige, their credibility, to deter states from testing the true quality of their arms in battle, and credibility is measured by a record of successes. Once a posture of confrontation is assumed, backing down, although rational for both together, is not rational (first best) for either individually if there is some chance that the other will back down first (the game of "chicken").[10]

Specific wars therefore arise from fear as a state seeking to avoid a surprise attack decides to attack first; from competitive emulation as states lacking an imposed international hierarchy of prestige struggle to establish their place; and from straightforward conflicts of interest that escalate into war because there is no global sovereign to prevent states from adopting that ultimate form of conflict resolution. Herein lie Thucydides's trinity of "security, honor, and self-interest" and Hobbes's "diffidence," "glory," and "competition" that drive states to conflict in the international state of war.[11]

Finding that all states, including liberal states, do engage in war, the Realist concludes that the effects of differing domestic regimes (whether liberal or not) are overridden by the international anarchy under which all states live.[12] Thus Hobbes does not bother to distinguish between "some council or one man" when he discusses the sovereign. Differing domestic regimes do affect the quantity of resources available to the state as Rousseau (an eighteenth-century Realist) shows in his discussion of Poland, and Morgenthau (a twentieth-century Realist) demonstrates in his discussion of morale.[13] But the ends that shape the international state of war are decreed for the Realist by the anarchy of the international order and the fundamental quest for power that directs the policy of all States, irrespective of differences in their domestic regimes. As Rousseau argued, international peace therefore depends on the abolition of international relations either by the achievement of a world state or by a radical isolationism (Corsica). Realists judge neither to be possible.

First, at the level of the strategic decisionmaker, Realists argue that a liberal peace could be merely the outcome of prudent diplomacy. Some, including Hobbes, have argued that sovereigns have a natural duty not to act against "the reasons of peace."[14] Individuals established (that is, should establish) a sovereign to escape from the brutalities of the state of nature, the war of all against all, that follows from competition for scarce goods, scrambles for prestige, and fear of another's attack when there is no sovereign to provide for lawful acquisition or regularized social conduct or personal security. "Dominions were constituted for peace's sake, and peace was sought for safety's sake"; the natural duty of the sovereign is therefore the safety of the people. Yet prudent policy cannot be an enforceable right of citizens because Hobbesian sovereigns, who remain in the state of nature with respect to their subjects and other sovereigns, cannot themselves be subjects.

Nevertheless, the interstate condition is not necessarily the original brutality only now transposed to the frontiers. The sovereign is personally more secure than any individual in the original state of nature and soldiers too are by nature timorous. Unlike individuals, states are not equal; some live more expansively by predominance, others must live only by sufferance. Yet a policy of safety is not a guarantee of peace. The international condition for Hobbes remains a state of war. Safety enjoins a prudent policy of forewarning (spying) and of forearming oneself to increase security against other sovereigns who, lacking any assurance that you are not taking these measures, also take them. Safety also requires (morally) taking actions "whatsoever shall seem to conduce to the lessening of the power of foreigners whom they [the sovereign] suspect, whether by slight or force."[15] If preventive wars are prudent, the Realists' prudence obviously cannot account for more than a century and a half of peace among independent liberal states, many of which have crowded one another in the center of Europe.

Recent additions to game theory specify some of the circumstances under which prudence could lead to peace. Experience; geography; expectations of cooperation and belief patterns; and the differing payoffs to cooperation (peace) or conflict associated with various types of military technology all appear to influence the calculus.[16] But when it comes to acquiring the techniques of peaceable interaction, nations appear to be slow, or at least erratic, learners. The balance of power (more below) is regarded as a primary lesson in the Realist primer, but centuries of experience did not prevent either France (Louis XIV, Napoleon I) or Germany (Wilhelm II, Hitler) from attempting to conquer Europe, twice each. Yet some, very new, black African states appear to have achieved a twenty-year-old system of impressively effective standards of mutual toleration. These standards are not completely effective (as in Tanzania's invasion of Uganda); but they have confounded expectations of a scramble to redivide Africa.[17] Geography—"insular security" and "continental insecurity"—may affect foreign policy attitudes; but it does not appear to determine behavior, as the bellicose records of England and Japan suggest. Beliefs, expectations, and attitudes of leaders and masses should influence strategic behavior. A survey of attitudinal predispositions of the American public indicate that a peaceable inclination would be enhanced by having at the strategic helm a forty-five-year-old, black, female, pediatrician of Protestant or Jewish faith, resident in Bethesda, Maryland.[18] Nevertheless, it would be difficult to determine if liberal leaders have had more peaceable attitudes than leaders who lead nonliberal states. But even if one did make that discovery, he also would have to account for why these peaceable attitudes only appear to be effective in relations with other liberals (since wars with nonliberals have not been uniformly defensive).

More substantial contributions have been made in the logic of game theory decision under differing military technologies. These technologies can alter the payoffs of the "security dilemma": making the costs of noncooperation high, reducing the costs of being unprepared or surprised, reducing the benefits of surprise attack, or increasing the gains from cooperation. In particular, Jervis recently has examined the differing effects of situations in which the offense or the defense has the advantage and in which offensive weapons are or are not distinguishable from defensive weapons. When the offense has the advantage and weapons are indistinguishable, the level of insecurity is high, incentives for preemptive attack correspondingly are strong. When offensive weapons do not have an advantage and offensive weapons are distinguishable the incentives for preemptive attack are low, as are the incentives for arms races. Capable of signalling with clarity a nonaggressive intent and of guaranteeing that other states pose no immediate strategic threat, statesmen should be able to adopt peaceable policies and negotiate disputes. But, this cannot be the explanation for the liberal peace. Military technologies changed from offensive to defensive and from distinguishable to nondistinguishable, yet the pacific union persisted and persisted only among liberal states. Moreover, even the "clearest" technical messages appear subject to garbling. The pre-1914 period, which objectively represented a triumph of the distinguishable defense (machine guns, barbed wire, trench warfare) over the offensive, subjectively, as Jervis notes, was a period which appeared to military leaders to place exceptional premiums on the offensive and thus on preemptive war.[19]

Second, at the level of social determinants, some might argue that relations among any group of states with similar social structures or with compatible values would be peaceful.[20] But again, the evidence for feudal societies, communist societies, fascist societies, or socialist societies does not support this conclusion. Feudal warfare was frequent and very much a sport of the monarchs and nobility. There have not been enough truly totalitarian, fascist powers (nor have they lasted long enough) to test fairly their pacific compatibility; but fascist powers in the wider sense of nationalist, capitalist, military dictatorships fought each other in the 1930s. Communist powers have engaged in wars more recently in East Asia. And we have not had enough socialist societies to consider the relevance of socialist pacification. The more abstract category of pluralism does not suffice. Certainly Germany was pluralist when it engaged in war with liberal states in 1914; Japan as well in 1941. But they were not liberal.

And third, at the level of interstate relations, neither specific regional attributes nor historic alliances or friendships can account for the wide reach of the liberal peace. The peace extends as far as, and no further than, the relations among liberal states, not including nonliberal states in an otherwise liberal region (such as the north Atlantic in the 1930s) nor excluding liberal states in a nonliberal region (such as Central America or Africa).

At this level, Raymond Aron has identified three types of interstate peace: empire, hegemony, and equilibrium.[21] An empire generally succeeds in creating an internal peace, but this is not an explanation of peace among independent liberal states. Hegemony can create peace by overawing potential rivals. Although far from perfect and certainly precarious, United States hegemony, as Aron notes, might account for the interstate peace in South America in the postwar period during the height of the cold war conflict. However, the liberal peace cannot be attributed merely to effective international policing by a predominant hegemon—Britain in the nineteenth century, the United States in the postwar period. Even though a hegemon might well have an interest in enforcing a peace for the sake of commerce or investments or as a means of enhancing its prestige or security; hegemons such as seventeenth-century France were not peace-enforcing police, and the liberal peace persisted in the interwar period when international society lacked a predominant hegemonic power. Moreover, this explanation overestimates hegemonic control in both periods. Neither England nor the United States was able to prevent direct challenges to its interests (colonial competition in the nineteenth century, Middle East diplomacy and conflicts over trading with the enemy in the postwar period). Where then was the capacity to prevent all armed conflicts between liberal regimes, many of which were remote and others strategically or economically insignificant? Liberal hegemony and leadership are important (see Section V below), but they are not sufficient to explain a liberal peace.

Peace through equilibrium (the multipolar classical balance of power or the bipolar "cold war") also draws upon prudential sources of peace. An awareness of the likelihood that aggressive attempts at hegemony will generate international opposition should, it is argued, deter these aggressive wars. But bipolar stability discourages polar or superpower wars, not proxy or small power wars. And multipolar balancing of power also encourages warfare to seize, for example, territory for strategic depth against a rival expanding its power from internal growth.[22] Neither readily accounts for general peace or for the liberal peace.

Finally, some Realists might suggest that the liberal peace simply reflects the absence of deep conflicts of interest among liberal states. Wars occur outside the liberal zone because conflicts of interest are deeper there. But this argument does nothing more than raise the question of why liberal states have fewer or less fundamental conflicts of interest with other liberal states than liberal states have with nonliberal, or non-liberal states have with other nonliberals. We must therefore examine the workings of liberalism among its own kind—a special pacification of the "state of war" resting on liberalism and nothing either more specific or more general.

IV

Most liberal theorists have offered inadequate guidance in understanding the exceptional nature of liberal pacification. Some have argued that democratic states would be inherently peaceful simply and solely because in these states citizens rule the polity and bear the costs of wars. Unlike monarchs, citizens are not able to indulge their aggressive passions and have the consequences suffered by someone else. Other liberals have argued that laissez-faire capitalism contains an inherent tendency toward rationalism, and that, since war is irrational, liberal capitalisms will be pacifistic. Others still, such as Montesquieu, claim that "commerce is the cure for the most destructive prejudices," and "Peace is the natural effect of trade."[23] While these developments can help account for the liberal peace, they do not explain the fact that liberal states are peaceful only in relations with other liberal states. France and England fought expansionist, colonial wars throughout the nineteenth century (in the 1830s and 1840s against Algeria and China); the United States fought a similar war with Mexico in 1848 and intervened again in 1914 under President Wilson. Liberal states are as aggressive and war prone as any other form of government or society in their relations with nonliberal states.

Immanuel Kant offers the best guidance. "Perpetual Peace," written in 1795, predicts the ever-widening pacification of the liberal pacific union, explains that pacification, and at the same time suggests why liberal states are not pacific in their relations with nonliberal states. Kant argues that Perpetual Peace will be guaranteed by the ever-widening acceptance of three "definitive articles" of peace. When all nations have accepted the definitive articles in a metaphorical "treaty" of perpetual peace he asks them to sign, perpetual peace will have been established.

The First Definitive Article holds that the civil constitution of the state must be republican. By republican Kant means a political society that has solved the problem of combining moral autonomy, individualism, and social order. A basically private property and market-oriented economy partially addressed that dilemma in the private sphere. The public, or political, sphere was more troubling. His answer was a republic that preserved juridical freedom—the legal equality of citizens as subjects—on the basis of a representative government with a separation of powers. Juridical freedom is preserved because the morally autonomous individual is by means of representation a self-legislator making laws that apply to all citizens equally including himself. And tyranny is avoided because the individual is subject to laws he does not also administer.[24]

Liberal republics will progressively establish peace among themselves by means of the "pacific union" described in the Second Definitive Article of the Eternal Peace. The pacific union is limited to "a treaty of the nations among themselves" which "maintains itself, prevents wars, and steadily expands." The world will not have achieved the "perpetual peace" that provides the ultimate guarantor of republican freedom until "very late and after many unsuccessful attempts." Then right conceptions of the appropriate constitution, great and sad experience, and good will will have taught all the nations the lessons of peace. Not until then will individuals enjoy perfect republican rights or the full guarantee of a global and just peace. But in the meantime, the "pacific union" of liberal republics "*steadily expands* [my emphasis]" bringing within it more and more republics (despite republican collapses, backsliding, and war disasters) and creating an ever expanding separate peace.[25] The pacific union is neither a single peace treaty ending one war nor a world state or state of nations. The first is insufficient; the second and third are impossible or potentially tyrannical. Kant develops no organizational embodiment of this treaty, and presumably he does not find institutionalization necessary. He appears to have in mind a mutual nonaggression pact, perhaps a collective security agreement, and the cosmopolitan law set forth in the Third Definitive Article.[26]

The Third Definitive Article of the Eternal Peace establishes a cosmopolitan law to operate in conjunction with the pacific union. The cosmopolitan law "shall be limited to conditions of universal hospitality." In this he calls for the recognition of the "right of a foreigner not to be treated with hostility when he arrives upon the soil of another [country]," which "does not extend further than to the conditions which enable them [the foreigners] to attempt the developing of intercourse [commerce] with the old inhabitants." Hospitality does not require extending either the right to citizenship to foreigners or the right to settlement, unless the foreign visitors would perish if they were expelled. Foreign conquest and plunder also find no justification under this right. Hospitality does appear to include the right of access and the obligation of maintaining the opportunity for citizens to exchange goods and ideas, without imposing the obligation to trade (a voluntary act in all cases under liberal constitutions).[27]

Kant then explains each of the three definitive articles for a liberal peace. In doing so he develops both an account of why liberal states do maintain peace among themselves and of how it will (by implication, has) come about that the pacific union will expand. His central claim is that a natural evolution will produce "a harmony from the very disharmony of men against their will."[28]

The first source derives from a political evolution, from a *constitutional law*. Nature (providence) has seen to it that human beings can live in all the regions where they have been driven to settle by wars. (Kant, who once taught geography, reports on the Lapps, the Samoyeds, the Pescheras.) "Asocial sociability" draws men together to fulfill needs for security and material welfare as it drives them into conflicts over the distribution and control of social products. This violent natural evolution tends toward the liberal peace because "asocial sociability" inevitably leads toward republican governments and republican governments are a source of the liberal peace.

Republican representation and separation of powers are produced because they are the means by which the state is "organized well" to prepare for and meet foreign threats (by unity) and to tame the ambitions of selfish and aggressive individuals (by authority derived from representation, by general laws, and by nondespotic administration). States which are not organized in this fashion fail. Monarchs thus cede rights of representation to their subjects in order to strengthen their political support or to obtain tax revenue. This argument provides a plausible, logical connection between conflict, internal and external, and republicanism; and it highlights interesting associations between the rising incidence of international war and the increasing number of republics.

Nevertheless, constant preparation for war can enhance the role of military institutions in a society to the point that they become the society's rulers. Civil conflict can lead to praetorian coups. Conversely, an environment of security can provide a political climate for weakening the state by constitutional restraints.[29] Significantly, the most war-affected states have not been liberal republics.[30] More importantly, the argument is so indistinct as to serve only as a very general hypothesis that mobilizing self-interested individuals into the political life of states in an insecure world will eventually engender pressures for republican participation. Kant needs no more than this to suggest that republicanism and a liberal peace are possible (and thus a moral obligation). If it is possible, then sometime over the course of history it may be inevitable. But attempting to make its date of achievement predictable—projecting a steady trend—he suggests, may be asking too much. He anticipates backsliding and destructive wars, though these will serve to educate the nations to the importance of peace.[31]

Kant shows how republics, once established, lead to peaceful relations. He argues that once the aggressive interests of absolutist monarchies are tamed and once the habit of respect for individual rights is engrained by republican government, wars would appear as the disaster to the people's welfare that he and the other liberals thought them to be. The fundamental reason is this:

> If the consent of the citizens is required in order to decide that war should be declared (and in this constitution it cannot but be the case), nothing is more natural than that they would be very cautious in commencing such a poor game, decreeing for themselves all the calamities of war. Among the latter would be: having to fight, having to pay the costs of war from their own resources, having painfully to repair the devastation war leaves behind, and, to fill up the measure of evils, load themselves with a heavy national debt that

would embitter peace itself and that can never be liquidated on account of constant wars in the future. But, on the other hand, in a constitution which is not republican, and under which the subjects are not citizens, a declaration of war is the easiest thing in the world to decide upon, because war does not require of the ruler, who is the proprietor and not a member of the state, the least sacrifice of the pleasure of his table, the chase, his country houses, his court functions, and the like. He may, therefore, resolve on war as on a pleasure party for the most trivial reasons, and with perfect indifference leave the justification which decency requires to the diplomatic corps who are ever ready to provide it.[32]

One could add to Kant's list another source of pacification specific to liberal constitutions. The regular rotation of office in liberal democratic polities is a nontrivial device that helps ensure that personal animosities among heads of government provide no lasting, escalating source of tension.

These domestic republican restraints do not end war. If they did, liberal states would not be warlike, which is far from the case. They do introduce Kant's "caution" in place of monarchical caprice. Liberal wars are only fought for popular, liberal purposes. To see how this removes the occasion of wars among liberal states and not wars between liberal and nonliberal states, we need to shift our attention from constitutional law to international law, Kant's second source.

Complementing the constitutional guarantee of caution, *international law* adds a second source—a guarantee of respect. The separation of nations that asocial sociability encourages is reinforced by the development of separate languages and religions. These further guarantee a world of separate states—an essential condition needed to avoid a "global, soul-less despotism." Yet, at the same time, they also morally integrate liberal states "as culture progresses and men gradually come closer together toward a greater agreement on principles for peace and understanding."[33] As republics emerge (the first source) and as culture progresses, an understanding of the legitimate rights of all citizens and of all republics comes into play; and this, now that caution characterizes policy, sets up the moral foundations for the liberal peace. Correspondingly, international law highlights the importance of Kantian publicity. Domestically, publicity helps ensure that the officials of republics act according to the principles they profess to hold just and according to the interests of the electors they claim to represent. Internationally, free speech and the effective communication of accurate conceptions of the political life of foreign peoples is essential to establish and preserve the understanding on which the guarantee of respect depends. In short, domestically just republics, which rest on consent, presume foreign republics to be also consensual, just, and therefore deserving of accommodation. The experience of cooperation helps engender further cooperative behavior when the consequences of state policy are unclear but (potentially) mutually beneficial.[34]

Lastly, *cosmopolitan law,* adds material incentives to moral commitments. The cosmopolitan right to hospitality permits the "spirit of commerce" sooner or later to take hold of every nation, thus impelling states to promote peace and to try to avert war.

Liberal economic theory holds that these cosmopolitan ties derive from a cooperative international division of labor and free trade according to comparative advantage. Each economy is said to be better off than it would have been under autarky; each thus acquires an incentive to avoid policies that would lead the other to break these economic ties. Since keeping open markets rests upon the assumption that the next set of transactions will also be determined by prices rather than coercion, a sense of mutual security is vital to avoid security-motivated searches for economic autarky. Thus avoiding a challenge to another liberal state's security or even enhancing each other's security by means of alliance naturally follows economic interdependence.

A further cosmopolitan source of liberal peace is that the international market removes difficult decisions of production and distribution from the direct sphere of state policy. A foreign state thus does not appear directly responsible for these outcomes; states can stand aside from, and to some degree above, these contentious market rivalries and be ready to step in to resolve crises. Furthermore, the interdependence of commerce and the connections of state officials help create crosscutting transnational ties that serve as lobbies for mutual accommodation. According to modern liberal scholars, international financiers and transnational, bureaucratic, and domestic organizations create interests in favor of accommodation and have ensured by their variety that no single conflict sours an entire relationship.[35]

No one of these constitutional, international or cosmopolitan sources is alone sufficient, but together (and only where together) they plausibly connect the characteristics of liberal polities and economies with sustained liberal peace. Liberal states have not escaped from the Realists' "security dilemma," the insecurity caused by anarchy in the world political system considered as a whole. But the effects of international anarchy have been tamed in the relations among states of a similarly liberal character. Alliances of purely mutual strategic interest among liberal and nonliberal states have been broken, economic ties between liberal and nonliberal states have proven fragile, but the political bond of liberal rights and interests have proven a remarkably firm foundation for mutual non-aggression. A separate peace exists among liberal states.

V

Where liberal internationalism among liberal states has been deficient is in preserving its basic preconditions under changing international circumstances, and particularly in supporting the liberal character of its constituent states. It has failed on occasion, as it did in regard to Germany in the 1920s, to provide international economic support for liberal regimes whose market foundations were in crisis. It failed in the 1930s to provide military aid or political mediation to Spain, which was challenged by an armed minority, or to Czechoslovakia, which was caught in a dilemma of preserving national security or acknowledging the claims (fostered by Hitler's Germany) of the Sudeten minority to self-determination. Far-sighted and constitutive measures have only been provided by the liberal international order when one liberal state stood preeminent among the rest, prepared and able to take measures, as did the United States following World War II, to sustain economically and politically the foundations of liberal society beyond its borders. Then measures such as the British Loan, the Marshall Plan, NATO, GATT, the IMF, and the liberalization of Germany and Japan helped construct buttresses for the international liberal order.[36]

Thus, the decline of U.S. hegemonic leadership may pose dangers for the liberal world. This danger is not that today's liberal states will permit their economic competition to spiral into war, but that the societies of the liberal world will no longer be able to provide the mutual assistance they might require to sustain liberal domestic orders in the face of mounting economic crises.

These dangers come from two directions: military and economic. Their combination is particularly threatening. One is the continuing asymmetry of defense, with the United States (in relation to its GNP) bearing an undue portion of the common burden. Yet independent and more substantial European and Japanese defense establishments pose problems for liberal cooperation. Military dependence on the United States has been one of the additional bonds helpful in transforming a liberal peace into a liberal alliance. Removing it, without creating a multilaterally directed and funded organization among the liberal industrial democracies, threatens to loosen an important bond. Economic instabilities could make this absence of a multilateral security bond particularly dangerous by escalating differences into hostility. If domestic economic collapses on the pattern of the global propagation of depressions in the 1930s were to reoccur, the domestic political foundations of liberalism could fall. Or, if international economic rivalry were to continue to increase, then consequent attempts to weaken economic interdependence (establishing closed trade and currency blocs) would break an important source of liberal accommodation.[37] These dangers would become more significant if independent and substantial military forces were established. If liberal assumptions of the need to cooperate and to accommodate disappear, countries might fall prey to a corrosive rivalry that destroys the pacific union.

Yet liberals may have escaped from the single, greatest, traditional danger of international change—the transition between hegemonic leaders. When one great power begins to lose its preeminence and to slip into mere equality, a warlike resolution of the international pecking order becomes exceptionally likely. New power challenges old prestige, excessive commitments face new demands; so Sparta felt compelled to attack Athens, France warred Spain, England and Holland fought with France (and with each other), and Germany and England struggled for the mastery of Europe in World War I. But here liberals may again be an exception, for despite the fact that the United States constituted Britains greatest challenger along all the dimensions most central to the British maritime hegemony, Britain and the United States accommodated their differences.[38] After the defeat of Germany, Britain eventually, though not without regret, accepted its replacement by the United States as the commercial and maritime hegemon of the liberal world. The promise of a peaceable transition thus may be one of the factors helping to moderate economic and political rivalries among Europe, Japan, and the United States.

Consequently, the quarrels with liberal allies that bedeviled the Carter and Reagan Administrations should not be attributed solely to the personal weaknesses of the two presidents or their secretaries of state. Neither should they be attributed to simple failures of administrative coordination or to the idiosyncracies of American allies. These are the normal workings of a liberal alliance of independent republics. There is no indication that they involve a dissolution of the pacific union; but there is every indication that, following the decline in American preponderance, liberal states will be able to do little to reestablish the union should the international economic interdependence that binds them dissolve and should the domestic, liberal foundations of its central members collapse. But should these republican foundations and commercial sources of interdependence remain firm, then the promise of liberal legacies among liberal regimes is a continuing peace, even when the leadership of the liberal world changes hands.

When in *The Snows of Kilimanjaro*, Julian (F. Scott Fitzgerald) tells his friend (Hemingway), "The very rich are different from you and me," his friend replies, "Yes, they have more money." But the liberals are fundamentally different. It is not just, as the Realists might argue, that they have more or less resources, better or worse morale. Their constitutional structure makes them—realistically—different. They have established peace among themselves. But the very features which make their relations to fellow liberals differ from the state of war that all other states inhabit also make their relations with nonliberals differ from the prudent, strategic calculation that Realists hope will inform the foreign policies of states in an insecure world. These failings are the subject of the second part of this article.

NOTES

This is the first half of a two-part article. The article has benefited from the extensive criticisms of William Ascher, Richard Belts, William Bundy, Joseph Carens, Felix Gilbert, Amy Gutmann, Don Herzog, Stanley Hoffman, Marion Levy, Judith Shklar, Mark Uhlig, and the Editors of *Philosophy & Public Affairs*. I have also tried to take into account suggestions from Fouad Ajami, Steven David, Tom Farer, Robert Gilpin, Ernest van den Haag, Germaine Hoston, Robert Jervis, Donald Kagan, Robert Keohane, John Rawls, Nicholas Rizopoulos, Robert W. Tucker, Richard Ullman, and the members of a Special Seminar at the Lehrman Institute, February 22, 1983. The essay cannot be interpreted as a consensus of their views.

1. The liberal-patriotic view was reiterated by President Reagan in a speech before the British Parliament on 8 June 1982. There he proclaimed "a global campaign for democratic development." This "crusade for freedom" will be the latest campaign in a tradition that, he claimed, began with the Magna Carta and stretched in this century through two world wars and a cold war. He added that liberal foreign policies have shown "restraint" and "peaceful intentions" and that this crusade will strengthen the prospects for a world at peace *(New York Times,* 9 June 1982). The skeptical scholars and diplomats represent the predominant Realist interpretation of international relations. See ns. 4 and 12 for references.
2. Immanuel Kant, "Perpetual Peace" (1795) in *The Philosophy of Kant*, ed. Carl J. Friedrich (New York: Modern Library, 1949), p. 453.
3. The actual rights of citizenship have often been limited by slavery or male suffrage, but liberal regimes harbored no principle of opposition to the extension of juridical equality; in fact, as pressure was brought to bear they progressively extended the suffrage to the entire population. By this distinction, nineteenth-century United States was liberal; twentieth-century South Africa is not. See Samuel Huntington, *American Politics: the Promise of Disharmony* (Cambridge, MA: Harvard University Press, 1981).
4. The sources of classic, laissez-faire liberalism can be found in Locke, the *Federalist Papers*, Kant, and Robert Nozick, *Anarchy, State and Utopia* (New York: Basic Books, 1974). Expositions of welfare liberalism are in the work of the Fabians and John Rawls, *A Theory of Justice* (Cambridge, MA: Harvard University Press, 1971). Amy Gutmann, *Liberal Equality* (Cambridge: Cambridge University Press, 1980), discusses variants of liberal thought.

   Uncomfortably parallelling each of the high roads are "low roads" that, while achieving certain liberal values, fail to reconcile freedom and order. An overwhelming terror of anarchy and a speculation on preserving property can drive laissez-faire liberals to support a law-and-order authoritarian rule that sacrifices democracy. Authoritarianism to preserve order is the argument of Hobbes's *Leviathan*. It also shapes the argument of right wing liberals who seek to draw a distinction between "authoritarian" and "totalitarian" dictatorships. The justification sometimes advanced by liberals for the former is that they can be temporary and educate the population into an acceptance of property, individual rights, and, eventually, representative government. See Jeane Kirkpatrick, "Dictatorships and Double Standards," *Commentary* 68 (November 1979): 34–45. Complementarily, when social inequalities are judged to be extreme, the welfare liberal can argue that establishing (or reestablishing) the foundations of liberal society

requires a nonliberal method of reform, a second low road of redistributing authoritarianism. Aristide Zolberg reports a "liberal left" sensibility among U.S. scholars of African politics that justified reforming dictatorship. (See *One Party Government in the Ivory Coast* [Princeton: Princeton University Press, 1969], p. viii.) And the argument of "reforming autocracy" can be found in J. S. Mill's defense of colonialism in India.
5. Fred Hirsch, *The Social Limits to Growth* (Cambridge, MA: Harvard University Press, 1977).
6. Charles Beitz, *Political Theory and International Relations* (Princeton: Princeton University Press, 1979) offers a clear and insightful discussion of liberal ideas on intervention and nonintervention.
7. There appear to be some exceptions to the tendency for liberal states not to engage in a war with each other. Peru and Ecuador, for example, entered into conflict. But for each, the war came within one to three years after the establishment of a liberal regime, that is, before the pacifying effects of liberalism could become deeply ingrained. The Palestinians and the Israelis clashed frequently along the Lebanese border, which Lebanon could not hold secure from either belligerent. But at the beginning of the 1967 War, Lebanon seems to have sent a flight of its own jets into Israel. The jets were repulsed. Alone among Israel's Arab neighbors, Lebanon engaged in no further hostilities with Israel. Israel's recent attack on the territory of Lebanon was an attack on a country that had already been occupied by Syria (and the P. L. O.). Whether Israel actually will withdraw (if Syria withdraws) and restore an independent Lebanon is yet to be determined.
8. Imperial Germany is a difficult case. The Reichstag was not only elected by universal male suffrage but, by and large, the state ruled under the law, respecting the civic equality and rights of its citizens. Moreover, Chancellor Bismarck began the creation of a social welfare society that served as an inspiration for similar reforms in liberal regimes. However, the constitutional relations between the imperial executive and the representative legislature were sufficiently complex that various practices, rather than constitutional theory, determined the actual relation between the government and the citizenry. The emperor appointed and could dismiss the chancellor. Although the chancellor was responsible to the Reichstag, a defeat in the Reichstag did not remove him nor did the government absolutely depend on the Reichstag for budgetary authority. In practice, Germany was a liberal state under republican law for domestic issues. But the emperor's direct authority over the army, the army's effective independence from the minimal authority of the War Ministry, and the emperor's active role in foreign affairs (including the influential separate channel to the emperor through the military attachés) together with the tenuous constitutional relationship between the chancellor and the Reichstag made imperial Germany a state divorced from the control of its citizenry in foreign affairs.

 This authoritarian element not only influenced German foreign policymaking, but also shaped the international political environment (a lack of trust) the Reich faced and the domestic political environment that defined the government's options and capabilities (the weakness of liberal opinion as against the exceptional influence of junker militaristic nationalism). Thus direct influence on policy was but one result of the authoritarian element. Nonetheless, significant and strife-generating episodes can be directly attributed to this element. They include Tirpitz's approach to Wilhelm II to obtain the latter's sanction for a veto of Chancellor Bethmann-Hollweg's proposals for a naval agreement with Britain (1909). Added to this was Wilhelm's personal assurances of full support to the Austrians early in the Sarajevo Crisis and his, together with Moltke's, erratic pressure on the Chancellor throughout July and August of 1914, which helped destroy whatever coherence German diplomacy might otherwise have had, and which led one Austrian official to ask, "Who rules in Berlin? Moltke or Bethmann?" (Gordon Craig, *The Politics of the Prussian Army* [New York: Oxford University Press, 1964], pp. xxviii and chap. 6). For an excellent account of Bethmann's aims and the constraints he encountered, see Konrad H. Jarausch, "The Illusion of Limited War: Chancellor Bethmann-Hollweg's Calculated Risk, July 1914," *Central European History* 2 (1969).

The liberal sources of Italy's decision are pointed out in R. Vivarelli's review of Hugo Buder's *Gaetano Salvemini und die Italienische Politik vor dem Ersten Weltkrieg* in the *Journal of Modern History* 52, no. 3 (September 1980): 541.

The quotation from President Wilson is from Woodrow Wilson, *The Messages and Papers of Woodrow Wilson*, ed. Albert Shaw (New York: The Review of Reviews, 1924), p. 378.

9. Thomas Hobbes, *Leviathan* (New York: Penguin, 1980), I, chap. 13, 62; p. 186.
10. Robert Jervis, "Cooperation Under the Security Dilemma," *World Politics* 30, no. 1 (January 1978).
11. Thucydides, *The Peloponnesian Wars*, trans. Rex Warner (Baltimore, MD: Penguin Books, 1954) 1:76; and Hobbes, *Leviathan*, I, chap. 13, 61, p. 185. The coincidence of views is not accidental; Hobbes translated Thucydides. And Hobbes's portrait of the state of nature appears to be drawn from Thucydides's account of the revolution in Corcyra.
12. Kenneth N. Waltz, *Man, the State, and War* (New York: Columbia University Press, 1954, 1959), pp. 120–23; and see his *Theory of International Politics* (Reading, MA: Addison-Wesley, 1979). The classic sources of this form of Realism are Hobbes and, more particularly, Rousseau's "Essay on St. Pierre's Peace Project" and his "State of War" in *A Lasting Peace* (London: Constable, 1917), E. H. Carr's *The Twenty Year's Crisis: 1919-1939* (London: Macmillan & Co. , 1951), and the works of Hans Morgenthau.
13. Jean-Jacques Rousseau, *The Government of Poland*, trans. Willmoore Kendall (New York: Bobbs-Merril], 1972); and Hans Morgenthan, *Politics Among Nations* (New York: Alfred A. Knopf, 1967), pp. 132–35.
14. Hobbes, "De Give," *The English Works of Thomas Hobbes* (London: J. Bohn, 1841), 2: 166–67.
15. *Ibid.*, p. 171.
16. Jervis, "Cooperation Under the Security Dilemma," pp. 172–86.
17. Robert H. Jackson and Carl G. Rosberg, "Why West Africa's Weak States Persist," *World Politics* 35, no. 1 (October 1982).
18. Interpreted from Michael Haas, *International Conflict* (New York: Bobbs-Merrill, 1974), pp. 80–81, 457–58.
19. Jervis, "Cooperation Under the Security Dilemma," pp. 186–210, 212. Jervis examines incentives for cooperation, not the existence or sources of peace.
20. There is a rich contemporary literature devoted to explaining international cooperation and integration. Karl Deutsch's *Political Community and the North Atlantic Area* (Princeton: Princeton University Press, 1957) develops the idea of a "pluralistic security community" that bears a resemblance to the "pacific union," but Deutsch limits it geo-

graphically and finds compatibility of values, mutual responsiveness, and predictability of behavior among decision-makers as its essential foundations. These are important but their particular content, liberalism, appears to be more telling. Joseph Nye in *Peace in Parts* (Boston: Little, Brown & Co., 1971) steps away from the geographic limits Deutsch sets and focuses on levels of development; but his analysis is directed toward explaining integration—a more intensive form of cooperation than the pacific union.

21. Raymond Aron, *Peace and War* (New York: Praeger, 1968) pp. 151–54. Progress and peace through the rise and decline of empires and hegemonies has been a classic theme. Lucretius suggested that they may be part of a more general law of nature: "Augescunt aliae gentes, aliae miniuntur/Inque brevis spatio mutantur saecula animantum,/Et quasi cursores vitai lampada tradunt." [Some peoples wax and others wane/And in a short space the order of living things is changed/And like runners hand on the torch of life.] *De Rer. Nat.* 11, 77–79.

22. Kenneth Waltz, *Theory of International Politics,* chap. 8; and Edward Gulick, *Europe's Classical Balance of Power* (New York: Norton, 1967), chap. 3.

    One of the most thorough collective investigations of the personal, societal, and international systemic sources of war has been the Correlates of War Project. See especially Melvin Small and J. David Singer, *Resort to Arms* (Beverly Hills, CA: Sage, 1982) for a more comprehensive list and statistical analysis of wars. J. David Singer ("Accounting for International War: The State of the Discipline," *Journal of Peace Research* 18, no. 1 [1981]) drew the following conclusions: "The exigencies of survival in an international system of such inadequate organization and with so pervasively dysfunctional a culture require relatively uniform response (p. 11). . . . domestic factors are negligible;" war "cannot be explained on the basis of relatively invariant phenomena" (p. 1).

    Michael Haas, *International Conflict,* discovers that, at the systemic level, "collective security, stratification, and hegemonization systems are likely to avoid a high frequency in violent outputs" (p. 453); but "no single [causal] model was entirely or even largely satisfactory" (p. 452). At the social level, war correlates with variables such as: "bloc prominence, military mobilizations, public perceptions of hostility toward peoples of other countries, a high proportion of gross national product devoted to military expenditures . . . " (p. 461). These variables appear to describe rather than explain war. A cluster analysis he performs associates democracy, development, and sustained modernization with the existence of peaceful countries (pp. 464–65). But these factors do not correlate with pacification duing the period 1816–1965 according to M. Small and J. D. Singer, "The War Proneness of Democratic Regimes," *Jerusalem Journal of International Relations* 50, no. 4 (Summer 1976).

    Their conclusions follow, I think, from their homogenization of war and from their attempt to explain all wars, in which a myriad of states have engaged. I attempt to explain an interstate peace, which only liberal regimes, a particular type of state and society, have succeeded in establishing.

23. The incompatibility of democracy and war is forcefully asserted by Paine in *The Rights of Man.* The connection between liberal capitalism, democracy, and peace is argued by, among others, Joseph Schumpeter in *Imperialism and Social Classes* (New York: Meridian, 1955); and Montesquieu, *Spirit of the Laws* I, bk. 20, chap. 1. This literature is surveyed

and analyzed by Albert Hirschman, "Rival Interpretations of Market Society: Civilizing, Destructive, or Feeble?" *Journal of Economic Literature* 20 (December 1982).

24. Two classic sources that examine Kant's international theory from a Realist perspective are Stanley Hoffmann, "Rousseau on War and Peace" in the *State of War* (New York: Praeger, 1965) and Kenneth Waltz, "Kant, Liberalism, and War," *American Political Science Review* 56, no. 2 (June 1962). I have benefited from their analysis and from those of Karl Friedrich, *Inevitable Peace* (Cambridge, MA: Harvard University Press, 1948); F. H. Hinsley, *Power and the Pursuit of Peace* (Cambridge: Cambridge University Press, 1967), chap. 4; W. B. Gallic, *Philosophers of Peace and War* (Cambridge: Cambridge University Press, 1978), chap, 1; and particularly Patrick Riley, *Kant's Political Philosophy* (Totowa, NJ: Rowman and Littlefield, 1983). But some of the conclusions of this article differ markedly from theirs.

    Kant's republican constitution is described in Kant, "Perpetual Peace," *The Philosophy of Kant*, p. 437 and analyzed by Riley, *Kant's Political Philosophy*, chap. 5.

25. Kant, "Universal History," *The Philosophy of Kant*, p. 123. The pacific union follows a process of "federalization" such that it "can be realized by a gradual extension to all states, leading to eternal peace." This interpretation contrasts with those cited in n. 24. I think Kant meant that the peace would be established among liberal regimes and would expand as new liberal regimes appeared. By a process of gradual extension the peace would become global and then perpetual; the occasion for wars with nonliberals would disappear as nonliberal regimes disappeared.

26. Kant's "Pacific Union," the *foedus pacificum*, is thus neither a *pactum pacis* (a single peace treaty) nor a *civitas gentium* (a world state). He appears to have anticipated something like a less formally institutionalized League of Nations or United Nations. One could argue that these two institutions in practice worked for liberal states and only for liberal states. But no specifically liberal "pacific union" was institutionalized. Instead liberal states have behaved for the past 180 years as if such a Kantian pacific union and treaty of Perpetual Peace had been signed. This follows Riley's views of the legal, not the organizational, character of the *foedus pacificum*.

27. Kant, "Perpetual Peace," pp. 444–47.

28. Kant, the fourth principle of "The Idea for a Universal History" in *The Philosophy of Kant*, p. 120. Interestingly, Kant's three sources of peace (republicanism, respect, and commerce) parallel quite closely Aristotle's three sources of friendship (goodness, pleasure or appreciation, and utility). See *Nicomachean Ethics*, bk. 8, chap. 3, trans. J. A. K. Thomson (Baltimore, MD: Penguin, 1955).

29. The "Prussian Model" suggests the connection between insecurity, war, and authoritarianism. See *The Anglo-American Tradition in Foreign Affairs*, ed. Arnold Wolfers and Laurence Martin (New Haven: Yale University Press, 1956), "Introduction," for an argument linking security and liberalism.

30. Small and Singer, *Resort to Arms*, pp. 176–79.

31. Kant, "The Idea for a Universal History," p. 124.

32. Immanuel Kant, "Perpetual Peace" in *The Enlightenment*, ed. Peter Gay (New York: Simon & Schuster, 1974), pp. 790–92.

    Gallie in *Philosophers of Peace and War* criticizes Kant for neglecting economic, religious, nationalistic drives toward war and for failing to appreciate that "regimes" make war in order to enhance their domestic political support. But Kant holds that these drives should be subordinated to justice in a liberal society (he specifically criticizes colonial wars stimulated by rapaciousness). He also argues that *republics* derive their legitimacy from their accordance with law and representation, thereby freeing them from crises of domestic political support. Kant thus acknowleges both Gallie's sets of motives for war but argues that they would not apply within the pacific union.

33. Kant, *The Philosophy of Kant*, p. 454. These factors also have a bearing on Karl Deutsch's "compatibility of values" and "predictability of behavior" (see n. 20).
34. A highly stylized version of this effect can be found in the Realist's "Prisoner's Dilemma" game. There a failure of mutual trust and the incentives to enhance one's own position produce a noncooperative solution that makes both parties worse off. Contrarily, cooperation, a commitment to avoid exploiting the other party, produces joint gains. The significance of the game in this context is the character of its participants. The "prisoners" are presumed to be felonious, unrelated apart from their partnership in crime, and lacking in mutual trust—competitive nation states in an anarchic world. A similar game between fraternal or sororal twins—Kant's republics—would be likely to lead to different results. See Robert Jervis, "Hypotheses on Misperception," *World Politics* 20, no. 3 (April 1968), for an exposition of the role of presumptions; and "Cooperation Under the Security Dilemma," *World Politics* 30, no. 2 (January 1978), for the factors Realists see as mitigating the security dilemma caused by anarchy.

    Also, expectations (including theory and history) can influence behavior, making liberal states expect (and fulfill) pacific policies toward each other. These effects are explored at a theoretical level in R. Dacey, "Some Implications of 'Theory Absorption' for Economic Theory and the Economics of Information" in *Philosophical Dimensions of Economics*, ed. J. Pitt (Dordrecht, Holland: D. Reidel, 1980).
35. Karl Polanyi, *The Great Transformation* (Boston: Beacon Press, 1944), chaps. 1–2, and Samuel Huntington and Z. Brzezinski, *Political Power: USA/USSR* (New York: Viking Press, 1963, 1964), chap. 9. And see Richard Neustadt, *Alliance Politics* (New York: Columbia University Press, 1970) for a detailed case study of interliberal politics.
36. Charles Kindleberger, *The World in Depression* (Berkeley: University of California Press, 1973); Robert Gilpin, *U.S. Power and the Multinational Corporation* (New York: Basic Books, 1975); and Fred Hirsch and Michael Doyle, "Politicization in the World Economy" in Hirsch, Doyle and Edward Morse, *Alternatives to Monetary Disorder* (New York: Council on Foreign Relations/McGraw-Hill, 1977).
37. Robert Gilpin, "Three Models of the Future," *International Organization* 29, no. 1 (Winter 1975).
38. George Liska identifies this peaceful, hegemonic transition as exceptional in *Quest for Equilibrium: America and the Balance of Power on Land and Sea* (Baltimore, MD: The Johns Hopkins University Press, 1977), chap. 4, p. 75. Wilson's speeches, including his "War Message," suggest the importance of ideological factors in explaining this transition: "Neutrality is no longer feasible or desirable where the peace of the world is involved and the freedom of its peoples, and the menace to that peace and freedom lies in the *existence* [emphasis supplied] of autocratic governments backed by organized force which is controlled wholly by their will, not by the will of their people." This quotation

is from Woodrow Wilson, *The Messages and Papers of Woodrow Wilson*, ed. Albert Shaw (New York: The Review of Reviews, 1924), p. 378. Ross Gregory in *The Origins of American Intervention in the First World War* (New York: Norton, 1971) offers an interpretation along these lines, combining commercial, financial, strategic, and ideological factors in his account of the policy which brought the United States onto a collision course with Germany.

2
Faulty Correlation, Foolish Consistency, Fatal Consequence

John Mueller

> A foolish consistency is the hobgoblin of little minds, adored by little statesmen and philosophers and divines.
> —Ralph Waldo Emerson (1841)

Democracy, a messy gimmick for aggregating preferences, has proven to be not only superior to alternative methods but also a remarkably simple form of government that can rather easily be established, or imposed, whenever elites decide to do so and remain uninhibited by thugs with guns. Democracy, however, has been elevated into something of a mystique by philosophers and divines who maintain that this system of governance efficiently aggregates and creates preferences. In addition, the rise of democracy has corresponded with the growing acceptance of another, essentially unrelated idea: war aversion. This faulty correlation has been thought to be causal. Putting theory into practice, American statesmen have sought to impose democracy on the Middle East partly operating under the foolish, if theoretically consistent, belief that this will cause peace and preferences favorable to U.S. foreign policy to blossom in the area. The consequences have been fatal.

DEMOCRACY AS A SUPERIOR GIMMICK

Democracy is a device for aggregating and expressing policy preferences. It is characterized by government that is necessarily and routinely responsive—although this responsiveness is not always fair—and it comes into existence when the people agree not to use violence to overthrow the government and when the government leaves them free to criticize, to pressure, to organize, and to try to overthrow it by any other means.[1] One is free to try to increase one's political importance by working in politics or by supplying money in appropriate places, or one can reduce it by succumbing to apathy and neglecting even to vote. In practice, then, democracy is a form of government in which the individual is left free to become politically unequal.[2]

Democracy is characterized by minority rule and majority acquiescence, and most of what democratic governments actually do on a day-by-day basis is the result not of elections but of pressure and petition—lobbying, it's called—and of the reactions and policy initiatives of the government. The history of the oldest large democracy supplies much evidence for this: although it is often against the interests and the desires of the majority, beekeepers gain price supports for honey, selected industries are insulated from competition, gun enthusiasts are protected from seizure, and artists are given medals and subsidies.

The ultimate appeal of democracy is not that it is, or could become, a perfect or ideal form of government, but that, however imperfect, it has distinct advantages when compared to other forms. In an essay first published in 1939, E. M. Forster (1951, 69–70) adopted just such an appropriate comparative approach when he observed that democracy "is less hateful than other contemporary forms of government." Or, as it is usually put: democracy is the worst form of government except for all the rest.[3]

Democracy is, and will always be, distressingly messy, clumsy, and disorderly, and people are permitted loudly and irritatingly to voice opinions that are clearly erroneous and even dangerous. Moreover, decision making in democracies is often muddled, incoherent, and slow, and the results are sometimes exasperatingly foolish, shortsighted, irrational, and incoherent.[4] And some, including James Bryce, have lamented that democracies do not often promote the best people in the society to political leadership—assuming, presumably, that the society would be better off with the best in those positions rather than in science, business, or medicine (Hess 1987). But the key question is, "Best compared to what?"

One might begin by looking at the quality of the people democracies have generally selected and compare them to leaders who have emerged in nondemocratic societies. In general, democracy looks pretty good when one compares the leadership and decision-making qualities of the tsars of Russia or the kaisers of Germany or the kings of Saudi Arabia or the dictators of just about any place with the prime ministers of Great Britain or Canada or the presidents of the United States. Only democracies generally have been able to establish effective review and succession arrangements, thereby solving an elemental problem of governance. Moreover, democracy furnishes a safety valve for discontent: those with complaints may or may not ever see relief of their grievances, but, rather than wallowing in frustration, they are supplied with the opportunity to express themselves and potentially change things.

In the end, William Riker's perspective (1982, 244–46) on all this seems sound: democracy is characterized not by "popular rule" but by various devices that provide for "an intermittent, sometimes random, even perverse, popular veto" that "has at least the potential of preventing tyranny and rendering officials responsive." He notes that this is "a minimal sort of democracy" but contends that it "is the only kind of democracy actually attainable."

The rise of this superior gimmick has essentially been the result of a 200-year competition of ideas, not the necessary or incidental consequence of grander changes in social, cultural, economic, or historical patterns. Democracy's promoters needed, first, to undermine the competition, to seize on and bring out its defects. Since democracy's chief competitor initially was monarchy, a rather bizarre form of government that had unaccountably been around forever (but was to be extinguished in most of the world in just one century), this was not a terribly difficult task. They also needed to create demand for values that, if embraced, would automatically help their product be accepted. For example, democracy will be aided (but its success will not necessarily be assured) if the notion becomes accepted that the government owes its existence and its perpetuation not to the dictates of God as expressed in the genetic process but to the general consent and approval of the people at large. In addition, the product had to be put into practice somewhere to show it could actually work. Promoters of democracy were lucky that they first test-marketed their product in Britain and America (in the United States it was explicitly called "the American experiment"), because, in the process, democracy came to be associated with countries that were admirable—that is, that became fashion leaders or role models—for reasons that were often quite irrelevant to the institution itself. War also played a role. As the European monarchy met its demise in World War I, fascism and Nazism, together with Japanese militarism, died, bloodied and discredited, in World War II.

In the last thirty years democracy has gained particularly wide acceptance (Huntington 1991; Mueller 1999, 214–27). The promoters improved neither the product nor the packaging. What changed was the receptivity of the customers: democracy caught on, at least among political elites, as an idea whose time had come. Indeed, just about the only countries where democracy has yet to penetrate deeply are the Islamic ones. As Samuel Huntington (1984, 216) has observed, Islam often associates democracy with the Western influences many who practice the religion oppose. Thus, the elites in many Islamic countries specifically do not find the Western democracies to be attractive fashion leaders even as those in, say, Hungary do. Moreover, where leaders have allowed elections in Muslim societies, as in Algeria and Iran in 1997, the voters displayed a considerable ability to differentiate and express their interest even though the choice of candidates and the freedom of speech were limited. And some Muslim states, such as Mali, Turkey, Pakistan, and Qatar, moved substantially toward democracy. That democracy could become fashionable even in the Middle East was suggested by the progressive emir of Qatar, who saw the most progress in regional states that adopted democratic rule.[5]

Democratic development, then, has principally been a matter of convincing leaders to "do" democracy.[6] In practice, it seems to be about as difficult to put on as a new suit of clothes, and democratic governance has spread not so much because it has been made cosmically inevitable by various economic or social developments, but because it has come into style: it's what just about everyone who is anyone is wearing this season. It is easy to establish and maintain because it is essentially based on giving people the freedom to complain—and, importantly, the freedom to organize with other complainers to attempt to topple or favorably influence the government. Complaining comes easily to most. Thus, as Americans should surely know by now, anyone can do democracy.

Democracy can also be established by force, although, absent favorable market conditions, the forceful imposition of democracy generally has not worked very well. For example, the United States has repeatedly and often evangelically urged democracy on its neighbors to the south and has often been prepared to use money (and sometimes military force) to coat the philosophic pill. Those efforts seem rarely to have made much lasting difference. Thus, in 1913 President Woodrow Wilson dramatically declared the United States to be the "champion" of democracy in the Americas and, to show he meant business, sent U.S. troops to Nicaragua, Haiti, and the Dominican Republic to establish democracy. But all three countries subsequently lapsed into extended dictatorships (Whitehead 1986, 6). Latin America's remarkable move toward democracy after 1975 was accomplished almost entirely by the people themselves when market conditions improved.

However, when conditions are propitious, force may work. The times seem to have been right for democracy by force at the end of World War II in some places. At the war's end, the victorious democracies set about foisting their form of government on the portion of Germany they occupied and on Italy, Austria, and Japan. By 1945 it must have seemed to the people of these countries that even democracy at its worst was better than the alternative that had just brought catastrophe on them, and they took up, or lapsed into, democracy without a great deal of apparent effort. Similarly, when Panama's Manuel Noriega calmly stole an election that went against him in 1989, in the midst of Latin America's transition, he was deposed by an American military invasion. Liberated from this anachronistic tyrant, Panama became a democracy. The United States also successfully imposed, or reimposed, democracy on Grenada in 1983. However, a somewhat similar process in Haiti in the 1990s met with far less success.

THE DEMOCRATIC PEACE: FAULTY CORRELATION

When ideas have spread throughout the world in the last few hundred years, they have tended to do so in one direction. There has been, for better or worse, a long and fairly steady process of what is often called "Westernization." Taiwan has become more like Canada than Canada has become like Taiwan; Gabon has become more like Belgium than Belgium has become like Gabon (see Nadelmann 1990, 484). Major ideas that have gone from the developed world to the less developed world include Christianity, the abolition of slavery, the acceptance of democratic institutions and Western economic and social forms, and the determined application of, and faith in, the scientific method. Not all of these have been fully or readily accepted, but the point is that the process has largely been unidirectional; so far there has been little in the way of a reverse flow of ideas.

In the last couple of decades there has been a burgeoning and intriguing discussion about the connection between democracy and war aversion.[7] Most notable has been the empirical observation that democracies have never, or almost never, gone to war with each other. This relationship seems more correlative than causal, however. Like many important ideas over the last few centuries, the idea that war is undesirable and inefficacious and the idea that democracy is a good form of government have largely followed the same trajectory: they were embraced first in northern Europe and North America and then gradually, with a number of traumatic setbacks, became more accepted elsewhere. In this view, the rise of democracy not only is associated with the rise of war aversion but also with the decline of slavery, religion, and capital punishment and with the growing acceptance of capitalism, scientific methodology, women's rights, environmentalism, abortion, and rock music.[8]

While democracy and war aversion have taken much the same trajectory, however, they have been substantially out of sync with each other: the movement toward democracy began about 200 years ago, but the movement against war really began only about a century ago (Mueller 1989, 2004). Critics of the theory of a democracy-peace connection often cite examples of wars or near-wars between democracies, most of which took place before World War I—that is, before war aversion had caught on.[9]

A necessary, logical connection between democracy and war aversion, accordingly, is far from clear. It is often asserted that democracies are peaceful because they apply their domestic penchant for peaceful compromise (something, obviously, that broke down in the United States in 1861) to the international arena or because the structure of democracy requires decision makers to obtain domestic approval.[10] Yet, authoritarian regimes must also necessarily develop negotiating skills in order to survive. They all have domestic constituencies that must be serviced, such as the church, the landed gentry, potential urban rioters, the *nomenklatura*, the aristocracy, party members, the military, prominent business interests, the police or secret police, lenders of money to the exchequer, potential rivals for the throne, and the sullen peasantry.[11]

Since World War I the democracies in the developed world have been in the lead in rejecting war as a methodology. Some proponents of the democracy-peace connection suggest that this is because the democratic norm of nonviolent conflict resolution has been externalized to the international arena. However, developed democracies have not necessarily adopted a pacifist approach, particularly after a version of that approach failed so spectacularly to prevent World War II from being forced on them. In addition, they were willing to subvert or to threaten—and sometimes to apply military force—when threats appeared to loom during the cold war. At times this approach was used even against regimes that had some democratic credentials, such as in Iran in 1953, Guatemala in 1954, Chile in 1973, and perhaps Nicaragua in the 1980s (Rosato 2003, 590–91). They have also sometimes used military force in their intermittent efforts to police the post–cold war world (Mueller 2004, chs. 7 and 8).

It is true that developed democracies have warred little or not at all against each other; and since there were few democracies outside the developed world until the last quarter of the twentieth century, it is this statistical regularity that most prominently informs the supposed connection between democracy and peace. However, the developed democracies hardly needed democracy to decide that war among them was a bad idea.[12] In addition, they also adopted a live-and-let-live approach toward a huge number of dictatorships and other nondemocracies that did not seem threatening during the cold war. In fact, they often aided and embraced such regimes if they seemed to be on the right side in the conflict with communism.

The supposed penchant for peaceful compromise of democracies has not always served them well when confronted with civil unrest and secessionist demands. The process broke down into civil warfare in democratic Switzerland in 1847 and savagely so in the United States in 1861. Democracies have also fought a considerable number of wars to retain colonial possessions—six by France alone since World War II. And these can in many respects be labeled civil wars (Fearon & Laitin 2003, 76). To be sure, democracies have often managed to deal with colonial problems peacefully, mostly by letting the colonies go. But authoritarian governments have done the same. The Soviet Union, for example, withdrew from its empire in Eastern Europe and then dissolved itself, all almost entirely without violence.

Thus, while democracy and war aversion have often been promoted by the same advocates, the relationship does not seem to be a causal one. And when the two trends are substantially out of step today, democracies will fight one another. Therefore, it is not at all clear that telling the elected hawks in the Jordanian parliament that Israel is a democracy will dampen their hostility in the slightest. And various warlike sentiments could be found in the elected parliaments in the former Yugoslavia in the early 1990s and in India and then-democratic Pakistan when these two countries engaged in armed conflict in 1999. If Argentina had been a democracy in 1982 when it seized the Falkland Islands (a very popular undertaking), it is unlikely that British opposition to the venture would have been much less severe. "The important consideration," observes Miriam Fendius Elman (1997, 484, 496), does not seem to be "whether a country is democratic or not, but whether its ruling coalition is committed to peaceful methods of conflict resolution." As she further points out, the countries of Latin America and most of Africa have engaged in very few international wars even without the benefit of being democratic. Of course, the long peace enjoyed by developed countries since World War II includes not only the one that has prevailed among democracies but also the even more important one between the authoritarian East and the democratic West. Even if there is some connection, whether causal or atmospheric, between democracy and peace, it cannot explain this latter phenomenon.

THE ROLE OF PHILOSOPHERS AND DIVINES

Democracy has been a matter of debate for several millennia as philosophers and divines have speculated about what it is, what it might become, and what it ought to be. Associated with these speculations has been a tendency to emboss the grubby gimmick with something of a mystique. Of particular interest for present purposes is the fanciful notion that democracy does not simply express and aggregate preferences but actually somehow *creates* (or should create) them. In addition, the (rough) correlation between democracy and war aversion has also been elevated into a causal relationship.

Democratic philosophers and divines have often come to conclude that, rather than simply being a process of interest aggregation, democracy actually creates, inspires, or requires certain modes of thought or policy preferences. However, although democracy does by definition require that opposition and contention and special interest activity be peacefully preserved, and although it may be a (comparatively) desirable gimmick for aggregating policy preferences, it does not create the policy preferences themselves. This should be clear from experience.

Over the course of time, democracies variously have banned liquor and allowed it to flow freely; raised taxes to confiscatory levels and lowered them to next to nothing; refused women the right to vote and granted it to them; despoiled the environment and sought to protect it; subsidized certain economic groups and withdrawn subsidies; stifled labor unions and facilitated their creation; banned abortion and permitted and subsidized the operation; tolerated drug use and launched massive "wars" on the practice; embraced slavery and determinedly sought to eradicate it; persecuted homosexuality and repealed or systematically failed to enforce the laws that did so; seized private property and turned over state assets to the private sector; discriminated against racial groups and given them preferential treatment; banned pornography and allowed it to be distributed freely; tolerated the organization of peaceful political opposition; and voted themselves out of existence by withdrawing the right to seek reelection indefinitely. Moreover, democracies have welcomed or committed naked aggression and fought to reverse it; devolved into vicious civil war and avoided it by artful compromise; embraced colonialism and rejected the practice entirely; tolerated and sometimes caused humanitarian disaster in other parts of the world and sought to alleviate it; adopted protectionist economic policies and been free traders; and gone to war with enthusiasm and self-righteousness and sought to outlaw the institution.[13]

Philosophers and divines not only have encased democracy in a vaporously idealistic or ideological mystique, they have done the same for the democracy-peace correlation. After all, if correlation is taken to be cause, it follows that peace will envelop the Earth right after democracy does. Accordingly, for those who value peace, the promotion of democracy, by force or otherwise, becomes a central mission.

This notion has been brewing for some time. Woodrow Wilson's famous desire to "make the world safe for democracy" was in large part an antiwar motivation. He and many others in Britain, France, and the United States had become convinced that, as Britain's Lloyd George put it, "Freedom is the only warranty of Peace" (Rappard 1940, 42–44). With the growth in the systematic examination of the supposed peace-democracy connection by the end of the century, such certain pronouncements became commonplace. Notes Bruce Russett (2005, 395), sentiments like those have "issued from the White House ever since the last year of the Reagan administration."

FATAL CONSEQUENCES: THE ROLE OF LITTLE STATESMEN

It was left to George W. Bush to put mystique into practice. As he stressed to reporter Bob Woodward (2004, 88–89) during the run-up to the war with Iraq, "I say that freedom is not America's gift to the world. Freedom is God's gift to everybody in the world. I believe that. As a matter of fact, I was the person that wrote that line, or said it. I didn't write it, I just said it in a speech. And it became part of the jargon. And I believe that. And I believe we have a duty to free people. I would hope we wouldn't have to do it militarily, but we have a duty." In an address shortly before the war, he confidently proclaimed, "The world has a clear interest in the spread of democratic values, because stable and free nations do not breed the ideologies of murder. They encourage the peaceful pursuit of a better life" (quoted in Frum & Perle 2003, 158).

In this, Bush was only trying to be consistent (foolishly so, perhaps), a quality that endeared him to so many of his followers. If democracy is so wonderful and inevitably both brings peace and creates favorable policy preferences, then forcefully jamming it down the throats of the decreasing number of nondemocratic countries in the world must be all to the good. Bush had already done something like that, with a fair amount of success, in Afghanistan; Bill Clinton had invaded Haiti and bombed Bosnia and Serbia with the same lofty goal at least partly in mind; George H. W. Bush had crisply slapped Panama into shape; and Reagan had straightened out Grenada. Further, the Australians had recently done it in East Timor and the British in Sierra Leone (Mueller 2004, ch. 7). Critics have argued that democracy cannot be spread at the point of a gun, but these cases, as well as the experience with the defeated enemies after World War II, suggest that it sometimes can be, something that supporters of the administration were quick to point out (Kaplan & Kristol 2003, 98–99; Frum & Perle 2003, 163). Even Russett (2005, 398–400), a prominent democratic-peace analyst, eventually conceded the possibility (see also Peceny & Pickering 2006).

However, George W. Bush and some of his supporters—particularly those in the neoconservative camp—foolishly, if consistently, developed an even more extravagant mystique. Not only would the invasion crisply bring viable democracy to Iraq, but success there would have a domino effect: democracy would eventually spread from its Baghdad bastion to envelop the Middle East. This would not only bring blissful peace in its wake (because, as we know, democracies never fight each other), but the new democracies would adopt all sorts of other policies as well, including, in particular, love of, or at least much-diminished hostility toward, the United States and Israel (because, as we know, the democratic process itself has a way of making people think nice thoughts). As Woodward (2004, 428) reported, Vice President Dick Cheney attested to Bush's "abiding faith that if people were given freedom and democracy, that would begin a transformation process in Iraq that in years ahead would change the Middle East."

Moreover, since force can establish democracy, and since democracies automatically embrace peaceful intentions toward each other, military force would be deftly applied as necessary to speed up the domino-toppling process wherever necessary in the area. Such extravagant, even romantic visions filled neoconservative calls to arms. In their book *The War over Iraq*, Lawrence Kaplan and William Kristol (2003, 104–5) applied due reverence to the sanctified correlation—"democracies rarely, if ever, wage war against one another"—and then extrapolated fancifully to conclude that the "more democratic the world becomes, the more likely it is to be congenial to America."

War architect Paul Wolfowitz also seems to have believed that the war would become an essential stage in the march toward freedom and democracy (Woodward 2004, 428). In an article proposing what he called "democratic realism," Charles Krauthammer (2004, 23, 17) urged taking "the risky but imperative course of trying to reorder the Arab world" with a "targeted, focused" effort that would, however, be "limited" to "that Islamic crescent stretching from North Africa to Afghanistan." And Kaplan and Kristol (2003, 124–25) stressed that "the mission begins in Baghdad, but does not end there.... War in Iraq represents but the first installment ... Duly armed, the United States can act to secure its safety and to advance the cause of liberty—in Baghdad and beyond."

With that, lamented Russett (2005), democracy and democratic peace theory became "Bushwhacked." Democratic processes of pressure and policy promotion were deftly used by a dedicated group to wage costly war to establish both peace and congenial policy in the otherwise intractable Middle East. It could be argued, then, that the little statesmen of the Bush administration had the courage of the mystical convictions of the democracy and democratic peace philosophers and divines. However, although Bush's faith in democracy had its endearing side, how deeply that passion was really shared by his neoconservative allies may be questioned. Did they really believe that the United States, which, as Francis Fukuyama (2004a, 60) noted, "cannot eliminate poverty or raise test scores in Washington, D.C.," could "bring democracy to a part of the world that has stubbornly resisted it and is virulently anti-American to boot?"

Although they hyped democracy, David Frum and Richard Perle (2003, 162–63) cautioned that "in the Middle East, democratization does not mean calling immediate elections and then living with whatever happens next" but rather "opening political spaces," "creating representative institutions," "deregulating the economy," "shrinking and reforming the Middle Eastern public sector," and, "perhaps above all," changing the educational system. Similarly, Krauthammer's "democratic realism" approach did not seem to stress democracy all that much.[14]

Most interesting was a plea issued by neoconservatism's champion, Norman Podhoretz (2002, 28), in the run-up to the war, who advocated expanding Bush's "axis of evil" beyond Iraq, Iran, and North Korea "at a minimum" to embrace "Syria and Lebanon and Libya, as well as 'friends' of America like the Saudi royal family and Egypt's Hosni Mubarak, along with the Palestinian Authority." However, Podhoretz proved to be less mystical (or simply less devious) than other neocons about democracy by adding, "The alternative to these regimes could easily turn out to be worse, even (or especially) if it comes into power through democratic elections.... It will be necessary for the United States to *impose* a new political culture on the defeated parties."[15] Although Podhoretz was more realistic than others about democracy, his extravagant notion that the United States would somehow have the capacity to impose a new political culture throughout the non-Israeli Middle East was, like Krauthammer's comparable vision, so fantastic as to border on the absurd.

Indeed, after looking beneath the boilerplate about democracy and the democratic peace, what seemed to be principally motivating at least some of these leaders was a strong desire for the United States to use military methods to make the Middle

East finally and once and for all safe for Israel (Drew 2003, 22; Fukuyama 2004a; Roy 2003). Most Bush advisers were devoted supporters of Israel and seemed to display far less interest in advocating the application of military force to deal with unsavory dictatorial regimes in other parts of the world that did not threaten Israel.

As John Mearsheimer and Stephen Walt (2006) observed in their discussion of what they called the "Israel Lobby," such policy advocacy is appropriate and fully democratic. Democracy, as noted earlier, is characterized by the contestation of isolated, self-serving, and often tiny special interest groups and their political and bureaucratic allies. What happened with Iraq policy was democracy in full flower. It does not follow, of course, that policies so generated are necessarily wise. Mearsheimer and Walt considered that the results of much of the lobby's efforts—certainly in this case—were detrimental to American (and even Israeli) national interest. Yet, their contentions that the lobby was "critical" or "a key factor" in the decision to go to war and that the decision would "have been far less likely" without the lobby's efforts need more careful analysis. In their view, the lobby has too much influence over U.S. foreign policy—a conclusion that is shared by 68 percent of more than 1,000 international relations scholars who responded to a 2006 survey.[16]

It should be noted, however, that although the neocons may actually have believed their prewar fantasies about the blessings that imposed democracy would in turn shower on the Middle East, the arguments they proffered for going to war stressed national security issues, not democracy ones. Specifically, these included the notion that Saddam's Iraq was a threat to the United States because of its development, or potential development, of weapons of mass destruction and because of its connections to terrorist groups out to get America (Roy 2003). The democracy argument rose in significance, noted Russett (2005, 396), only after those security arguments for going to war proved to be empty. As Fukuyama (2005) put it, a prewar request to spend "several hundred billion dollars and several thousand American lives in order to bring democracy to . . . Iraq [would] have been laughed out of court." Moreover, when given a list of foreign policy goals, the American public has consistently ranked the promotion of democracy lower—often *much* lower—than such goals as combating international terrorism, protecting American jobs, preventing the spread of nuclear weapons, strengthening the United Nations, and protecting American businesses abroad.

Support for the Iraq war eroded more slowly than one might have expected given the demise of the initial casus belli for going to war and the unexpectedly high American casualty numbers (Mueller 2005, 45). This may reflect the fact that many people still connected the effort there to the campaign, or "war," against terror, an enterprise that continued to enjoy huge domestic support. In addition, the toppling of Saddam Hussein remains a singular accomplishment, one the American people had been spoiling for since the Gulf War of 1991 (Larson & Savych 2005, 132–37).

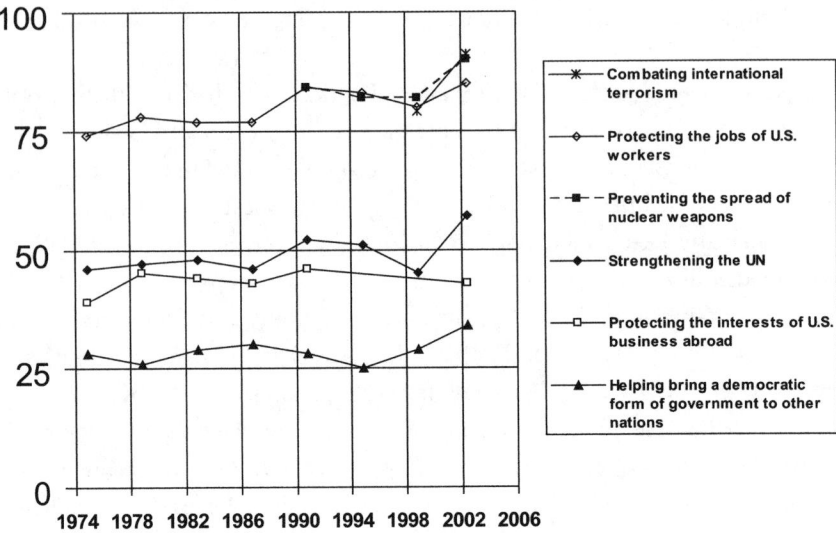

Figure 2.1. The Public and U.S. Foriegn-Policy Goals: Percent Saying "Very Important." Source: Chicago Council on Foreign Relations, quadrennial surveys.

However, the persistence of support for the war may be partly the result of acceptance by the American public, despite its pervasive cynicism about democracy in practice, of some of the democratic mystique so sonorously spun out by philosophers and divines over the decades.

SAVING DEMOCRACY AND PEACE

The cynicism (or realism) about democracy expressed by Podhoretz has proven to be sound, of course. As peace builders in Bosnia have repeatedly discovered, elections lead to the rise of people who can best engage and manipulate the political process to attract voters, and the winners are not necessarily the ones preferred by intervening foreign well-wishers.

Thus, if the people detest Israel and the United States and let that passion influence their vote, they will elect politicians who voice—indeed, stoke—hatred for Israel and the United States. Such hatreds have been very much enhanced by the U.S. and British invasion of Iraq and by Israel's military actions against Palestinians during an internal rebellion between 2000 and 2005 and later against Lebanon in 2006. Nearly two-thirds of those elected to the Iraq parliament in late 2005 explicitly advocated a stronger role for Islam in politics (Gause 2006). Muslim Brotherhood candidates did very well in Egyptian elections at the same time and would have done even better had it not been for great electoral restrictions imposed by the government. And the militantly anti-Israel group Hamas triumphed in elections in Palestine in January 2006.

This is not to argue that efforts to force democracy on Iraq have necessarily failed. Following the minimal—but realistic—definitions of democracy proposed at the outset of this chapter, Iraq is acting very much like a standard democracy, albeit one with exceptionally high rates of crime and violence. Politicians are squabbling continuously, interest groups are seeking to loot the public treasury as best they can, people are rather freely expressing themselves even where this may entail the airing of ethnic and racial hatreds (those who use violence to do so are not democratic, however), and politicians are seeking to manipulate the system to benefit their supporters.[17] If the violence eventually comes under control, it is entirely possible that the country will remain democratic—though the demand for security may lead to a takeover by a strongman welcomed by the desperate population. However, even if democracy does survive in Iraq, it is to be expected that those in charge will remain loyal to the wishes of their constituencies. That may well mean, as Podhoretz suggested, intensified hostility to Israel and ungrateful animosity toward Iraq's naive, clumsy, and destructive democratic liberators.

On the brighter side, there is at least some hope that the disastrous experience in Iraq will terminally undercut both the democracy mystique and the democratic peace mystique that are so adored by philosophers, divines, and little statesmen. There are some signs that this may already be in process. Egypt's elected leaders made innumerable speeches seeking to prod that country into a more democratic direction, but this cheerleading ceased after the election with its discouraging, if democratic, results. It is all rather similar to the nonreaction of George H. W. Bush when in 1992 the Algerian military cancelled elections likely to bring Muslim fundamentalists to power shortly after Bush had taken deep umbrage and instituted sanctions against Haiti, where the military had done much the same thing.

There is, however, a considerable danger that the disastrous experience with democracy promotion in the Middle East will become a major setback to the rise of democracy there. The unwillingness of the United States to accept the results of elections in Egypt and especially in Palestine because they did not come out "right" has led to understandable, and essentially correct, accusations of hypocrisy. An additional danger is that the disastrous chaos visited on Iraq by the American invasion will come to be associated with democracy, substantially discrediting the institution in the area.

In the end, someone may explore the possibility that the supposed democracy-peace connection has been reversed in all this. The correlation between democracy and peace may not mean that democracy causes peace but that peace causes, or facilitates, democracy—at least when other conditions are right. This already seems to hold for the relationship between peace and trade. Although expanding trade and interactions may enhance or reinforce the process, attitude toward war is likely to be the key explanatory variable in the relationship. Thus, it has frequently been observed that militarized disputes between countries reduce trade between them (Pollins 1989a, 1989b; Li & Sacko 2002). In contrast, if countries that have previously enjoyed a conflictual relationship lapse into a comfortable peace and become extremely unlikely to become involved in war, businesses in both places may well be inclined to explore the possibilities for mutually beneficial exchange.

Similarly, although international institutions and norms often stress peace, they, like expanded trade flows, are not so much the cause of peace as its result. Many of the institutions that have been fabricated in Europe, particularly ones like the coal and steel community so carefully forged between France and Germany in the years following World War II, have been specifically designed to reduce the danger of war between erstwhile enemies. It is difficult to see why these institutions should get the credit for the peace that has flourished between those two countries for the last half-century.[18] They are among the consequences of the peace that has enveloped Western Europe since 1945, not a cause. For institutions of collective security, "peace is the premise of the system, not the product" (Betts 1992, 23–24; see also Schweller 2001, 183).

Something like that may hold for the democracy-peace connection: peace causes—or, more likely, facilitates—democracy (see also Pietrzyk 2002; Payne 2006). Countries often restrict or even abandon democracy when domestic instability or external military threat seems to loom. An Iraqi who had been imprisoned by the Saddam Hussein regime and who gleefully helped pull down a statue of the tyrant in 2003 became disillusioned by subsequent calamity and concluded in 2007, "We regret that Saddam Hussein is gone, no matter how much we hated him" (Raghavan 2007). After the chaos of the 1990s, Russians continue to approve highly of their order-providing, if democracy-eroding leader, Vladimir Putin. By the same token, when they are comfortably at peace, people may come to realize that they no longer require a strongman to provide order and can afford to embrace the comparative benefits of democracy, even if those might come with somewhat heightened uncertainty and possibly with the potential for less reliable leadership.

If this is so, the prospects for continued democratization seem to be quite good. As it happens, there has been a remarkable decline in the incidence of war—both civil and international—over the last decade to the point where, outside of Iraq and Afghanistan, scarcely any exist anywhere in the world (Mueller 2007). That is, although there has been a considerable increase in the number of democratic countries in the world as noted earlier, trends in war aversion seem to have considerably outrun it. Thus, if this pattern holds and if fashionable yearnings for democracy continue to grow, peace may help these yearnings to be realized. If so, however, this desirable development is not likely to owe much to little statesmen, philosophers, and divines and the damaging and sometimes fatal mystiques they cherish and nurture.

NOTES

1. For further development of these ideas, see Mueller (1999, ch. 6). This approach can be used to set up a sliding scale of governmental forms. An *authoritarian* government may effectively and sometimes intentionally allow a degree of opposition—a limited amount of press disagreement, for example, or the freedom to complain privately, something sometimes known as the freedom of conversation. Yet it will not tolerate organized attempts to overthrow it, even if they are peaceful. A *totalitarian* government does not allow even those limited freedoms found under authoritarianism. On the other end of the scale is *anarchy*, a condition that holds when a government "allows" the use of violence to try to overthrow it, presumably mainly out of weakness or ineffectiveness.
2. See also Schmitter and Karl (1991, 83–84); Dahl (1956, ch. 4).
3. The most famous expression of this sentiment comes from Winston Churchill (1950, 200), who, in a House of Commons speech in November 1947, observed, "It has been said that democracy is the worst form of government except all those other forms that have been tried from time to time." Twenty years earlier William Ralph Inge (1919, 5) put it this way: "Democracy is a form of government which may be rationally defended, not as good, but as being less bad than any other."
4. De Tocqueville (1990, 235), for example, argued in the 1830s that, particularly with respect to foreign policy, democracy "can only with great difficulty regulate the details of an important undertaking, persevere in a fixed design, and work out its execution in spite of serious obstacles. It cannot combine its measures with secrecy or await their consequences with patience."
5. On Qatar, see also Jehl (1997); on Iran, see Bakhash (1998).
6. On elite transformations, see Higley and Gunther (1992).
7. See, for example, Doyle (1986); Russett (1990); Singer and Wildavsky (1993); Russett and Oneal (2001).
8. On this process, see Mueller (1995, 181–82; 1999, ch. 8); Nadelmann (1990, 484).
9. For example, Layne (1994); Rosato (2003, 591-92); Elman (1997, chaps. 1–3); Pietrzyk (2002).
10. For a discussion, see Russett and Oneal (2001, 53–58).
11. See also Rosato (2003, 593–94, 596–97).
12. Nor is it likely they needed "American preponderance" to do so, as Rosato (2003, 599–600) suggested.
13. See also Schweller (2002, 184); Rosato (2003, 594–96).
14. The theory's extravagant calls for massive warfare over a very substantial portion of the globe, only "limited" in comparison to Bush's expansive view, suggested it was lacking in realism as well.
15. Richard Perle issued a similar litany of targets, adding, for good measure and possibly in jest, France and the U.S. State Department. He also suggested that "a short message"

should be delivered to other hostile regimes in the area: "You're next" (Mearsheimer & Walt 2006).
16. Maliniak et al. (2007, 66). The complete survey results are at http://www.wm.edu/TRIP (accessed July 9, 2009).
17. Alternatively, using the notions sketched out earlier, Iraq could be considered mostly to be in a state of anarchy because of the inability of the government to sufficiently police political violence.
18. But they do: "The creation of a security community has made armed conflict between France and Germany . . . unthinkable" (Russett & Oneal 2001, 158). See also Ikenberry (2001, ch. 6).

3
The Common Origins of Democracy and Peace

Erik Gartzke

The origins of democracy and the causes of peace constitute two of the central and most enduring subjects of inquiry in world affairs. Democracy has recently proliferated after being virtually an anomaly for most of recorded history. Similarly, interstate warfare appears increasingly rare in the modern world, after eons in which such warfare was essentially synonymous with, and perhaps critical to, the formation of government.[1] The normative appeal of each of these processes needs little explication. Instead, I focus on their positive logic and common origins.

It seems natural to relate peace with democracy. Scholarship on the precursors of liberal government emphasizes the need for social, economic, and political stability; war can ruin an established democracy or prevent democracy from taking hold. Similarly, research on the democratic peace—the observation that democracies are much less likely to fight each other, though no less likely to use force in general—has been preoccupied with explaining how democracy makes nations less warlike, if only toward each other. The success of the democratic peace as an observation, however, has not been matched by consensus as to its causes. Researchers really do not know why democracy produces a separate peace.

Perhaps instead of viewing them as two related phenomena, it makes more sense to think of peace and democracy as one. Rather than imagining democracy and peace as independent variables, each causing the other, suppose that democracy and peace are each the product of common underlying forces. In this sense, democracy and peace do not just coincide but are really better thought of as different manifestations of a common economic and political transformation. A little over a century ago, physicists were struggling to characterize two apparently fundamental features of the physical world, energy and matter. Separate fields had developed to address each subject, with their own literatures, nomenclature, and scholarly hierarchy.

Then an obscure Swiss patent clerk posed the possibility that energy and matter were actually different manifestations of the same unified physical entity.

We can make a rough parallel to politics, where peace is a requisite for democracy and democracy is by its very nature a form of peace. This duality mirrors the physical duality between energy and matter. This relationship would help explain the historical scarcity of democracy and peace. Likewise, it addresses their simultaneous rise in recent decades even though largely relegated to certain parts of the globe. Politics is always much more complicated and "noisy" than physics, so the identity is far from fixed or complete. But thinking about democracy and peace as related products of the same fundamental political transformation will perhaps be useful, and more accurate, in understanding our world.

THE CAUSES OF PEACE, DEMOCRACY, AND DEMOCRATIC PEACE

Students of international affairs have traditionally been divided over whether world politics is inherently fractious or whether anarchy can be mitigated, or at least warfare subdued, by social, political, or moral mechanisms. Optimists, intellectual liberals, idealists, and others conceived of politics as ultimately malleable; constraints could be raised or preferences altered that would improve the human condition (Kant 1985 [1795]; Wilson 1918; Doyle 1986). This transformation varies in its details and locus. Some have argued for individual human improvement as a vehicle for social change. Others emphasize social reform, since societies link individuals and form the basis for international politics. Critics, mostly realists, charge that human nature is basically unalterable (Carr 1939; Morgenthau 1948). Even if human nature does evolve, the character of nations does not change much in the face of incentives to compete in an anarchic world (Waltz 1959; Mearsheimer 2001).

Historically, the arguments of optimists necessarily relied on unproven logic, or often on wishful thinking, while the pessimists could lean more heavily on experience. This difference between normative and positive focus meant that the ascendance of a particular view was driven as much by the prevailing mood of optimism or pessimism—in turn driven by contemporary world events and by stylistic issues such as personal preferences—as by reason and evidence. The core statistical finding of the democratic peace—that democracies seldom fight each other—has recently changed the nature of the debate, putting optimists on the offensive (so to speak) and forcing realists to rethink their conviction that politics begins at the water's edge. This relationship has been reproduced often enough to achieve "lawlike" status (Levy 1988).[2] Studies by Oneal and Russett (1997, 1999a, 1999b, 1999c, 2001); Oneal, Maoz, and Russett (1996); Oneal, Russett, and Berbaum (2003); Russett (1993, 1995); Russett and Oneal (2001); and Russett, Oneal, and Davis (1998) constitute the core research program narrowing the Kantian conception of peaceful liberal republics to a special peace unique to democratic dyads. Work by Hegre (2000), Mousseau (2000), and Mousseau, Hegre, and Oneal (2003) further delimits the scope of the peace largely to developed countries. Kant's original vision that republican governments were more benign has shrunk from a general claim to a special observation about pairs of democracies and then to just developed democratic dyads.

Some of my own work suggests that it is not democracy per se that brings peace but economic development, a common worldview among Western liberal states, and global markets (Gartzke 2007). New modes of production change the interests of developed countries so that they prefer commerce to conquest (Gartzke 2006). Globalization allows leaders to obtain better information about whether some opponents are bluffing in the poker game of international politics (Gartzke & Li 2003). Finally, a common worldview among powerful liberal states makes it possible to prefer similar international policies (Gartzke 1998). Essential elements of these arguments go back, in evolving formulations, to even before the Kantian model of democratic peace (Montesquieu 1989; Paine 1986; Cobden 1903; Angell 1909). The apparent failure of liberal peace in both world wars led to a general repudiation of liberal theories of international relations, while only the democratic variant was thoroughly revised and resurrected as world communism began to collapse. Indeed, it was the advancement of liberal economic policies, as much as arms racing or rhetoric about democracy, that led to the collapse of the Soviet Union and to victory by the West in the cold war. This victory was not without its own violence, but the cold war was much cooler militarily than it might have been. Leaders in the Soviet Union and elsewhere were forced to yield power in large part because liberal reforms in the West had made their economies uncompetitive, while authoritarian politics was incompatible with efforts to raise productivity.

Several researchers have noted the possibility of reverse causality (Thompson 1996; James, Solberg, & Wolfson 1999; Rasler & Thompson 2004), suggesting that peace may produce or facilitate democracy, leading to a spurious correlation between democracy and peace. While the validity of this critique has been debated (Oneal & Russett 2000; James, Solberg, & Wolfson 2000), the argument is considerably different from the one offered here. While existing attempts to endogenize democracy (that is, explain democracy with the thing democracy is said to cause) focus on the impact of conflict or its absence on liberal government, I explore the possibility of a common set of causes for both peace and democracy.

Economic development is widely viewed as a cause of democracy. The notion that modern economic processes lead to political liberalization is well established in the literature (Lipset 1959; Burkhart & Lewis-Beck 1994; Epstein et al. 2006). Certainly, there are counterarguments. Acemoglu and Robinson (2006) argue that there is no connection between economic development and democratization. Olson

(1982) suggests that democracy may lead to development. Others find that, while development does not cause democracy, a lack of development leads to the failure of democratic governments. Thus, while not undisputed, the connection between development and democracy is often viewed as virtually "lawlike" as that of the democratic peace.

As with the democratic peace, questions remain about the reasons that democracy is rare historically but relatively abundant in recent decades. Olson (1993), in a classic study, lays out the riddle of democratization most intuitively in a parable about two groups, bandits and peasants. Before the advent of states or formal government (i.e., under anarchy), bandits roam the countryside, plundering the farms and workshops of peasants. Since there are other bandits, it does not do to leave anything unplundered. Since bandits take everything, peasants have no incentive to work hard or save; they produce only what they need and what they think they can consume before the bandits return. Since the peasants produce very little, both the peasants and the bandits suffer. The relationship represents a classic problem of the commons. Bandits would benefit if they could commit to refrain from "overconsuming" peasant assets, since this would lead the peasants to produce more, but roving bandits cannot credibly make such a promise, given incentives to renege.

It turns out that both the bandits and the peasants are better off if the bandits settle down, guarding and protecting one set of peasants but also laying exclusive claim to their plunder. These sedentary bandits create an economic transformation by creating domestic politics. Sedentary plunder is like farming. The farmer has incentives to keep his fields fertile. Bandits as sovereigns benefit most if they let the peasants keep some of the surplus from toiling on the land or in workshops. Peasants will produce more if they expect to be able to keep some of the surplus for themselves. Provided the increase in productivity is enough, bandits can prefer being sedentary.

Thus, Olson has a very simple and intuitive explanation for the formation of government. Predation by the state ("rent seeking" in social scientific terms) is better for everyone involved than predation by roving groups. Note that this argument has none of the trappings of the legalistic notion of the social contract favored by Enlightenment theorists, but nonetheless it arrives at a similar conclusion about the viability of the state. Sovereigns do not make fundamental bargains with their citizens precisely because there is no way for the public to enforce such agreements once the state has the sole prerogative on force. Instead, contractlike norms of interaction evolve given compatible unilateral incentives for the sovereign and the population. The notion that only self-enforcing bargains are genuinely stable is something that runs in parallel between domestic and international politics, as indeed these two distinct spheres come into being only through the self-enforcing bargain of the state.

Seeking a theory of democracy, Olson then takes his argument one step further, pointing out that a competition among bandit groups for power in which peasants are allowed to select their new rulers is better for the peasants. Oligopolistic competition among the bandits causes the bandits to limit their predation even further than by simply being sedentary. However, Olson does not explain why such a system would come to pass. Precisely because the bandits cannot steal as much from the population if they have to compete for power, they should prefer a system in which their rule is not subject to review by the populace. The very logic of self-enforcing bargains, which makes Olsen's story about bandits and peasants such a convincing parable of state formation, seems to defy Olson's interest in democracy. Olson thus leaves us with a riddle: what might make sedentary bandits prefer competing for power to ruling as autocrats? The fact that answers are not immediately clear suggests the reason that democracy is historically rare. That there are such conditions is belied by the logic of state formation in which bandits voluntarily limit their predation in return for a bigger absolute payoff. Democracy is attainable in Olson's world if there are ways that sedentary bandits prosper by yielding even more political power.

Boix (2003) provides one such solution. In Olson's story the bandits can take from the population but limit their haul because taking everything would mean that nothing was produced in subsequent years. Boix argues that modern economic processes lead to a shift in wealth from fixed factors of production (particularly land) to mobile ones (financial capital). Capital mobility provides incentives for sedentary bandits to limit rent seeking since holders of capital will simply move abroad if there is too much predation. The theory Boix offers is compelling, but it is presented in a negative form. Democracies cannot survive while the wealthy face redistribution through popular rule. Holders of landed wealth must retain political power in order to stave off the natural incentives of majoritarian hordes to take their land. Yet there are several limitations to this argument. First, it is generally true of government that it represents an opportunity for redistribution. Whether autocratic or otherwise, the intuition is that those in power, if they wish and are able to do so, will use the sovereign power of the state to take whatever is worth having. Those with wealth must be in office to remain wealthy in any land where the state has the power to redistribute. Conversely, if the state is not an effective mechanism for taking things of value, then democracy can result, but democracy still is not necessarily a product of such an economic system. In other words, Boix offers an insight into when democracy is possible but does not explain why it should be inevitable.

One positive explanation for democracy is that it is efficient. If one were only concerned that government do the most good at the least cost (if, for example, no one sought distributional advantages through government), then the appeal of democracy is that it spreads the cost of monitoring public officials very widely while minimizing the cost of constraining the public. If under some circumstances we can limit the incentives of citizens to use the state for personal gain, then a society may prefer democracy as a more equitable and less burdensome way of paying for government. Boix's argument may then lead to democracy if landed elites resist democracy (redistribution) while mobile elites do not, whereupon democracy is accepted as a better way of governing.³

The logic Boix offers as to what makes democracy possible (namely, that political power is no longer necessary to maintain one's wealth) can be generalized. Anything that makes the state less effective at taking private property, or the population more effective at evading state redistribution, should make it more feasible to liberalize politics. Not only capital mobility but also increases in any factor mobility should lead to a greater likelihood of democratization. The opening up of the American and Australian frontiers, a revolution in transportation technology, and liberal immigration and emigration policies all contributed to the advent of democracy. Similarly, the nature of human intellectual capital makes it difficult for the state to profit from this increasingly important input into the production process. When entrepreneurial spirit, know-how, and creativity become important components of productivity, nations must begin to choose whether they will continue to stifle growth by attempting to coerce these inputs or accept a curtailed role in the lives of citizens. Much as roving bandits could do better by settling down and taking a smaller share of the surplus, leading the surplus to grow, modern governments have consistently found that they have more to tax if they take relatively less of the surplus created by creative people. Those who doubt this must ask themselves whether engineers, scientists, and entrepreneurs are taxed more lightly than they might be given that they are typically better paid than most of their fellow citizens. Almost nowhere is the tax structure such that everyone has the same net income. We continue to allow productive people to keep more of their money because we want productive people to prosper and to benefit us and others.

Three more insights related to Boix's argument may prove useful. First, if it is even minutely costly to move capital from place to place, then the distance traveled should affect the appeal of relocating. Physically large countries should be less likely to become democratic because it is harder to leave them and go somewhere else, at least until very recently. Second, democracy should tend to cluster geographically. Once one state liberalizes, it becomes a relative safe haven, and the pressure on neighbors to liberalize must be more intense than if no safe haven states were available nearby. Finally, the population size of a polity should condition the cost and benefits of autocratic rule. Studies of coercion suggest that countries with larger populations may be more prone to autocracy than countries with smaller populations. Size also exacerbates collective action problems, making it harder for citizens in large countries to organize against the government. At the other extreme, very small polities lack economies large enough to allow the kinds of specialization necessary for a repressive state. In fact, we observe historically that democracy is more common among small states (physical size or population) than among large countries and that democracy tends to cluster geographically in a few locations around the globe (Gleditsch 2003).

Anarchy cannot be remedied directly without erecting a world government, but whether this implies that war is inevitable in international relations is unclear. The distinction between the politics of nations and politics within nations has been overdone. Within a society, central authority remedies the "natural" state of war among individuals or groups—but only by making war on everyone. Arguments for world government typically miss the fact that a global central authority would bring peace among nations only by also risking replacing anarchy with tyranny. Since autocracy (and tyranny) is much more common domestically than is democracy, it would appear dangerous to assume that world government is destined to be virtuous. In contrast, peace can exist among individuals or between countries when the incentives to compete are absent, or when political power is no longer an effective instrument for obtaining the spoils of political victory. These self-enforcing incentives exist with or without the state apparatus. As such, these incentives are independent of, and more fundamental than, the presence or absence of political institutions. Rather than looking for institutions or attitudes that can transform domestic and international politics, we may be better off finding peace where there is an absence of interest in war both within and among nations. Only then can government (domestic or international) be pursued with confidence that it will be democratic.

DEFINING DEMOCRACY

These minimalist definitions are not meant to comprehensively characterize democracy and interstate peace. Indeed, there is much that I would want to include with peace and democracy that is absent here. Other attributes enrich democracy and peace. They may even be necessary in their own right, but none can suffice in the absence of these minimal conditions:

Minimum definition of democracy: A system of domestic politics in which defeated or dissatisfied agents (political elites) prefer to remain defeated or dissatisfied, rather than resorting to force

Minimum definition of interstate peace: A system of international politics in which defeated or dissatisfied agents (states) prefer to remain defeated or dissatisfied rather than resorting to force

Again, these definitions are not sufficient, but they do appear to be necessary. Any system that does not provide for the peaceful selection of leaders is not democratic.

If democracy involves elections, then democracy ceases to function when the loser of an election refuses to accept defeat and instead relies on coercion, deceit, or force to obtain political office. Indeed, democracy is the only system of domestic politics that essentially terminates when one political faction takes up arms against another. Monarchy can persist despite revolution and dictators can be overthrown by force, but democracy requires that political contestation be peaceful to be legitimate and democratic.

Similarly, international peace requires successful deliberation, negotiations, or some other form of bargaining among states. We can think of the status quo as a constant state of tacit or overt bargaining, where one state or coalition prefers the status quo to any changes in international conditions and the other state or coalition prefers accepting the preferences of the first group to using force to impose change. Bargaining may be formal (as in debates and voting in an intergovernmental organization), informal (as in diplomatic wrangling among states), or tacit (as when nations unilaterally adjust their policies in anticipation of the reactions of other nations). The important distinction is that war and peace are complementary avenues of political competition (Clausewitz famously called war a continuation of politics by other means).

Finally, as the definitions make clear, the distinction between domestic and international politics is much less important than apparent. The difference is one of venue, while the process of conducting politics in both contexts looks remarkably similar. In essence, democracy makes the domestic system look more international (less hierarchical), while peace makes the international system look more like domestic politics (more stable).[4] Other attributes of democracy or international relations are arguably less important than generally believed. The lack of central authority in international relations requires bargaining and consensus or at least majorities of countries to get things done. The same is true of representative democracy. The leviathan does make domestic politics different from international anarchy, but democracy reduces the leviathan. Coercion is no longer the central mechanism of domestic politics as the autocratic sovereign who makes war on all of his or her citizens gives way to majoritarian mechanisms.[5]

A PROTOTHEORY OF DEMOCRACY AND PEACE

At its simplest, politics consists of two basic processes: redistribution and collective goods provision. Redistribution involves using the power of the state to take assets or prerogatives from one individual or group and to give them to another. Thus, redistributive politics is inherently conflictual.[6] Collective goods provision involves the use of social mechanisms (the state) to address individual incentives to underprovide items of collective benefit. Classic examples of public goods that can be remedied by government efforts include fighting pollution, providing for national defense, or maintaining public parks or the road network. Public goods that increase economic productivity or social welfare provide a fundamental normative rationale for government.

The search for peace and democracy parallels the discovery of conditions where the redistributive role of government has become limited in some way while the public goods function of government maintains or increases in importance. When and where does cooperation trump conflict in politics? Olson (1993), in his discussion of roving bandits, provides an interesting nonanswer. The search for security (a public good) leads to the Hobbesian state, but the Hobbesian state in turn is simply monopoly control on predation. The same military might that can be used to protect a society from foreign marauders can be used to enrich the sovereign and his cronies (redistribution). Individuals or groups can resist the Hobbesian state, but, even if successful, the historical temptation is to perpetually recreate this structure. More is required than human or social virtue, apparently, since "the great man" too often must resort to Hobbesian mechanisms to survive. A failure to use the power of the state to destroy competitors means the likely demise of even the most virtuous sovereign, which of course ensures that the most virtuous sovereign looks no different, in practice, from the most vile. A "good king" can rule in the interest of many only by adopting the same implements of power (an army, a castle, etc.) as a "bad king." Power corrupts in such a system because nothing is done without retaining power, and power cannot be retained without its exercise. The implements of predatory government persist even if occasionally the sovereign is motivated to act outside his or her narrow self-interest. The only way to ensure good government is to rely on constant and uniform adherence to altruism by political elites.

Historically, almost all large civilizations were, or wanted to be, police states (many governments may have lacked coercive capabilities despite the will of the sovereign). Political winners have used the power of the state to force political losers to accept defeat and often to weaken or destroy the loser. Political losers faced even greater insecurity with the nearly constant prospect that those in power would decide to rid themselves of a prospective menace. Winners could not remain secure with the prospect of usurpation of their power, and losers could not credibly claim to have no desire to usurp. The prospect that someone might use the power of the state to deprive others of their property, freedom, or even their lives meant that few with the opportunity to wield power could deny themselves the opportunity to be safe and prosperous at another's expense.

The insecurity created by aspirants to sovereignty and to their subjects parallels the conditions said to give rise to warfare in international relations. The security dilemma—a condition in which states are aggressive because they cannot be sure they will not be attacked by others—exists just as much in the autocratic world within a state as it does between countries. Hobbes's leviathan is an endgame, not an equilibrium. The desire of the sovereign to achieve conditions of the leviathan and the resistance this engenders from those who are trod underfoot makes the exercise of sovereignty more circumspect. Kings had supporters and opponents within the realm just as much as they had allies and enemies abroad. On occasions where the state did indeed become the leviathan, an entity that no citizen could resist, the competition within the coalition supporting the sovereign became even more intense. Since the gains to be had from wielding power grow as the sovereign becomes more powerful, those around the king or dictator become more aggressive in their attempts to control the crown. Purges and power plays eliminate friends when enemies are vanquished, absent, or retreat. As the value of political office rises, attempts to usurp power intensify as the sovereign centralizes authority.

In addition to obvious concerns about the immorality of unrepresentative political systems, there are two other problems. First, coercion is inherently costly. Some portion of the resources of the society is expended on coercion. Productive labor is spent on policing and intelligence gathering. Other productive labor is spent on plotting and rebelling. Some of this occurs even in the freest societies, but it stands to reason that much more effort is expended in repressive societies. Second, the problem of insecurity is ongoing. Since those in power cannot credibly promise to rule with a light hand and those out of power cannot credibly promise not to plot against those in power, the sovereign must either permanently destroy part of the productive population or spend a considerable amount of available resources in constant readiness for internal war. The same is true for international politics. A system of international relations involving coercion and redistribution also requires near-constant readiness for warfare.

Thus, the police state (or proto–police state) functions best where coercion is cheap to manufacture and where predation is relatively effective. If the cost of labor-intensive policing rises, the effectiveness of using the state to extract rents decreases, or the power to coerce opponents declines, then the police state becomes less desirable for those in power as well as for those out of power.

The key element in the rise of free politics is that politics itself becomes relatively trivial. Freedom follows when no one cares very much about capturing the state because there is relatively little benefit from being the king (and little cost or risk involved in not being the king). In addition, if public goods become more important to economic productivity (and to human welfare), then popular rule is an effective and relatively inexpensive way to monitor the political system and to ensure efficiency. Politics is never trivial when the incentives or the ability to redistribute are strong or when societies face a high degree of uncertainty about fundamental policy choices. Again, the same is true for the politics of nations. Countries may be at peace when the effort required to redistribute territory or other tangible assets exceeds the benefits that can be thus acquired and when countries share common perspectives on key questions of policy. Nations fight when most of the wealth available in a society is available to steal, either by individuals, the state, or a foreign power, or when important differences exist in policy preferences or beliefs about the future.

The argument here poses an interesting conundrum for intellectual calls for political activism. It may be that the popular dislike for "politics" may actually foster democracy. When issues are too important to overlook, political agents can begin to refuse to accept peaceful political defeat. Democracy is possible when it is bad to be the king. To attain democracy, it must be relatively unimportant to be the leader. Otherwise, those defeated in peaceful political contests (such as elections) may prefer resorting to force to have their way or to protect themselves and their interests from predation by those in office. When losing in politics is acceptable, it can be done peacefully. Conversely, when defeat is unthinkable, force follows, and we can expect neither peace nor democracy.

We can now offer a solution to Olson's riddle: when public goods increase in salience for the society or when opportunities for distribution decrease, peaceful competition for temporary rule is feasible. Given that autocracy is necessarily more expensive, since part of the wealth of the society must be dedicated to quelling the many by the few, there is no point in taking office through force when the benefits of office are relatively small and diffuse (as in the provision of public goods). Democracy is a cheaper form of government because higher nominal consent of the governed does not require as much coercion and an increase in public goods makes democracy more popular.

Yet in a democracy, distribution also must have a high degree of nominal consent. Taxes must appear to be spent for the public good, not to enrich the few. If in fact they are being used largely to line the pockets of those in power, then autocracy is a more useful form of government. Citizens in developing countries not infrequently cheer when the army takes power or when a democrat becomes a dictator, often because they believe that there will be less corruption. Democracy fails when the state remains the most effective instrument for advancing the interests of those in office.

Autocracy will be used where the factors of production are fixed and the surplus is readily extractible by state force. Democracy is an equilibrium where the factors of production are mobile (and where exit from the society by these factors is possible) or where the surplus is not easily extractible except by the consent of the governed. Knowledge workers in Silicon Valley can withhold much of their wealth because the state cannot coerce the basis for their productivity. As creativity becomes a larger portion of the value of a good or service, it becomes harder to remove this benefit from a worker by force. For the same reasons that firms are forced to raise wages and provide incentive pay, the state must accept that its ability to compel creativity is limited. The rise of the middle class is associated with democracy not because the middle class uniquely values participation in politics but rather because the existence of well-paid workers is indicative of productive citizens that are also difficult to coerce. Similarly, if the extraction technology available to the state is not very efficient because of factors such as high labor costs for police and the limited ability to monitor intellectual capital, then no one wants the job of king. Societies then default to democracy because public monitoring minimizes the cost for elites of "good" government and ensures the efficient use of public funds for public goods.

If "Dutch disease" occurs where extractable assets become the basis for the national economy, discouraging private and public investment in human and economic productivity, then we may also consider a "Dutch cure," where the absence of resources removes the curse of predatory government and replaces it with incentives to use the state to create stability and prosperity. In the seventeenth and eighteenth centuries, intellectual and financial capital flowed into Holland. A relatively free society encouraged writers, thinkers, entrepreneurs, and other creative people to immigrate from all corners of Europe. Holland flowered with commerce and prospered primarily because of the large number of creative people who were present together in a relatively small place. The productivity of creative people seems to multiply as their numbers increase. Universities are valuable centers of innovation not just because they are chock full of smart people but also because they create a critical mass of such people, who then build on one another's ideas. Getting a large number of creative people together and giving them the freedom to build, start new businesses, and invent is much more powerful than the power of the state to coerce or rent-seek. Just as bandits may have settled down to take a smaller share of a larger pie, modernity, mobility, and intellectual creativity have conspired to make the holding of state power relatively unimportant.

FROM PEACEFUL GOVERNMENT TO WORLD PEACE

The same forces that lead politics within nations to become democratic cause politics among nations to become pacific. If domestic elites cannot capitalize on political power through force, foreign elites facing similar conditions presumably cannot either. Rich countries stopped invading one another to take territory and productive populations because the populations and land they could conquer were not particularly productive in modern terms, while the most productive populations and places were no longer amenable to conquest. It makes no more sense to become the dictator of Silicon Valley as a foreigner than as a local. In either case, the value in high-tech industries is not readily extractible through force. Creative people must desire to create and benefit from their own creativity. They will willingly return some of this benefit to the common coffers if they believe that their contributions will make the community more productive through collective goods provisions by the state, but they cannot be forced to be productive by external measures.

Invading a democracy with an expensive army to subdue the population and profit is a non sequitur. One could still profit by using an army of the very poor, but these poor would lack the skills to make up a military force likely to conquer any portion of the developed world, while soldiers capable of winning on the twenty-first-century battlefield are too expensive to make conquest pay. Poor states and their sovereigns still want empire, but they cannot achieve it. Developed economies can and do support large armies, but the desire to enlarge a nation's physical space is gone.

We can characterize this condition as "Hadrian's Wallet." The Roman emperor Hadrian erected a wall across what is now northern England sometime after AD 122. The wall is popularly conceived as a defensive fortification preventing incursions of the "barbarian" tribes of modern Scotland and north England. In truth, it was probably more significant as a delineation of the border and as a demarcation of two very different spheres of Roman influence. North of the wall, Rome was not bothered to attempt to instill order. Low population densities and limited agricultural productivity meant that it was not worth the cost of Roman legions and administration to make that region part of the empire. Rome still traded with the barbarians, but it did not attempt to make them subjects. Hadrian built the wall as protection for the portion of the British Isles that was worth protecting from roving bandits. Thus, where Hadrian put his wall had more to do with his "wallet" and with the marginal returns of the protection racket we now remember as the Roman Empire than with defense.

In effect, modernity makes much of the world beyond the wall. Yet, rather than being insecure, our roving bandits have moved on. Armies in the developed world are now used to protecting populations (not so much territories), to influencing international politics among developing states, and to meting out punishment to foreign sovereigns who fail to conform to expectations. Unlike the Roman legions, modern armies are not used to sitting on populations and extracting tribute. In large part this is because the tribute one could extract does not pay for the modern legions, and where benefits are more intense, they are not easily extracted by force. The developed world, heavily invested in territorial empire a century ago, has all but given up on controlling territory in the developing world. It is far cheaper to let the locals govern themselves or, more often, to look the other way as a petty dictator behaves much as the kings our ancestors faced wherever we are from. The United States and other developed countries continue to intervene abroad, but typically this is in a punitive manner, to force local leaders to conform to preferred foreign or domestic policies or to replace leaders who have become unresponsive to the demands of Washington, London, or Paris. Saddam Hussein is one such example. In his invasion of Kuwait in 1990, Saddam managed to secure all of Kuwait's oil and none of its substantial reserve of cash. As the modern world continues to look more like the Kuwait of electronic funds transfers and less like the Kuwait of oil wells, it becomes increasingly difficult to capture anything of value through force.

Peace may still fail when states have different policies. Countries may want very different things in the world, as when Sudan and Egypt clash over the influence of fundamentalist Islam. States may have very different conceptions of cause and effect, as with the clash of West and East during the cold war. If this dialectic has ended, then fighting over ideological paradigms may be passé (Fukuyama 1992), but more is needed to secure peace than a consensus about policy, at least if contention remains about who gets what. Madison and the Federalists emphasized the inadequacy of individual or social transformation in cementing democracy. Those who seek good government through individual or social improvement expect more of their peers and institutions than prudence should require. The Federalists, though they had no faith in individual betterment as a mechanism for perpetuating democracy, emphasized institutions and placed their hopes on divided government, though more through an absence of alternatives than from genuine confidence in the mechanisms they had contrived. Even the advocates of federal democracy in the United States at its founding recognized that ultimately institutions cannot prevent tyranny. It was largely for this reason that the Founding Fathers were pessimistic about the prospects for their experiment.

The founders were more than a little lucky. Democracy existed in the colonial era because at first the British Empire could not be bothered to govern, and when it attempted to do so, its effort turned out to be futile. Officials in the colonies attest in their writings to the difficulty of imposing the state on a society with open frontiers. As the colonies became countries and then states, the ability of anyone to use the government as a mechanism of coercion remained extremely limited. Labor was very expensive—a large standing army would have cost much more than it was likely to recoup, particularly when disgruntled citizens could simply head west. The western frontier and the weakness of the federal system in the first 100 years meant that government had a soft hand on the population. In the second century, industrialization and heavy immigration meant that it was easier to get and stay rich outside government than in, while again the ability of those in power to use the state to steal was limited by the evolving nature of industrial production.

Exceptions in the case of the United States are almost as illustrative as the general trend. Americans did attempt to coerce one another over policy. The intensity of differences in policy preferences over slavery and the incompatibility of those preferences ensured that war resulted when neither side could continue to exist with the other ascendant. Slavery itself attests to the willingness of citizens in a democracy to tolerate abominable treatment of others when seen as expedient. Moral or institutional constraints that fail to thwart such a gross violation of the spirit of democracy must be very tenuous indeed. Even today we can find examples of how liberty is compromised when convenient, even among democratic states. Black African slaves were quite specifically used in the Americas because they could not use the frontier or other avenues of escape to avoid the theft of their labor. Similarly, an expansionist United States continued to use force to impose its will on the weaker nations of Native Americans, as co-optation suited settlers. Interestingly, on several occasions, independent frontier nations were established, but these were folded into the United States as these smaller republics felt the threat of Mexico.

Internationally, the United States, like other democracies, was never any less warlike, but it gave up on Canada and later Mexico as it found that gradually improving military power was not equal to profitable conquest. Experiments with empire in the Philippines were an abject failure, as they were far more expensive in losses to U.S. troops and equipment than in benefits gleaned through access and added trade. Once Spanish influence was removed from the Caribbean and Asia, it made little sense to transport expensive soldiers to distant lands to subdue a society with little left to steal. A peace of sorts prevailed—not because the United States was more virtuous than it had been previously but because it had become cheaper to pay foreigners for their labor than to prey on them as statist roving bandits or to establish or retain sedentary domains as colonies. At the same time, the forces that made empire inefficient made territorial conquest among the developed powers pointless. Peace and democracy have come to an increasing portion of the globe not because humanity had been improved or institutions perfected but because economics has made most forms of state-based predation inefficient.

CONCLUSION

People and societies coexist peacefully when the use of state power for theft is expensive relative to what can be stolen. This may occur when the factors of production are cheap and abundant relative to the factors used intensively in predation, when productive factors become more mobile, or when the technology of predation is relatively inefficient. These effects are magnified as collective action becomes a larger component of productivity (i.e., through specialization) and when mechanisms exist to remedy informational problems that can lead to conflict. In simple terms, development leads to the creation of societies where it is easier to make than to take. Government is no longer primarily a means to acquire wealth but is primarily tasked with public goods provision. The same economic changes that encourage democracy (the end of predation from within) lead also to interstate peace (the end of predation from without). Peace and democracy are then linked through common, fundamental changes in the nature of economic production and factor mobility.

The argument offered here is only a sketch, but perhaps it suggests a more integrated approach to explaining the impact the liberal transformation of the global economy is having on interstate peace and domestic politics. At its simplest, democracy is a system of government in which elites prefer peaceful political defeat to some possibility of victory through force. Similarly, peace prevails internationally when nations prefer the status quo to attempts at change requiring the possibility of warfare. Historically, both conditions have been rare. Democracies did not exist in many places, or for long, because issues invariably arose in which deliberative defeat was unacceptable to some faction that was able to use force. Nations regularly experienced interstate conflict for similar reasons; the prospect of ceding territory or of conceding major policy issues was such in international relations that many states preferred war and some chance of victory to peace and the certainty of defeat. Defeat is acceptable when the differences faced in winning and losing are not that great, as happens when the victor is limited in its ability to capitalize on the possession of greater power. Being the king, both domestically and internationally, is no longer so good.

Students of international relations have long drawn a strong distinction between international anarchy and domestic hierarchy. The leviathan ensures peace (or at least stability) domestically by retaining the sole prerogative on the legitimate use of force. However, this assumes that the control of the sovereign is itself secure and that any (latent or overt) challenge from within the society is nonexistent. Such challenges, or the risk of such challenges, are perennial in an autocracy, so the distinction between domestic security and international insecurity is illusory. Indeed, as I have suggested, the security dilemma is equally applicable to domestic affairs and international relations. The difference between politics within one state and that between states starts to erode further when democracy is practiced at home and when peace prevails abroad. In both spheres, politics becomes the product of deliberation and negotiation. Rather than deriving from the externalization of democracy, as some have suggested, the increasing parallels reflect a more profound congruence of causes.

One of the myths of the modern era is that we can export democracy, as if it is some commodity devoid of context or content. Why should we expect that popular self-rule will take hold in places where losing office means losing one's livelihood or possibly one's life? As long as politics is too important a game to lose, it will not be "just a game," trivial enough to make democracy viable. I am always concerned when students or acquaintances tell me about a place where the people care deeply about politics, where ordinary citizens while away hours discussing events in the capital. These are places where winning in politics is winning in life and where democracy is in jeopardy. Before democracy can be exported, one must first "export" the conditions that make peaceful political defeat tolerable, if not preferred. Making politics trivial in most places means making much of what matters to people beyond the reach of those who hold political power in a society. As far as I can tell, this can be achieved only through a shift in the economy away from rooted factors of production (land, minerals, unskilled labor) and toward mobile or intangible factors (intellectual and financial capital). Democratization campaigns without this kind of development effort are largely ineffective. Worse, they create political uncertainty and instability that exacerbate the violence of political competition. One need look no further than contemporary Iraq to find a place where toppling a dictator has brought not only elections but also atrocious bloodshed.

Democracy and world peace are hard work. Perhaps the hardest thing to accept for many is that they are not going to come from good intentions, or even considerable effort. Two thousand years passed before Western societies attempted to reignite the torch of democracy and community that existed in ancient Greece. In the interim, untold suffering was inflicted within and between societies in the search for security. If we seek to liberalize polities without first establishing economic and social conditions in which it is fruitless to be king, we are inviting violent usurpations of power, as occur episodically in much of the developing world. The efforts of the West to achieve democracy for the rest of the world sometimes appear to reflect the same impatience that has given us fast food and ATM machines. Instant democratization is not going to work in most cases and has already caused considerable harm in the world. What is needed is a careful, gradual laying of foundations for liberal transformation and peace. Promoting trade, education, and free emigration, together with development focusing on intellectual and financial intensive industries, are all better avenues to both democracy and interstate peace than direct intervention.

NOTES

1. For a discussion of how war makes the state, see Tilly (1985, 1992). Downing (1992) argues that the need to field larger armies made it necessary for political elites to broaden suffrage.
2. The empirical literature on the democratic peace is voluminous and is not detailed here. Chan (1993, 1997) and Morgan (1993) offer reviews, though these sources are somewhat dated.
3. Normative arguments for democracy should not be ignored. The claim here is simply that incentives to democratize have changed, while the rationale for democracy was well established in classical writings. It must also be remembered that practical democracy is representative. Given principal-agency problems and other concerns with direct rule, the defense of representative democracy over "true" democracy is largely based on expediency. It is not efficient for a society to gather together all its members to vote on every piece of legislation or to make every executive decision. That citizens in democracies use concerns about inefficiency to limit the scope of democracy suggests that citizens elsewhere may use efficiency as a criteria to advocate or oppose democracy generally.

4. Waltz (1959) emphasized the distinction between domestic politics and international relations. Substantial criticism in recent years led researchers to reemphasize what Waltz described as "second image politics" (Russett 1993; Bueno de Mesquita 2002). The debate largely fails to reflect a third dynamic involving common trends in politics at domestic and international levels.
5. It is an interesting question why other, more limited forms of franchise are so rare. The predominance of universal adult suffrage suggests a "tipping point" in which numbers of participants become an advantage and what is being given up in terms of relative political influence is no longer all that important. Whether political power is divided up into 10 million or 20 million tiny pieces becomes academic, while the effort required to resist the franchise for a large portion of the population is eventually too great.
6. Redistributive politics is equivalent to what pundits mean when they use the term *politics* in a derogatory manner. Even so, determining who gets what is essential for a society (or among societies) and of course involves conflict.

4

Democracy, the State, and Global Capitalism

Daniel Egan

Since its origins in the seventeenth century, the nation-state has been a contested terrain. It provided the foundations for capitalist development, ensuring the rise of a class devoted to the pursuit of capital accumulation regardless of the human cost, and continues to provide the political cohesion necessary for the reproduction of capitalism. At the same time, the very social institutions that facilitated the process of capital accumulation also provided opportunities for subordinate social forces to extend political, economic, and social rights that had the potential to place substantial limits on the power of capitalists and state officials. The relationship between democracy and capitalism is thus a contradictory one.

This complex relationship between democracy and capitalism is revealed in contemporary discussions of "globalization." It has become commonplace to argue that the nation-state has already abdicated or must transfer much of its traditional sovereign control over economic policy to multilateral institutions such as the International Monetary Fund (IMF) and the World Trade Organization (WTO). This transfer of sovereignty has been accompanied by a consensus that nation-states, within the context of these multilateral institutions, must orient themselves toward the reduction or elimination of all economic, social, and political obstacles to free trade. The pursuit of a comprehensive global trade system, however, comes at the expense of intensified social inequality, as nationally based economic and social policies protecting citizens from the negative consequences of markets are abandoned and markets penetrate deeper into more levels of social life.

Discursively, the most powerful contradiction between democracy and capitalism within globalization is the widely shared assumption that globalization is an inevitable process. If globalization is inevitable, driven by forces outside the control of society or any particular social group, then democracy becomes increasingly irrelevant. Democratic participation in politics and the substantive benefits of democracy do not matter if the nation-state is compelled out of necessity to act only to maximize competitiveness within global capitalism.

A critical appreciation of the relationship between democracy and globalization is essential for understanding the prospects for a more peaceful world. Kant's 1795 (1985) essay "Perpetual Peace" has served as the foundation for the argument that democracies are less likely to go to war with each other (see Brown, Lynn-Jones, & Miller 1996; Ray 1998). Democratic peace theorists argue that an international system defined by the presence of democratic states will be characterized by norms making compromise and negotiation more likely than war as a means of resolving conflict. At the same time, liberal democratic states face internal constraints to war resulting from the necessity for securing the consent of their citizens, a complex process. With regard to capitalism, the founders of sociology generally agreed that the transition from traditional to modern society would lead to a reduction in war (Shaw 1988). Modern society would replace military-oriented institutions with those based on market exchange, and the resulting economic interdependence of states would facilitate more peaceful interaction internationally. Indeed, democratic peace theorists have pointed to the important role that markets play in facilitating democratic peace (Mousseau 2000). In its broadest form, the strength of democratic peace theory rests in large part on the strength of the presumed equivalence of democracy and capitalism. This is a fundamentally problematic assumption.

Scholars committed to a truly democratic world order must confront the contradiction between democracy and capitalism contained within globalization. Such a project has two interrelated tracks. First, we must acknowledge globalization as the creation of specific social forces operating within particular economic, political, and cultural constraints. Globalization is the product of a political-economic struggle taking place simultaneously at the national and transnational levels. Second, the very concept of globalization must be replaced by the recognition of multiple possible globalization*s*. Capitalist globalization that maximizes market liberalization at the expense of democracy in both its procedural and substantive forms is clearly hegemonic, but it is not the only alternative. By restoring agency to the analysis of globalization, we may acknowledge that a globalization from below that expands democratic rights and social welfare rather than the power of markets is possible.

CAPITALISM AND THE NATION-STATE

Neoclassical economic theory conceptualizes the capitalist market as an institution completely independent of the state. Rational individuals acting on their preferences engage in self-seeking activity, which produces efficient, socially optimal outcomes.

The only legitimate role for the state is that of a "night watchman," protecting private property rights so that individuals may pursue their self-interest free of outside interference. Such an understanding of the state's role in capitalist systems, however, is fundamentally flawed. In its pursuit of elegant theoretical abstraction, neoclassical economic theory ignores how individual preferences are shaped by social institutions, the significance of power in shaping individuals' activity within the market, and the importance of history in changing both the nature of social institutions and the character of individuals living within a specific historical period (Pressman 2006). The failure of neoclassical economics to provide a coherent understanding of the state's relationship to capitalism has, thankfully, not gone unnoticed. A rich literature in the social sciences has emerged to provide a critical analysis of this relationship, one grounded in empirical reality rather than abstraction. The following literature review is in two parts. First, I examine the functions played by the state in capitalism and the social relationships between the state and capital that drive these functions. Second, I consider how these relationships reflect a specific understanding of democracy.

What Is "Capitalist" about the Capitalist State?

The nation-state performs a number of essential functions in a capitalist system. With regard to the economic functions of the state, in such a system the state is not involved in direct production. Concluding, however, that this means the state is not an important economic actor in the market is incorrect. The state subsidizes private capital through social capital expenditures, spending that provides necessary resources or infrastructure for private economic activity such as education, transportation, research, and development. Since the cost of these resources is beyond the ability of individual capitalists to provide on their own, the state supports capital by socializing these expenditures. The state also covers the social costs associated with capitalist development, which include "externalities" arising from private economic activity such as pollution, poverty, crime, and international conflict. Moreover, the state frequently serves as a lender of last resort for industries or companies that are deemed "too big to fail." In so doing, the state provides the social stability, both at home and abroad, necessary for capital accumulation.

As the institution possessing the monopoly on the legitimate use of force (Weber 1964), the state is the agent that disciplines subordinate social forces both domestically and globally. Coercive state power was instrumental during the formation of capitalism, when it was directed against the peasantry to force them off the land and compel them to serve as "free labor." It has also been important in the reproduction of the working class by criminalizing deviant behaviors that are the consequences of subordination and by defending the interests of capital against challenges from popular movements (Parenti 2008; Reiman 2007). Outside national borders, the state has served to defend and extend colonial power, thereby ensuring access to cheap labor and natural resources as well as markets for core countries' manufactured goods. Luxemburg (1968) takes this further, arguing that the destruction of war and the reconstruction that follows are opportunities for capital accumulation. As Baran and Sweezy (1966) point out, the absorption of surplus that results from militarism reduces the severity of capitalist crises resulting from underinvestment.

Coercion, however, is by itself insufficient for the state to ensure a disciplined society. The state must at the very least obscure the class divides that characterize capitalistic societies, but ideally it seeks to win the consent of subordinate social forces to capitalism. In other words, the state serves the ideological function of ensuring that workers accept capitalism and their status within capitalism. In Gramsci's (1971, 260) famous phrase, the state serves as "educator." For example, the law constructs people within capitalist systems as "individuals," thereby facilitating the private ownership of capital and the symbolic deconstruction of classes (Althusser 1971; Poulantzas 1974). At the same time, through various state rituals and the state's role in providing education, these "individuals" are then reconstituted as members of an "imagined community" (Anderson 1983) called the nation, a community that appears as a more natural alternative to class. Education conveys other "commonsense" ideas, such as individualism, competition, and scarcity, that make capitalism appear desirable or at least unchangeable.

Yet identifying the functions performed by the state in capitalist systems does not explain why the state fulfills these functions in the manner that it does. In order to understand this, we need to examine the social relationship between state and capital. Critical scholars have argued that capital exercises control over state policy through a number of mechanisms. Domhoff (2005) and Miliband (1969) argue that members of the capitalist class participate directly in state institutions either as elected officials or as officials appointed to administrative or legal positions. Other channels of influence include the provision of financial resources for political campaigns, ownership of news media, and support for the network of policy planning organizations, such as foundations and think tanks, that serve increasingly as the source for political ideas. Other scholars, such as Block (1987) and Offe (1984), emphasize the state's dependence on private capital, rather than the participation of capital in the state, for making the state a capitalist state.

Since the state does not organize production directly, it is dependent on the activity of private capital for the revenue necessary for state functions. Without the taxes that flow from private economic activity, the state will not be able to provide services to its citizens. As a result, state officials encounter structural pressure to develop policies that support capitalism. In addition, since the fate of state officials rests in large part on perceptions of economic success, including the provision of services and employment, the failure to meet expectations is likely to come at the cost of being evicted from office. State officials are thus in a bind: the state is held responsible for the economic well-being of its citizens, but, lacking its own forces of production, the state is dependent on private capital for the resources necessary to achieve this goal. If state officials fail to orient state policy toward the interests of capital, they are likely to be chastised by a "capital strike" that causes economic slowdown or collapse.

Gramsci (1971, 57–58) argued that the dominance of the ruling class is not simply based on economic power or political-military coercion but is also a function of its ability to provide cultural and moral leadership. In his view, the supremacy of a social group manifests itself in two ways, as "domination" and as "intellectual and moral leadership." A social group dominates antagonistic groups, which it tends to "liquidate" or subjugate, perhaps even by armed force; it leads kindred and allied groups. A social group can, and indeed must, already exercise "leadership" before winning governmental power (this indeed is one of the principal conditions for the winning of such power); it subsequently becomes dominant when it exercises power, but even if it holds power firmly in its grasp, it must continue to "lead" as well.

In this context, a class is hegemonic to the extent that it offers an integrated system of values and beliefs that is supportive of the established social order and that projects a particular set of class interests as the general interest. Hegemonic power is not imposed on subordinates but instead is a negotiated process. Both within the dominant coalition of capital, state managers, and intellectuals and in their relations with subordinate social forces, dominant groups must negotiate with subordinate groups in order to secure the latter's consent to their rule. This process of negotiation, which Gramsci referred to as *trasformismo*, or "passive revolution," may make some accommodation to the economic interests of subordinate groups and may even appropriate their symbols and discourse, but it will not question fundamental social relations (Boggs 1976; Showstack 1987).

The powerful critiques that these theories of the state offer do not imply a determinist understanding of the relationship between capitalism and the state. To say that capital exercises power as a ruling class and that the state functions to reproduce capitalism does not mean that capital *always* wins or that subordinate social forces *always* lose. The concept of the relative autonomy of the state is found in all of the critical perspectives just discussed. The state's relation to capital is not a simple correspondence of the former to the needs of the latter. The state must exercise a certain historically specific degree of autonomy from capital if it is to successfully serve its reproductive functions for capital. This is most clearly seen in the work of theorists who examine the state's structural dependence on capital as well as in Gramsci's theory of hegemony. For theorists such as Block and Offe, the state's relative autonomy from capital gives legitimacy to its capital-oriented policies. For Gramsci, state power is exercised through the ability of the dominant class to incorporate the interests of a variety of classes and class factions into a ruling coalition. The dominant class must be able to make concessions to the interests of coalition partners, but these concessions will not go so far as to undermine fundamental capitalist social relations. Even those theorists who see capital as exercising direct power over the state through participation in state policymaking, however, accept that the state is relatively autonomous from capital.

The concept of relative autonomy is what makes discussions of the relationship between capitalism and democracy meaningful. If the "democratic state" were simply a reflection of the interests of capital, then we could swiftly dispense with the supposedly "democratic" nature of the state. In this case, democracy would be an ideological cover for the unconstrained power of capital. It is because the state is relatively autonomous from capital that the nation-state has been a contested terrain since its origins. Capital's rule through the nation-state is not automatic but must be constantly reorganized and managed to account for the development of capitalism both nationally and globally and for resistance that comes from subordinate social forces. At the same time, subordinate social forces have sought to democratize the state, sometimes in ways that emphasize the procedural features of democracy and sometimes in ways that extend the meaning of democracy to include economic and social, as well as political, rights.

The Contradiction Between Capitalism and Democracy

As Held (1987, 4) argues, models of democracy may be divided into two types. The first is liberal or representative democracy, which is "a system of rule embracing elected 'officers' who undertake to 'represent' the interests and or views of citizens within the framework of the 'rule of law.'" The second is direct or participatory democracy, which is "a system of decision-making about public affairs in which citizens are directly involved." Liberal/representative democracy has been most closely associated with capitalism. There is, of course, no natural connection between capitalism and liberal/representative democracy. Indeed, capitalism has also been associated with fascism and with authoritarian, often military-led political systems. For this reason, it is important to not simply assume an affinity between capitalism and democracy but instead examine critically the relationship between the two.

A review of U.S. history, for example, does not readily suggest an easy association between capitalism and democracy. Despite the value U.S. culture places on it, democracy has been perceived to be a threat by dominant social forces since the country's earliest years (Zinn 2005; M. Parenti 2007). Many, if not most, of the delegates at the Constitutional Convention in 1787 saw democracy as a threat to the interests of the propertied classes and therefore believed that political power should be concentrated in their hands. In this context, the Constitution's separation of powers, its provision for the indirect election of senators by state legislatures and of presidents by the Electoral College, and other articles reflect not some abstract commitment to limit the potentially tyrannical power of government but a very special concern that popular participation in politics, which might threaten the interests of "the few," be constrained (M. Parenti 2007). Held (1987, 66), in his analysis of Madison's famous critique of factions in the Federalist Papers No. 10, puts it quite succinctly: "Madison was in favor of popular government so long as there was no risk that the majority could turn the instruments of state policy against a minority's privilege."

This concern that democracy creates opportunities for "the people" to challenge class privilege is reflected in the disparaging imagery with which "the people" are portrayed in liberal/representative democratic theory. The liberalism of Locke, for example, is based on the concept of consent, but Locke's understanding of consent is not necessarily one in which the active, positive assent of individuals is secured. To the extent that consent is "implied" by state officials, there may be no meaningful consent. Schumpeter (1976, 262) saw any further participation by citizens beyond voting as interfering with the efficient operation of the political system: "the typical citizen drops down to a lower level of mental performance as soon as he enters the political field. He argues and analyzes in a way that we would readily recognize as infantile within the sphere of his real interests. He becomes a primitive again." Lipset (1963), with his concept of "working class authoritarianism," argued that the working class was that class most likely to possess anti-democratic, intolerant attitudes and least likely to possess the civic orientations Lipset deemed necessary for a pluralist system to work.

This understanding of democracy is perhaps best represented by a 1975 report of the Trilateral Commission (an organization of academics, corporate executives, and state managers from the United States, Western Europe, and Japan) entitled *The Crisis of Democracy* (Crozier, Huntington, & Watanuki 1975). In a subsequent book, Huntington (1981, ch. 3) argued that the civil rights, women's, antiwar, environmental, and other social movements that emerged during the 1960s threatened "the governability of democracy" by raising excessive demands on the system: "some of the problems of governance in the United States today stem from an excess of democracy. . . . Needed instead is a greater degree of moderation in democracy." In referring to "the democratic distemper," Huntington suggested that "too much" democracy is dysfunctional. More recently, neoliberalism has returned to the critique of democracy that characterized the debates on the U.S. Constitution. For writers such as Nozick (1977) and Hayek (1994), the democratic use of state power should not interfere with the principle of individual liberty; the natural right to use one's property as one sees fit is superior to all others. Indeed, to the extent that neoliberalism understands society to be a collection of self-interested individuals rather than a separate entity, the legitimacy of the democratic state is itself called into question.

If one accepts as a given the existing distribution of resources in society, then it is easy to see democracy as a potential threat to stability and order. In contrast to this top-down class perspective on democracy, a bottom-up perspective sees history as a series of attempts by people, who at various times and for various reasons were excluded from or marginalized by the political process, to make real the promise of democracy. Advances in democracy and equality are the result of conflict, of mobilization by marginalized, oppressed, and exploited social groups that challenge the legitimacy of existing social institutions. In their most radical form, labor, feminist, antiracist, and other social movements have all rejected the apparent separation of the political from the social that is characteristic of capitalism. While citizens are formally equal in the political sphere, since each citizen has one vote and no citizen's vote counts more than another's, as individuals in civil society they are subjected to class, racial, gender, and other forms of social inequality.

This distinction is problematic for two reasons. First, social inequality creates barriers to meaningful political participation by citizens in subordinate social positions. To the extent that money is an essential resource for electoral campaigns, for example, class inequality provides wealthy individuals and corporations with a means of political participation that is not available to most citizens. Second, political power is a major means of maintaining social inequality. The state not only engages in repression of critical social movements, it helps to construct "commonsense" ways of looking at the world that legitimize inequality. In response, social movements have attempted to socialize politics by seeking to create and (re) distribute the social resources necessary for meaningful participation in politics.

This perspective recognizes that citizenship (in the sense of being an active, participating member of a polity) is not defined by law but, rather, is socially constructed. At the same time, these movements have sought to politicize society by extending democracy to the economy, education, popular culture, mass media, and other social institutions. From this perspective, politics is not restricted to government or public policy-making. Rather, all social activity is necessarily political and therefore subject to democratization.

The Transnational State?

This contradictory relationship between capitalism and democracy has taken new forms within global capitalism. The contemporary politics of global capitalism are defined by neoliberalism, which is a coherent program of market liberalization, state deregulation, and privatization that privileges market forces above all else (Tabb 2001; Teeple 2000). All nonmarket forces that might challenge the hegemony of the market run the risk of being either marginalized or absorbed through commodification. At the same time, labor and other subordinate social forces are disciplined by legal restrictions on union activity, punitive reductions in social welfare provision, and the extension of formal institutions of social control. In addition to these concrete policies, an essential component of neoliberalism is the ideological argument that capitalist globalization is an inevitable process that operates independently of human agency (Steger 2002).

One important expression of this ideological argument is the suggestion that global capitalism has led to the supersession of the nation-state. The political authority of the nation-state is seen as inadequate to limit the transnational movement of capital, and so the best that state officials may do is make their national territories more competitive in order to attract hypermobile capital (Friedman 1999). Peripheral regions have always been subordinated to the needs of capital, whether in the form of slavery and colonialism or in the more recent form of IMF structural adjustment policies, which require recipients of loans to reduce or eliminate subsidies for food, transportation, and education; cut public employment; and privatize publicly owned industries. Another example is the WTO's imposition of intellectual property rights at the expense of more traditional, locally controlled forms of agriculture and medicine. What is new, it is argued, is that core regions have increasingly been subjected to the same disciplinary power.

The argument that the nation-state has been increasingly marginalized by global capitalism, while a consistent feature of mainstream political debate, has also found expression in more critical social science circles. Teeple (2000, 81, 157), for example, argues that neoliberal policies are "the last national policies to be promulgated, the final act of the independent nation-state." A post-Fordist system of production has simultaneously dispersed and integrated production globally and has been accompanied by the rise of "a relatively coherent multiplicity of supranational agencies and organizations, dominated by the U.S., . . . that oversee the broad reaches of the global economy in the interests of corporate private property."

Sklair (2001, 16, 4, 10), in his outline of global systems theory, makes a similar argument. Global systems theory offers "a decisive break with state-centrism" by examining transnational practices, "practices that cross state borders but do not originate with state agencies or actors," at three interrelated levels. First, political transnational practices are institutionalized in a transnational capitalist class consisting of "globalizing bureaucrats, politicians, and professionals." Second, economic transnational practices are institutionalized in transnational corporations, which provide the material base for the transnational capitalist class. Third, cultural/ideological transnational practices are institutionalized in the dominance of consumerism as a value system.

Transnational historical materialists (see Cox 1987; S. Gill 2003, 1993; van der Pijl 1998) argue that a hegemonic bloc of transnational capital, political officials from core capitalist states and multilateral economic institutions, and global intellectuals has emerged and is exercising power through its construction of a consensus for capitalist globalization. An important part of this hegemonic power has been the fundamental reorientation of the nation-state toward supporting global, rather than national, capital accumulation. The nation-state now serves to facilitate global capital accumulation as well as insulate new supranational economic institutions from democratic accountability from below. It also helps to secure a generalized acceptance of globalization as a "commonsense" description of an uncontrollable, inevitable, and ultimately desirable process. Finally, Hardt and Negri (2000, xii) have received considerable acclaim for their argument that the globalization of markets and production has been accompanied by a transformation of political power. The power of nation-states, which is no longer capable of regulating global economic and cultural flows, has been replaced by a network of national and supranational institutions referred to as "empire." They define this new form of global sovereignty, as "a *decentered* and *deterritorializing* apparatus of rule that progressively incorporates the entire global realm within its open, expanded frontiers."

Neoliberalism has called into question, both theoretically and materially, the social democratic welfare states that arose out of World War II. It has, with its privileging of private property and the market above all else, its dismantling of social welfare provision, and its weakening of labor unions and labor-oriented political parties, intensified national and global social inequalities (Kloby 2003). Neoliberalism also reflects a major assault on democracy; it is capital's reaction to the "democratic distemper," which the Council on Foreign Relations saw in the 1970s. Through privatization and deregulation, the state's powers to impose a degree of democratic accountability on capital, which emerged after long struggles in the nineteenth and twentieth centuries, have been either dismantled or rendered inert. Likewise, there has been a shift in the balance of power within the state toward those agencies most concerned with monetary policy, which are precisely those agencies, such as the Federal Reserve, that are more insulated from democratic forces. In addition, established global economic institutions, such as the IMF and the World Bank, and new ones, such as the WTO, have imposed significant constraints on the power of states to regulate capital (McMichael 2003).

The WTO, for example, is committed to the principles of "standstill," in which no new restrictions are placed on the activities of capital, and "rollback," in which existing restrictions are to be eliminated. National laws protecting labor, consumers, and the environment are defined as "nontariff barriers to trade" that must be removed. In the event that a country chooses, on the basis of democratic political debate and elections, to develop such policies, corporations may sue for unlawful "expropriation" of their property. Unlike national courts, which are transparent public agencies, WTO panels are held in secret, with no right for citizens to participate or observe, and while decisions are made public, the testimony given in these panels is not. For example, WTO decisions have overturned regulations in the United States requiring cleaner gasoline and sea turtle–friendly forms of shrimp fishing as well as European Union regulations privileging smaller banana farmers in former European colonies over larger corporate banana plantations. At the same time that the WTO has weakened regulations on capital, it has provided capital with new protections, such as global intellectual property rights. Indeed, global institutions such as the WTO have created a new form of citizenship in which the only legitimate actors are corporations, states, and multilateral institutions themselves. Subordinate social forces and organized social movements are conspicuously excluded from this new global citizenship (Sassen 1996).

The development of transnational institutions to manage global capitalism clearly has important consequences for democracy. This does not necessarily mean, however, that the nation-state is being relegated to secondary status within a newly transnationalized state. This may be most clearly seen through an examination of the most significant institutional *failure* in the current process of globalization: the defeat of the Multilateral Agreement on Investment (MAI) (Egan 2001). The MAI was an effort initiated by the Organization for Economic Cooperation and Development (OECD) in 1995 to construct an agreement that would do for global flows of finance capital what the WTO has done for global trade in goods and services. Despite three years of negotiations, the proposed MAI ultimately failed.

The defeat of the MAI reveals important limits on the transnationalization thesis. Differences in nation-state political cultures were important in undermining the MAI. First, there was disagreement over where the negotiations for the MAI should be located. European Union countries, many of which face the political constraints of established Left parties with representation in both national parliaments and the European Parliament, initially argued for the MAI to be negotiated in the WTO. While this would have provided greater legitimacy (within accepted neoliberal boundaries) for an agreement, it would also have provided opportunities for poorer countries to express opposition to increased liberalization or at least for their interests to be taken into account in the final agreement.

The United States, which does not face the same institutionalized level of political opposition to liberalization, argued forcefully and successfully for using the OECD as the proper forum for the MAI. Following the collapse of the MAI, U.S. representatives floated the idea of using the IMF's Articles of Agreement to create a de facto MAI. With voting power in the IMF based on monetary contributions, the United States has an effective veto and would thus have sufficient power to ensure an agreement in line with its commitment to maximum liberalization. In other words, differences in national political cultures were important in shaping strategy for the proposed agreement.

In addition, national political cultures were important in pressuring negotiators to protect states from many of the core elements of the MAI. A number of countries, including Australia, Canada, and France, sought to limit foreign takeover of nationally based companies and, in the case of Canada and France, to protect French-language culture and media industries. For its part, the United States sought to reserve the right to exempt subsidies given by U.S. states and localities and sought to maintain the Helms-Burton Act, which imposes sanctions against foreign companies investing in Cuba. In all, more than 400 specific exemptions were made, suggesting that the particular interests of nation-states interfered significantly with the conclusion of a strong, inclusive agreement. State participation in transnationalization is thus a function not only of historically specific levels of political organization and commitment to political-economic values but also of nationally specific levels of organization and instrumental power among economic sectors.

In addition to conflicts between states, subordinate social forces played a major role in the fate of the MAI. Although negotiations were conducted in secret and the draft agreement did not recognize popular forces as legitimate global actors, negotiations stimulated considerable international opposition by labor and environmental groups after the February 1997 draft treaty was leaked and posted on the Internet. Nongovernmental organizations (NGOs) initiated national and international campaigns of sufficient strength to compel the OECD to organize informal consultations with NGO representatives. The inclusion of language in the agreement calling on MAI members to honor national laws concerning labor and the environment, however weak and tentative, was the OECD's attempt to grant concessions to subordinate social forces that did not challenge the core elements of the agreement.

This attempt to co-opt MAI opponents ultimately failed. Concerned NGOs rejected the MAI's combination of strong, enforceable, supranational provisions for liberalizing global movements of capital and voluntary, unenforceable, national labor and environmental regulations. Instead, the NGOs called for binding supranational agreements on environmental, labor, health, safety, and human rights standards and on the creation of democratic, transparent mechanisms of accountability for global capital. In contrast to the OECD, NGOs preferred strong supranational regulatory regimes that ensure a harmonization of standards in the interest of labor and the environment.

Finally, the MAI was sidetracked because those forces that would most directly benefit from its creation—global capital interests—began to question whether this particular agreement could deliver what they sought. Corporate lobbying groups from the United States, Europe, and Japan opposed the inclusion of any language, even nonbinding language, referring to labor or environmental standards. As OECD negotiators granted concessions on labor and the environment in the hopes of winning the consent of subordinate social forces, they progressively alienated corporate lobbying groups. At the same time, the volume of country-specific exemptions, from capital's perspective, made the MAI look less impressive as a means of liberalizing capital flows than its architects intended. For capital, the combination of significant country-specific exceptions and the inclusion of language on labor and the environment rendered the MAI so problematic that no agreement was preferred to a watered-down agreement that did not deliver maximum liberalization.

The three sets of conflicts that contributed to the defeat of the MAI—conflicts among OECD member states, between the OECD and subordinate social forces, and, ultimately, between the OECD and important elements of multinational capital—reveal the contradictory nature of globalization. Rather than following an inexorable or monolithic path of development, globalization is a process in which nation-states and national political cultures play a leading role. Despite their commitment to a neoliberal global economic order, state managers are still dependent on national political and economic interests for legitimacy and material resources, and both capital and nation-states are not so all-powerful that they may ride roughshod over social forces opposed to liberalization.

This contradiction between the nation-state's active role in liberating capital globally from constraints that were imposed as the result of political struggles and its continued structural dependence on national political and economic forces places important limits on capitalist globalization. Capitalist globalization is the product of strategic action by powerful social actors. But, in Marx's words, people—even those in the dominant class—do not make history as they choose. The contradictions of capitalist globalization provide structural opportunities for antiglobalization and anticapitalist movements to resist capitalist globalization and offer the possibility of a more democratic globalization from below.

DEMOCRATIC GLOBALIZATION: THERE *IS* AN ALTERNATIVE

The democratization of the nation-state has been an uneven process. To the extent that liberal/representative democratic institutions are characteristic of the capitalist core, this is in large part the result of the relations of subordination experienced by the periphery over the past 500 years (C. Thomas 1984). The transfer of wealth from periphery to core that has characterized the history of capitalism has provided core countries with the resources necessary to win consent among their populations. At the same time, the loss of human and natural wealth because of the historical experience of slavery and colonialism and of contemporary forms of exploitation, such as free trade, debt, and structural adjustment, makes it more difficult for these states to exercise power based on consent. Without the resources with which to bargain for consent, these states have been more likely to exercise power through coercion. Strikingly, the argument for the supercession of the nation-state by a transnational state, defined by institutions that actively suppress liberal/representative democracy, comes before the full potential of the liberal/representative democratic state has been realized globally. As we have seen, however, even this potential is limited by powerful structural forces through which liberal/representative democracy is associated with capitalism. The creation of a democratic alternative to capitalist globalization is thus simultaneously the creation of a new global society as well as new national institutions.

Challenges to the oft-cited claim that "there is no alternative" to capitalist globalization have been an important feature of the process of globalization (McNally 2006). Capitalist globalization has stimulated the rise of social movements, challenging the hegemony of the market and offering a vision of a democratic globalization committed to social justice and equality. The same technologies that have allowed capital to decentralize production across the globe have allowed labor, environmental, women's, peace, and human rights movements the opportunity to share experiences and strategies of resistance on a global level. Likewise, capitalist globalization has forced social movements to move beyond the confines of national boundaries to embrace goals, strategies, and organizational forms that are increasingly transnational in character.

Resistance to structural adjustment policies in Venezuela in 1989, the brutal suppression of which led to the deaths of hundreds of civilians, and the Zapatista uprising that began in 1994 are examples of early challenges to capitalist globalization. The defeat of the MAI is another, as it was the first major defeat of capitalist globalization within the capitalist core. Prior to the MAI, the network of transnational institutions managing capitalist globalization had operated safe from public scrutiny, much less any coordinated challenge, and within a technocratic worldview that saw globalization as a purely economic (that is, market-oriented) phenomenon. What were once quiet gatherings of technical experts and state officials, however, are now occasions for mass protest and resistance to global capitalism. The "battle of Seattle" in 1999 and subsequent protests at meetings of the WTO, World Bank, and other institutions of capitalist globalization in Genoa, Montreal, Washington, and other cities is evidence that capitalist globalization may no longer proceed uncontested. That the architects of capitalist globalization have recognized this is reflected in a trend within multilateral economic institutions toward increased attention, if only at a relatively superficial level, to the relevance of democracy, sustainable development, environmental protection, and other nonmarket issues. Opponents of capitalist globalization, however, reject such accommodations as insufficient and instead seek more thorough changes to national and international institutions.

One of the most important expressions of this alternative to capitalist globalization is the World Social Forum (WSF) (Fisher & Ponniah 2003; Leita 2005; de Sousa Santos 2006). The WSF, which met for the first time in Porto Alegre, Brazil, in 2001, represents an attempt to construct a global civil society that emphasizes participatory democracy and social justice in contrast to the market-oriented values of capitalist globalization. This alternative vision of globalization is characterized by a radical redistribution of wealth, the replacement of market-driven growth with forms of sustainable social development that are centered on meeting human needs for meaningful work and a healthy environment, and the elimination of institutionalized inequalities and structural violence. The specific means of achieving these goals have been the subject of intense debate.

Fisher and Ponniah (2003) argue that WSF debates have revolved around a number of questions. First, can existing transnational institutions be sufficiently reformed to achieve democratic globalization, or must these institutions be dismantled and replaced by new ones? Second, can the need for economic development to provide employment and necessary goods and services be balanced with that of managing ecologically sustainable development? Third, how are human rights to be defined and enforced? How can claims for universal human rights, which have ironically emerged from the capitalist core, take into account the experiences and perspectives of the global South? Finally, how can the "different geographies of political demands"—including the local, the national, and the global—be reconciled?

In addition to the substantive goals and debates that distinguish it from transnational institutions of capitalist globalization, the WSF is notable for its internal organization. As Bandy and Smith (2005, 231) point out in their volume on transnational social movements, "transnational civil societies are often not so civil." The problematic nature of global civil society arises from the inequalities of power, resources, and organizational capacity that characterize global capitalism. Successful transnational movements must acknowledge these inequalities, subject them to open debate and discussion, and redistribute power and resources within a democratic organizational culture. As a result, the WSF's organizational commitment to participatory democracy is just as important as its substantive goals, since the debates noted above can be resolved satisfactorily only through a transparent, participatory process. This integration of a democratic procedure that simultaneously is based on and contributes to social justice is a powerful repudiation of the liberal/representative model of democracy that has been associated with capitalism.

Just as capitalist globalization has not meant the diminution of the nation-state's role in capitalism, so too the significance of the WSF as a model for a democratic globalization from below does not mean that the nation-state has been replaced by a new, transnational field of struggle. In Bandy and Smith's (2005, 12) words, "an effective struggle against the ideological and structural hegemony of global neoliberalism will likely depend upon efforts to strengthen institutions for democratic accountability and participation at the national level as well as transnationally." Nationally based liberal/representative democratic institutions are constrained by the realities of class power in capitalism.

Yet the relative autonomy of the state from capital provides opposition movements with structural opportunities to challenge both the state and capital. Contrast this with the more severe constraints that exist within transnational institutions of capitalist globalization, where the very concept of citizenship has been redefined to exclude these movements. Also, to the extent that social movements are facilitated by the absence of repression, struggles to democratize the nation-state, where coercive state power is still concentrated, will make a major contribution to the development of transnational social movements. Finally, to the extent that the nation-state remains the principle institution through which social welfare provision occurs, a major component of globalization from below is the struggle over how this may be organized at the national level in more humane and less market-oriented ways.

CONCLUSION

Here I have offered a critique of democratic peace theory that calls both core components—democracy and peace—into question. Capitalist globalization represents a dramatic reassertion of the power of the market. This has resulted in an intensification of social inequality and pressures for the commodification of everyday life. This, in turn, has disturbing consequences for democracy. As class power becomes more concentrated, the contradictions of liberal/representative democracy become more obvious. The discourse of citizenship that is central to this form of democracy is increasingly being undermined by a neoliberal discourse of *homo economicus*—of isolated, abstract individuals interested only in profit-maximizing behavior. In such a world, democracy is no longer relevant, as the society whose will it is supposed to represent has been atomized; at best, democracy survives as a commodity.

The nation-state, the institutional form through which liberal/representative democracy has been expressed, is not a passive victim of capitalist globalization. Instead, capitalist globalization is a process that "takes place in, through, and under the aegis of states; it is encoded by them and in important respects even authored by them; and it involves a shift in power relations within states that often means the centralization and concentration of state powers as the necessary condition of and accompaniment to global market discipline" (Panitch 1996, 86).

The state's powers to mobilize for and conduct war have been an essential feature of capitalist development, both globally and within national boundaries, for the past 500 years. In the context of the "globalization" that has taken place since the end of the Second World War, it is clear that core states have used military power to impose neoliberalism and discipline those states that sought to chart an independent form of social development. During this period, the record of the United States, which used overt or covert military force to overthrow democratically elected governments in Guatemala, Iran, Brazil, the Dominican Republic, Chile, Nicaragua, and Haiti, gives pause to democratic peace theory's assertions about the connection between democracy and peace. If "democracies are less likely to go to war with each other," this may be limited to those core democratic states that share both a limited conception of democracy and a commitment to maintaining global capitalism; alternative conceptions of democracy, particularly those that are critical of the market, are unlikely to stimulate among the core capitalist states the peaceful forms of conflict resolution outlined in democratic peace theory.

At the same time, the United States' permanent war economy has facilitated the imposition of neoliberalism at home. Unlike in other core capitalist states, which had extensive social welfare systems that ameliorated the social consequences of capitalist markets and which had to be dismantled (with some success and much resistance) as part of the neoliberal project, state intervention in the U.S. economy was more heavily oriented toward military spending. The result was the displacement of social welfare policies that could have had a more substantial impact on social inequality and served as an obstacle to neoliberalism (Martin & Torres 2004; Melman 2001). Democratic peace theory's argument that electoral accountability serves as an obstacle to war is called into question by the intensification of social inequality associated with neoliberalism. Consent becomes more problematic and meaningless with the rapid growth in coercive and disciplinary forms of power associated with the "war on terror" (C. Parenti 2004, 2008).

"Commonsense" assertions of the inevitability of globalization and the resulting decline of the nation-state are thus powerful tools for justifying neoliberal state policy regarding trade and investment, the dismantling of social welfare, and the disciplining of subordinate social forces. They also are important resources for demobilizing resistance to such policies (Hirst & Thompson 2001; Piven & Cloward 1997). In contrast to this view, I argue that if nation-states remain central to global capitalism, then so too do the contradictions of the nation-state. As such, the nation-state continues to provide resources for resisting capitalist globalization and for developing an alternative globalization characterized by participatory democracy and social justice.

5
Poverty and Democratic Consolidation in Sub-Saharan Africa

Abdulahi A. Osman

INTRODUCTION

The theory of democratic peace is not limited to great powers or even industrialized states. All countries are presumably involved, with their security policies linked directly to their own regime types and that of their potential enemies. For this reason, it is worth undertaking a focused review of the most impoverished region of the world, sub-Saharan Africa, and considering to what extent the expansion of democratic rule may affect regional relations—and, more broadly, the universal validity of the theory.

The African continent has witnessed greater democratization since the end of the cold war, with more than seventy competitive national elections held in the region between 1989 and 2000. Today the majority of African states maintain legislatures with representatives from at least two political parties, a remarkable distinction when contrasted with previous years. Still, fewer than half of the forty-eight countries in sub-Saharan Africa were considered in 2006 to have electoral democracies.[1] Only Botswana, Mauritius, and Senegal have been fully democratic for an extended period of time.

Why are there so many failures of democratization in this region? One major factor is the conceptual confusion that surrounds how democracy is defined, applied, and practiced. More specific to the African setting are the tensions between state and society. Most African states have their roots in colonial rule, hardly a training ground for democratic governance. Hence, the majority of the postcolonial states in Africa have lacked the legitimacy and acceptance of the populace. Compounding this political problem, the subcontinent is mired in severe poverty, social strife, and militarized conflict, all of which serve as obstacles to democratic development.

The 1990s presented conditions that ultimately dashed many Africans' high hopes for stability and development, hopes that were first sparked during the independence period of the 1960s. Most countries emerged out of decades of colonial rule only to be shattered by a lack of representative government and economic opportunity. The 1990s, the first decade after the cold war, brought a "second wave" of hope in many African countries (Adedeji 1999). Unfortunately, dreams of stability and prosperity succumbed to the realities of the decade: inattention from the industrialized world to the outbreak of violence in several areas in the early 1990s (unlike these countries' response to the crisis in southern Europe); failed democratic transitions, despite the holding of elections for the first time in many states; and heightened poverty, exactly the opposite of the economic revival that had been widely anticipated (Gurr et al. 2000, 11). The outbreak of the HIV/AIDS epidemic across sub-Saharan Africa, claiming a countless number of lives, furthered the suffering and demoralization.

Many scholars and policymakers have blamed the lack of democratic development for both the increased poverty and the instability in Africa. After the collapse of the Soviet Union, democracy was pushed as a remedy for the poverty and conflicts in the developing world. Many societies that had long lived under autocratic regimes were transformed into democratically elected states, a pattern that increased the percentage of free states around the world from 26 percent to 47 percent between 1976 and 2006 (Freedom House 2007). Understandably, the "third wave" (Huntington 1991) of democratization raised expectations of a golden age of freedom (see Fukuyama 1992; Pye 1990). As time progressed, however, it became clear that democratic regimes neither exist uniformly nor function effectively in all cases. Although many states adopted constitutions that spelled out political freedoms of speech, information, religion, and other forms of self-expression, rampant violations of human rights continued (Finer 1999; Rose 2001).

The United States stood as a foremost advocate of democratic reforms across the developing world. To the former U.S. secretary of state, Colin Powell, "Democracy and the love of freedom are universal values that transcend culture and history."[2] His comment, though well-meaning, suggested that, for democracy, "one size fits all." As some scholars have concluded, however, democracy may take several forms, and Western models promoted by Powell and other leaders have proven to be ill-suited to the African context (Diamond 1989).

On achieving independence the new African states adopted several types of democratic governments, including presidential, parliamentary, and mixed systems. Often these systems were imported from the departing colonial power's political system. In 1960, for example, Nigeria adopted a British parliamentary government, until its leaders were overthrown in 1966. Two decades later Nigeria attempted a U.S.-style presidential system, until once again it was toppled by military generals.

Since 1999 Nigeria has had an elected civilian government, and recent elections that brought Uamru Yar'Adua to power marked the first civilian succession in Nigeria since independence.

All of this raises many fundamental questions: How is democracy to be defined? Is the Western model replicable in all places? Given Africa's economic and political realities, can most African states complete democratic transitions? This chapter examines these questions and confronts the many dilemmas African societies face in the process of democratic reform. The chapter will be divided into three parts. The first part explores the conceptual definitions of democracy and their relative benefits from a normative perspective. The second part examines the contemporary African state and its evolution, particularly the role of colonial rule. The third part of the chapter considers the functional relationship between poverty and democracy in the region. The chapter ends with some concluding remarks and revisits the democratic peace theory and its applicability to the African reality.

DEMOCRACY AND AFRICA: A CONCEPTUAL MISMATCH?

There is little doubt that the first post–cold war decade witnessed a dramatic increase in African democracy (see Bratton & van de Walle 1997). As the number of free and partly free countries rose, those without democratic government became fewer in number. As Africa's widening adoption of democratic rule gained momentum after the cold war, there was much confusion as to what the term *democracy* meant and how it should be practiced.

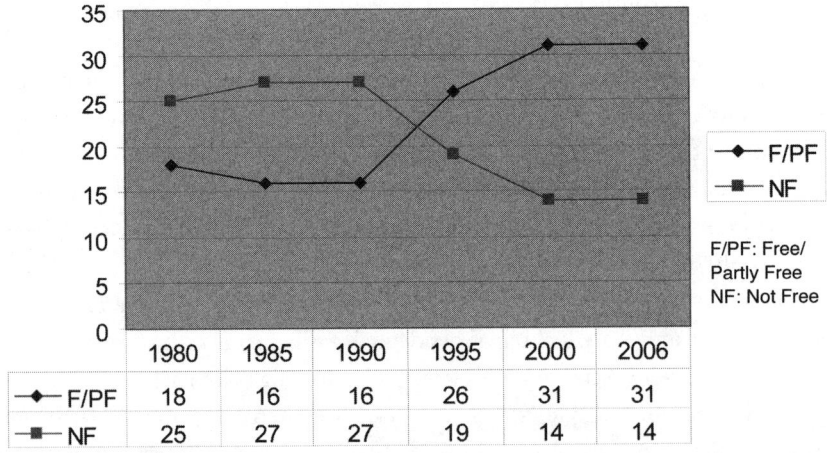

Figure 5.1. Freedom in sub-Saharan Africa, 1980–2006. Source: www.freedomhouse.org.

This conceptual disarray was hardly novel; the notion of democracy has long suffered from a lack of concise definition. Although ancient Greece is commonly accepted as democracy's birthplace, Athenian democracy actually resembled an oligarchic rather than a democratic system. The state did not represent all Athenians; only free male citizens of the city-state participated, while women, foreigners, and slaves were excluded from political life. The modern democratic system took shape amid the French and American revolutions of the eighteenth century and amid the industrial revolution of the same era that brought many citizens into urban areas. Societal changes, largely economic in nature, fueled demands for greater individual rights (Weiner & LaPalombara 1966; Sartori 1976).

While a singular conception of democracy remained elusive, there are today several agreed-on features, such as free electoral competition and respect for individual freedoms of thought, expression, and assembly. But the most difficult aspect of democracy is how it is to be implemented into functioning statehood. Debates among democratic theorists can be placed along a continuum that ranges from maximalist to minimalist approaches. Representing the former, Dahl (1989, 221) advances three essential conditions for the functions of a multiparty democracy: extensive competition by political candidates and their respective parties; widespread political participation among the electorate; and civil and political liberties that enable citizens to express themselves without fear of punishment. At the other end of the spectrum, minimalists argue that democracy is merely "a method by which decision-making is transferred to individuals who have gained power in a competitive struggle for the votes of the citizens" (Schumpeter 1942, 269).

Both of these definitions reflect a Western, specifically Anglo-American, bias that tends to reduce the concept of democracy to elections, multiparty systems, and universal suffrage. Any deviation from this model is considered anomalous. Yet this model of democracy has often failed in sub-Saharan Africa because of fundamental differences between the West and Africa in how society organizes itself. In many parts of Africa, political parties are mainly organized around ethnic or clan identity and interest, whereas in the West parties are generally organized around economic class interests. Thus the contemporary Western insistence on multiparty politics for the most part ignores indigenous cultural values and encourages multiparty electoral politics to degenerate into ethnic or communal conflicts. Moreover, because of the lack of consensus on democratic norms, coupled with insufficient pressure from civil societies, many African leaders have repressed rights and engaged in government corruption. In many places where competitive elections have occurred, minorities have been excluded from the political process and continue to face an insecure future (see Rothchild 2000).

Political systems generally result from the experiences shaped by a given society's values and historical experiences. As noted earlier, democratic reform in Africa has so far achieved mixed results. This does not, however, mean that African cultures are devoid of democratic norms. Most societies in the pre- and postcolonial eras have maintained systems of government based on self-determination. Traditional African political systems respected democratic values in various forms, including patrimony, communalism, strong voluntary participation, and, most importantly, accountability. Many African indigenous governments were open and inclusive, and most of the African societies had leaders who ruled with the consent of members of the society who recognized their rights and responsibilities. Despite many centuries of European intervention through slavery and colonialism, many democratic qualities can be observed in parts of Africa. Two examples are the Dighil and Mirifle communities in southern Somalia, which practice consensus building in most of their deliberations and have created indigenous institutions that are accountable to the populace. A typical village has institutional structures that effectively function as legislative, executive, and judicial branches. The leader of the village is the Malaaq, who is responsible for directing the social and economic activities of the village. However, the Malaaq must consult with village elders and religious leaders before making any decision. One such institutional structure is the defense system of the village. Before war is declared among the Dighil and Mirifle, the warrior leader must get permission from the Malaaq (Mukhtar & Kusow 1994).

These examples are not exclusive to the Dighil and Mirifle communities and can be observed in many parts of the subcontinent. Other cases illustrate the extent to which democratic norms are inherent in the ruling system of many African societies.

DEMOCRATIC STATE BUILDING IN AFRICA

Despite the existence of democratic practices in Africa, as illustrated above, many African societies are seen as lacking democratic norms. We must recognize, however, that what is lacking is a *Western* democratic system and not democratic norms per se. The major factor behind the lack of Western democracy in Africa is the fundamental difference between Western individualism and African communalism, the latter of which is based to a large extent on ethnic identity. In order to understand this strong cultural adherence to ethnic identity, one must examine the role of colonialism in shaping the primacy of ethnic identity in the current political systems in Africa.

Colonial powers used ethnic identity as a tool that facilitated their exploitative ambitions. Throughout the colonial era, European colonial states relied heavily on the local chiefs and other traditional leaders. This reliance on ethnic structures was utilized, at different levels, in both the indirect rule of the British and the assimilation system of direct rule of the French (Welsh 1996; Mamdani 1996; Young 1994).

Colonial states encouraged local groups to advance their interests through tribal organizations, seeking the patronage of tribal leaders and thereby strengthening ethnic, clan, and tribal loyalties.

Today, these ethnic divisions are the source of much of Africa's violent politics, the prevalence of weak political institutions, and the lack of economic growth across most of the continent (Berman 1998). Since independence, power in many states has come to be concentrated in the hands of a few elites who benefit disproportionately, often through nepotism and corruption (Chazan et al. 1999). As a result, the postcolonial state in sub-Saharan Africa became a highly visible and contested resource because of the wealth and power it possessed (see Braathen et al. 2000; Schroeder 2000; Adedeji 1999). Moreover, most of the colonial states functioned as dictatorships, run by appointed governors whose primary task was the extraction of wealth. Colonial rulers had little or no interest in promoting African-led, autonomous, and viable political systems.[3]

As pressure for political rights and independence mounted at the end of World War II, colonial states imprisoned many of the opposition movement leaders, such as the late Jomo Kenyatta, former head of Kenya's Mau Mau movement and the country's first president after independence in 1963. Unfortunately, many leaders of the postcolonial states in Africa copied their former colonial powers and used the same authoritarian measures. Most Africans had little or no opportunity for any political participation until the very end of the colonial period, when elections began to be held.

To many observers, multiethnic state identities were to blame for the lack of economic development, democracy, and stability in sub-Saharan Africa. In order to remedy this problem, many leaders in the region resorted to the discourse of nationalism both in the colonial and postcolonial periods. As the movement toward independence strengthened after World War II, the search for national identity came further to the forefront. This brand of nationalism, however, had two major shortfalls. First, it was a reaction against the harsh colonial practices that strictly demarcated and enforced social separation based on ethnic or clan lines. Second, it was perhaps the only way to appeal to the largest popular support for the anticolonial struggle. As a result, most political parties claimed national unity and tried to dismiss underlying tribal and clan affiliations.

The sudden burst of nationalism, consequently, lacked a deeply grounded ideological basis and was superficial at best. Davidson (1992, 199) viewed nationalism in this context as "a mobilizing and emotively compelling slogan [that] had small meaning in the Africa of 1950s. Its history was as little known as its credentials.... Nobody was thinking about the implications of nationhood." In a similar vein, as Fanon (1961, 119) asserted, "National consciousness [has become] a crude and fragile travesty of what might have been."

In sum, colonialism created arbitrary borders that incorporated diverse and often contentious peoples into a single territory and imposed alien political institutions on them that stymied the process of democratic state building. The postcolonial states faced the challenges of building both a nation (a strong and cohesive common identity) and a state (effective governing institutions). Whereas Europe had many years for building strong institutions and a common identity, resulting in powerful central governments obeyed by the citizens, the African states had to build both nation and state simultaneously and in a very short time.

After gaining independence, most African rulers eliminated political competition in the name of national unity. One of the most brutal dictators in Africa, Zaire's late president Mobutu Sese Seko, once said, "Democracy is not for Africa. There was only one African chief and he ruled for life. Here in Zaire we must make unity" (quoted in Ayittey 1998, 93). In order to consolidate their power, the rulers utilized different methods, including the elimination of all aspects of federalism or the power of the regional authorities. The late president of Ghana, Kwame Nkrumah, for example, claimed that regional authorities were a divisive hindrance to the unity of the state (Chazan et al. 1999, 48). Other methods of forced unification included the declaration of opposing parties as "divisive." Julius Nyerere of Tanzania, who ruled from 1964 until 1985, argued that the one-party system was part of the "norm of consensus" in Africa. Similarly, the president of Cote d'Ivoire, Felix Houphouet-Boigny, said, "'There is no number two, three or four in Cote d'Ivoire. There is only a number one: that is me and I don't share my decisions" (quoted in Ayittey 1993, 64).

Many leaders of postcolonial states promoted a cult of personality. Sandbrook (1993, 49) summarized the centrality of the African leader as follows:

> The strongman, usually the president, occupies the centre of the political life. Front and centre stage, he is the centrifugal force around which all else revolves. Not only the ceremonial head of state, the president is also the chief political, military and cultural figure: head of government, commander-in-chief of the armed forces, head of the governing party (if there is one) and even chancellor of the local university. His aim is typically to identify his person with the "nation." He is present everywhere: his picture is hung on public walls, billboards, government offices, and even private homes. His portrait also embellishes stamps, coins, paper currency, and even stationary of state corporations. Schools, hospitals, and stadiums are named after him. The state-controlled media herald his every word and action, no matter how misguided.

Postcolonial leaders in Africa had two hegemonic ambitions that concurrently facilitated their control of the state. The first ambition, the maximization of personal wealth, prompted these leaders to create large public bureaucracies that facilitated their wealth extraction through taxes and other rents. The second and related ambition involved the creation of a large security apparatus whose primary mission was to protect the leaders and their palaces from political enemies. This security apparatus, however, was a drain on the weak economies of many sub-Saharan countries. The combined impact of these hegemonic ambitions was to render control of the state a zero-sum game, as evidenced by the frequent and violent transfer of political power in the form of coups d'état (Adedeji, 1999, 3).

Finally, the dynamics of the cold war also played into the hands of the postcolonial leaders of Africa, who opportunistically turned to the United States and Soviet Union for foreign aid in exchange for diplomatic allegiance. This military and economic support made the African states dependent less on their people's support and legitimation than on external entities such as the cold war superpowers and their allies (including several former colonial powers in Europe). It is this aid that further strengthened the hegemonic ambition of many ruling elites in the region. Such support provided by the cold war superpowers sustained "abusive and incompetent African governments" for years, often decades (see Jackson 1992).

The subsequent push toward democratization after the cold war, much like the support of dictators during the conflict, was not applied uniformly but selectively, in keeping with the security and economic interests of the great powers. For example, the French government's recent advocacy of democratic reforms in its former colonies exempted such states as Gabon and Congo-Brazzaville. Similarly, the U.S. government's democratization campaigns since the presidency of Jimmy Carter have consistently bypassed Egypt because of security concerns in the Middle East. The same can be said more recently for large volumes of U.S. aid to Pakistan and other front-line states in the "war on terrorism."

In all of these ways, the Africans' early experience with "home-grown" democracies that reflected diverse cultural identities and norms was ignored at the very time the subcontinent's long-awaited liberation had come. Instead, Western models prevailed in many cases that ill-suited the environments in which they were erected. The consequences of this have been dire with regard to regional security, and the flawed process of state-building both reflected and perpetuated the chronic economic underdevelopment that continues to haunt sub-Saharan Africa today.

DEMOCRACY AND POVERTY IN AFRICA

The linkage between democracy and socioeconomic development has a long tradition in the social sciences. A central thesis in the scholarly literature has been that democracy and development are positively related (Lipset 1959). Additionally, development is said to foster a population's interest in and capacity for political participation and to engender pressures for democratization. The main presumption of this school of thought is that a high level of development must be achieved first for democracy to emerge.

To Moore (1966), economic development facilitated the historic rise of democracy in the West. He asserted that both industrialization and democratization were transformations without precedent. Moore's investigation led to his famous expression "no bourgeois, no democracy." More recently, Przeworski and colleagues (2000) argued that sufficient socioeconomic development must occur for sustained democracy to be established. This research team systematically examined the relationship between economic development and democracy of 141 countries that were classified as democracies or autocracies between 1950 and 1990. It found a strong relationship between economic development and democratic regimes. Dictatorships were largely concentrated among the most impoverished societies.

After the former Soviet Union collapsed in 1990 and the world system approached a unipolar balance of power, the West began to push democracy as a remedy for the economic woes that many developing countries faced during the 1980s. Additionally, the increased number of civil wars that occurred after the cold war cried out for explanation and new remedies of conflict resolution. International financial institutions (IFIs) also advocated political reforms and the staging of multiparty elections across the developing world. In this instance, the Western leaders pledged not to support autocratic leaders, as they had during the cold war in the cases of Mobutu, Siad Barre of Somalia, Kamuzu Banda of Malawi, and many others. Backed by the "Washington consensus," the IFIs conditioned aid flows on dual reforms in recipient countries' economies (structural adjustment) and governments (democratization).

There is no scholarly consensus regarding the "development first" model. Still, it is widely held that sustained economic development in the developing world is possible only under democratic regimes. This remains visible in the provisions for aid imposed by donor states and aid agencies, which identify democracy as a primary condition for their support and for legitimization of the African states. This push toward democratization, however, comes at the expense of the effectiveness of many states (Osman 2007). Although political reforms and state effectiveness are needed for the proper functioning of any government, externally imposed democratization produces a confusing environment in many cases because of the multiple conceptions of democracy and a lack of clear guidance on how it should be practiced in very different contexts. Despite the fact that democracy has become more common in Africa, frequently the outcome of such transitions is the emergence of "illiberal" democracies (Zakaria 2003) that lack transparency and the rule of law. Corruption is also endemic, and elections are often uncontested, as in the recent cases of Burkina Faso, Djibouti, Egypt, and Uganda.

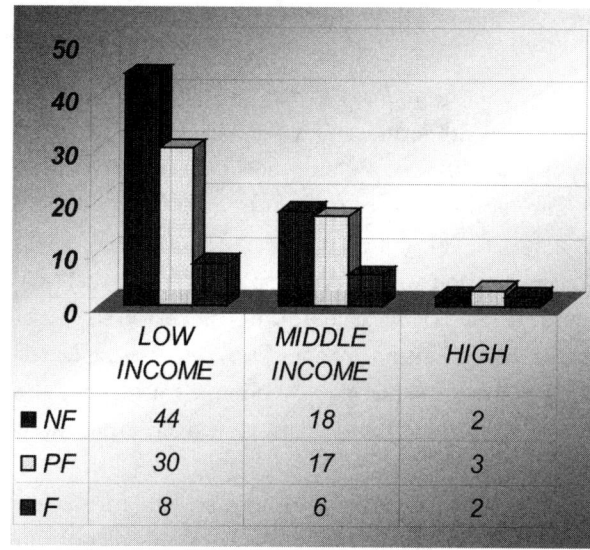

Figure 5.2. Freedom status and GDP per capita, 1980–2000. Source: www.freedomhouse.org.

The prevalence of poverty in sub-Saharan Africa represents the major obstacle to the formation and strengthening of democracy in the region.[4] Still, affluent governments and IFIs present democratic governance as the only way for African states to achieve sustained economic growth. The reality, however, remains that stability and state effectiveness are often the results of a state's ability to enforce rule of law within its borders. In many non-African cases, authoritarian states such as Russia, China, South Korea, and Singapore have experienced economic growth even in the midst of strict government curbs on civil liberties.[5] This trend illustrates the potential for economic power to strengthen rather than weaken authoritarian states, which have become more sophisticated and better endowed with the resources needed for oppression. The desire of citizens for democratic freedoms has not ceased in these cases, but their governments have proven highly capable of resisting mass movements toward actual democracy.

Still, there is a relationship between wealth and democracy that can be observed in sub-Saharan Africa. Countries with higher incomes have experienced greater democratic development compared to their counterparts. Yet the functional relationship between these two developmental patterns, political and economic, remains obscure, and it has yet to be demonstrated that democracy itself can lead Africa to a more prosperous future.

AFRICAN ECONOMIC PERFORMANCE IN PERSPECTIVE

Sub-Saharan Africa presents a paradox of human societies and their development. On the one hand, the region is rich with fertile land, rivers, oil, and vast mineral wealth. On the other hand, this wealth has not produced adequate living standards for the majority of Africans. Chronic poverty coexists in many areas with civil wars, displaced populations, and a host of devastating diseases, including HIV/AIDS. Africa is falling behind even in comparison to other developing regions and routinely suffers the lowest levels of living standards as measured by the Human Development Index (HDI).[6] For example, in 2004 the bottom 28 (out of 177) countries ranked in the HDI were from the African continent. While global economic growth grew at a healthy rate in the 1990s, 54 countries, most of them in Africa, actually experienced economic declines.[7]

The cycle of optimism and disappointment experienced across Africa is not limited to the post–cold war period. Despite predictions of economic revival and many ambitious bilateral and multilateral aid initiatives in the immediate postcolonial years, the number of Africans living in abject poverty (on less than $1 per day) increased from 90 million in 1960 to 234 million in 1990 (Ayittey 2005, 5). Two-thirds of the countries in the region had a lower GDP per capita in 1997 than in 1980; during this period the average annual growth rate in sub-Saharan Africa was 1.5 percent lower than that of other developing countries in Asia and Latin America. The region had the lowest GDP per capita of any region in the world in 1997 and continues to hold this distinction today (Collier & Gunning 1999, 3–4; World Bank 1999b, 191; Ndulu & O'Connell 1999, 42–44).

One of the major factors behind the stagnant growth in the region is the role of foreign aid and the resulting debt crisis facing many African states. During the 1970s these states received large volumes of official development assistance (ODA) in the midst of low and declining levels of foreign direct investment (FDI). Whereas net ODA receipts amounted to less than 10 percent of national incomes in 1970, this level grew to nearly 40 percent by 1987. In East Asia, however, the reverse was the case, as ODA levels decreased while the level of FDI nearly tripled from 12 percent to 33 percent of the national income (Adedeji 1993, 6). Similarly, foreign aid to the manufacturing sector, which constituted less than 12 percent of total official aid to sub-Saharan Africa at the start of the 1980s, fell to approximately 7 percent by 1989 (UNIDO 1989).

During this period Africa's foreign debt grew from $3 billion in 1960 to $225 billion in 1992. As a result, of the 32 countries worldwide with the highest levels of debt, 25 were located in sub-Saharan Africa (World Bank 1995). This debt crisis and deficit were further compounded by declines in commodity prices, which fell by more than half between 1970 and 1992 (Nafziger 1993, 67–71). Additionally, food production began to decline during the 1970s, and Africa's share of the world market for agricultural commodities decreased while food imports grew at three times the rate of population increase (World Bank 1982, 45; see also Herbst 1993).

There has been no shortage of diagnoses of what is ailing Africa. Some (e.g., Adedeji 1993) have blamed poor economic management, while others (e.g., World Bank 1989; Braathen, et al. 2000) have focused on flawed governing systems. Still others (e.g., Ayittey 1998) have cited social problems, mainly tribalism and clanism, as the source of Africa's lack of development. Most of these diagnoses concentrate on the political institutions and their failure to spark social and economic development and bring stability to their societies. But, as noted earlier, the main reason behind this failure is the fact that most postcolonial states in the region often lack legitimacy and popular acceptance through democratic norms. Possessing few of the characteristics associated with the normative functions of a democracy, these states became known as "weak" (Migdal 1988), "predatory" (Fatton 1992), or even "criminal" (Bayart, Ellis, & Hibou 1999). Callaghy (1987) described the African state as a "lame leviathan"; Ayittey (1998) likened this state to a vampire.

The analysts that examine African states' failure to develop economically and politically can be grouped into two opposing paradigms: *institutionalist* and *structuralist*. For institutionalists, the failure is the result of Africa's states and their institutions. The proponents of this viewpoint include the World Bank and IMF, which assume that after independence these countries essentially had the freedom to choose their fate. Common cases in point, Botswana and Lesotho endured all the historical barriers, including colonialism, neocolonialism, and the geopolitical and ideological pressures of the cold war.[8] Yet they still managed to preside over some of the fastest-growing economies in the world between 1960 and 1985 (Englebert 2000; World Bank 1993).

For structuralists, however, Africa's political and economic woes are part of the greater international setting. These include inherited social, historical, and ecological issues, coupled with the highly intrusive cold war and neocolonialism, which negatively impacted Africa's infant states. The main subscribers to this school include dependency theorists, who argue that the world is divided into core and periphery. The core has over the years become capable of exploiting the periphery as a result of colonialism, imperialism, and a global system of economic production that created and enforced mechanisms for exploitation. Therefore, according to structuralists, the current abundance of stagnation and violence in Africa, and in many other developing countries, was set up and has been maintained through economic and military support to many peripheral autocratic and dictatorial regimes that were rewarded for their support of the core.

The fate of African states cannot be so easily predetermined, however. There are important exceptions to be considered, states that were able to maintain democracy and growth, such as Botswana, Lesotho, Swaziland, Seychelles, Cape Verde, and Mauritius. A closer look reveals that these six countries have relatively small and homogeneous populations, as compared to those of other states and societies in sub-Saharan Africa. Englebert's (2000) seminal book argues that the legitimacy of the state in Africa is correlated with its capacity to spark development. State legitimacy was higher in countries like Botswana, where its first president, Seretse Khama, grandson of son of Khama III, king of the Bamangwato, came to power with greater acceptance from the populace. In a country such as the Democratic Republic of the Congo (formerly Zaire), however, unlike Botswana, the legitimacy of its leaders was for the most part absent. As a result, the Congolese people, despite greater natural wealth, including vast cultivable land and strategic minerals, continue to suffer from unending conflicts and harsh dictatorial rule that is legitimized and supported by the West.

This partial failure of Western-style democracy in Africa generally stems from two major sources. First is the economic marginalization of Africa, which is the result of its dependency on the global economic system. As argued, over the years the African politics and economy have been continuously shaped by years of colonialism, neocolonialism, and the cold war. Most African countries are overwhelmingly part of the periphery, and their economies have been dependent on commodities that have proven to be unreliable, with fluctuating prices.

Second, and more importantly, is the mismatch between Western individualism and African communalism, which continues to impede and might perhaps be antithetical to the success of Western-style democracy in sub-Saharan Africa (Ake 1991). The imposition of outside political structures, reflecting ideas and values that are alien to Africa's experience, cannot inspire democracy, prosperity, and peace.

CONCLUSION

The expansion of democratic rule in many parts of sub-Saharan Africa is a welcome trend. A closer look, however, reveals that what is being instituted is mainly an *illiberal* democracy empty of the civil liberties that usually accompany democratic rule. Many African states hold elections that are mainly designed to satisfy the appetite of outsiders rather than of their own people. African democratization during the 1990s was driven in large measure by pressure from Western countries that won the cold war. Moreover, democracy was pushed as a remedy for Africa's poverty and conflicts. Unfortunately, after a decade and a half of increased democratization, neither the poverty rate nor the frequency of conflicts has declined significantly.

I argue here that two factors are behind this failure. The first involves the vague and confusing nature of democracy, both in concept and practice. Earlier African societies featured political systems that promoted liberal values and mechanisms for checks and balances, but these indigenous forms of democracy were disrupted during European colonialism. Today one can observe a mismatch between Western individualism and African communalism as central to the failure of institutionalizing democracy in Africa. Since independence, many Africans have demanded democracy in their own countries, but throughout the cold war their demands mainly fell on deaf ears. Afterward, the external pressures to democratize reflected the cultural biases of Western states and international financial institutions and failed to incorporate both the indigenous democratic cultures and local and communal demands for democracy.

Second, the prevalence of poverty represents a persistent obstacle to democratization in Africa. Since the 1980s many African countries have fallen into a seemingly bottomless pit of economic decline coupled with conflicts and genocide. More importantly, the democratic wave of the 1990s followed a pattern of selective democratization that was determined by each country's ability to sustain itself through aid and rent seeking. Resource-rich countries such as Angola and Congo proved capable of rejecting the pressure to democratize, and Western democratizers were more than willing to overlook their shortcomings. At the same time, poorer and more vulnerable countries, such as Benin, Mali, and Senegal, were quick to accept the political conditions for aid imposed by the West.

In the future, democratic state builders in Africa need to consider several factors. First they must incorporate the indigenous cultures' democratic practices and give voice to local demands. Second, the continent's economy—destroyed through colonialism, neocolonialism, and the cold war—must be rebuilt. Unlike the economic recovery and strong democratic systems that emerged in post–World War II Europe as a result of the Marshall Plan, Africans remained mired in postcolonial oppression. Both indigenization and economic reconstruction need to be instituted in order to achieve sustainable and peaceful democracy in Africa. The achievement of this endeavor is equally the responsibility of Africans, who must institute their own forms of "good governance" in accordance with the rule of law, and of the international community, which must forge an equal partnership with its African counterparts rather than prolong the historic pattern of alternating neglect and hegemonic manipulation.

This review of political and economic development in sub-Saharan Africa does not pose a threat to democratic peace theory. It does, however, suggest that a more nuanced conception of democracy that accommodates contextual variation is essential. Democratic governments have emerged in a variety of historical, geopolitical, and cultural settings, and the variation in these processes has implications for regional relations and stability. As the most distressed region in the world, sub-Saharan Africa must be understood as a distinctive test case for the theory. The profound challenges facing its nation-states at their founding, just a generation or two ago, manifest in ongoing difficulties today, create dilemmas for both democracy and peace across the region.

Since the end of the cold war, democracy has been pushed as a remedy to the rampant poverty and instability in many parts of the developing world, including sub-Saharan Africa. Moreover, this push toward democracy has shown mixed results in this subregion, where neither poverty nor instability has been significantly reduced despite the increased number of countries with democratically elected legislative and executive branches. Democratic peace theory, which suggests the absence of war between democracies, is in most cases inapplicable in the subregion since interstate wars are rare as compared to intrastate (or civil) wars. Still, democratic peace theory provides a foundation on which the push toward democratization around the globe has been built.

Nevertheless, over the years democracy has been pushed neither uniformly nor equally, and, more importantly, the rhetoric did not match the reality. During the cold war, the West pushed democracy as anticommunism while at the same time often embracing autocratic regimes in Africa and overlooking many human rights violation committed by dictators such as Mobutu of Zaire. After the collapse of the former Soviet Union in 1991, democratization became a precondition for African countries that sought foreign aid and loans, especially from IFIs, in order to remedy their political and economic crises. As a result, political reform in Africa since the cold war era has been dependent on the economic circumstances of each country.

All of this brings to mind one fundamental question: Is Africa unstable because it is not democratic, or is Africa not democratic because it is unstable? The continent has been shaped by years of slavery, colonialism, and postcolonialism, and by the cold war and post–cold war eras, during which political and economic reforms were imposed for the enhancement of the interest of actors mainly in the West. These reforms have over the years destabilized many countries on the continent—quite the opposite of their stated intentions. Thus, the lack of peace in Africa is not the result of a lack of democracy. Rather, there are other factors that must be taken into account. The theory of democratic peace must be mindful of these complex factors rather than blindly accepting democracy (or the lack thereof) as the cause of and cure for Africa's woes.

NOTES

1. Of the 48 countries in sub-Saharan Africa, 11 were considered "free" by Freedom House, 23 "partly free," and 14 "not free" (Freedom House 2006, 4).
2. See http://www.america.gov/st/washfile-english/20040302173540AJesroMO.650448.html (retrieved Aug. 30, 2009).

3. Berman (1998, 329) described the colonial state as "an authoritarian bureaucratic apparatus of control and not intended to be a school of democracy."
4. As Lipset (1959) pointed out, the more affluent a nation, the better its chances of transforming itself into a democracy.
5. Recent history reveals a variety of states with high rates of economic growth that are not accompanied by political reforms (Bueno de Mesquita & Downs 2005). China and Russia are prime examples of this phenomenon. China's economy has undergone massive growth over the last twenty-five years, yet it has opened little politically. And in Russia the political reins continue to tighten even as the economy improves. This trend illustrates the potential for economic power to strengthen rather than weaken authoritarian states, which have become more sophisticated and better endowed with the resources needed for oppression. Citizens' desire for democracy hasn't ceased in these cases, but governments have proven highly capable of resisting potential movements toward actual democracy.
6. The Human Development Index is published annually by the United Nations Development Program (UNDP). It is a combination of indicators including health care, education, and income. The index is intended to provide data for achievements in the most basic human capabilities: living a long life, being knowledgeable, and enjoying a decent standard of living.
7. For example, according to the World Bank *Africa Database 1998/99*, the average per capita growth in sub-Saharan Africa (including South Africa and Nigeria) in 1965 was $499; by 1995 this figure stood at $494 (in constant 1987 U.S. dollars).
8. Although Lesothos's economy has been dependent on South Africa, it has shown steady growth. For example, the manufacturing sector, which accounted for 7 percent of the GDP in 1980, rose to 18 percent by 1995 (World Bank 1997; see also Englebert 2000).

Part Two
Democratic Peace in Practice

6

Kant, Liberal Legacies, and Foreign Affairs, Part 2

Michael W. Doyle

VI

Even though liberalism has achieved striking success in creating a zone of peace and, with leadership, a zone of cooperation among states similarly liberal in character, liberalism has been equally striking as a failure in guiding foreign policy outside the liberal world. In these foreign relations, liberalism leads to three confusing failings: the first two are what Hume called "imprudent vehemence" and, conversely, a "careless and supine complaisance";[39] the third is the political uncertainty that is introduced by the moral ambiguity of the liberal principles which govern the international distribution of property.

Imprudent vehemence is the most familiar failing. In relations with powerful states of a nonliberal character, liberal policy has been characterized by repeated failures of diplomacy. It has often raised conflicts of interest into crusades; it has delayed in taking full advantage of rivalries within nonliberal alliances; it has failed to negotiate stable mutual accommodations of interest. In relations with weak states of a nonliberal character, liberal policy has succumbed to imperial interventions that it has been unable to sustain or to profit from. Its interventions, designed to create liberal societies by promoting the economic development and political stability of nonliberal societies, have frequently failed to achieve their objects. Confusion, drift, costly crusades, spasmodic imperialism are the contrasting record of liberal foreign policy *outside* the liberal world. A failure to negotiate with the powerful and a failure to create stable clients among the weak are its legacies.[40] Why?

These failures mainly flow from two sources. First, outside the pacific union, liberal regimes, like all other states, are caught in the international state of war Hobbes and the Realists describe. Conflict and wars are a natural outcome of struggles for resources, prestige, and security among independent states; confusion is an unsurprising accompaniment in a state of war without reliable law or organization.

Second, these failures are also the natural complement of liberalism's success as an intellectual guide to foreign policy among liberal states. *The very constitutional restraint, shared commercial interests, and international respect for individual rights that promote peace among liberal societies can exacerbate conflicts in relations between liberal and nonliberal societies.*

If the legitimacy of state action rests on the fact that it respects and effectively represents morally autonomous individuals, then states that coerce their citizens or foreign residents lack moral legitimacy. Even Kant regarded the attitude of "primitive peoples" attached to a lawless liberty as "raw, uncivilized, and an animalic degradation of humanity."[41] When states reject the cosmopolitan law of access (a rejection that authoritarian or communist states, whether weak or powerful, can often find advantageous and, indeed, necessary for their security), Kant declares that they violate natural law:

> The inhospitable ways of coastal regions, such as the Barbary Coast, where they rob ships in the adjoining seas or make stranded seamen into slaves, is contrary to natural law, as are the similarly inhospitable ways of the deserts and their Bedouins, who look upon the approach of a foreigner as giving them a right to plunder him.[42]

Nevertheless, Kant rejects conquest or imperial intervention as an equal wrong. The practice of liberal states, which in many cases only applies liberal principles in part, has not been so forbearing.

According to liberal practice, some nonliberal states, such as the United States' communist rivals, do not acquire the right to be free from foreign intervention, nor are they assumed to respect the political independence and territorial integrity of other states. Instead conflicts of interest become interpreted as steps in a campaign of aggression against the liberal state. Of course, powerful authoritarian or totalitarian states, such as Nazi Germany or the Soviet Union, sometimes wage direct or indirect campaigns of aggression against liberal regimes. And totalitarian diplomacy is clouded by the pervasive secrecy these societies establish. But part of the atmosphere of suspicion can be attributed to the perception by liberal states that nonliberal states are in a permanent state of aggression against their own people. Referring to fascist states, Cordell Hull concluded, "their very nature requires them to be aggressive."[43] Efforts by nonliberal states at accommodation thus become snares to trap the unwary. When the Soviets refuse to negotiate, they are plotting a world takeover. When they seek to negotiate, they are plotting even more insidiously. This extreme lack of public respect or trust is one of the major features that distinguishes relations between liberal and nonliberal societies from relations among liberal societies.

At the same time, lack of public trust constrains social and economic exchanges. Commercial interdependence can produce conflict as well as welfare when a society becomes dependent on foreign actions it cannot control. Among liberal societies the extent and variety of commercial exchanges guarantee that a single conflict of interest will not shape an entire relationship. But between liberal and nonliberal societies, these exchanges, because they are limited for security considerations, do not provide a counterweight to interstate political tension nor do they offer the variety that offsets the chance that a single conflict of interest will define an entire relationship.

Furthermore, the institutional heritage of liberal regimes—representation and division of powers—opens avenues for special interests to shape policy in ways contrary to prudent diplomacy. As George Kennan has noted, this form of government "goes far to rule out the privacy, the flexibility, and the promptness and incisiveness of decision and action, which have marked the great imperial powers of the past and which are generally necessary to the conduct of an effective world policy by the rulers of a great state."[44] And these features may be compounded by the incentives for exaggerated claims that competitive electoral politics tends to encourage. The loss of these attributes is not harmful to interliberal relations (in fact, their absence is more likely to be beneficial), but the ills of ready access to foreign policy created by representation and the division of power multiply when a lack of trust is combined with the limited economic and social connection of extra-liberal relations. Together they promote an atmosphere of tension and a lobby for discord that can play havoc with both strategic choice and moral intent.

These three traits affect liberal relations both with powerful nonliberal states and with weak nonliberal societies, though in differing ways.

In relations with *powerful* nonliberal states the consequences of these three features have been missed opportunities to pursue the negotiation of arms reduction and arms control when it has been in the mutual strategic interest and the failure to construct wider schemes of accommodation that are needed to supplement arms control. Prior to the outbreak of World War I, this is the charge that Lord Sanderson levelled against Sir Eyre Crowe in Sanderson's response to Crowe's famous memorandum on the state of British relations with Germany.[45] Sanderson pointed out that Crowe interpreted German demands to participate in the settlement of international disputes and to have a "place in the sun" (colonies), of a size not too dissimilar to that enjoyed by the other great powers, as evidence of a fundamental aggressiveness driving toward world domination. Crowe may well have perceived an essential feature of Wilhelmine Germany, and Sanderson's attempt to place Germany in the context of other rising powers (bumptious but not aggressively pursuing world domination) may have been naive. But the interesting thing to note is less the conclusions reached than Crowe's chain of argument and evidence. He rejects continued accommodation (appeasement) with Germany not because he shows that Germany was more bumptious than France and not because he shows that Germany had greater potential as a world hegemon than the United States, which he does not even consider in this connection. Instead he is (legitimately) perplexed by the real uncertainty of German foreign policy and by its "erratic, domineering, and often frankly aggressive spirit" which accords with the well-known personal characteristics of "the present Ruler of Germany."

Similar evidence of fundamental suspicion appears to characterize U.S. diplomacy toward the Soviet Union. In a fascinating memorandum to President Wilson written in 1919, Herbert Hoover (then one of Wilson's advisers), recommended that the President speak out against the danger of "world domination" the "Bolsheviki"—a "tyranny that is the negation of democracy"—posed to free peoples. Rejecting military intervention as excessively costly and likely to "make us a party in reestablishing the reactionary classes in their economic domination over the lower classes," he proposed a "relief program" designed to undercut some of the popular appeal the Bolsheviks were garnering both in the Soviet Union and abroad. Although acknowledging that the evidence was not yet clear, he concluded: "If the militant features of Bolshevism were drawn in colors with their true parallel with Prussianism as an attempt at world domination that we do not stand for, it would check the fears that today haunt all men's minds." (The actual U.S. intervention in the Soviet Union was limited to supporting anti-Bolshevik Czechoslovak soldiers in Siberia and to protecting military supplies in Murmansk from German seizure.)[46]

In the postwar period, and particularly following the Korean War, U.S. diplomacy equated the "international Communist movement" (all communist states and parties) with "Communist imperialism" and with a domestic tyranny in the U.S.S.R. that required a cold war contest and international subversion as means of legitimizing its own police state. John Foster Dulles most clearly expressed this conviction, together with his own commitment to a strategy of "liberation," when he declared: " . . . we shall never have a secure peace or a happy world so long as Soviet communism dominates one third of all the peoples that there are, and is in the process of trying at least to extend its rule to many others."[47]

Liberalism has also encouraged a tendency to misread communist threats in the Third World. Since communism is seen as inherently aggressive, Soviet military aid "destabilizes" parts of Africa in Angola and the Horn; the West protects allies. Thus the People's Republic of China was a "Soviet Manchukuo" while Diem was the "Winston Churchill of Asia." Both the actual (and unstable) dependence of these regimes on their respective superpowers and anticolonialism, the dominant force of the region, were discounted.

Most significantly, opportunities for splitting the Communist bloc along cleavages of strategic national interest were delayed. Burdened with the war in Vietnam, the United States took ten years to appreciate and exploit the strategic opportunity of the Sino-Soviet split. Even the signal strategic, "offensive" success of the early cold war, the defection of Yugoslavia from the Soviet bloc, did not receive the wholehearted welcome that a strategic assessment of its importance would have warranted.[48] Both relationships, with Yugoslavia and China, become subject to alternating, largely ideologically derived, moods: visions of exceptionalism (they were "less ruthless," more organic to the indigenous, traditional culture) sparred with bouts of liberal soul-searching ("we cannot associate ourselves with a totalitarian state"). And these unresolved tensions continue to affect the strategic relationship with both communist independents.

A purely Realist focus on the balance of power would lead one to expect the hostility between the two superpowers, the United States and the Soviet Union, that emerged preeminent after the defeats of Nazi-Germany and Japan. Furthermore, a bipolar rivalry raises perceptions of zero-sum conflict (what one gains the other must lose) and consequently a tendency toward overreaction. And liberalism is just one of many ideologies prone to ideological crusades and domestic "witch hunts."[49] But, Realists have no reason to anticipate the hesitation of the United States in exploiting divisions in the Communist bloc and in forming strategic relationships with the USSR's communist rivals. U.S. cold war policy cannot be explained without reference to U.S. liberalism. Liberalism creates both the hostility to communism, not just to Soviet power, and the crusading ideological bent of policy. Liberals do not merely distrust what they do; we dislike what they are—public violators of human rights. And to this view, laissez faire liberals contribute antisocialism and social democratic liberals add a campaign for democracy.

One would think this confused record of policy would have produced a disaster in the East-West balance of forces. Squandered opportunities to negotiate East-West balances of interest and erratic policy should have alienated the United States' allies and dissipated its strategic resources. But other factors mitigated liberal confusion and crusades. Communist nuclear weapons and state power dictated prudence, and mutual survival has called for detente. The liberal alliance was deeply rooted in the pacific union and almost impervious to occasional crises over alliance policy toward the Soviet Union. And the productivity of market economies provided resources that could be mobilized to sustain the strategic position of the liberal West despite a confusion of aims and strategy.

Dilemmas and disasters are also associated with liberal foreign policy toward weak, nonliberal states; no greater spirit of accommodation or tolerance for noninterventionist sovereignties informs liberal policy toward the many weak, nonliberal states in the Third World. Indeed, liberalism's record in the Third World is in many respects worse than in East-West relations, for here power is added to confusion. This problem affects both conservative liberals and welfare liberals, but the two can be distinguished by differing styles of intervention.[50]

Both liberal strains appear congenitally confused in analyzing and in prescribing for situations of intervention. The liberal dictum in favor of nonintervention does not hold. Respecting a nonliberal state's state rights to noninterference requires ignoring the violations of rights they inflict on their own populations. Addressing the rights of individuals in the Third World requires ignoring the rights of states to be free of foreign intervention. Bouts of one attitude replace bouts of the other; but since the legitimacy of the nonliberal state is discounted, the dominant tendency leads toward interventionism.

A liberal imperialism that promotes liberalism neither abroad nor at home was one result of this dilemma. Protecting "native rights" from "native" oppressors, and protecting universal rights of property and settlement from local transgressions, introduced especially liberal motives for imperial rule. Kant's right of universal hospitality justifies nothing more than the right to visit and exchange. Other liberals have been prepared to justify much more. Some argue that there is a universal right of settlement under which those who cannot earn a living in their own countries have a right to force others—particularly nomads and tribal hunters—to cede parts of their territory for more intensive settlement. J. S. Mill justifies even more coercive treatment of what he calls the "barbarous nations." They do not have the rights of civilized nations, "except a right to such treatment as may, at the earliest possible period, fit them for becoming one." He justifies this imperial education for "barbarous" nations, while requiring nonintervention among "civilized" nations, because the former are not capable of reciprocating in the practice of liberal rights, and reciprocity is the foundation of liberal morality.[51]

Ending the slave trade destabilized nineteenth-century West African oligarchies, yet encouraging "legitimate trade" required protecting the property of European merchants; declaring the illegitimacy of suttee or of domestic slavery also attacked local cultural traditions that had sustained the stability of indigenous political authority. Europeans settling in sparsely populated areas destroyed the livelihood of tribes that relied on hunting. The tribes, quite defensively, retaliated in force; the settlers called for imperial protection.[52] The protection of cosmopolitan liberal rights thus bred a demand for imperial rule that violated the equality of American Indians, Africans, and Asians. In practice, once the exigencies of ruling an empire came into play, liberal imperialism resulted in the oppression of "native" liberals seeking self-determination in order to maintain imperial security: to avoid local chaos and the intervention of another imperial power attempting to take advantage of local disaffection.

Thus nineteenth-century liberals, such as Gladstone, pondered whether Egypt's protonationalist Arabi rebellion (1881–82) was truly liberal nationalist (they discovered it was not) before intervening to protect strategic lifelines to India, commerce, and investment.[53] Britain's Liberal Party faced similar dilemmas in managing Ireland; they erratically oscillated between coercion and reform. These foreign disasters contributed to the downfall of the Liberal Party as Parliament in 1886 chose to be ruled by a more aristocratic and stable Conservative Party. The Conservatives did pursue a steadier course of consistent coercion in Ireland and Egypt, yet in their effort to maintain a paramountcy in southern Africa they too were swept away in a campaign to protect the civic and property rights of British settlers (*uitlanders*) in the Boer's theocratic republics. These dilemmas of liberal imperialism are also reflected in U.S. imperialism in the Caribbean where, for example, following the Spanish-American War of 1898, Article III of the Platt Amendment gave the United States the "right to intervene for the preservation of Cuban independence, the maintenance of a government adequate for the protection of life, property, and individual liberty . . ."[54]

The record of liberalism in the nonliberal world is not solely a catalogue of disasters. The North American West and the settlement colonies—Australia and New Zealand—represent a successful transplant of liberal institutions, albeit in a temperate, underpopulated, and then depopulated environment and at the cost of Indian and aborigine rights. Similarly, the twentieth-century expansion of liberalism into less powerful nonliberal areas has also had some striking successes. The forcible liberalization of Germany and Japan following World War II and the long covert financing of liberal parties in Italy are the more significant instances of successful transplant. Covert financing of liberalism in Chile and occasional diplomatic demarches to nudge aside military threats to noncommunist democratic parties (as in Peru in 1962, South Korea in 1963, and the Dominican Republic in 1962[55] and again in 1978) illustrate policies which, though less successful, were directed toward liberal goals. These particular postwar liberal successes also are the product of special circumstances: the existence of a potential liberal majority, temporarily suppressed, which could be reestablished by outside aid or unusually weak oligarchic, military, or communist opponents.[56]

Elsewhere in the postwar period, when the United States sought to protect liberals in the Third World from the "communist threat," the consequences of liberal foreign policy on the nonliberal society often became far removed from the promotion of individual rights. Intervening against "armed minorities" and "enemies of free enterprise" meant intervening for other armed minorities, some sustaining and sustained by oligarchies, others resting on little more than U.S. foreign aid and troops. Indigenous liberals simply had too narrow a base of domestic support.

To the conservative liberals, the alternatives are starkly cast: Third World authoritarians with allegiance to the liberal, capitalist West or "Communists" subject to the totalitarian East (or leftist nationalists who even if elected are but a slippery stepping stone to totalitarianism).[57] Conservative liberals are prepared to support the allied authoritarians. The communists attack property in addition to liberty, thereby provoking conservative liberals to covert or overt intervention, or "dollar-diplomacy" imperialism. The interventions against Mossadegh in Iran, Arbenz in Guatemala, Allende in Chile, and against the Sandinistas in Nicaragua appear to fall into this pattern.[58]

To the social welfare liberals, the choice is never so clear. Aware of the need to intervene to democratize the distribution of social power and resources, they tend to have more sympathy for social reform. This can produce on the part of "radical" welfare liberals a more tolerant policy toward the attempts by reforming autocracies to redress inegalitarian distributions of property in the Third World. This more complicated welfare-liberal assessment can itself be a recipe for more extensive intervention. The large number of conservative oligarchs or military bureaucracies with whom the conservative liberal is well at home are not so congenial to the social welfare liberal; yet the communists are still seen as enemies of liberty. They justify more extensive intervention first to discover, then to sustain, Third World social democracy in a political environment that is either barely participatory or highly polarized. Thus Arthur Schlesinger recalls President Kennedy musing shortly after the assassination of Trujillo (former dictator of the Dominican Republic), "There are three possibilities in descending order of preference, a decent democratic regime, a continuation of the Trujillo regime [by his followers] or a Castro regime. We ought to aim at the first, but we can't really renounce the second until we are sure we can avoid the third." Another instance of this approach was President Carter's support for the land reforms in El Salvador, which was explained by one U.S. official in the following analogy: "There is no one more conservative than a small farmer. We're going to be breeding capitalists like rabbits."[59]

Thus liberal policy toward the Third World state often fails to promote individual rights. Its consequences on liberalism at home may also be harmful. As Hobson pointed out in his study of imperialism, imperial security and imperial wars may enhance in the short run the position of nonliberal domestic forces, such as the military, and introduce in the longer run issues into the political debate, such as security, that raise the role of nonliberal coalitions of conservative oligarchy or technocracy.[60]

One might account for many of these liberal interventions in the Third World by geopolitical competition, the Realists' calculus of the balance of power, or by the desire to promote the national economic interests of the United States. The attempt to avoid Third World countries coming under the hegemony of the USSR or to preserve essential sources of raw materials are alternative interpretations of much of the policy attributed to liberalism which on their face are plausible. Yet these interventions are publicly justified in the first instance as attempts to preserve a "way of life": to defend freedom and private enterprise. The threat has been defined as "Communism," not just "Sovietism" or "economic nationalism."

Expectations of being punished electorally, should they abandon groups they had billed as democratic allies contributed to the reluctance of U.S. politicians to withdraw from Vietnam. The consistent policy of seeking a legitimating election, however unpromising the circumstances for it (as in Vietnam), reflects the same liberal source.[61] Moreover, few communist or socialist Third World states actually do seek to cordon off their markets or raw materials from the liberal world economy. And the radical movements, first and foremost anticolonialist, against which the United States has intervened, have not been simple proxies for the Soviet Union.

Furthermore, by geopolitical considerations alone, the large interventions may have been counterproductive. The interventions have confirmed or enhanced the coherence of the Soviet bloc as the Chinese Civil War (U.S. logistical support for the KMT) and the drive to the Yalu of the Korean War, the Vietnam War, and the Angolan War served to increase the dependence of the PRC, Vietnam, and Angola on the USSR. In each of these interventions, U.S. geopolitical interests might have been served best by supporting the communist side and encouraging its separation from the Soviet bloc. But because the United States failed to distinguish communism from Soviet power, this separation was impossible. Had the Soviet Union been a capitalist authoritarian superpower, geopolitical logic also would have led the United States to intervene against the expansion of its bloc.[62] But the United States intervenes against the expansion of communism regardless of geopolitical considerations just as it (along with Britain) did against Soviet communism following World War I.[63]

Is the United States anticommunist because communism is the ideology adopted by the Soviet Union; or are liberals anti-Soviet because the Soviet Union is the headquarters of communism? In encouraging intervention, the imprudent vehemences of geopolitics and the liberalisms cannot be clearly separated in a bipolar contest between a communist and a liberal superpower. Nonetheless, liberalism does appear to exacerbate intervention against weak nonliberals and hostility against powerful nonliberal societies.

VII

A second manifestation of international liberalism outside the pacific union lies in a reaction to the excesses of interventionism. A mood of frustrated withdrawal—"a careless and supine complaisance"—affects policy toward strategically and economically important countries. Just as interventionism seems to be the typical failing of the liberal great power, so complaisance characterizes declined or not quite risen liberal states.[64] Representative legislatures may become reluctant to fund the military establishment needed to play a geopolitical role. Rational incentives for "free riding" on the extended defense commitments of the leader of the liberal alliance also induce this form of complaisance. During much of the nineteenth century, the United States informally relied upon the British fleet for many of its security needs. Today, the Europeans and the Japanese, according to some American strategic analysts, fail to bear their "fair" share of alliance burdens.

A different form of complaisance is charged by Realists who perceive ideologically based policies as self-indulgent. Oligarchic or authoritarian allies in the Third World do not find consistent support in a liberal policy that stresses human rights. They claim that the security needs of these states are neglected, that they fail to obtain military aid or more direct support when they need it (the Shah's Iran, Humberto Romero's El Salvador, Somoza's Nicaragua, and South Africa). Equally disturbing from a Realist point of view, communist regimes are shunned even when a detente with them could further United States strategic interests (Cuba, Angola). Welfare liberals particularly shun the first group, while laissez faire liberals balk at close dealings with the second. In both cases the Realists note that our economic interests or strategic interests are slighted.[65]

VIII

Lastly, both variants of liberalism raise dilemmas in North-South economic relations and particularly in the international distribution of property or income. Not expecting to have to resolve whether freedom of enterprise should extend to doing business with the followers of Marx and Lenin, conservative, laissez faire liberals have become incensed over the attractiveness to American and European corporations of profits made in the communist world. And the commitment of liberals—both social welfare and laissez faire liberals—to the efficiency and the political advantages of international free trade is severely tested by the inflow of low-cost imports from newly industrializing countries of the Third World. These imports threaten domestic industries, which tend to be politically active and affiliated with the extremes of conservative or welfare liberalism. Some of these have strongly resisted domestic, union organization (for reasons of cost) and thus strongly support domestic laissez faire, conservative liberalism (among these, most prominent are some textile firms). The welfare liberals face similar political dilemmas in their association with well-organized labor in related industries (for example, the garment industry) or in industries just recently threatened by imports (for example, steel or autos).[66]

In addition, the welfare liberal faces international moral and domestic political dilemmas. If the disadvantaged are rightly the objects of social welfare, redistribution should be directed toward the vast preponderance of the world's poor who are in the Third and Fourth Worlds. Three arguments reveal facets of the moral and political problems welfare liberals face.

First, there is the obligation of humanitarian aid. Peter Singer has argued that the humanitarian obligation an individual has to rescue a drowning child from a shallow pool of water (when such a rescue would not require a sacrifice of something of comparable moral importance, for example, one's own life) should be extended to international aid to famine victims and the global poor.[67] Recently, Brian Barry has provided a strong defense against skepticism concerning this obligation.[68] But he concludes that, while it is hard to doubt that .25 percent of national income (the U.S. figure for foreign aid) is too low, there does not seem to be a clear limit on how much aid of the enormous amount needed is obligatory. One should add that since this aid is required by needy individuals (mostly) in the Third and Fourth Worlds and not clearly owed to their states, the logistics of distributing humanitarian aid will prove difficult. And since this aid is due from individuals in the wealthy North, a limitless personal obligation to the world's poor threatens a form of tyrannical morality. Nor is the burden easily shifted to liberal governments in the North. Political obstacles to taxing rich liberal societies for humanitarian aid are evident. The income of the American poor places them among the world's more advantaged few. But the demand for redistributing income from the United States to the world's poor meets two domestic barriers: the United States poor *within* the United States are clearly disadvantaged, and our democratic politics places the needs of disadvantaged voting citizens above those of more disadvantaged but foreign people.

The second and third problems arise with respect to claims to international redistribution based on obligations of justice. Both establishing a just global society and justly distributing resources in an unjust international society raise apparently insuperable barriers.

In cases of extreme inequality and political recalcitrance within a country, the welfare liberals find justifiable a developmental, redistributing dictatorship to equalize opportunity as a necessary foundation for a just liberal society.[69] The liberal justification for such a dictatorial redistribution on a national scale is that without it authentically democratic liberal politics and social economy are rendered ineffective. The enormous social inequalities of the international order might—however implausibly—suggest the same prescription should apply to the international order. But extended to global scale, this prescription runs up against a fundamental liberal constraint. It is not clear that an effective global, liberal polity can be formed. Kant regarded global sovereignty, whether liberal in aim or not, as equivalent to global tyranny due to the remoteness of the representation it would entail. If the maximum effective size of a legislature is about 500, a global constituency would have to be of the order of 8 million persons. Confederal solutions that mix direct and indirect elections further attenuate the political life of the citizen or they create the grounds for serious conflict between the local government and the remote confederation. In short, the redistribution that can be justified on liberal grounds does not stretch beyond liberal government. Since modern states may already be too large for effectively liberal politics, global government cannot be a liberal aim. Yet without the prospect of moral autonomy through representative government this form of international redistribution is not justified on liberal grounds.

The dilemma of justly redistributing income in an international society of independent states is addressed by Brian Barry. After rejecting "just requitals" (just prices) for past exploitation as being inadequate justice for poor societies lacking any resources whatsoever and after rejecting justice as "fair play" (reciprocal obligations) for being ill-suited to the minimally integrated international economy, he settles on justice as equal rights.[70] He follows Hart's argument that special rights (to property) presuppose general rights (to property) and that natural resources (or inherited endowments) cannot be justly acquired without consent. Without consent, all have an equal right to global resources. The contemporary rich countries, therefore, owe a share of their income or resources to poor countries. Moreover, they owe this share without the requirement that it be directed to the poorest in the poor countries, because the rich have no right to impose conditions on income or property to which all have an equal right. If rich countries can dispose of global income autonomously, poor countries should have the same right.[71]

There are two objections that I think should be made against accepting Barry's principle of indiscriminate interstate justice. First, if justice is determined by the equal rights of individuals to global resources or inheritances, then rich *countries* only acquire income justly when they acquire it justly from individuals (for example, by consent). Only just countries have rights over the autonomous disposition of national income. An unjust rich state has no right to dispose or hold income. A just rich country, conversely, has the right to dispose autonomously of national income, provided that national income represents its just share of global income. Any surplus is owed to *individuals* who are poor or to (just) poor states that have acquired a right to dispose of income or resources by the consent of their citizens. Neither unjust poor states nor unjust rich states should (by the argument of equal rights of individuals) have rights over global income. If there were justice among "thieves," it might call for distribution without condition from unjust rich states to unjust poor states. But there is no reason why that scheme should apply to the surplus of just rich states beyond that which they distribute to just poor states. Some form of trust for the global poor (for present lack of such an institution, perhaps the World Bank or UNICEF) seems a better recipient than an unjust poor state. An obligation of equal justice that requires, say, Norway or Sweden to tax its citizens to provide direct transfers to a Somoza or a Duvalier in preference to funding the IDA of the World Bank or UNICEF is morally bizarre.[72]

The second objection reflects the residual insecurity of the contemporary order. As long as there is no guarantee of security, indiscriminate obligations of justice to redistribute income and resources (including redistribution to potential security threats) cannot be justified. Obliging Israel to tax itself for Syria, or Japan for China, or even the United States for Cuba threatens the rights of individuals within these states to promote their territorial integrity and political independence.

These two objections to the application of just redistribution should not apply within the pacific union. States within the liberal union do rest on consent and do not constitute threats to one another. Between the union's rich and poor members, obligations of justice to distribute global resources and income supplement humanitarian obligations applicable globally to aid the poor. (Of course, obstacles are daunting. Among them are how to raise international revenue in a just fashion; how to distribute this revenue in an efficient manner; and how to persuade democratic citizens to support a lengthy program when some mismanagement is likely and when strategic ties to authoritarian allies make competitive demands on the revenues they have become accustomed to raise for foreign purposes. These obstacles may even make a public recognition of the obligation unlikely, but that does not mean it should not be recognized.)

To counterbalance these costly dilemmas in relations between liberal and nonliberal states, liberalism has had two attractive programs. One is a human rights policy that counters the record of colonial oppression and addresses the ills of current domestic oppression in the Second and Third Worlds. The other is a policy of free trade and investment. But neither has had the impact it might have. The attraction of human rights has been tarnished by liberal practice in supporting dictatorships; complementarily, human rights holds little attraction to dictatorial governments in the Third World. The market has been tarnished by unequal bargaining, and now that the bargaining has become more equal, by a mounting "new protectionism."

Liberal principles and economic institutions retain their attractive potential even though they alone cannot satisfy Third World needs such as creating national unity or reducing social inequalities. Releasing this potential from the burden of liberal practice is a feat the liberal world has yet to accomplish.

Thus liberalism has achieved extraordinary success in relations among liberal states as well as exceptional failures in relations between liberal and nonliberal states. Both tendencies are fundamentally rooted in the operation of liberalism within and across national borders. Both are liberalism's legacy in foreign affairs.

IX

No country lives strictly according to its political ideology and few liberal states are as hegemonically liberal as the United States.[73] Even in the United States, certain interests and domestic actors derive their sense of legitimacy from sources other than liberalism. The state's national security bureaucracy reflects an approach to politics among nations that focuses on other states, particularly threatening states. Its policies correspondingly tend to fall into the Realist, national interest frame of reference. Certain of the West European states and Japan have more syncretic and organic sources of a "real" national interest. But in the United States, and in other liberal states to a lesser degree, public policy derives its legitimacy from its concordance with liberal principles. Policies not rooted in liberal principles generally fail to sustain long term public support. I have argued that these principles are a firm anchor of the most successful zone of international peace yet established; but also a source of conflicted and confused foreign policy toward the nonliberal world. Improving policy toward the nonliberal world by introducing steady and long-run calculations of strategic and economic interest is likely to require political institutions that are inconsistent with both a liberal policy and a liberal alliance: for example, an autonomous executive branch or a predominance of presidential and military actors in foreign policy so as to obtain flexible and rapid responses to changes in the strategic and economic environment. In peacetime, such "emergency" measures are unacceptable in a liberal democracy. Moreover, they would break the chain of stable expectations and the mesh of private and public channels of information and material lobbying that sustain the pacific union. In short, completely resolving liberal dilemmas may not be possible without threatening liberal success.

Therefore, the goal of concerned liberals must be to reduce the harmful impact of the dilemmas without undermining the successes. There is no simple formula for an effective liberal foreign policy. Its methods must be geared toward specific issues and countries. But liberal legacies do suggest guidelines for liberal policy making that contrast quite strikingly with the Realists' advocacy of maximizing the national interest.

First, if "publicity" makes radically inconsistent policy impossible in a liberal republic, then policy toward the liberal and the nonliberal world should be guided by general liberal principles. Liberal policies thus must attempt to promote liberal principles abroad: to secure basic human needs, civil rights, and democracy, and to expand the scope and effectiveness of the world market economy. Important among these principles, Kant argued, are some of the "preliminary articles" from his treaty of perpetual peace: extending nonintervention by force in internal affairs of other states to nonliberal governments and maintaining a scrupulous respect for the laws of war.[74] These, as J. S. Mill argued, imply a right to support states threatened by external aggression and to intervene against foreign intervention in civil wars.[75] Furthermore, powerful and weak, hostile and friendly nonliberal states must be treated according to the *same* standards. There are no special geopolitical clients, no geopolitical enemies other than those judged to be such by liberal principles. This policy is as radical in conception as it sounds. It requires abandoning the national interest and the balance of power as guidelines to policy. The interests of the United States must be consistent with its principles. We must have no liberal enemies and no unconditional alliances with nonliberal states.

Second, given contemporary conditions of economic interdependence, this policy could employ economic warfare to lead a liberal crusade against communism and against Third World authoritarians of the left or the right. It could also lead to a withdrawal into isolationism and a defense of only one principle: the right of the United States to territorial integrity and political independence. Both of these policies are consistent with liberal principles, but neither promotes security in a nuclear age nor enhances the prospects for meeting the needs of the poor and oppressed. To avoid the extremist possibilities of its abstract universalism, U.S. liberal policy must be further constrained by a geopolitical budget. Here the Realists' calculus of security provides a benchmark of survival and prudence from which a liberal policy that recognizes national security as a liberal right can navigate. This benchmark consists of prudent policies toward the most significant, indeed the only, strategic threat the United States faces—the USSR. Once the Realists set a prudent policy toward the USSR, the liberals can then take over again, defining more supportive and interdependent policies toward those countries more liberal than the USSR, and more constraining and more containing policies toward countries less liberal than the USSR.[76]

And third, specific features of liberal policy will be influenced by whether voting citizens choose to be governed by a laissez faire or by a social democratic administration. But both of these liberalisms should take into account more general guidelines to a prudent, liberal foreign policy—such as those that follow.

In relations with the USSR, a prudent set of policies calls for a frank acceptance of our political incapacity to sustain a successful reforming crusade. Instead mutually beneficial arrangements should be accepted to the extent they do not violate liberal principles or favor long-run Soviet interests over the long-run interests of the United States and the liberal world. Arms control would be central to this as would the expansion of civilian trade. We would encounter difficulties when our liberal allies can gain economic benefits from trade deals (for example, the sale of computer technology) that might in the long run favor the USSR. These situations may be exceptionally difficult to resolve diplomatically since assessments of strategic advantage tend to be uncertain and since the particular nature of the benefits (say, sales of grain as opposed to sales of computers) can influence the assessment of the strategic risks entailed. Liberals will also need to ensure that ties of dependence on the USSR (such as the gas pipeline) are not a major constraint on liberal foreign policy by providing alternative sources (for example, uranium) for allies or by equalizing the import costs of energy and by assuring alternative sources in an emergency. Given the Soviet Union's capacity to respond to bottlenecks imposed by the West, there will be few occasions (fortunately for the coherence of the liberal alliance) when it can be clearly shown that an embargo would unambiguously hamper the Soviet Union and help the liberal alliance.[77]

In relations with the People's Republic of China, similar liberal principles permit trade that includes arms sales to a state no more restrictive of its subjects' liberty but much less restrictive of the liberty of foreign peoples than is the USSR. But strategic temptations toward a further alliance should be curbed. Such an alliance would backfire, perhaps disastrously, when liberal publics confront policymakers with the Chinese shadows of antiliberal rule.

Arms control, trade, and accommodation toward nonliberal Third World nations must first be measured against a prudent policy toward the Soviet Union and then should reflect the relative degrees of liberal principle that their domestic and foreign policies incorporate. Although our policy should be directed by liberal principles, it should free itself from the pretension that by acts of will and material benevolence we can replicate ourselves in the Third World. The liberal alliance should be prepared to have diplomatic and commercial relations as it does with the USSR with every state that is no more repressive of liberal rights than is the USSR. For example, North Korea and Mozambique might receive PRC level relations; Vietnam, with its foreign incursions, and Angola, with its internal ethnic conflict, Soviet-level relations. Being one of the few states that deny the legal equality of its subjects, South Africa should be treated as Amin's Uganda and Pol Pot's Khmer Republic should have been, in a more containing fashion than is the USSR. No arms should be traded, investment should be restricted with a view to its impact on human rights, and trade should be limited to humanitarian items that do not contribute to the longevity of *apartheid*.

Elsewhere, the liberal world should be prepared to engage in regular trade and investment with all Third World states no more restrictive of liberty than is the PRC, and this could include the sale of arms not sensitive to the actual defense of the liberal world in regard to the USSR. Furthermore, the liberal world should take additional measures of aid to favor Third World states attempting to address the basic needs of their own populations and seeking to preserve and expand the roles of the market and democratic participation. Much of the potential success of this policy rests on an ability to preserve a liberal market for Third World growth; for the market is the most substantial source of Third World accommodation with a liberal world whose past record includes imperial oppression. To this should be added mutually beneficial measures designed to improve Third World economic performance. Export earnings insurance, export diversification assistance, and technical aid are among some of these. (And social democrats will need to take steps that begin to address the humanitarian obligations of international aid and the limited obligations of international justice rich countries have to poor individuals and to [just] poor countries.)

Liberals should persevere in attempts to keep the world economy free from destabilizing, protectionist intrusions. Although intense economic interdependence generates conflicts, it also helps to sustain the material well-being underpinning liberal societies and to promise avenues of development to Third World states with markets that are currently limited by low income. Discovering ways to manage interdependence when rapid economic development has led to industrial crowding (at the same time as it retains massive numbers of the world's population in poverty) will call for difficult economic adjustments at home and institutional innovations in the world economy. These innovations may even require more rather than less explicit regulation of the domestic economy and more rather than less planned dis-integration of the international economy. Under these circumstances, liberals will need to ensure that those suffering losses, such as from market disruption or restriction, do not suffer a permanent loss of income or exclusion from world markets. Furthermore, to prevent these emergency measures from escalating into a spiral of isolationism, liberal states should undertake these innovations only by international negotiation and only when the resulting agreements are subject to a regular review by all the parties.[78]

Above all, liberal policy should strive to preserve the pacific union of similarly liberal societies. It is not only currently of immense strategic value (being the political foundation of both NATO and the Japanese alliance); it is also the single best hope for the evolution of a peaceful world. Liberals should be prepared, therefore, to defend and formally ally with authentically liberal, democratic states that are subject to threats or actual instances of external attack or internal subversion.

Strategic and economic Realists are likely to judge this liberal foreign policy to be either too much of a commitment or too little. The Realists may argue that through a careful reading of the past we can interpret in a clear fashion a ranked array of present strategic and economic interests. Strategically beneficial allies, whatever their domestic system, should be supported. The purposes of our power must be to maximize our present power. Global ecologists and some on the left claim an ability to foresee future disasters that we should be preparing for now by radical institutional reforms.

But liberals have always doubted our ability to interpret the past or predict the future accurately and without bias. Liberalism has been an optimistic ideology of a peculiarly skeptical kind. Liberals assume individuals to be both self-interested and rationally capable of accommodating their conflicting interests. They have held that principles such as rule under law, majority rule, and the protection of private property that follow from mutual accommodation among rational, self-interested people are the best guide to present policy. These principles preclude taking advantage of every opportunity of the present. They also discount what might turn out to have been farsighted reform. The implicit hope of liberals is that the principles of the present will engender accommodating behavior that avoids the conflicts of the past and reduces the threats of the future. The gamble has not always paid off in the past (as in accepting a Sudeten separatism). It certainly is not guaranteed to work in the future (for example, in controlling nuclear proliferation or pollution). But liberalism cannot *politically* sustain nonliberal policies. Liberal policies rest upon a different premise. They are policies that can be accepted by a liberal world in good faith and sustained by the electorates of liberal democracies.

In responding to the demands of their electorates, liberal states must also ascribe responsibility for their policies to their citizenry. The major costs of a liberal foreign policy are borne at home. Not merely are its military costs at the taxpayers' expense, but a liberal foreign policy requires adjustment to a less controlled international political environment—a rejection of the status quo. The home front becomes the front line of liberal strategy. Tolerating more foreign change requires a greater acceptance of domestic change. Not maintaining an imperial presence in the Persian Gulf calls for a reduction of energy dependence. Accepting the economic growth of the Third World may require trade and industrial adjustment. The choice is one between preserving liberalism's material legacy of the current world order at the cost of liberal principles or of finding ways of adjusting to a changing world order that protect liberal principles.

FIRST ADDITION

Kant argued that the natural evolution of world politics and economics would drive mankind inexorably toward peace by means of a widening of the pacific union of liberal republican states. In 1795 this was a startling prediction. In 1981, almost two hundred years later, we can see that he appears to have been correct. The pacific union of liberal states has progressively widened. Liberal states have yet to become involved in a war with one another. International peace is not a Utopian ideal to be reached, if at all, in the far future; it is a condition that liberal states have already experienced in their relations with each other. Should this history sustain a hope for global peace?

Kant did not assume that pacification would be a steady progress; he anticipated many setbacks. Periods of history since 1795, among them the Napoleonic Wars and the two World Wars, have fully justified his pessimism. The future may have more fundamental setbacks in store.

First, human beings have been driven into forming liberal republics by the pressures of internal and external war. Discord has thus created the essential institutions on which liberal pacification rests. But the Kantian logic of war may find itself supplanted by a nuclear logic of destruction. However persuasive a moral foundation for peace a global wasteland might make, it would make a poor material foundation for its survivors. Indeed, the erratic and lengthy process of educative wars that Kant anticipated appears impossible under nuclear conditions. Long before the nations completed their process of graduation into republicanism, a nuclear wasteland might well have reduced them to barbarism. Yet nuclear logic also calls forth a sense of caution (the balance of terror) that could accelerate the process of graduation into peace even before republics established a homogeneous governance of the world.[79]

Second, Kant assumed that republics formed an endpoint of political evolution: "the highest task nature has set mankind." The increasing number, the longevity, the spread of republics to all continents and to all cultures that are free from foreign domination lend credence to his judgment. Nonetheless, a great and long depression or a runaway inflation could create the conditions that lead to authoritarian or totalitarian regimes. Having access to the new technology of surveillance to root out domestic dissidents, such regimes might prove difficult for their populations to dislodge. And nuclear deterrence might provide them with external security.[80]

Third, Kant relied upon international commerce to create ties of mutual advantage that would help make republics pacific. But past technological progress that lowered the costs of transport and that developed rapidly and unevenly—together encouraging international trade—could change direction. Instead, a trade-saving path of technical progress such as emerged in the Roman Empire could reemerge. If the technological progress of transportation develops less quickly than the spread of manufacturing technology, if current trends toward resource-saving technology continue, if economic development tends to equalize capital-labor ratios, or if states choose economic stability over growth and prefer domestic manufacturing, agriculture and services to trade, then world trade could decline even as global economic development continued. The educative force of international exchange would thereby decline.[81]

But, if we assume that these setbacks do not emerge and that, as Kant argued, a steady worldwide pressure for a liberal peace continues, can the past record of liberalism's expansion lead us to any sense of when it might ultimately triumph?

SECOND ADDITION

Extrapolating Nature's Secret Design

Kant's argument implies two dynamic paths toward peace: one transnational, the other international. The first operates through the ties of trade, cultural exchange, and political understanding that together both commit existing republics to peace and, by inference, give rise to individualistic demands in nonrepublics whose resolution requires the establishment of republican government. The second operates through the pressure of insecurity and of actual war that together engender republican governments—the domestic constitutional foundations of peace. While the second appears fundamental, the first is not merely dependent. The transnational track conveys the impression of a global society expanding from one country to the next, encompassing an ever larger zone of peace, and yet working on each society in an independent even though connected and similar fashion. The international track—war—is basically a set of epidemics become, in the larger perspective, endemic to the international state of war. It operates conjointly, on one because it is operating on another. It is inherently relational and interdependent.

In all likelihood, the past rate of progress in the expansion of the pacific union has been a complex and inseparable combination of the effects of both tracks. But if we imagine that progress had been achieved solely by one track or the other, we can deduce the outer limits of the underlying logics of the transnational and international progresses toward peace.

Table 3. The Pacific Union

	1800	1800–1850	1850–1900	1900–1945	1945–(1980)
Number of Liberal Regimes	3	8	13	29	49
Transnational Track		+5	+5	+16	+20
International Track		>2x	<2x	>2x	<2x

The second row represents the transnational track of an underlying arithmetic widening of the zone of peace accomplished by linking republics together and creating pressures, incentives, and ideals leading more nations to become republican. An expanding rate of absolute progress reveals itself as the base develops each century—in the nineteenth adding 5 per 50 years, in the twentieth more than tripling to approximately 18 (i.e., $^{16:20}/_2$) per 50 years. Thus if the rate triples again in the twenty-first century to approximately 50 liberal states per 50 years and if the state order remains fixed at roughly 150 states, the pacific union will not become global until, at the earliest, the year 2101. The third row, a geometric progression that corresponds to the interdependent logic of war, may be the better indicator of Kantian progress. There republics more than double in number during warlike periods such as 1800 to 1850 or 1900 to 1950, less than double in more pacific times (1850–1900 or perhaps 1945–2000, when there have so far been many wars, but no "great" or world wars involving many states akin to the Napoleonic War or World Wars I and II). Thus if we assume continuing preparation for war and petty wars—akin to the period 1850 to 1900—and a similar ratio of expansion (13/8) then global peace should be anticipated, at the earliest, in 2113.[82]

Of course, this pacific calculus further assumes that, as Kant required in his "Second Supplement," a "Secret Article" be included in the treaty for a Perpetual

Peace: "The maxims of the philosophers concerning the conditions of the possibility of public peace shall be consulted by the states which are ready to go to war." To this proviso, we need add that the greater complexity of international relations today calls for economists, political scientists, sociologists, and psychologists as well as natural scientists to add their advice to that of the philosophers. This increase in the costs of consultation would, however, be fully justified if even a small war or two were thereby indefinitely delayed, wars being so much more destructive than they were in Kant's day.

NOTES

This is the second half of a two-part article. In addition to those mentioned in the first half, I would also like to thank the Ford Foundation, whose grant supported some of the research on which this article draws, the Institute for Advanced Study, Exxon, and the National Endowment for the Humanities. The themes of Parts 1 and 2 of this essay were first developed in a paper written in June 1981. That paper drew on a short presentation delivered at the Conference on the Future of American Liberalism, Princeton, New Jersey, 3–4 April 1981.

39. David Hume, "Of the Balance of Power" in *Essays: Moral, Political, and Literary* (1741–1742) (Oxford University Press, 1963), pp. 346–47. With "imprudent vehemence," Hume referred to the English reluctance to negotiate an early peace with France and the total scale of the effort devoted to prosecuting that war, which together were responsible for over half the length of the fighting and an enormous war debt. With "complaisance," he referred to political exhaustion and isolationism. Hume, of course, was not describing fully liberal republics as defined here; but the characteristics he describes, do seem to reflect some of the liberal republican features of the English eighteenth century constitution (the influence of both popular opinion and a representative [even if severely limited] legislature). He contrasts these effects to the "prudent politics" that should govern the balance of power and to the special but different failings characteristic of "enormous monarchies," which are prone to strategic overextension, bureaucratic, and ministerial decay in court intrigue, praetorian rebellion (pp. 347–48). These failings are different from those of more, even if not fully, republican regimes. Indeed just as the eighteenth century English failings illuminate aspects of contemporary liberal diplomacy, the failings of his universal monarchy seem to be reflected in some aspects of the contemporary authoritarian and totalitarian predicament.

40. A careful statistical analysis that has just appeared, R. J. Rummel, "Libertarianism and International Violence," *Journal of Conflict Resolution* 27, no. 1 (March 1983), empirically demonstrates that "libertarian" states engaged neither in war nor in other forms of conflict with each other in the period 1946–1980. (But his definition of libertarian appears to be more restrictive than my definition of liberal states.) He also finds that between 1946 and 1980 libertarian states were less likely to engage in any form of conflict than were states of any other domestic political regime. The extensive history of liberal imperialism and the liberal role in conflicts and wars between liberal and nonliberal states for the

longer period from the 1970s that I survey lead me to conclusions which differ from his second point. Both George Kennan's *American Diplomacy* (New York: Mentor, 1951) and Hans Morgenthau's *Politics Among Nations* (New York: Alfred A. Knopf, Inc., 1973), esp. p. 147, are cogent criticisms of the impact of American liberalism. Different but related analyses of the impact of liberal principles and institutions on U.S. foreign policy are made by Stanley Hoffmann, *Gulliver's Troubles* (New York: McGraw-Hill, 1968), esp. pp. 114–43.

41. Kant, "Perpetual Peace," in Friedrich, ed., p. 442.
42. Ibid., p. 446.
43. Cordell Hull, Radio Address, 9 April 1944, excerpted in Norman Graebner, *Cold War Diplomacy* (New York: Van Nostrand, 1977), p. 172.
44. George F. Kennan, *A Cloud of Danger* (Boston: Little, Brown & Co., 1977), p. 4.
45. Memoranda by Mr. Eyre Crowe, 1 January 1907, and by Lord Sanderson, 25 February 1907, in G. P. Gooch et al, eds., *British Documents on the Origins of the War, 1898–1914*, 3 (London: HMSO, 1928), pp. 397–431.
46. Herbert Hoover to President Wilson, 28 March 1919, excerpted in *Major Problems in American Foreign Policy*, II, ed. Thomas Paterson (Lexington, MA: D.C. Heath and Co., 1978), p. 95.

    Fear of Bolshevism may have been one of the factors precluding a liberal alliance with the Soviet Union in 1938 against Nazi aggression. But the connection liberals draw between domestic tyranny and foreign aggression may also operate in reverse. When the Nazi threat to the survival of liberal states did require a liberal alliance with the Soviet Union, Stalin became for a short period the liberal press's "Uncle Joe."

47. U.S. Senate, *Hearings Before the Committee on Foreign Relations on the Nomination of John Foster Dulles, Secretary of State Designate*, 15 January 1953, 83rd Congress, 1st Session (Washington, D.C.: G.P.O., 1953), pp. 5–6.
48. Thirty-three divisions, the withdrawal of the Soviet bloc from the Mediterranean, political disarray in the Communist movement: these advantages called out for a quick and friendly response. An effective U.S. ambassador in place to present Tito's position to Washington, the public character of the expulsion from the Cominform (June 1948), and a presidential administration in the full flush of creative statesmanship (and an electoral victory) also contributed to Truman's decision to rescue Yugoslavia from the Soviet embargo by providing trade and loans (1949).

    Nonetheless (according to Yugoslav sources), this crisis was also judged to be an appropriate moment to put pressure on Yugoslavia to resolve the questions of Trieste and Carinthia, to cut its support for the guerrillas in Greece, *and* to repay prewar (prerevolutionary) Yugoslav debts compensating the property owners of nationalized mines and land. Nor did Yugoslavia's strategic significance exempt it from inclusion among the countries condemned as "Captive Nations" (1959) or secure most-favored-nation trade status in the 1962 Trade Expansion Act. Ideological anticommunism and the porousness of the American political system to lobbies combined (according to Kennan, ambassador to Yugoslavia at that time) to add these inconvenient burdens to a crucial strategic relationship. (John C. Campbell, *Tito's Separate Road* [New York: Council on Foreign Relations/Harper and Row, 1967], pp. 18–27; Suctozar Vukmanovic-Tempo, in Vladimir Dedijer, *The Battle Stalin Lost* [New York: Viking, 1970], p. 268; George F. Kennan, *Memoirs, 1950–1963* [Boston: Little, Brown & Co., 1972], chap. 12.)

49. Like the *original* crusades (an earlier instance of transcendental foreign policy), the first were expeditions that created strategic littorals (Lithuania, Estonia, Latvia, and Poland in 1918 to 1920 for Antioch and Jerusalem): the second and third (1947 to 1949 for the crusades of the monarchs) new logistical reinforcements, or anticommunism in Europe; the fourth (the crossing of the 38th Parallel for Constantinople) was a strategic diversion. A McCarthyite (Albigensian) crusade at home followed. The fifth and sixth crusades extended the range of the conflict to the Third World (for Damietta); and later crusades were excuses for reequipping armies.

50. See Robert A. Packenham, *Liberal America and the Third World* (Princeton: Princeton University Press, 1973), for an interesting analysis of the impact of liberal ideology on American foreign aid policy, esp. chaps. 3 and pp. 313–23.

51. See Hobbes, *Leviathan*, Pt II, chap. 30, and Pt I, chap. 15. This right is discussed in Michael Walzer, *Spheres of Justice* (New York: Basic Books, 1983), p. 46. Mill's remarks on colonialism are in "A Few Words on Nonintervention," pp. 377–79, and in "Civilization" he distinguishes "civilized" nations from "barbarous" nations, not on racial or biological grounds but on the basis of what our contemporary scholars now call socioeconomic modernization or development. Mill declared, "Their minds are not capable of so great an effort [as reciprocity], nor their will sufficiently under the influence of distant motives." Both essays are in J. S. Mill, *Essays on Literature and Society*, ed. with an introduction by J. B. Schneewind (New York: Collier, 1965). Perhaps the most interesting memorial to liberal imperialism is the inscription, written by Macaulay, on the base of Lord William Bentinck's statue in Calcutta: "He abolished cruel rites; he effaced humiliating distinctions; he gave liberty to the expression of public opinion; his constant study was to elevate the intellectual and moral character of the natives committed to his charge" (cf. Mill). It is excerpted in Earl Cromer, *Ancient and Modern Imperialism* (London: Longmans, 1910), p. 67.

52. Alexis de Tocqueville, *Democracy in America*, vol. I (New York: Vintage, 1945), p. 351. De Tocqueville describes how European settlement destroys the game; the absence of game reduces the Indians to starvation. Both then exercise their rights to self-defense. But the colonists are able to call in the power of the imperial government. Palmerston once declared that he would never employ force to promote purely private interests—commercial or settlement. He also declared that he would faithfully protect the lives and liberty of English subjects. In circumstances such as those de Tocqueville described, Palmerston's distinctions were meaningless. See Kenneth Bourne, *Palmerston: The Early Years* (New York: Macmillan, 1982), pp. 624–26. Other colonial settlements and their dependence on imperial expansion are examined in Ronald Robinson, "Non-European Foundations of Imperialism," in Roger Owen and Bob Sutcliffe, eds., *Studies in the Theory of Imperialism* (London: Longmans, 1972).

53. Gladstone had proclaimed his support for the equal rights of all nations in his Mid-lothian Speeches. Wilfrid Scawen Blunt served as a secret agent in Egypt keeping Gladstone informed of the political character of Arabi's movement. The liberal dilemma—were they intervening against genuine nationalism or a military adventurer (Arabi)?—was best expressed in Joseph Chamberlain's memorandum to the Cabinet, 21 June 1882, excerpted

in J. L. Garvin and J. Amery, *Life of Joseph Chamberlain* (London: Macmillan & Co., 1935) 1, p. 448. And see Peter Mansfield, *The British in Egypt* (New York: Holt, Rinehart and Winston, 1971), chaps. 2–3; Ronald Hyam, *Britain's Imperial Century: 1815–1914* (London: Batsford, 1976), chap. 8; and Robert Tignor, *Modernization and British Colonial Rule in Egypt* (Princeton: Princeton University Press, 1966).

54. On Ireland and its relation to British parties, Conor Cruise O'Brien, *Parnell and His Party, 1880–1890* (Oxford: Clarendon Press, 1964); on South Africa, G.H.L. LeMay, *British Supremacy in South Africa 1890–1907* (London: Oxford University Press, 1965). A good representative of liberal attitudes on force and intervention is the following comment by Vice Admiral Humphrey Smith:

"I don't think we thought much about war with a big W. We looked on the Navy more as a World Police Force than as a war-like institution. We considered that our job was to safeguard law and order throughout the world—safeguard civilization, put out fires on shore, and act as guide, philosopher, and friend to the merchant ships of all nations." Vice Admiral Humphrey Smith, *A Yellow Admiral Remembers* (London, 1932), p. 54 in Donald C. Gordon, *The Dominion Partnership in Imperial Defence: 1870–1914* (Baltimore, MD: The Johns Hopkins University Press, 1965), p. 47.

The Platt Amendment is excerpted in *Major Problems in American Foreign Policy*, ed. Thomas Paterson (Lexington, MA: D.C. Heath and Co., 1978) 1, 328.

55. During the Alliance for Progress era in Latin America, the Kennedy Administration supported Juan Bosch in the Dominican Republic in 1962. See also William P. Bundy, "Dictatorships and American Foreign Policy," *Foreign Affairs* 54, no. 1 (October 1975).

56. See Samuel Huntington, "Human Rights and American Power," *Commentary*, September 1981, and George Quester, "Consensus Lost," *Foreign Policy* 40 (Fall 1980), for argument and examples of the successful export of liberal institutions in the postwar period.

57. Jeane Kirkpatrick, "Dictatorships and Double Standards," *Commentary* 68 (November 1979): 34–45. In 1851 the liberal French historian Guizot made a similar argument in a letter to Gladstone urging that Gladstone appreciate that the despotic government of Naples was the best guarantor of liberal law and order then available. Reform, in Guizot's view, meant the unleashing of revolutionary violence. (Philip Magnus, *Gladstone* [New York: Dutton, 1964], p. 100.)

58. Richard Barnet, *Intervention and Revolution: The United States in the Third World* (New York: Meridian, 1968), chap. 10; and on Nicaragua, see *The New York Times*, 11 March 1982, for a description of the training, direction, and funding ($20 million) of anti-Sandinista guerrillas by the United States.

59. Arthur Schlesinger, *A Thousand Days* (Boston, MA: Houghton Mifflin, 1965), p. 769, and quoted in Richard Barnet, *Intervention and Revolution* (New York: Meridian, 1968), p. 158. And for the U.S. official's comment on the Salvadoran land reform, see L. Simon and J. Stephen, *El Salvador Land Reform 1980–1981* (Boston, MA: Oxfam-America, 1981), p. 38. See Zolberg, n. 4, above.

60. John Hobson, *Imperialism: A Study* (Ann Arbor: University of Michigan Press, 1965), pp. 145–47.

61. Leslie Gelb and Richard Belts, *The Irony of Vietnam* (Washington, D.C.: Brookings, 1979). Frances Fitzgerald, *Fire in the Lake* (New York: Vintage/Random House, 1972), chap, 11,

portrays the elections of 1967 in this way. Allan Goodman, *Politics in War* (Cambridge, MA: Harvard University Press, 1973), disagrees, but does find that the elections of 1971 fit this description.

62. Robert W. Tucker, *The Radical Left and American Foreign Policy* (Baltimore, MD: The Johns Hopkins University Press, 1971).

63. Although geopolitical anti-Sovietism and the effects of the two liberalisms complemented each other throughout the postwar period and together usually led to intervention; less frequently, geopolitics and liberalism worked together to restrain intervention. Once recognized, the defection of *established* Communist regimes such as Yugoslavia and China was welcomed, though neither defection was fully exploited. Both the geopolitical interest and the prospects of increased trade or development were served by Yugoslav and Chinese separation from the Soviet bloc. In other instances this particular complementary restraint may have had less welcome effects. The most serious harm to American national economic interests inflicted in the postwar period was the OPEC embargo and price revolution of 1973–74. Geopolitical factors dictated no intervention because the Iranian "regional policeman" needed funds to purchase its arms. Conservative liberals rightly perceived no substantial attack on U.S. oil corporations. Welfare liberals had come to believe in improving the terms of trade for Third World exports, and oil appeared a good place to begin. None of these sources of restraint appear in quite the same light in 1982.

64. Robert Gilpin, *War and Change in World Politics* (New York: Cambridge University Press, 1981), discusses the sources of change in the foreign policies of rising and declining hegemonies.

65. Kirkpatrick points out our neglect of the needs of the authoritarians, see n. 4. Theodore Lowi argues that Democratic and Republican policies toward the acquisition of bases in Spain reflected this dichotomy; "Bases in Spain" in *American Civil-Military Decisions*, ed. Harold Stein (University: The University of Alabama Press, 1963), p. 699. In other cases where both the geopolitical and the domestic orientation of a potential neutral might be influenced by U.S. aid, liberal institutions (representative legislatures) impose delay or public constraints and conditions on diplomacy that allow the Soviet Union to steal a march. Warren Christopher has suggested that this occurred in U.S. relations with Nicaragua in 1979. Warren Christopher, "Ceasefire Between the Branches," *Foreign Affairs*, Summer 1982, p. 998.

66. On economic policy, and pressure groups, see J. J. Pincus, "Pressure Groups and the Pattern of Tariffs," *Journal of Political Economy* 83, August 1975, and L. Salamon and J. Siegfried, "Economic Power and Political Influence," *American Political Science Review* 71, September 1977.

67. Peter Singer, "Famine, Affluence, and Morality," *Philosophy & Public Affairs* 1, no. 3 (Spring 1972): 229–43.

68. Brian Barry, "Humanity and Justice in Global Perspective" in *Ethics, Economics, and the Law; Nomos XXIV*, ed. J. Roland Pennock and John W. Chapman (New York: New York University Press, 1982), chap. 11.

69. John Rawls, *A Theory of Justice* (Cambridge, MA: Harvard University Press, 1972), pp. 352–53.

70. Barry, "Humanity and Justice," p. 234. For an exposition of the implications of a Rawlsian argument ("fair play") concerning international justice, see Charles Beitz, *op. cit.*, Part III. And for a criticism of the extension of Rawls's arguments to international justice, see Christopher Brewin, "Justice in International Relations," in *The Reason of States*, ed. Michael Donelan (London: George Allen and Unwin, 1978), pp. 151–52.
71. Ibid., p. 248.
72. None of the points raised in the first objection to Barry's argument of international distribution devalue the right of nationality or justify liberal imperialism. Both nationality and property are national-state rights derived from the equal rights of individuals, but they are different. Nationality can only be enjoyed collectively, property can retain an individual form of appropriation. No international scheme of provision a global affiliation can substitute for nationality when the nation is the accepted center of loyalty; international provision of income to individuals can substitute for or bypass a corrupt state.
73. Louis Hartz, *The Liberal Tradition in America* (New York: Harcourt, Brace, and World, 1953). The United States is one of the few liberal states both of whose leading political fractions (parties) are liberal. Others have shared or competitive fractions: aristocratic or statist-bureaucratic fractions contesting more centrally liberal fractions.
74. See Kant's "Preliminary Articles," pp. 431–36; and for a contemporary application of liberal views that shares a number of positions with the policies suggested here, see Richard Ullman, "The Foreign World and Ourselves: Washington, Wilson, and the Democrats Dilemma," *Foreign Policy*, Winter 75/76, and Stanley Hoffmann; *Duties Beyond Borders* (Syracuse: Syracuse University Press, 1981), chaps. 2–4. Michael Walzer in *Just and Unjust Wars* (New York: Basic Books, 1977), has reformulated and revised the major liberal propositions concerning the justice of wars and justice in wars.
75. Interestingly, even a liberal imperialist of a Millian persuasion would now accept that the right to nonintervention should extend to the contemporary Third World. Since the criteria set forth in "Civilization" (commercialization, security) are now met by all nations, Mill would find that we no longer have "barbarous nations" requiring imperial rule.
76. These points benefited from comments by Fouad Ajami, Thomas Farer, and Richard Ullman. For a recent example of a prudential argument for detente, see Stanley Hoffmann, "Detente Without Illusions," *New York Times*, 7 March 1983. And for a coherent exposition of a liberal foreign policy which has helped inform my views on this entire question, Marshall Cohen, "Toward a Liberal Foreign Policy," which will appear in *Liberalism Reconsidered*, ed. by D. MacLean and C. Mills (Totowa, NJ: Rowman and Littlefield, 1983).
77. *The Economist Study* of Soviet technology, June 1981, and an extensive literature on the use of economic sanctions, including F. Holtzman and R. Portes, "Limits of Pressure," *Foreign Policy*, Fall 1978.
78. These and similar policies can be found in Fred Hirsch and Michael Doyle, and in C. Fred Bergsten et al., "The Reform of International Institutions," and Richard N. Cooper et al., "Towards a Renovated International System" (Triangle Papers 11 and 14), both in *Trilateral Commission Task Force Reports: 9–14* (New York: New York University Press, 1978).
79. For a thorough survey of these issues see Michael Mandelbaum, *The Nuclear Question* (New York: Cambridge University Press, 1979).

80. Gilpin, *War and Change*, p. 229. Senate Judiciary Committee, *Committee Print: Surveillance Technology* (Washington, D.C.: GPO, 1976).
81. In this connection, an interesting hypothesis that either a frontier, a rapidly growing industrial sector, or an improved educational system are the only hopes for preserving an essential foundation for modern democracies has been advanced by Marion Levy, "A Revision of the Gemeinschaft-Gesellschaft Categories and Some Aspects of the Interdependences of Minority and Host Systems," in *Internal War,* ed. Harry Eckstein (London: Collier-Macmillan, 1964), p. 261.
82. In the last sentence of "Perpetual Peace," Kant expressed a hope for a similar rate of expansion of the pacific union. "It is to be hoped that the periods in which equal progress is achieved will become shorter and shorter." Kant, "Perpetual Peace," in Friedrich, p. 476.

7

Competing Values in U.S. Democratization Policy

R. WILLIAM AYRES

> Wherever the standard of freedom and Independence has been or shall be unfurled, there will [America's] heart, her benedictions and her prayers be. But she goes not abroad, in search of monsters to destroy. She is the well-wisher to the freedom and independence of all. She is the champion and vindicator only of her own.
>
> —John Quincy Adams, 1821

Following the end of the cold war, American leaders began to converge around the idea that "democratization"—spreading democratic government as far and wide as possible—is in the fundamental interest of the United States. Reasons for this have varied; some cited the commercial advantages of free markets, globalization, and intercultural communication; others pointed to the "democratic peace" thesis that democracies do not fight wars with other democracies. Some of this discussion has harkened back to the grand visions of Woodrow Wilson, who urged the United States to "make the world safe for democracy." The two greatest goals of U.S. foreign policy, prosperity and peace, thus seemed to meld into one general policy: to spread democracy to as many countries as possible. The post-Vietnam debates about American action abroad could be put to rest, and foreign policy could return to its historic roots—bringing the blessings of the American vision to the world (Smith 1994; Brands 1998). All that was left was to argue about the details.

The U.S.-led wars in Iraq and Afghanistan in the early years of the twenty-first century have thrown this emerging bipartisan consensus into question. Doubts have been raised about the wisdom of making democratization a key goal in U.S. foreign policy, about the means used to spread democracy to other societies, and about the effects of such efforts at home. In particular, both Iraq and Afghanistan called into question the use of force as a tool for democratization. Despite these questions, U.S. policy in Iraq has changed only slowly under the Obama administration, while the Afghan campaign has been stepped up in the name of securing human rights and democratic development.

To ask whether the spreading of democracy should be a central U.S. foreign policy goal, and whether force should be used to do so, raises three separate questions. First, are efforts at using force to spread democracy effective? Second, are democratized states more peaceful? Finally, what are the effects on domestic U.S. politics of pursuing democratization by force? Can democracy be exported forcefully and still be maintained at home?

The first two of these questions are empirical, and ample evidence already exists in both areas. Other chapters in this volume address these questions well. The third question is theoretical and thus is the most underexamined. Despite decades of calls to examine foreign policy in both its international and domestic contexts, studies of the domestic effects of foreign policy choices are still rare. This chapter attempts to close this gap by posing important foreign-domestic interaction questions: What effect does democratization by force abroad have on democracy at home? Given the U.S. government's founding principles and structures, is democratization by force consistent with the country's origins or political system? This chapter then presents a theoretical argument for why democratization by force abroad is inconsistent with, and damaging to, democracy at home. A central concern is the tension between liberty and power, a perennial question in all of politics. The first section introduces the questions of particular interest: What values undergird American democracy? Why does the United States seek to spread those values abroad? What effect does that effort have at home? The second section outlines the basic values of American democracy, with an emphasis on the original logic on which the country's governing structures were founded. This is followed by an examination of what factors encourage the United States to spread these values abroad, looking particularly at both the substance of the values themselves and at the opportunities that the international system has presented. A discussion of the consequences of democratization policies for democracy at home is then presented. Finally, the chapter concludes with implications for future U.S. foreign policy, including a reexamination of the consensus surrounding democratization and possible alternatives.

TWO CENTRAL QUESTIONS

Two fundamental questions can be posed to address these issues. First, what ideas and values drive the U.S. to seek to democratize other nations? Second, are these values consistent with each other and with the values underlying democracy in the United States itself? The central focus of this analysis involves the *values* and *ideas* that drive the American understanding of its place in the world and of the best ways to govern society and that therefore undergird U.S. foreign policy choices.

The notion that values are central to U.S. foreign policy decision making is hardly a new or novel one. A wide range of authors have examined the ideals that make American foreign policy unique. Some have argued that the U.S. national style has created a paradox in which U.S. cultural-political values exist in growing tension with its place in the world and the international forces that act on it (Hook 2005). Others make the same point by embedding the study of U.S. foreign policy within U.S. society and belief structures and point to fundamental tensions between values and national security issues (Rosati & Scott 2007). Still other analysts argue that approaches that contrast interests and values miss the point, because "values are simply an intangible national interest" (Nye 2002, 139). Even individual-level studies acknowledge that leaders' values and beliefs are central to the foreign policy decisions that they make (George 1980, 3–5; Holsti & Rosenau 1988).

The first question—What values drive the U.S. government to seek democratic reforms elsewhere?—has two elements. First, what is the U.S. understanding of democracy? What do Americans believe about how government should be run and how society ought to be governed? The substance of democracy matters because it forms the bedrock goals of any democratization project—the definitions of what the United States is trying to accomplish if it sets democratization as a priority. Second, why is it important to spread those beliefs to others? Much of the literature on democratic peace theory equates democratization with U.S. material and strategic interests, arguing that the spread of democracy makes the world more peaceful and therefore more conducive to things the United States presumably cares about (trade, cultural interchange, travel, etc.). While these are valuable arguments that have merit, the approach I take here will look for an answer not in material interests but in the values themselves. There are elements within the system of values that Americans identify with "democracy" that lend justification to efforts to spread that system, apart from calculations of interest. At minimum, such elements, if shared broadly by the population, make it easier to mobilize support for a foreign policy of democratization, even forceful democratization.

Given a desire to spread democracy abroad, supported by elements of the U.S. value structure, the second question then turns the focus around and asks what effect this policy thrust has on the functioning of democracy in the United States itself. What are the consequences to the way the U.S. is governed of its efforts to democratize others? How does the implementation of such policies affect government institutions, public opinion and participation, and civil society? This is both a theoretical and an empirical question, although the emphasis in this chapter will be on the latter, tracing the logical consequences of ideas. A more systematic analysis of empirical evidence is left to future study.

The underlying assumption in most treatments of values in foreign policy is that they are essentially consistent. This may be a paradigmatic assumption—because belief systems are assumed to be internally consistent (Jervis 1976, 117–202)—or simply a way of framing American political values to incorporate them into models of foreign policy. The approach here assumes the opposite—that there are value contradictions inherent in U.S. efforts to democratize other societies and crossover between the foreign and domestic policy arenas. In short, while most Americans tend to view foreign and domestic policy as emanating from the same set of values, there are some strands of foreign policy, supported by other values, that are inimical to the core political values that most Americans embrace.

What Are American Values of Democracy?

If the argument here is that American values are the driving force behind U.S. democratization policies, it is important to understand what those values are. These values fall into two categories: the fundamental goals and objects of government and the means of government by which these goals are to be pursued.

It should be noted that although we popularly use the term *democracy* to refer to the U.S. form of government, and talk about the U.S. "democratizing" other countries through its foreign policies, the U.S. system of government was not understood as a *democracy* by those who founded it. The founders of the American system understood a democracy to be "a society consisting of a small number of citizens, who assemble and administer the government in person" (Madison 1787). This kind of direct democracy was considered dangerous and unwise, both because it could not encompass more than a small community and because "in a democracy, where a multitude of people exercise in person the legislative functions, and are continually exposed, by their incapacity for regular deliberation and concerted measures, to the ambitious intrigues of their executive magistrates, tyranny may well be apprehended, on some favorable emergency, to start up in the same quarter" (Madison, 1788c). The preferred system of government was understood to be a *republic*, which consists of government by elected representatives accountable to the people, rather than government by the people themselves. In the Federalist Papers the term *democracy* is mentioned only three times—and all three are negative references intended to demonstrate the dangers of direct democracy. By contrast, nearly forty of the papers extol the virtues of republicanism and republics, a contrast of some significant import.

The ends of American government—that is, the purposes that the new form of government was supposed to serve—are chiefly two: to provide for the "common good" and to preserve liberty. The function of republican governments is to navigate and in some measure reconcile the tension between these two objectives. Liberty was clearly on the minds of those who wrote the Constitution; it is a subject in nearly half of the Federalist Papers. Many of those arguments dealt with this basic theme: "In framing a government which is to be administered by men over men, the great difficulty lies in this: you must first enable the government to control the governed; and in the next place oblige it to control itself" (Hamilton 1788). The great challenge of the "first wave" of democracy was to design governments that were sufficiently powerful to provide for the common good (defense against enemies, an orderly basis for commerce, etc.) while being restrained enough not to trample of the liberty and freedom of citizens. Republican government is therefore different from other forms, not in its duty to provide for the welfare of its citizens but in its determination to do so in a way that does not infringe on their liberty. The fundamental tension at the core of American political beliefs lies between liberty and power. As observers of American politics have noted, *political* liberty was created to augment the existing *social* liberty of American society, which through its colonial origins freed itself from the social constraints of the feudal and class-bound structures of Europe (Hartz 1952; Lipset 1963). Political liberty thus flows from the basic social recognition of the fundamental equality of all citizens.

In foreign policy it is tempting to equate this tension with the familiar dichotomy between *realism* and *idealism,* between those who think foreign policy should be based largely on power considerations and those who think it should be based on normative values or ideals. Proponents of realism themselves have made this argument. Morgenthau (1985, 5, 12) argued that state interests are "defined in terms of power" and that there is an "ineluctable tension between the moral command and the requirements of successful political action." Neorealists went a step further in removing values from the equation, arguing that world politics is fundamentally a function of the structure of the anarchic interstate system rather than of ideologies or values and that "the only remedy for a strong structural effect is a structural change" (Waltz 1979, 111).

This dichotomy—interests versus values—is often taught as a central one in the study of U.S. foreign policy. As realism has come to dominate the intellectual study of international affairs, it has defined the terms of debate regarding U.S. foreign policy, even for other theorists who want to suggest alternative models. But for the purposes of this chapter, this dichotomy between realism and idealism—between the amoral realm of power and the values-driven world of the idealist—is a false one, not useful for answering the questions posed here. Indeed, a compelling argument can be made that, whatever its analytical utility in studying foreign policy, realism has rarely if ever driven the *making* of that policy (Gottfried 2007). Historically there have been few avowed practitioners of realism in positions of authority in U.S. foreign policy (Henry Kissinger and, to a lesser degree, George Kennan being major exceptions). Prominent contemporary realists have come out against the Iraq War as an unwarranted assertion of universal values (see Mearsheimer & Walt 2002).

Indeed, realists have frequently been critics of American foreign policy precisely because that policy has been inconsistent with realist notions of putting the practical national interest and power considerations ahead of ideological goals. Vietnam was a particular favorite for criticism, since the country was far from U.S. shores, much closer to the core of Communist power (China and the Soviet Union) than to the United States, and represented a marginal player in a remote region on the world stage. And while the subsequent U.S. intervention in Panama made realist sense because of the canal, repeated U.S. meddling in the Dominican Republic, Nicaragua, and elsewhere over decades is difficult to justify on realist grounds.

To focus on a tension between interests and values is thus to miss an important point about U.S. foreign policy—that it has *always* been ideological. This is, in fact, a point frequently made about American politics in general. In his classic work *The Liberal Tradition in America*, Hartz (1952, 10–11) argued that the "American way of life" constitutes in effect a "moral unanimity" in which central beliefs—liberalism in its classic sense—are fundamental and universally held. In his seminal work on American politics, Lipset (1963) emphasized a discernible "American character" that was defined by values of equality and individual achievement. More recently, Brands (1998) made a similar, if more nuanced, argument regarding U.S. foreign policy: that it has been, for the most part, not a struggle between amoral power on the one hand and high ideals on the other but a tactical argument between "vindicationist" and "exemplarist" arguments about how America should best translate its values into global reform.

If preservation of liberty is the primary goal of the American way of politics, what is this liberty and how is it to be preserved? Liberty consists of two things: a recognition of the rights of individuals to enjoy freedom in broad spheres of their lives and the establishment of various mechanisms to limit the power of government and to ensure that it does not infringe on those rights (Mill 1859). The former is generally a broad category, encompassing all areas (social, economic, political) in which there is no pressing cause to restrict an individual's freedom of choice and action in the name of preserving the common good. The *political* application of this idea of liberty has thus focused on the latter element: the tools and mechanisms by which government power is restrained from abridging liberties in pursuit of aims other than the common good. The key question of liberty is therefore not *whether* it is worth pursuing, but *how* to pursue it.

For the Founders of the United States, this was the primary benefit of what they termed *republicanism*. Madison (1787) defined a republic as "a government in which the scheme of representation takes place," choosing by election a "body of citizens, whose wisdom may best discern the true interest of their country." Thus, "the whole power of the proposed government is to be in the hands of the representatives of the people" (Hamilton 1787b). Accountability to the people being the primary check on government power and abuse, the elected legislature—in the American system, the only branch of government *directly* elected by the people—was assumed to be the most important (Hamilton 1788). To preserve the value of liberty while allowing for effective governance, therefore, government needs to be representative and accountable to the will of the people. This is why Founders made such a distinction between democracies and republics—the latter incorporate representation and accountability, while the former do not.

American democracy, what the Founding Fathers called "republicanism," thus has one basic end and three principles of process to support that end. The end is the *preservation of liberty* from the potential depredations of power.[1] The means by which this end is to be attained are representation, accountability, and divided government. Any modern American definition of democracy, the system we seek to uphold ourselves and encourage other societies to adopt, is built on these basic values.

Why Do These Values Lead the United States to Spread Democracy?

If these are the founding values of American democracy, why would the United States adopt a foreign policy whose intent is to spread them to other societies? There is nothing inherent in this list of values itself that demands such a course, and the extent to which the United States should or should not share its wisdom with the world was the subject of much debate in the eighteenth and nineteenth centuries, as noted in the Adams quote that opens this chapter (see also Brands 1998).

It is tempting to fall back on a dichotomy commonly taught to students: that the United States began its history as an "isolationist" country and at some point became an "internationalist" one. This story so permeates the teaching of U.S. history and foreign policy as to be nearly universal, to the point that this basic narrative is put forth in almost any U.S. foreign policy text one encounters (e.g., Spanier & Uslaner 1994; Wittkopf, Kegley, & Scott 2003).[2] As with the realist/idealist framing discussed above, the isolationist/internationalist framing is not very useful for examining the questions raised here. As some authors have pointed out, the United States has never been isolationist, if by that term we mean unconcerned with or unconnected to the rest of the world (Rosati & Scott 2007, 15). Yet, the question of interest here is how the U.S. views its system of government in relation to other systems and what it chooses to do about perceived differences.

There is little doubt that the originators of American democracy considered the system of government they built to be superior to others in their era. The Founding Fathers were fond of drawing basic contrasts:

Societies exist under three forms sufficiently distinguishable:
1. Without government, as among our Indians.
2. Under governments wherein the will of everyone has a just influence, as is the case in England to a slight degree, and in our states, to a great one.
3. Under governments of force: as is the case in all other monarchies and in most of the other republics. (Jefferson 1787)

It was recognized that the first condition, while ideal, would be "inconsistent with any great degree of population," while the third "is a government of wolves over sheep" under which people live with "the curse of existence" (Jefferson 1787).[3] There was a good deal of morality in this argument, as the contrast between tyrannical monarchies and republics was frequently described in terms of evil and good. Thus, Jefferson (1786) argued, "if anybody thinks that kings, nobles, or priests are good conservators of the public happiness send them here [to France]. It is the best school in the universe to cure them of that folly. They will see here with their own eyes that these descriptions of men are an abandoned confederacy against the happiness of the mass of the people. . . . [The people are] loaded with misery by kings, nobles and priests."

Madison argued that the superiority of republican over other forms of government was so evident to all that to restrict states from adopting "antirepublican Constitutions" would "hardly be considered as a grievance" (Madison 1788a). The origins of modern American democracy are thus grounded in a sense of the moral superiority of the American system. This sense of exceptionalism has been much remarked on by observers of American politics. Lipset (1963) saw the American ethos of egalitarianism has the hallmark and defining value of American politics, although that same impulse also drove Americans to be extremely sensitive to the opinions of others.

This sense of superiority sprang in part from observations about the results of different forms of governance (as with Jefferson's experiences in monarchical France) and in part from the intellectual context in which American democracy was created. The Constitution was written and the United States created within the broader context of the Enlightenment, which sought to enshrine reason and the search for truth as the highest goals. The superiority of the new American form of government was not merely because of its better outcomes but because republicanism was superior in a reasoned theoretical sense than other forms of government. In this context, Hamilton (1787a, emphasis added) warned against "the honest errors of minds led astray by preconceived jealousies and fears. So numerous indeed and so powerful are the causes which serve to give a false bias to judgment, that we, upon many occasions, see wise and good men *on the wrong as well as on the right side of questions of the first magnitude to society.*" The moral superiority of the American system was thus rooted in the belief that truth could be arrived at through reason and that once achieved, its rightness could not be overturned.[4]

The belief in reason also provided a sense of *universality* to the American way of government. Since reason is presumably objective and (given the proper information and protection from normative bias) always arrives at the truth, what is true for one must be true for another. It was widely assumed that republicanism not only would make Americans better off, but that such advances as England had achieved were because of its republican characteristics and, if applied to France or other societies, would inevitably improve conditions for people there as well, both in terms of their political liberties and their material lives. The earliest foreign policy debates of the republic turned on the question of how to respond to the revolution in France. In the ensuing debate, both sides agreed that liberty was indeed better than monarchy and that French citizens would be better off if it was obtained. The only question was the tactical one of what the new country should (or should not) do about it (Brands 1998, 1–4).

American democracy has at its root a sense of universal moral superiority founded on the Enlightenment notion that conclusions reached by reason are unassailable and superior to other kinds of knowledge—a foundation labeled "American exceptionalism" or the "American way of life" (Hartz 1952, 11). This sense of having found the "right" answer to government is deeply ingrained and gives rise to the question: If the American system of democracy is better than all alternatives, how should the United States interact with other countries with different forms of government? Should there be an effort to spread the benefits of democracy to other, presumably benighted societies? Belief that one has the universally better answer is a necessary condition for even asking this question: democratization makes no sense unless one believes that democracy is better than all alternatives.[5] American political values thus set the stage—but do not require—efforts by the United States to spread its system of governance around the world. Indeed, some have argued that it is this very question that is at the heart of U.S. foreign policy. The danger of exceptionalism is that it does not tolerate difference easily. "An absolute national morality is inspired either to withdraw from 'alien' things or to transform them: it cannot live in comfort constantly by their side" (Hartz 1952, 286).

Exceptionalism may provide a justification for expanding democracy to other countries, but the United States is only in a position to do so provided that its power is sufficient to give it leverage over others. In this sense, the realists' insistence on the importance of power in the international system is important because power provides the enabling force for any foreign policy. An America that had no sense of moral exceptionalism would have no impetus to spread its system abroad; an America without significant power would have no opportunity. Power thus provides the opportunity to moral exceptionalism's motive.

In fact, America's democratization policy has fairly closely followed its power opportunities. Despite John Quincy Adams's arguments, the United States quickly adopted hegemonic ambitions toward the fledgling governments of Latin America, which were weak enough and close enough to the United States to be influenced by the latter. The result was the Monroe Doctrine of 1823, in which President Monroe made a clear case for the distinction of political systems and the importance of the American system prevailing in the Western hemisphere: "The political system of the allied powers [of Europe] is essentially different in this respect from that of America. . . . It is impossible that the allied powers should extend their political system to any portion of either continent [North or South America] without endangering our peace and happiness; nor can anyone believe that our southern brethren, if left to themselves, would adopt it of their own accord" (Monroe 1823).

Similarly, President Lincoln's claim that American democracy offered a promise to the world, not just to the United States, coincided with the centralization of government power and the growth of the federal government, thus laying the groundwork for more extensive efforts abroad (DiLorenzo 2003). The founder of twentieth-century American liberal globalism, Woodrow Wilson, also presided over the greatest modern expansion of U.S. federal government power: the creation in 1913, via the Sixteenth Amendment, of the federal income tax. And U.S. efforts to combat communism after World War II, when America found itself in a new power position as one of only two superpowers, were heavily laden with moral references to the evils of communism and the benefits of democracy (Ayres 2007).

American political values thus contain an impetus toward a foreign policy of democratization, stemming from the belief in the superiority of the American system and its universal applicability. The history of democratization as an American foreign policy goal is a long-running one, going back to the early days of the republic. That history has tended to track America's position in the world system and the availability of power, giving rise to the reasonable supposition that, given the opportunity, the United States will tend to seek to spread its governance system abroad and that there are few, if any, countervailing domestic political values prevent such efforts.

Given that the United States tends to seek to spread its governance system abroad—and history has shown that it does—what are the consequences of such a policy? In particular, this chapter is interested in the consequences under two conditions: when the U.S. is the primary (hegemonic) power in the international system, thus giving it maximum latitude to pursue policies, and when the effort to democratize another society involves the use of force as a major component. These two conditions describe current and recent U.S. circumstances but are also more generally applicable and important theoretically.

If power is an enabling force, then democratization efforts should be expected to rise and fall with America's power position (an expectation that is at least superficially supported by major points in history). Questions of the effects of democratization are therefore least interesting when the country is at its low ebb in power and, correspondingly, most interesting at its peak. Even during the cold war, U.S. foreign policy could be offset by the countervailing efforts of the Soviet Union. In the absence of any power with either the interest or the capacity to oppose U.S. democratization, therefore, there is little in realist systemic power terms to stand in the way.[6] The post–cold war period thus affords the greatest possible opportunities for democratization abroad, which has sparked tremendous interest in the subject.

Democratization by force likewise presents us with an "extreme case." A wide range of authors array foreign policy action along a continuum of exertion or effort, with diplomatic or other primarily verbal means on one end and the use of force on the other.[7] Democratization by force thus represents the most active version, imposing the highest costs on the state. Because it involves greater cost and effort, forceful democratization is also more likely to have side effects at home as well as abroad. Forceful democratization is therefore a useful case in which we should expect to see emerging contradictions most strongly.

This said, it should be noted that the United States has never been shy about using force in pursuit of essentially ideological goals. Some U.S. military interventions, like the 1989 invasion of Panama, have an obvious realist explanation: great powers use force when things of geopolitical importance (like the canal) are at stake. Yet even in that case, it is striking the extent to which it was sold to American citizens as an effort to protect democracy in Panama. Perhaps more striking are U.S. interventions in a wide range of other cases—Haiti, the Dominican Republic, Bosnia, Somalia—where U.S. material and power interests were essentially nil and where some version of the American ideological vision was held up as the impetus to action. And although motives for the invasions of Iraq and Afghanistan were mixed and will be debated for many years, the goal of bringing democracy to repressed peoples was always a large part of the public sales pitch. Indeed, one is hard pressed to find examples of U.S. military interventions post–cold war that are not in some fashion involved with the spreading of democracy, either as an immediate or long-term goal. It is the very presence of this apparent consensus that makes examining democratization by force empirically as well as theoretically important.

It is important to look at the effects of forceful democratization on American politics in three dimensions. First, and most obvious, are effects on state capacity and institutions. A foreign policy of democratization by force can be expected to have serious consequences for how the government runs, which may in turn interact with existing values about how government is supposed to be run. Second, forceful democratization pursued abroad and the changes it brings may affect patterns of political participation. As government changes the way it works, people will change the way they think about and interact with government. Finally, these outcomes can be expected to produce broader changes in civil society. As people's interactions with government change, their understanding of the way society at large is supposed to work may change as well. At the very least, values in conflict with each other may be expected to pull in different directions, with contradictory and self-destructive consequences.

Forceful democratization efforts will involve, first and foremost, a change in state capacities. Although the discussion above identifies the international balance of power as an enabling factor, position within the international system is not enough by itself. Power has to be mobilized in order to be useful. The United States, as the "world's only superpower," must still mobilize its resources in order to accomplish its goals. What sorts of resources are necessary for a strategy of democratization by force?

The primary use of force in a democratization effort would be to remove a recalcitrant government, one that refuses to democratize voluntarily. Given the moral universalism of democracy, one could even argue that powerful countries have a moral duty to the oppressed peoples living under tyrannical systems to aid them in their natural quest for liberty. Secondarily, one might use force after the fall of a government to establish order during a transition to democracy and to protect a fledgling democracy from external threats intended to reimpose nondemocratic rule. All of this requires the United States to possess a standing military capable of carrying out such missions. It should be large and diverse enough to fight a war with the military of another state and win and supplied with sufficient capacity to extend its reach over long distances, since most targets of democratization are likely to be relatively far away from American shores. In other words, in order to engage in forceful democratization, the United States must have a sizeable and independent military—army, navy, and air force.

This seems unremarkable in the modern era, but the authors who designed the American democracy spent a great deal of time discussing and debating the wisdom of standing armies. Again, no fewer than six Federalist Papers were dedicated to the subject. The universal theme of these was that standing armies are dangerous to liberty, though necessary (at least in small quantities) for the defense of the country from outside threats. That standing armies pose a threat to liberty was thought to be true for two reasons: because armies can become instruments of tyranny in the hands of the wrong rulers and because the upkeep of such armies requires an enormous and perpetual tax burden thought to be injurious to both liberty and prosperity. Therefore, the authors of the Constitution went to great lengths to ensure that any force the United States raised would be explicitly constrained (by requiring the Congress to debate and renew the existence of the army every two years) and carefully controlled (by granting Congress the power to declare war and the president the authority to wage it).

To establish a standing military of sufficient size and strength to project force abroad thus runs afoul of some of the initial values of the American political system. Of the two issues above, direct threats to liberty through military coercion have not yet materialized in any great degree. There have certainly been incidents—the shootings at Kent State University in 1970 perhaps most prominent among them—but by and large, through legal and political barriers the U.S. military has not engaged domestically in any sort of coercive role. The tax burden of the military establishment, however, is substantial and far beyond anything originally envisioned in the early days of the republic. Modern military spending takes up about 25 percent of the U.S. government budget. Total public indebtedness reached nearly 65 percent of the U.S. economic output by 2005, and after the near-collapse of 2008, the figure reached nearly 100 percent. To the extent that government taxation represents a threat to the liberty of citizens, which the Founding Fathers clearly thought that it did, their initial concerns appear to be justified.

Beyond the marshaling of resources, however, a strategy of forceful democratization requires a different sort of institutional decision making from the one envisioned under the basic American political values system. Democratization by force is a polite way of saying democratization by war. Accountability (one of the key values of American democracy) in matters of war was to be ensured by giving Congress the power to declare war and the president the power to conduct wars so declared. Yet it is unlikely that a body reflective of the will and opinions of the people would freely choose to declare war on another country in order to democratize it. The American public has certainly tended to shy away from supporting the use of force to alter other countries' politics, at least before the fact (Jentleson 1992). So, an accountable system in which the will of the public has its "just influence" is unlikely to support such a policy.

In order to get around this problem—to enable the United States to engage in forceful democratization despite the lack of prior public support—one (or both) of two things must be done. First, decision-making power over issues of war and peace can be moved from the legislative to the executive branch, from Congress to the president. That this has been done is widely acknowledged in the study of American foreign policy (see Hook 2005; Rosati & Scott 2007).[8] Yet to do so violates the basic principle of separation of powers, one of the basic mechanisms supposed to restrain government power and protect the liberty of citizens.

Second, an executive bent on pursuing forceful democratization could engage in a strategy of persuasion. Since the use of force in self-defense is generally regarded as universally legitimate, and therefore is more likely to be supported by the American public, an effort could be made to persuade the public that forceful democratization abroad is necessary to blunt a threat to American security. This was a popular strategy during the Bush administration in 2002 and 2003, although doing so required a tremendous amount of verbal contortion and in some cases outright falsification (Kaufman 2004). Similar arguments could be made regarding the claims of the George H. W. Bush administration with respect to Panama in 1989. This approach, however, tends to undermine another basic presumption of Enlightenment thought—that the people ought to have full and correct information and if given that information they will arrive at the truth, or at least be able to ascertain their own best interests free from the biasing influence of passion.

Forceful democratization efforts thus require the United States government to undergo at least three institutional transformations contradictory to basic principles of American democracy. First, the government must bring in significant tax revenues to support a standing army, which poses a double threat (fiscal and coercive) to citizens' liberty. Second, power and decision-making authority must be concentrated in the executive branch, in violation of the separation of powers. And third, the government must find means other than reason (i.e., passion or false information) to persuade citizens to support positions they would not otherwise find in their interest. In short, it would appear that forceful democratization cannot be pursued by a government that actually adheres to the principles it is presumably trying to spread.

These institutional changes, in turn, can be expected to affect political participation patterns—how citizens interact with their government. If standing armies and high taxes to support them are maintained long enough, people will become accustomed to them and cease raising questions about whether standing armies are a direct or indirect threat to liberty. This has the effect of changing minds without actually winning the argument, since the citizens will have come to accept something by habit that has not been tested by reasoned debate. Arguments for standing armies based more on passion than reason will engender in citizens the habit of conversing with their government in terms of passions (fears, hatreds, love of country) rather than logic and evidence. Likewise, arguments in favor of forceful democracy based on falsehoods or "spin" will tend to engender in an alienated public the expectation that reasoned debate is not a part of the political process. Political participation thus becomes increasingly based on passion or cynicism, neither of which is conducive to the conduct of democracy as it is generally understood.

Shifting decision-making authority to a centralized executive also affects the way people view and interact with the government. It shifts focus away from the legislature, developing the assumption (contrary to Hamilton's argument) that the executive is the appropriately dominant wing of government. Focusing on war as a tool of policy and thereby advancing reasons for why decision-making authority needs to be centralized also tends to take attention away from divided-government arguments about checks and balances. The more power is centralized over time, the more citizens are likely to expect centralized decision making and the less they will consider the importance of divided government as a guarantor of liberty. Given that other institutions in society also tend toward centralized decision making—CEOs of corporations, religious leaders, many NGOs—patterns of political participation that assume central authority tend to reinforce support for, or at least acquiescence in, such structures.

This leads to potential effects at the broader level of civil society. We tend to organize our activities along the lines of familiar patterns. Models that we learn in one sphere are often applied to others. It is no accident, for example, that the Episcopal Church of the USA—the transplanted Church of England—has a bicameral legislature organized along representational, republican lines with a very weak central executive authority. As political participation and citizen-government interactions become increasingly modeled on centralized authority systems, we should expect that experience to be reflected in other aspects of society as well. A government that centralizes authority in the executive, that relies on coercive mechanisms (violence) to achieve its goals, and that eschews reasoned debate is likely to be reflected in a civil society increasingly dominated by authoritarian structures that pursue coercive solutions and that conduct their business based on passion rather than reason. Those patterns, in turn, will lend further support to centralized, coercive, emotion-driven government.

In such centralized systems, the role of the individual is very different from the presumptive role of the citizen in a democracy. In the latter, citizens are assumed to be primarily self-interested, to define and follow their own goals, which is the purpose of liberty. They are expected to participate in the reasoned debate and discussion of society over definitions of the common good and to elect and converse with representatives who are tasked with the business of governance. In such a republic, all authority ultimately derives from the citizen. In a centralized, coercion-driven system, however, the individual's primary role is to support the government through the payment of taxes and through agreement with centrally made decisions. Since a unified executive has no room for deliberative dissent (unlike a representative legislature), individuals are not expected to engage in dialogue with the government over issues but instead to support decisions made from the center. In other words, embarking on a policy of forceful democratization in other countries—a foreign policy decision—tends to have the effect of making the United States less like a democracy at home. In foreign policy, we see the truth of Hartz's warning that while the American political doctrine is "a glorious symbol of individual liberty . . . [,] in America its compulsive power has been so great that it has posed a threat to liberty itself" (Hartz 1952, 11).

CONCLUSION

This chapter has laid out two chains of logic. The first demonstrated the connections between the initial values and ideals of American democracy and the desire to spread that system to other countries. American political ideals rest on the goal of preserving liberty in the face of power through means of representation, accountability, and divided government—all undergirded by Enlightenment assumptions regarding the role of reason in reaching conclusions. Because this system was derived by reason, and because of the overwhelming value given the political ideal of liberty, democracy is assumed to be superior to all other political arrangements and universally applicable to humanity. This universality and faith in the value of reason encourages the policy of spreading democracy to other societies. Thus, the seeds of a policy of democratization are contained in the founding ideas of American democracy itself.

The second chain worked backward, starting from an assumed policy of forceful or coercive democratization under conditions of hegemony (an important test case) to logically necessary and potential changes to domestic politics and civil society. Here it was noted that forceful democratization abroad requires a significant standing army, which in turn requires a continual tax base—both identified as potential threats to liberty. It also requires centralized decision-making power and a co-option of the deliberative process of public debate by either institutional or rhetorical means (or possibly both) to the effect that questions of war are concentrated in the executive branch and public deliberations about those questions are governed by passion and false information, not reason. These effects, in turn, tend to color interactions between citizens and the government, which in turn affect broader patterns of interaction and organization in civil society. The net effect of all of these changes, starting with the policy of forced democratization, is to make both government and society less democratic and conducive to the values that American democracy was established to foster. In short, spreading democracy abroad tends to make the United States less democratic at home.

The observation that American values are in tension with American foreign policy actions is nothing new. Most basic foreign policy texts have some discussion about "tensions between democracy and national security" (Rosati & Scott 2007), and prominent essays have been written on the discord between "American ideals versus American institutions" (Huntington 1982). Some of these discussions imply that this is simply the way things are, and so it may be. Others suggest that the situation is untenable in the long run and that changes will likely take place in one direction or another. This, too, is a fruitful avenue of inquiry. Can this tension persist over time, or does the United States have to make a choice between certain kinds of policies and its own democratic identity? From a public policy standpoint, these are probably the most important questions to ask.

Finally, it is worth noting that the dynamic outlined here—leading from democratic values to a particular policy back to reverberations of an antidemocratic nature—is not a closed or isolated loop. Coercive democratization abroad is not the only policy that may both spring from and be damaging to American democracy, although in the early part of the twenty-first century one might argue that it is the most important one. Arguments have been made by many that, for various historical or political reasons, American democracy has been undermined and is now far from its intended form (DiLorenzo 2003; Perkins 2004). Responses to such arguments tend to be impassioned, not reasoned, which is not unexpected given the values at stake. Nevertheless, to the extent that the American political system has drifted away from its founding values—has become, in that sense, less democratic—this is probably the function of a number of forces and events, not simply the advent of coercive democratization in the early twenty-first century. What should perhaps be said is that these policies do not by themselves create these effects, but logic suggests that they certainly *add to them* and are likely to accelerate them for the future.

Recent U.S. democratization efforts in Haiti, Panama, Iraq, and Afghanistan and future coercive democratization policies elsewhere help create a less democratic America—an irony of history, perhaps, but one that requires a rethinking of U.S. foreign policy in the future. American support for these efforts—strong at some times, tepid or wavering at others—is based on the assumption that democracy can be spread abroad while being maintained at home. If the argument presented here is correct, that assumption needs to be reexamined in the public realm with an eye toward creating a new, sustainable, democratically based policy that is truly consistent with American political values. The argument was made best by Madison, who warned, "Of all the enemies to public liberty, war is perhaps the most to be dreaded, because it comprises and develops the germ of every other. War is the parent of armies; from these proceed debts and taxes; and armies, and debts, and taxes are the known instruments for bringing the many under the domination of the few" (quoted in Hartmann 2002).

NOTES

1. It was widely assumed by the founders that concentrated power was inimical to liberty and that those who had too much power or who held it for too long would inevitably seek to undermine or reduce the liberty of the population to further their own ends. In this sense, although they are sometimes labeled "idealists" for having led a revolution based on ideals, Madison, Hamilton, and their contemporaries were very much realists in the classic sense, comfortable with the observations on human nature made by Hobbes and other early "realist" authors. Thus, Jefferson (1786) argued that "there is no King, who, with sufficient force, is not always ready to make himself absolute."
2. To be fair, some have added an "imperialism" period into the mix, particularly in the late nineteenth century (e.g., Wittkopf, Kegley, & Scott 2003, 30–33). There is also some dispute about whether current U.S. internationalism traces its roots to Franklin Roosevelt and World War II or to Woodrow Wilson and World War I. But this does not take away from the basic structure of the argument, which is that the United States began as an "isolationist" power and is now an "internationalist" or "global" one. Even authors who do not accept this narrative are forced to deal with it forcefully, understanding that it is conventional wisdom. It should be noted, too, that this debate is a normative as well as a historical one. Isolationism has a nearly universally negative connotation in the U.S. political context, and the implicit assumption in most of these narratives is that the change from isolationism to internationalism is a good one.
3. It should be noted that Jefferson spent much of the Constitution drafting period as emissary to France, then still under prerevolutionary monarchy, and he often commented on the contrast of living conditions enabled by the respective forms of government.
4. Ironically, Hartz (1952) saw that while the origins of American national character lay in the rationalism of Locke, it quickly became a centerpiece of liberal orthodoxy. Thus, while the origins of the system of thought are in reason, the political character of the United States became irrationally dogmatic in defense of those supposedly rationalist values.
5. In recent years, the democratic peace hypothesis—based on the observation that democracies do not fight wars with each other—has lent a practical dimension to this argument. The logic of this theory, being practical and empirical, supplements but does not displace the theoretical argument made here.
6. This is not to say that being in a position of systemic strength guarantees the success of democratization efforts, only that the opportunities will appear to be greatest. Connecting power to outcomes is a tricky business, and the powerful do not always get their way (see Habeeb 1988). But the concern here is not whether the United States will be successful in democratizing other countries but what effects the attempt will have on other values the United States cares about. The effort to mobilize power has effects of its own apart from the success or failure of the attempted policy.
7. See, for example, Craig and George (1990) or many of the popular empirical datasets on international affairs.
8. It should be noted that forceful democratization abroad is not the only impetus for this change, which has had a wide range of motivations. The point nevertheless remains that a policy of forceful democratization requires such a change to be in place, and that change contradicts other fundamental values in American democracy.

8

The Forgotten Element of Democratization

Bringing the Citizen Back In

Andrea Kathryn Talentino

While not explicitly a democratizing effort, contemporary nation building has become a common facet of international involvement in postconflict situations because of a broad consensus that states will be better—more effective, more stable, more law abiding at home and abroad—if they are more liberal. The creation of democratic habits is seen to dovetail with conflict resolution efforts because it is assumed that democracy will make citizens happier and polities more stable (see Peceny 1999). Internal conflicts are often driven by economic and political exclusion, competition over resources, or weak and unaccountable governments. Democratization may solve these problems by introducing mechanisms of voice and accountability that give citizens a stake in the government and ensure governmental responsiveness. Democracy is also considered a means of halting the human rights crises that are associated with conflict and collapse. Although best known for its impact on external relations, democratic peace theory has an internal component as well. Democratization through nation building is seen not only as a means of creating governments that are less aggressive internationally but also less aggressive toward their own citizens and thus less prone to collapse.

In recent years, nation building has also been touted as a tool of counterterrorism, further rooting it within the democratic peace. The concern that weak or failed states might become host to a variety of transnational actors with extralegal and violent interests makes democratic behavior desirable as a means of stabilizing such states and ensuring their international cooperation (Rotberg 2003; Fukuyama 2004b). Democracy, it is hoped, will transform them from permissive environments into places that respect rules and enforce regulations. That makes it harder for criminal groups to operate and strengthens coordinated international efforts to uproot them. Thus, democracy and security go hand-in-hand, internally and externally. Elections are often one of the first steps in the process of postconflict peace building because they create a basis for participation and transparency and convey a sense of legitimacy that previous governments may have lacked. From there, international actors seek to liberalize political and economic interactions, thereby encouraging more effective, fair, and peaceful governments.

In spite of this conviction, if we examine the record of international nation building, the prospects for exporting democracy seem quite thin. The few true successes, such as Germany and Japan, were from a different time and context, when a victory

Table 1. The Record of Nation-Building Cases

Country	NB tenure	Catalyst	Comments
Afghanistan	2002–present	Bonn agreement	U.S. invasion to remove Taliban and al-Qaeda with UN assisting in political rebuilding and NATO assisting with security. Structure of elected government brokered in international conference at Bonn.
Bosnia	1995–present	Dayton Accords	Dayton agreement wrote new constitution for a multiethnic state and provided for NATO intervention. Office of High Representative established by international community to be highest civilian authority in country. Rehabilitation effort now led by European Union.
Burundi	2000–present	Arusha Peace Agreement	International community involved in brokering peace accords and bringing rebel groups into talks with government. Now limited to humanitarian operations.
Dem. Rep. of Congo	2002–present	Global and Inclusive Agreement on the Transition in the DRC	International efforts focused on developing inclusive political system and bringing resources back under control of central state. Effort seeks to end both internal upheaval and international war, which involved six other African nations deploying troops to the Congo.
Haiti	2004–present	Consensus on the Political Transition Pact	Consistent upheaval since first democratically elected government in 1994. Violence led to removal of president in 2004 and UN effort to broker inclusive, non-personalistic government.
Iraq	2003–present	Coalition Provisional Authority	US brokered new political system/constitution with local elites and limited input of UN after removal of Saddam Hussein's government. Seeking to create intersectarian/ethnic government combining Kurd, Shia, and Sunni elements.
Kosovo	1999–present	UNSCR 1244	Region run as UN trusteeship since 1999 with no agreement on its final status, either independence from or future within Serbia.
Liberia	2003–present	Accra Peace Agreement	International pressure forced removal of President Charles Taylor in 2003. UN began operation to dismantle personalistic and predatory rule.
Sierra Leone	1999–present	Lome Agreement	Democratically elected government restored to office and working with UN to change warlord structure of state.
Timor-Leste	1999–2002	UNSCR 1272	UN monitored elections and oversaw transition to soverign state after referendum declaring independence from Indonesia.

in war, the capability provided by occupation, and the sense of strategic need drove U.S. efforts. The more recent cases of nation building, those taking place since 1990, have a far more mixed record. Bosnia, the longest-running example, is still partially run by an international overseer who has coerced most of the significant reforms while politics remain fractious and dominated by group agendas. Of the ten cases that could currently be considered nation building, five are still mired in conflict while the other five remain unstable and at high risk for future violence.[1]

This chapter adheres to a restrictive definition of nation building that includes only cases where entirely new structures of government were created. The media tend to lump almost any example of international intervention under the term, but very few cases achieve a scope comprehensive enough to earn the label. Nation building has emerged in the post–cold war period as a particular type of intervention that is usually pursued by multilateral means and that involves a broad program of reform which seeks to transform political, economic, and even social interactions (see Talentino 2005). It does more than simply reform existing structures; rather, it creates entirely new means of governance. In truth, contemporary nation building is actually state building. It focuses less on the ethos of belonging commensurate with true nationhood and more on the techniques of governing. International actors place most of their emphasis on the mechanisms of democratic government and the creation of the parties, parliaments, and presidents that make it work. Yet, the approach is intended to change attitudes as well. The hearts and minds aspect of nation building often lags behind the technical effort to build institutions, but the hope is that transforming political life will create a civic identity that ultimately transcends whatever social divisions might have been at the heart of the conflict.

Many populations, particularly those emerging from conflict, are hungry for democracy and enthusiastically embrace the prospect of change and their role in it, often at great personal risk. The sight of Afghans and Iraqis flocking to the polls in the face of ongoing violence was a poignant reminder of the value placed on the right to choose. Though citizens rarely understand fully what democracy means, they crave the opportunity to cast their vote and often treat the ballot with much more reverence than do publics in the West. How, then, might the seemingly receptive ground for democratization be reconciled with the poor record of achievement? While the issue has been debated at great length in the academic world, one factor is both frequently mentioned and significantly overlooked: successful examples of democratization require the commitment and active participation of the citizenry. This is the forgotten element in internationally led efforts to democratize. International actors focus on creating the form of a democratic government but neglect to mobilize and educate the citizenry. Beyond the actual moment of voting, few avenues are provided through which citizens may engage with or influence political developments.

Furthermore, many reforms are determined at the international level and have the perverse effect of separating citizens from a process that requires their involvement. The participation of citizens is sterile in that it is primarily limited to a one-time option and then has little capacity to effect change. At the same time, entrenched elites who favor the status quo because of the benefits it provides them resist international efforts to reform, so the top-down effort is obstructed while the bottom-up effort never begins. Although international observers often think of democracy as a contractual arrangement, a matter of holding a vote and establishing checks and balances, the populace is its lifeblood. Participation by the mass of society is essential to limit governmental power and build the political culture necessary to sustain democratization. It gives substance to the structure of democracy. But while the emphasis on building the structures of the state is important, it neglects the more intangible facet of building the attitudes that support democracy and cement the actual nation.

This chapter examines democratization and participation in the context of international nation building in order to assess how nation building inhibits participation, in spite of stated objectives to the contrary, and to suggest ways in which it might be increased. The analysis will focus on both why citizens are a necessary engine of change and how to motivate the local hearts and minds that are so often referenced in, but rarely linked to, the democratization effort. The primary question facing international actors is how to move nation-building efforts from a largely technical exercise in establishing structures and processes to a more substantive effort that builds the habits and culture of democracy among the citizenry in a way that allows the consolidation of democratic reforms without being excessively oppressive or heavy-handed.

DEMOCRACY AND THE CITIZEN

The involvement of the populace in building effective polities is a central part of democratic theory. Man behaving as citizen is seen as an important aspect of political life and a foundation of responsive institutions. Although theorists differ on what participation means, all accord some agency to the citizenry in terms of developing the substance of democracy. For John Stuart Mill (1998), the "spirit of combination" brings the populace together to achieve a mutual whole, while for Alexis de Tocqueville (2001), the progress of the public spirit by continuing democratic education allows for the maintenance of democratic institutions. Unlike other theorists, these writers did not conceive explicitly of the idea of a social contract between ruler and ruled, but they did consider public values essential to democratic success. The willingness to work for the common good encourages both civic involvement and the ability to compromise, which together sustain democracy.

Similarly, for John Locke and Jean-Jacques Rousseau, success is measured in part by the ability of the populace to conceive of political life as a shared and mutually beneficial task. Rousseau argued that only through participation can individuals develop the capacity for socially responsible action, which in turn provides the possibility of just law (Rousseau 1968). Participation also gives individuals a sense of control, which both connects them to government and creates a sense of commitment to the state's well-being. Agency conveys legitimacy and, through support, capacity. So, "the act of association implies a mutual undertaking between the body politic and its constituent members," with each person serving a duty to both his neighbors and the sovereign people as a whole (Barker 1962, 182). Rousseau took the idea of association further than Locke in terms of its virtuous aspects, arguing that participation is necessary to maintain individuals' identity as part of the whole, rather than just filling individual needs. Beyond its tangible and utilitarian benefit to individuals, it also builds the sense of community and common identity.

Crucially, all these theorists emphasize that the liberal state is a representation of the mass of citizens' will and preference. That is, the state derives from what the population prefers, fitting Abraham Lincoln's famous dictum of being of the people and for the people. Participation serves a role well beyond making choices or casting votes. Indeed, the larger value of participation is its ability to inculcate respect and virtue by forcing citizens to consider other perspectives and interests within political life. For Immanuel Kant, recognizing oneself as a participatory citizen should also lead to recognizing others as similarly capable, which in turn leads to respect for and recognition of the needs and dignity of others. The self-control, patience, and moderation that participation develops create a broad sense of civic virtue. Much like Rousseau, Kant believed first that this civic-mindedness can spring only from participation and, second, that it is essential to consolidating republican government. He described this mind-set as the "duty of right," meaning the obligation to act out of respect for others (Roulier 2004).

These ideas are taken up in a more contemporary way by Ian Shapiro (2003), who notes that the preferences of citizens within a democratic polity are shaped not only by institutional arrangements but also by education and acculturation. While process can serve to introduce some measure of democracy, it should also be accompanied by an effort to create a substantive commitment to democratic behavior, or essentially the public spirit that earlier writers emphasize. A conception of civic identity, which means a willingness to invest in and work for the larger good, is necessary to sustain effective democratic structures. "In short, it is prudent to assume that if democracy is to survive, people will have to be persuaded to value it for more than its short-term institutional benefits" (Shapiro 2003, 91). This distinction between short- and long-term perspectives is echoed in the literature on spoilers in peace-building processes. Marie-Joelle Zahar (2006) argues that individuals may adhere to peace agreements for one of four broad reasons: a simple belief that they must comply with the terms, a belief that the institutions created within the peace process will benefit them, a commitment to peace building, or to change the values and ideals within politics and society (see also Stedman 1997; Walter 1997; Richmond 2006). The first two are short-term and instrumental perspectives defined by expected benefits. Only the last encompasses a long-term view emphasizing the creation of a broader social identity defined by political process.

Civil society is a central building block of democratic acculturation and serves as a source of social capital because it creates structures of reciprocity and cooperation. By banding together in various associations, citizens will theoretically learn the habit of combination and become motivated to pursue their interests. They should also transcend narrow and rigid social divides to develop a shared civic interest. Studies suggest that civic engagement leads to higher levels of institutional success by creating the associations and social networks that make democracy durable (Shapiro 2003, 91; Verba & Nie 1998; Booth & Richard 1998). Through these means, "the idea of sharing in common life and acting on the basis of reciprocity to create the 'common good' can develop" (Scarff 1975, 449). Importantly, civil society refers to groups that encompass "pluralism and diversity" and does not include exclusive organizations that seek to prevent the involvement of others or to define legitimacy by their own values (see Diamond 1999).

Not all social organizations count as civil society; the category refers only to those that exert influence on political decision making by seeking mutual interests and building bridges of trust and interaction among groups. That in turn helps to engage the mass public in the "never-ending quest to deepen democracy beyond its formal structure" (Diamond 1999, 219). Groups based on rigid and narrow affiliations that seek to discredit or exclude other perspectives or identities, as are often present in postconflict contexts, do not constitute civil society as understood in the academic literature. Ian Shapiro, Larry Diamond, and others use the term to refer to a specific kind of social engagement that is based on mutual benefit and reciprocity.

Thus far, participation has been discussed in terms of its ability to cultivate mindsets. Its value is assessed by its ability to make people more open to government and to each other. Participation also has a more instrumentalist meaning, however, that is perhaps more reflective of the specific group interests so dominant after internal war. Lawrence Scarff describes this view of participation as "more closely related to influence and power than to justice and community, for it stresses the idea of protecting one's rights and advancing one's interests within a competitive context" (Scarff 1975, 455; Parsons 1966; Verba & Nie 1998; Goodin & Dryzek 1980). Here participation serves the purpose of gaining advantage and preserving position for the individual or group. This viewpoint focuses on the distribution of power to suggest that citizens participate primarily for tangible gain. It therefore corresponds to a rational actor model of value-seeking individuals functioning within society. Failure to participate puts one at a disadvantage. Even with its instrumental functions, however, participation still has important associational effects. Studies show that the act of participating, both directly and indirectly, links the public more closely with policy and makes individuals more supportive of the government and its actions (Baer & Jaros 1974). Even beyond what individuals might expect to gain, therefore, participation does increase the sense of connection to policy and conveys ownership, both of which help the regime establish legitimacy.

The literature on transitions from authoritarian rule to democracy also emphasizes the importance of participation. In examining the "third wave" of democratization, Samuel Huntington notes that the movements for change were led by the middle class and that some form of mass action took place in almost every case. Citizen demand did not always play a central role, but it did help catalyze the demand for governmental accountability and the expansion of economic opportunity (Huntington 1991). The involvement of citizens serves to provide moral pressure, in Graeme Gill's (2000) view, and thus helps influence how elites act. Yet the role of individuals also goes well beyond serving as a catalyst for change. Organized civil society is necessary to channel continued participation and provide an enduring means of both articulating demands and pressuring the regime to respond to them. "A robust civil society, with the capacity to generate political alternatives and to monitor government and the state[,] can help transitions get started, help resist reversals, help push transitions to their completion, help consolidate, and help deepen democracy" (Linz & Stepan 1996, 9; see also Diamond 1999). Citizens operating through organizations thus provide an essential means of holding the state accountable both legally and in accordance with mass expectation. By contrast, the atomization of society impedes transition partly because it inhibits the development of cohesive interests and partly because it leaves elites free to make their own decisions with little concern for accountability to their constituents.

The composition of civil society is also important for transition. Gill (2000) criticizes theorists who define it mainly through political parties and thus elite actors. He argues that democratization will be compromised when politics remains an elite activity. Mass involvement is necessary to pressure the leaders and serve as a repository for democratic values. It constitutes "the basis upon which any stable democratic regime which issues from a process of transition must rest" (Gill 2000, 180). Political culture and popular legitimation also play a central role in Diamond's (1999, 179) arguments about democratic consolidation. The cases he cites suggest that consolidation of transition is most likely when the major political groups share a preference for democracy and accept both its legitimacy and efficacy. Consolidation is far more difficult if a common perspective on the proper direction of politics is absent.

Where preference for democracy is manifest, it typically derives from a belief in efficacy, which is the idea that a democratic system can have a positive effect on social and economic problems. Although Huntington argues that the performance issue is less crucial in democracies because their legitimacy is assumed, Diamond suggests that performance may be important in ensuring continued support. If citizens lean toward democracy because they expect it to deliver, they may be quick to disassociate themselves if it fails, regardless of their perceptions of legitimacy. The political culture that creates a preference for democracy, therefore, can only be sustained if it proves to have value. Without performance, citizens may become much more ambivalent, which will then serve to undermine the development of the values and identities that other theorists note are important.

This concern is particularly important in postconflict societies because the change of societal norms heightens uncertainties and vulnerabilities. New systems are, by definition, unfamiliar and, because of the absence of a track record, untrustworthy. What's more, they often begin to operate in radicalized contexts where demands on the system are high and support is low. Transitional actors "must satisfy not only vital interests but vital ideals" or conceptions of right and justice that tend to differ among the different groups in society (O'Donnell & Schmitter 1986, 70). Common perspectives are notably absent. The transition of norms does not simply create confusion but an environment in which anything goes, where individuals see opportunities to maximize their position, are fearful of others doing the same, and have few constraints to consider. This serves as a powerful inhibitor of the ability to entrench democratic values and perspectives, particularly in terms of building trust among social groups.

Prevailing uncertainty and distrust also serve to alienate citizens. "Actors find it difficult to know what their interests are, who their supporters will be, and which groups will be their allies or opponents" (Karl 1990, 6). Although Terry Lynn Karl suggests that this will make party development easier as actors try to create broad constituencies, in some cases it can lead instead to stronger group identification and a hardening of social divisions. Legitimacy and authority tend to be fragmented throughout society, which makes it easier to mobilize individuals through narrow group appeals. Unless and until loyalties can be directed away from smaller groups and toward the emerging structures of government, a strong likelihood exists that the society will remain divided and chaotic.

The literature on both democratic theory and democratic transitions, therefore, raises certain expectations about the importance and role of citizens. From the point of view of democratic theory, citizen involvement in political life is a necessary means of inculcating the values that support democratic behavior. Participation leads to the broadening and deepening of democratic principles, which ultimately strengthens democracy through habituation. Even if one views participation from a more utilitarian viewpoint, it is still important in driving the commitment to processes and structures that allow citizens to expect payoffs down the line. Instrumental participation does not represent the absence of democratic values, merely the perception that they are tied to tangible rather than moral benefits.

The literature on transition examines participation from a more goal-oriented standpoint, arguing that mass involvement, particularly through civil society, provides both the means of developing democratic habits and the means of limiting state behavior. In the first instance, the act of involvement will allow citizens to gain greater commitment to democratic processes and to begin to transcend narrow social divides. In the latter case, civil society becomes a sort of guardian of right by creating pressures that bring the state into conformity with the limits, regulations, and expectations established through constitutional means. Importantly, however, the relationship is symbiotic. If elites show disregard for the process of democracy, particularly its rules and limits, over time this will shape citizen perceptions as well. Elite behavior can thus have a demonstrable effect on citizens, encouraging involvement when elites are responsive to demands and encouraging impunity when elites ignore citizen interests and repeatedly break the rules.

CITIZENS IN NATION BUILDING

Although the importance of the citizen is central to democratic theory and transition theory, and although hearts and minds are frequently referenced in nation building, international actors give astonishingly little attention to the role of individuals. Beyond the notion of building political parties and holding elections, the populace is left out of the process almost entirely. The literature on peace and nation building tends to focus on the process of state building (see Crocker, Hampson, & Aall 2001; Stedman, Rothchild, & Cousens 2002; Cousens & Kumar 2001). The emphasis in these works is on creating and consolidating the institutions that can lead to effective governance. Although opinions differ as to approaches and timeframes, all studies emphasize processes over attitudes. Other studies analyze the development of peace agreements more specifically, but here too the emphasis is on structures rather than individuals (Fortna 2004; Walter 1997, 1999). Although most studies note that local actors need to be involved and satisfied in some way, few venture into examining how those actors affect and even define the success of international efforts.

The actual practice of nation building also tends to exclude the citizenry because it focuses on macro-level, top-down reforms that create structures rather than commitments. Through power-sharing agreements and inclusive arrangements, international actors expect to build incentives for groups to work together. Yet, the social divides that helped drive fear and violence do not disappear once war ends. Instead, they are often heightened by people's experiences during the conflict and the usual increase in nationalist fervor. The postwar circumstances are highly polarized, so groups within the target society are often distrustful of change, convinced of their actual or potential victimization at international hands, and suspicious of reforms that do not satisfy the demands of their ethnic, religious, or cultural group. In this atmosphere biases and fears play a large role. Perceptions of both local antagonists and international actors will affect how individuals and groups respond to changes and their capacity to engage in consensual decision making, as will the availability of local mechanisms that provide a consistent and visible means of agency and seem to have a more direct impact on daily life. A request made solely for the purpose of burden sharing might easily be perceived as prejudice and a new political structure as hostile in such an atmosphere. Agendas will be established on these gut reactions. While difficult to understand from the outside, they play an important role in determining the extent of the transition from war to peace.

Altogether, these three factors or tendencies of nation building serve to repress the capacity of the populace to participate, either by channeling their involvement into structures that enhance divisiveness or by excluding them altogether. The result is to inhibit the citizens' role in developing democratic processes or assisting in consolidation. These factors serve to alienate the citizenry and reduce rather than increase participation. Importantly, they also tend to create cultures of impunity in which neither elites nor citizens trust the new structures of government or find reasons to give them support. These factors represent broad categories of potential participation and division and thus in many cases encompass several different dynamics. Space allows only limited attention to each factor here, but they are important issues for further study and likely play a central role in the success of nation-building efforts.

THE EXTERNAL IMPETUS OF TRANSITION

As noted, nation building is a top-down process that focuses on the creation of government structures. International actors deal primarily with elites and rarely venture beyond the confines of the capital city in terms of discussing or brokering transition agreements (see Stedman, Rothchild, & Cousens 2002; Fortna 2004; Doyle & Sambanis 2006). While most discussions of democratic transition assume that internal dynamics drive the process, originating in either elite flexibility or mass demand, nation building presents a new context in which the transition is stimulated and implemented from the outside. Even where citizens may prefer democracy, from the outset they are generally outside looking in as international actors negotiate with elites about the structure of the new government. The resulting structures represent international preference rather than citizen will. In a few cases, elections may have preceded intervention, thus providing some indication of an indigenous push for transition. In Haiti and Sierra Leone, for example, the citizenry had a hand in demanding elections and opposing those who overthrew the elected governments. Thus, these two cases fit more neatly the pattern analyzed in the transition literature.

In most cases, however, the form of government is substantially negotiated by outside actors, either through the outright creation of a constitution, as in Bosnia, or via the international management of a transitional process intended to yield a new constitution (e.g., Afghanistan, Burundi, Democratic Republic of Congo [DRC], Liberia, Timor-Leste).[2] The movement toward transition sidelines the citizenry to an important degree, since they are dependent on the deals made at negotiating tables and have little capacity to generate demands or expectations. The fact that Bosnia's governmental structure was negotiated in Ohio and Afghanistan's in Bonn says much about the separation of the citizenry from the process.

Beyond the actual creation of a transition process, implementation does little to invite the citizen in. Peace builders generally work with what Rama Mani (2002) calls "programmatic minimalism," which focuses on mechanics rather than substance and provides little guidance on how to incorporate citizen needs or develop systems of fairness and dignity throughout society. Although she discusses this specifically in the context of justice, the problem is pervasive throughout international operations. A very tangible manifestation may be seen in Bosnia, where the international tribunal had no ties to local courts, did little to educate the citizenry about or involve them in its activities, and thus became a focus of criticism and disappointment (see Fletcher & Weinstein 2004). Importantly, the special court in Sierra Leone has enjoyed far more local support, largely because it is linked to the local structure, includes Sierra Leonean judges, and was the subject of an extensive education campaign.

The separation of the citizenry from the transition process often becomes manifest in a sense of imposition, a belief that international actors are forcing changes that are not reflective of or sensitive to local interests (see Talentino 2007). Governance is not viewed as being of or by the people. While positive local views give reforms life and legitimacy and can help form a symbiotic relationship between emerging political structures, which need citizen support, and the citizens themselves, who need effective government, negative views can essentially cut off reform's oxygen, asphyxiating nascent governments through citizen dissociation. Even in cases where international intervention may initially be welcomed, such as Kosovo and Liberia, the sometimes oppressive international influence over the shape and pace of reform can whittle away public support. Furthermore, international actors' continued hold on power gives citizens little reason to believe in their own agency. Kosovo is one example, and there international control is heavily resented. Similar patterns are seen in almost every current case. Few tools of government lie in Afghan hands, even after five years, and most political decisions receive no public discussion either in the legislature or other forums. Citizens in Iraq believe, rightly or wrongly, that the United States rules and so they have little motivation to seek involvement save through violent means. In Bosnia, local "ownership" of reform remains limited; in most advances, international pressure was key (ICG 2006a).

The collapse of public support often comes not from a deliberate attempt to undermine or obstruct new structures but rather from a collective distrust of external interference and a sense of separation from the structures it creates. Nation building creates the grounds for alienation. The involvement of nongovernmental organizations (NGOs) also complicates matters, because although they provide needed assistance, they also often take on de facto policymaking roles, further diluting citizen agency. In West Africa and Afghanistan in particular this dynamic has been important, with the very activity and efficiency of aid organizations serving to alienate the citizenry and separate them from the process of transition.

In addition to the elite-level focus and hold on power at the international level, the lack of citizen connection to the nation-building process likely stems from a critique expressed by international officials themselves: personnel changes are frequent and lead to short tours of duty by individuals who may be unable or unwilling to invest in real capacity building for local actors. Consistency is weak and officials are often playing catch-up or engaging in crisis management. "For the astute ear, the recurrent whisper through this examination is public confidence. The blatantly missing element in . . . reform is engagement of populations inhabiting war-torn societies" (Mani 2002, 84). This is indeed a perverse outcome, since the purpose of nation building is to increase participation and bring the citizen into the state. However, the reality is far different. Almost every reform serves to keep the citizen at arm's length and to limit the development and effectiveness of civil society.

The Office of the High Representative in Bosnia was and remains the primary force trying to limit state power and enforce the implementation of reform. Citizens have little input. In Afghanistan and Iraq, populations remain excluded politically and economically, and the need to find means to survive has driven them to separate even further by engaging in the illicit economy and following regional or sectarian political leaders who run fiefdoms independent of the central state. The few social organizations that develop in these cases fail to meet the criteria of pluralism and diversity necessary for an effective civil society. Instead, they tend to mirror the same social divides that often served as a catalyst for violence. Where strong civil society does exist, as in Liberia, leaders complain that they have been distanced by the state-building process.

Citizens feel little connection to the state that comes out of the nation-building process. One of the most telling examples comes from Congo, where, in response to the survey question "If the state was a person how would you interact with him?"

the frequent answer was, "kill him" (ICG 2006b). Although this is an extreme case, the disconnect between the citizens and the government it signals is not unusual. A majority of citizens in the Congo are dissatisfied with the information they receive about the country's political situation, which likely increases their antipathy, and are disgusted with a government they view as corrupt and ineffective (UNDPKO 2005). Afghanis, Iraqis, Haitians, and Bosnians likewise feel little connection to or involvement with their respective governments, often viewing officials as little more than crooks who exploit their position for personal gain. In Iraq, the government is tainted by U.S. involvement and so may be expected to gain less support because of frustrations stemming from the sense of external imposition and excessive U.S. manipulation. In the other cases, however, the creation of a new political system was met, at least initially, with enthusiasm and support. Even so, when the initial creation of government did not lead to aggressive efforts to involve the citizenry over the period of implementation, the population was left adrift to form other allegiances. The result is often the extreme fragmentation of politics and a government that has no means to establish legitimacy.

THE UNINTENDED COST OF ELECTIONS

Elections are an obvious tool to create participation, but they often have the paradoxical effect of separating citizens further from the political process rather than drawing them in. On the one hand, elections are necessary to establish some kind of perceived mandate for emerging domestic political structures. By generating involvement and giving citizens a voice, they are intended to create legitimacy for the new leaders (Sisk 2001). On the other hand, that participation can be extraordinarily dangerous precisely because it brings highly mobilized groups into a political process with limited and weak regulatory structures. Furthermore, few citizens accord legitimacy just on the basis of having a choice, without seeing concrete evidence of a government's effectiveness. In stable societies, elections can convey legitimacy because they give a functioning government the imprimatur of popular selection. Yet when a government is unknown and often ineffectual, an electoral mandate does not convey any substantive support. This is particularly true when elections are a new phenomenon. In such cases, the process of voting is more an expression of hope than a commitment to new structures. A demonstrated capacity to govern effectively is necessary to sustain that hope. Elections can thus generate greater distrust, at least in the short term, and serve to further divide the groups vying for political recognition (see Rapoport & Weinberg 2001; Guelke 2001). As described by Terrence Lyons, "Elections attempt to instill democracy by enshrining new political institutions and rules of competition" (Lyons 2002, 215). The record suggests, however, that their more common effect is to transfer societal competition into the new bodies of government, creating a political impasse that impedes further development.

While holding elections may be exciting, prompting massive turnouts, their outcome often leads to alienation or division. The former situation is seen in Afghanistan, where the electoral rolls themselves raised doubts. Well-known warlords ran for office unimpeded and tried to influence turnout by intimidating prospective voters. Their participation brought the entire enterprise into question because the commanders, as they are called, were legally barred from running for office. Although some 200 of the blacklisted candidates identified by the Electoral Complaint Commission were initially disqualified, most of them were subsequently restored to the ballot (see Sissener & Kartawitch 2005). Numerous non-warlord candidates fingered the warlords as being the most difficult challenge they faced in running for office because the various campaigns of intimidation made candidates reluctant to express their views publicly. Most citizens consider the warlords the main source of instability in the country and now believe they are a central obstacle to building an effective parliament.

The system of voting in Afghanistan also strengthened the ability of entrenched networks to influence the outcome. Large, established, ethnic parties with the capacity to mobilize across a single issue did well, while newer groups that pursued a more complex platform were at a disadvantage. The campaign became a contest of powerful individuals rather than agendas and was dominated by the commanders. The election, which was set up in large part to legitimize democratic structures and take power away from the warlords, did just the reverse. As the International Crisis Group (ICG) explains, "Millions put themselves at risk to vote, demonstrating their enthusiasm for democracy, but they have yet to see the government demonstrate that it is on their side" (ICG 2006a). The lack of connection to or belief in the government has also made it easier for radical organizations, including the resurgent Taliban, to recruit adherents.

In other cases, the problem with elections has been their tendency to enshrine ethnic or sectarian divisions within the political system. The ICG decried early elections in Bosnia for precisely this reason, arguing that the compressed time frame did not allow moderate groups to develop or establish agendas and so rewarded the existing, ethnically centered, hard-line parties. In the decade since then, hard-liners have proved to be remarkably resilient and continue to define political lines. At the same time, even where elections take place later rather than sooner, there is little evidence that this problem can be avoided. In Iraq the composition of the Interim Governing Council (IGC) gave Kurdish and Shiite groups an institutional advantage but, more importantly, encouraged groups to think within the context of identity politics. Sunnis believe that the roots of today's sectarian animosity started with the creation of the rough quota system, a situation that was reinforced by the interim constitution drafted by the IGC and then perpetuated by the Sunnis' boycott of the first round of elections.

While this may seem to be the inevitable result of the ethnic and religious balance within Iraq, there is no evidence that it should have been. Sectarian identification has now become the primary force in society, but it was not dominant in the early days of post-Saddam Iraq. Nonsectarian elements have been weakened first by the IGC and then by the series of political developments that came after, including the historic elections and the creation of the constitution. Both the January and December 2005 elections were "confessional exercises," as mosques were turned into the headquarters of political action and campaigns, with many clerics becoming politicians. The ICG says that through those two elections the secular center of Iraq disappeared "into the maelstrom of identity politics" (ICG 2006c). The elections served to reinforce communal identities and both legitimized and institutionalized the concept of sectarian political development.

In practical terms, this division manifests itself in splintered support for the government. The process of the elections and political development to date has taught the citizens that each group can be represented only by its own members. While overall, 5 percent of Iraqis disapproved of Shia prime minister Nouri al-Maliki's performance, there are distinct differences in support among confessional groups. Only 3 percent of Sunnis approved, compared to 67 percent of Shias. This divide carried over into perceptions of the parliament as well, with a majority of the population saying that members of the national assembly were not willing to make the necessary compromises to bring peace. Yet once again huge disparities exist among groups. While 57 percent of Shias supported the assembly, only 9 percent of Sunnis did.[3] Holding elections, therefore, created a form of political participation, but it made the prospect of cooperation and civic-mindedness far less likely. By institutionalizing group identities, the elections served to harden separations within society and impeded the capacity to generate either trust or a sense of common enterprise.

In addition, efforts to establish local structures of democracy lagged behind in almost every case of nation building. This is a crucial problem because support for emerging institutions may develop where citizens have local experience with democratic processes and thus a means through which to begin developing the values and behaviors that theorists cite as critical to success. Yet mechanisms for building trust have been neglected. The Provincial Councils in Afghanistan, potentially important institutions in countering the strength of the regional commanders and building commitment to democratization, were left undefined, with no clear description of their role and responsibility. Municipal and district councils, the lowest (and perhaps most important) tier of representative government, were also unformed.

Similarly, the local elections in the DRC, originally scheduled for 2006, have now been pushed back to 2008, which means that the success of democratization will rest entirely with the central government. At present it has extremely limited capacity and is known mostly for its corruption. Local government was likewise given little priority by the United States in Iraq, and the initial Iraqi authorities viewed it with some suspicion. Although the Coalition Provisional Authority did establish some provincial and municipal advisory councils, which Iraqis enthusiastically joined, they were forgotten in the rush to transfer sovereignty and the shifting series of reconstruction initiatives that followed. The program is slowly getting back on track with programs to educate citizens on democracy and train local leaders, but, like the country as a whole, progress is held hostage by the ongoing violence.

The international community's neglect of the local level is unfortunate because it has the potential to help diminish the problems of alienation and division that may arise through national elections. Mill argued that local-level involvement is essential to build the habits of democracy, since that is where citizens can both see agency and perhaps imagine themselves serving in government. Voting on a national level is not adequate because it is infrequent and has little impact on citizens' habits or beliefs. As Mill said (quoted in Pateman 1970, 31), "'It is only by practicing popular governance on a limited scale, that the people will ever learn how to exercise it on a larger." Much as civil society functions in part to educate the citizenry and involve them in political life, local representation may, with effort, bring groups together over mutual interests, demonstrate effectiveness, and serve as a path for representing and articulating needs. It also helps convince the people that government may be effective and that they can help make it so.

Indeed, the absence of official local government in Afghanistan is precisely what has left the citizenry adrift and served to strengthen the hold of the regional commanders. Similar privatization of government is seen in the DRC, where local leaders have their own tax and security systems and operate outside legal bounds. The often divisive nature of national-level elections combines with the absence of local structures of government to create a context of anomie. Citizens have no means of participation and no reason to support the government, which in turn serves to strengthen alternative structures and further undermine democratization.

THE ECONOMIC CULTURE OF IMPUNITY

Economic development is not required for democratization to take place, but in the postconflict context it is essential to gain citizen support for the government and involve them in the political process. Importantly, as Diamond points out, elite behaviors guide mass behaviors. If elites break the rules and otherwise show contempt for the system, the citizens will too. That creates a culture of impunity that impedes development of the political culture necessary to sustain democracy: the type of system that everyone believes "is worth obeying and defending" and where groups of all types are committed to the process (Diamond 1999, 66). Unfortunately, however, nation building often perpetuates the war economies it was at least partially intended to break and so contributes to a culture of impunity. Analysis of the economic impact of peacekeeping shows that some peace-building operations may actually have negative demonstration effects, convincing people that engaging in dishonest and corrupt economic practices is the only means to succeed (Carnahan, Durch, & Gilmore 2006). Just as people with questionable records may gain recognition, or the illegal use of power may bring rewards, so the insulated decision-making process at the international level encourages citizens to pursue activities that operate outside that process.

Two economic factors are particularly important for nation building to address: access to jobs and corruption. Jobs matter because they may generate loyalty to the regime or turn citizens away from it. Corruption, particularly the involvement of political officials, creates a culture of impunity that directly impedes the culture of democracy. In most cases of nation building, the employment facts are grim, with unemployment generally greater than 50 percent and in some cases as high as 85 percent. This is a serious problem in Iraq, where unemployment and inflation were both near 70 percent in late 2006, pushing people to desperation (IRIN News 2005). Most reports and surveys on Iraq's economic condition since 2004 have focused on the difficulty of finding work and the decline of many families from a middle-class to a poverty-ridden existence despite reform efforts. Needless to say, resentment and frustration accompanied these developments and served as a potent recruiting tool for the opposition and terrorist groups in the country. In 2005, the *Washington Post* reported that insurgents would pay people as much as $50 per day to plant explosives or shoot policemen; the number of people in need of that money has substantially increased (Finer & Fekeiki 2005).

Elsewhere, demobilization efforts have foundered because of a lack of jobs. Agriculture, which plays a prominent role in West African economies, was mostly ignored as an outlet for ex-combatants in Liberia and Sierra Leone for a variety of traditional and cultural reasons. Instead, the international community focused on training people for jobs as carpenters, plumbers, and auto mechanics. But in depressed economies, few people can afford these services. In other cases, individuals selected jobs because of the resale value of the training kits, having no intention of performing the work. Neither country has managed to solve one of the primary issues that helped the war spread—the lack of opportunities for youth.

While jobs are obviously crucial, nation building also needs to limit corruption, particularly where it involves political actors (Godson 2003). Overall, the goal is to increase transparency and accountability, both of which ensure that criminal connections are hard to maintain and end the perception that corruption is a way of life for the government and therefore should be for citizens as well. The political-criminal nexus in Burundi is one reason why a culture of impunity has developed in that country. Similarly, in 2004 the citizens of Sierra Leone cited corruption as the country's second-biggest security threat (behind the rebel militia) and a major cause of war. In many ways an informal economy may be beneficial because it provides outlets for economic activity that transitioning states cannot, but enterprises in the informal sector also have limits on their capacity to grow, are difficult to integrate into production chains, do not pay taxes, and make corruption easier.

Afghanistan provides a good example of the problems posed by informal relationships. The political-criminal nexus is strong and makes economic development more difficult. The warlords-turned-politicians now have a legal position of authority even while they maintain criminal networks that convey real power. Many of the major customs posts in Afghanistan are in regions under the warlords' control, and their command of smuggling networks, along with their ability to impose transit fees on goods, gives them powerful incentives to keep the central government weak. Some commanders view the governmental process as "window dressing," and their position and authority allow them to undermine the government by questioning its competence and co-opting its resources (USIP 2003). This becomes a self-reinforcing cycle, because without resources the government cannot increase its competence and so becomes a virtual sideshow to the authority of the commanders. Caught in the middle, citizens gravitate toward leaders who have the most immediate impact on their economic well-being and security: the commanders. By creating alternative sources of authority, perpetuating the illegal economy, and undermining the authority of the central government in both word and deed, they effectively inhibit widespread democratization at the local level.

Similar problems are witnessed in the DRC. Much of the money intended for disarmament was reportedly stolen by members of the transition government, bringing the effort to a halt and leaving many of the demobilized jobless. The country also has many areas that are cut off from the government. Although Congo covers 900,000 square miles, it has only 300 miles of paved roads. In the remote villages, the government has no authority and all interactions are outside of regularized structures. Citizens pay their taxes to the local warlord and receive services in return. The government has focused on making deals with the warlords to control the violence but has not made an effort (perhaps largely because it cannot) to control the informal economic system that gives warlords their power. Indeed, in at least one case government soldiers serve under the command of the warlord's officers, demonstrating just how much power informal systems may bring (Gettleman 2007).

Iraq is a particularly interesting case in this regard because it had a strong informal sector prior to the U.S. invasion in 2003. The long-running sanctions, which shrank the public sector, and the dominance of the oil industry combined to make the informal sector approximately 35 percent of GDP under Saddam Hussein's rule. Neither the current violence nor the political rehabilitation effort could be fingered for having created the informal sector. Its share as a percentage of GDP, however, has increased to well over half of output. The ongoing conflict is certainly to blame, but so is the lack of official jobs. Informalization and corruption keep revenue and capacity out of the hands of government. The practices also keep citizens distrustful of the new institutions since they cannot provide basic necessities. Evidence of corruption at the official level is rampant and further alienates citizens (see Allawi 2007).

Interestingly, twelve years of international effort in Bosnia have fostered a growing informal sector rather than promoting transparency. The World Bank estimated in 2006 that the informal economy equaled 34 percent of GDP and accounted for most job creation. The costs and difficulties of doing business in the formal sector are high, so most people prefer to go informal; entrepreneurs would rather pay bribes than negotiate arduous and more costly regulations. Moreover, among those who do have licit firms, 47 percent stated that the legal system was seldom or never honest, and 45 percent felt that decisions were seldom or never enforceable (World Bank 2005a, 76; see also World Bank 2005b). The incentives for doing business legally are very low, even after ten years of international nation building. The role of the legal system is important because its ability to guarantee that agreements will be kept affects how businesses work. Here, too, the political-criminal nexus likely has an indirect effect. Although some judges may be connected to criminal networks, they are more probably guided by nationalist identifications and the political-criminal nexus of the politicians with whom they are affiliated.

In an economic market freed from regulation, all manner of activities become commonplace, from standard racketeering to trafficking in drugs and humans. From an economic standpoint, the problem is significant enough, but it is exacerbated by the involvement of government officials. Political position and economic activity thereby become entwined, entrenching criminal behaviors within formal institutions and providing officials with reasons to obstruct reform. The loss of revenue harms the government and simultaneously aids the expansion of criminal behavior. Officials who may sincerely want to benefit the country and citizens and businesses that may prefer to observe the rules find the playing field very uneven, tilted against legal activity.

Importantly, officials need not take any specific action in order to become enmeshed in criminal activity. The official who is in a position to stop something and simply looks the other way is also implicated in the nexus and helps undermine economic development. Either way, a government riddled with corruption cannot gain popular support.

Every case studied here has a similar story, with government officials closely implicated in illegal activities. In the DRC the creation of the transitional government in 2003 was considered a signal of hope and of moving beyond crisis, but the government engaged in what Global Witness (2006) described as "systematic" abuses and corruption of the country's vast mineral wealth. Although some revenues have been reinvested in industry, particularly mining, much of this investment rewarded a small group of political and economic elites. The national customs service, intelligence agency, mines ministry, and assorted other national- and local-level officials are all part of the illegal activities, which include both smuggling undeclared quantities of resources and extorting money for the various stages of the work process. Much as in Afghanistan, many candidates in the 2006 election were leaders of the same criminal gangs and militia groups that have been vying for control of resources throughout the war. The elections merely institutionalized criminal relationships, therefore adding to the number of government officials with vested interests in illegal activity.

Bosnia shows what little impact outsiders may have even in a country less fraught than the DRC with competition over lucrative resources. The lack of effective procurement laws in the first six years of the nation-building effort meant that it was easy for Bosnian officials to misuse funds, a problem that has not been effectively remedied. Transparency remains very low because of the profusion of administrative layers. Few elements of the economy are centralized, allowing economic power to dovetail with political connections and remain in the hands of unofficial mafias.[4] The unpredictability of the legal and policy environment discourages investment and prevents the emergence of a competitive business environment (World Bank 2001). Perhaps the most difficult consequence, however, is the erosion of morale and of confidence in the rules. Virtually all economic activity is controlled, directly or indirectly, by politicians and their cronies. Honest people are thus discouraged from pursuing legal interactions and encouraged to view the government as illegitimate.

BRINGING THE CITIZEN IN

This analysis reveals that international nation building has not been effective in developing participation from either a value-based or instrumental perspective. There is no opportunity for a sense of social responsibility to develop in these cases because the process of nation building keeps citizens at arm's length and serves to increase rather than decrease social divisions and a corresponding distrust. Individuals look to group affiliations first and, through that lens, see politics as a means to short-term value and the protection of group needs rather than as a common enterprise to benefit the whole of society. Although that has some elements of instrumental participation, it proceeds only in the most exclusive of ways, with each group trying to reduce the benefits of others rather than simply securing its own place within a structure benefiting all. The performance of the national-level government is also compromised in most cases by a limited capacity to implement or initiate programs, which serves to further alienate citizens and push them toward local leaders and illegal economic interactions. These incentives create a self-perpetuating cycle in which incapacity increases illegal activity and illegal activity increases incapacity by keeping legitimacy and revenue away from the government. The government itself often falls into illegal activity and faces little organized criticism from the society that might enforce accountability. As a result, there is no opportunity for a democratic political culture to develop, and so the structure exists in name only. While meeting the narrow Schumpeterian criterion of holding elections, the government exhibits little else that might suggest democratic behaviors.

This is a disturbing problem for many reasons, not least of which is that semi-democracies are very unstable governments. Transition periods make aggressive behavior more likely. Although it may be true that mature and stable democracies are the least likely states to fight one another, those that combine both authoritarian and democratic characteristics are, conversely, among the most likely to go to war (Mansfield & Snyder 2007). The pressures on their leadership push them to pursue war as a means of establishing legitimacy. Not only are such semi-democracies more war-prone in general, but they are likely to fight democratic states, placing an important qualifier on assumptions about the democratic peace.

This finding has implications for nation building because most of its targets qualify as semi-democracies. Of the seven cases that have lasted five years or longer, at least five (Afghanistan, Bosnia, Burundi, Sierra Leone, and Timor-Leste) combine electoral systems with an executive power that overshadows and undermines other parts of government. These countries are more shadows of democracy than the real thing and so fall into the category that Edward Mansfield and Jack Snyder (2007) identify as particularly dangerous. The dynamics of nation building may therefore be directly contradictory to the effort's objectives. Rather than making states more peaceful through democratization, nation building may make them less peaceful. Pushed into a netherworld defined by neither entirely democratic nor authoritarian characteristics, the states that are targeted for nation building may in the end be prone to violent policies at home and abroad.

The task ahead, therefore, is to develop strategies to avoid that outcome. Involving the citizen cannot be of secondary importance; nor should it be assumed that participation will become naturally entrenched once an electoral process starts. Instead, international actors need to draw up participatory strategies from the outset and focus on making them work. One of the reasons democracies are assumed to be more peaceful is because of citizen participation and people's unwillingness to support wars that are costly in both financial and human terms. Leaders that engage their militaries internationally will find themselves vulnerable to opposition unless extreme security needs are present. Leaders that persecute or repress groups internally will likewise have to answer at the ballot box. In both cases, policy is expected to be more cautious and accountable as a result. Motivating citizens by giving them an interest in and reason for loyalty to the process of government is important in placing restrictions on the aggressive behavior of states.

Building local-level mechanisms for participation should be an obvious pillar of any such strategy. By themselves, they do not guarantee progress; but their absence likely guarantees a lack of progress. A variety of benefits come from local-level representation. First, it engages citizens at a point where their direct impact is immediately clear. Local government bodies will make decisions on economic and social issues that affect people's everyday lives. Those are the things that postconflict societies care most about and that they need most in order to move forward. Second, local representation introduces the concept of cooperative governance. It is likely to be painful and halting at first, but there is anecdotal evidence showing that local institutions can unite divided ethnicities, religions, or other groups in the interest of immediate and common needs. Examples have been seen in Bosnia with the building of houses in the Brcko district, in Sierra Leone with economic cooperatives, and in the DRC with women's initiatives. Once the groups see evidence that working together can provide mutual benefit, they are more likely to do so in the future and may even begin, over time, to see their success in a cooperative rather than exclusive way. Finally, local representation provides the ownership of change that the international community considers important yet finds difficult to convey. When success comes, it is the result of citizen effort, not the distant decision of international actors.

Another important tool in the effort to build participation is education. Some of this has been done with representatives of intergovernmental organizations, and NGOs sometimes holding town hall–style meetings, addressing different groups and disseminating information. Yet the effort to educate the populace and thereby galvanize its interest and energy needs to be made a more central part of international strategies. It needs to be more than a periodic effort, and it needs to be done on every issue. Handing out printed material, which often passes for education, or relying on the local media is not enough. Instead, international officials need to hold frequent meetings and travel throughout the country explaining, informing, discussing, and listening. This may help citizens feel more aware of the changes that are taking place and therefore more connected to policy outcomes. It may also help build civil society and generate a common perspective that democracy is the best means of ordering political life. The last strategy noted above, listening, is also extremely important in helping citizens believe that their views are treated with respect. Creating momentum for democracy is difficult when the citizenry—the very group all theorists believe needs to approve of a government—is not asked for its views on the matter. The education effort should therefore be as much about gathering information as it is about disseminating it.

A final point of focus should be increasing governmental capacity. That is easy to say and hard to do. Even so, thus far nation-building efforts have not shown an ability to create effective governmental structures that can regulate economic activity and centralize political power. Case after case reveals a persistent and damaging fragmentation of authority that aids in the perpetuation of the illegal economy, enables corruption, and undermines the government. So while nation building needs to focus on the grassroots approach through local representative structures, it also needs to focus on making the national level effective. Local government cannot long be sustained if the national government fails to give it direction or provide the ability to enforce laws and limitation. Strengthening one means strengthening the other.

At the national level this is complex and requires a diverse set of activities, from building more effective security systems to breaking identity-based politics. This latter goal may be the most important because it makes progress in other areas more possible. One answer may be to make elections the end of the transition process (or perhaps the middle) rather than the beginning. We have seen that elections can serve to harden and institutionalize the divisions that both generated and were generated by violence. Delaying national elections by five or six years and using local nominating processes to bring together a coalition that governs in the interim may create more room for moderate agendas to develop and may prevent the difficulties encountered thus far.

Arguing that greater attention needs to be focused on participation raises as many questions as it seeks to solve. One crucial concern is how to maintain legitimacy in the absence of early elections. I argue, however, that the present approach provides neither legitimacy nor effectiveness. It is therefore time to try something else. There seems to be little sense in perpetuating policies that do not yield the intended outcome and indeed, in terms of the propensity for violence of semi-democracies, may yield quite the opposite of what is intended. Nation building will not contribute to stability through democratization if it builds fragile states that are guided by belligerency. Participation has been one of the most neglected aspects of nation building thus far; although its appearance is established, its substance is not. Recognizing the importance of participation and making it the focus of new policies will surely bring no worse results.

NOTES

1. Cote d'Ivoire and Sudan might eventually merit inclusion, but as of mid-2009 they were still struggling to enact lasting reforms.
2. Kosovo exists in something of a netherworld because it still remains part of Serbia and has not had a process of movement toward independence officially declared.
3. The Kurds fall into the middle on the first measure, with 60 percent supporting Maliki, but are the most supportive of the legislature, as 61 percent believe it can make the necessary compromises (O'Hanlon & Campbell 2007, 44–48).
4. The political-economic nexus is particularly acute because Bosnia's thirteen administrative units include five different levels of government: state, entity, canton, city, and municipality.

9
Sanctioning for Democracy

A. COOPER DRURY AND DURSUN PEKSEN

For millennia, economic sanctions have been used to coerce nations. Indeed, discussions of economic coercion appear in works as early as Sun Tzu and Thucydides, who explored the impact of commerce on political interactions among states. Economic strength may be a formidable weapon and, according to these realists, ought to be used as one. Simply put, states have sought to weaken one another's economies in order to undermine their adversaries' military capability. In what is referred to as economic warfare, states have attempted to bleed an opponent's economy dry—and thus, its military—by tactics such as denying access to resources and trade routes. Sun Tzu promoted this idea of winning a conflict without engaging in military action by weakening the opponent to the point of surrender.

In the formative years leading to the creation of the United States, Alexander Hamilton argued that the newborn nation's economy should be used as a form of influence, as a weapon. Driven by mercantilist ideas, the political use of economic power—economic statecraft—would allow the U.S. to expand its influence in the world while still maintaining a degree of detachment from European affairs of state, or at least abstaining from military engagement in those affairs. Hamilton's vision is evident throughout American diplomatic history, as the United States has employed economic sanctions more frequently than any other state (Drury 2005).

In the past century, economic statecraft has employed tactics beyond economic warfare. On the coercive side, imports and exports have been curtailed, quotas imposed, aid cut off, assets frozen, and loans and debt rescheduling blocked (often covertly). However, economic incentives have also been offered in the form of favorable trade deals, aid, and arms sales. States have used these economic measures to destabilize enemy regimes, curtail communism and terrorism, increase or maintain access to markets and resources, solidify alliances, and promote democracy and human rights.

These foreign policy instruments not only have a long history in the world but also have become increasingly common. Since the end of the cold war, more economic sanctions have been used throughout the world than in any other period. Though used for a variety of purposes, economic coercion is most commonly applied to promote democracy. During the cold war a quarter of all sanctions were aimed at improving democratization or human rights within the targeted country. Since then the proportion has more than doubled to 51 percent. The majority of economic sanctions imposed since the cold war has been aimed at the promotion of democratization, political and civil liberties, and human rights.

Despite this wide and increasing use of sanctions—particularly to encourage democratization—many scholars and policymakers have concluded that economic sanctions typically fail. Although experts widely differ on the frequency of failure, a consensus exists that sanctions are ineffective and counterproductive in achieving their objectives. Given this record, together with the increasing use of sanctions, it is surprising that little scholarly attention is paid to the impact economic coercion has on democracy promotion. Quite possibly, the proliferating efforts to promote democratization through economic coercion are actually setting back the efforts to liberalize autocratic countries.

Foreign policymakers, therefore, routinely use economic sanctions as a means to promote liberalization in the world without knowing whether or not their policies are doing more harm than good. While democracy promotion is a laudable goal, thanks to the many benefits often attributed to liberal regimes, the best policies to promote democratization have not been assessed.

In this chapter we examine empirically the effect economic coercion has on democratization in sanctioned states. We find that when countries are sanctioned to promote democratic reforms, they actually become less democratic. Under sanctions, these nondemocratic countries begin to centralize their power and develop more autocratic regimes. We explain the process through which sanctions are meant to work and why they often do not work and then specify the effect they have on a country's regime and on the struggle for democratic reform. The chapter concludes with a discussion of the consequences and policy implications of these patterns.

HOW ECONOMIC COERCION OFTEN FAILS

The logic behind economic coercion is rather simple. One state (the "sender") levies some financial cost on another state (the "target") by increasing tariffs, banning the sale of specific products, freezing assets, limiting or banning travel, and/or reducing aid. This list is by no means exhaustive. In the 1970s, the U.S. government went on a campaign to destabilize the Allende regime in Chile. As part of this covert operation, the White House blocked debt rescheduling from banks and international agencies, rendering Chile's financial situation exceedingly difficult to sustain. The United States also cut aid and the sale of spare parts to all government agencies with the exception of the military—the group that would later lead a successful coup against Allende. In another case, the U.S. government froze Iranian assets after the American embassy in Teheran was invaded and diplomats taken hostage. These assets were significant and made it more difficult for the Iranians to cover the costs of the Iran-Iraq War—one reason they were interested in conceding to U.S. demands to release the hostages by late 1980.

Once sanctions have been deployed, the sender must either wait for the target to acquiesce or apply more economic, diplomatic, or military pressure. In most cases, the cost of the sanctions is much less than the cost of what is being demanded by the sender state. In the case of the long-standing U.S. sanctions on Cuba, the White House has demanded regime change—the cost of which is much higher than open access to the U.S. economy. No Cuban head of state would consider his fall from power a good trade for U.S. tourism and investment dollars.

In some cases, however, the cost of economic coercion is so high that the target regime complies. Russia's restrictions on Uzbekistan after 1991, aimed at securing access to natural gas deposits and protecting the sizable ethnic Russian minority left from the Soviet Empire, were a resounding success. The Uzbeks saw that the serious cost of these sanctions far exceeded their initial policy positions. Likewise, unlike the demands, the sanctions posed a real threat to the ruling Uzbek elites.

Note that it is the target state that determines whether sanctions will be effective or ineffective. Countries such as South Africa, Rhodesia, and North Korea have held out for decades against significant costs imposed by the international community. Although the sender or senders decide when to impose the economic costs, the target determines the outcome of the sanctions—success, failure, or continued stalemate.

Sanctioning other states to encourage or coerce democratization follows the same process. One or more countries deploy economic sanctions in the hope that the target regime will choose a liberal reform agenda. These demands for liberal reforms can be extreme; they may foster regime change or fundamentally challenge sovereignty, prospects that all leaders take seriously. In the post–cold war era, autocrats must be even more protective of their regimes, because democracy has become the hegemonic system, with a group of countries seeking to push this new religion on the rest of the world. Autocrats thus face greater pressure to reform, pressure often applied in the form of economic sanctions.

The question we seek to answer here is not whether sanctions can be effective or not. Many scholars have already made assessments along these lines and concluded almost universally that sanctions are not very effective. Instead, we seek to show what other consequences sanctions have on the balance of autocracy and democracy and on civil liberties in the targeted state. Thus, we show what happens to civil and physical liberties within a state after sanctions are imposed.

THE IMPACT OF SANCTIONS ON DEMOCRATIC FREEDOMS

We maintain that economic sanctions may inadvertently diminish citizens' civil and political liberties in target countries. In many cases, sanctions reinforce the repressive capacity of the targeted leadership, destabilizing domestic politics and leading to fewer accommodations for political liberalization. Here we identify four interrelated causes that explain the process through which sanctions may threaten rather than enhance democratic freedoms.

Controlling Scarce Resources

Contrary to the expectation (or hope) of sender countries, economic pressure often fails to destabilize the targeted political regimes by restricting or denying them essential and often scarce resources. Specifically, the expectation is that as the sanctions deny the political leadership access to critical military and economic resources, they will lose both their coercive capacity (as the sanctions limit military capabilities) and support from key political and social groups (as the sanctions limit the ability to pay off those groups).

Yet according to growing research, targeted elites can mitigate the negative effect of sanctions by maintaining their access to scarce economic and military resources through transnational black markets and illegal smuggling (Andreas 2005; Gibbons 1999). North Korea is a prime example of this tactic. The regime in Pyongyang is able to sustain itself and even flourish by maintaining a supply of money, military resources, and luxury goods from illegal arms sales, drug smuggling, and money laundering. Moreover, by controlling the allocation of public resources, particularly those now made scarce by the sanctions, the target leadership further reduces the effect of economic coercion by diverting the cost of economic pressure to ordinary civilians, all the while paying off political supporters (Weiss et al. 1997; Weiss 1999). Therefore, against all the expectations and hopes of the sanctioning states, it is unlikely that the target regime will be militarily and economically weakened—particularly to the extent that new political space is opened—to allow antigovernment groups to challenge the authoritarian system and consequently achieve a power shift in their favor.

On the contrary, in allocating the resources made scarce by the sanctions, target regimes will receive more support from key groups, such as those in military and police forces, by granting them access to public resources in return for their loyalty to the regime. As a result, economic sanctions inadvertently enhance the ties between the patrons and their clients. Since maintaining a repressive regime depends on the support of powerful groups (Bueno de Mesquita, et al. 2003), it follows that economic coercion allows the targeted leadership to strengthen its repressive governance by enhancing the relationship between the political elites and their supporters. The leadership is able to escape the cost of economic coercion and to increase support from essential groups. It consequently maintains its coercive capacity and uses even more oppressive measures against citizens demanding liberties.

A good example involves the economic sanctions imposed on Haiti (1991–94) in response to the military overthrow of President Jean-Bertrand Aristide. Although the U.S. government aimed at restoring democratic governance in Haiti, the case evidence suggests that economic sanctions were counterproductive and led to further restrictions of political liberties (Gibbons 1999). The sanctions and later comprehensive embargo strengthened the military rule and its repressive regime by giving the Haitian army the power to control the supply and distribution of scarce resources. The strict control of scarce resources in turn allowed the military regime to starve prodemocracy groups while permitting army officers to make huge profits, especially from black market fuel. Furthermore, the profit from the domestic and transnational black market, encouraged by the close ties between Haitian and Dominican army officials, was also used by the Haitian military to retain necessary army supplies and resources to continue to crack down on civilians opposing the military regime. Overall, Gibbons's (1999, 39) assessment of the impact of Haitian sanctions on civilians concludes that "the mechanics of sanctions operation in a society reinforces the power of repressive regimes at the same time they weaken the power of the population to either resist or survive."

INCREASING GRIEVANCES

The second way in which economic sanctions may undermine the democratic rights of citizens is by creating more economic grievances among the citizenry, which will likely lead to more domestic violence in the society and subsequent repression by the government. A large body of scholarly research has suggested that economic coercion has a disproportionate impact on ordinary citizens in the form of increasing poverty, unemployment, and poor public health conditions (e.g., Weiss et al. 1997; Weiss 1999; Cortright et al. 2001; Cortright & Lopez 1995, 2000). This is partially explained by the fact that political elites and their supporters—especially in authoritarian regimes—remain unharmed by economic pressure as they divert the cost of the sanctions to societal groups without economic or political influence. Therefore, since sanctions worsen the economic well-being of average citizens, there will likely be more dissatisfaction with the target leadership among disadvantaged groups. Growing economic grievances and frustration with the regime will in turn lead to more violent acts against the established regime (Allen 2004). As a result, as political violence increases in the society, the state will be more likely to resort to coercive measures, including the use of military force, and to restrict civil and political liberties in order to maintain political stability.

Heightening Nationalism

A third detrimental effect economic coercion will have on democratic freedoms in the target is to allow the political elite to exploit the sanctions as an external threat to the integrity of the country. As shown in the much-cited case study of Rhodesia (Galtung 1967), the apartheid Ian Smith government used the economic sanctions to emphasize the importance of national cohesion to overcome foreign influence or meddling. As this reveals, political elites blame the sanctioning countries for the ensuing economic deprivation in the society and attempt to rally the public behind their leadership as the sole authority to fight the external aggression. In these cases, sanctions will enhance the legitimacy of the established regimes and give them more leverage to suppress any opposition groups under the excuse of maintaining the status quo.

In the case of Cuba, Fidel Castro was able to suppress any opposition against his rule by framing U.S. sanctions as an imperialistic attack on the Cuban people (Miyagawa 1992, 84–86). With the sanctions thus portrayed as an external threat to the country, Castro oppressed anti-Communist groups by either exiling or imprisoning them with the justification that he was maintaining domestic cohesion in a time of national crisis. Economic coercion, therefore, allowed the Communist regime to eliminate prodemocratic opposition movements and thereby preserve the authoritarian regime on the island.

Encouraging Retrenchment

The final impact economic sanctions have on democratic freedoms is a rather perverse one. As the targeted regime comes under pressure to reform and begins suffering from the economic coercion, there is an incentive to actually decrease the level of democratic freedoms and human rights. Once the sanctions are in place, the leadership has two choices. First, it may reform and hope that the sender countries will accept the reforms and lift the sanctions. It is possible, however, that the senders will see these reforms as a signal that more may be gained if continual pressure is applied. If this is the case, then the target will have instituted reforms for nothing. The other choice open to the leadership is to further repress its people politically and physically. Since demands for democratic reforms are often a threat to the regime's survival, once the sanctions are applied, the leadership may as well seize the opportunity to retrench. Subsequently, the target regime may adopt limited reforms, hoping that the senders will accept them as a sign of good faith and lift or decrease the sanctions.

Thus, the sanctions themselves create a moral hazard. Their imposition generates an incentive for the target leadership to actually reduce any civil and physical liberties in the country. After killing or jailing its opposition, the target regime may offer reforms and even prisoner releases as bargaining chips to the sender countries in an effort to end the sanctions. One may imagine a scenario in which the target cracks down severely after the sanctions, undermining democratic rights, and then, after several years under sanctions, lifts some of its repressive laws, increasing personal liberties but still holding them below their presanction levels. While such reforms might be enough to prompt the senders to remove the sanctions, the country would actually be worse off than before the sanctions began. In such a case, the sanctions would have worsened the situation.

In sum, economic sanctions are often counterproductive policy tools—particularly when promoting civil and political liberties—because of their inadvertent bolstering of the coercive capacity of the targeted regime, their potential to heighten political instability or decrease the tolerance for opposition, and their likelihood of providing perverse incentives for targets to repress domestic freedoms.

It is worth emphasizing the serious threat that democratic reforms pose to an autocratic regime. In addition to the four causes discussed, the target's negative reaction to democracy-promoting sanctions arises from different perceptions of the issue held by the sender and target (Ang & Peksen 2007). While the imposition of economic pressure to promote civil liberties for citizens in a repressive regime is considered a symbolic act for sanctioning states (Lindsay 1986), the targeted regime usually perceives the foreign pressure demanding change in its repressive policies as a threat to its survival. Sanctioning states, especially the United States and European countries, widely use economic coercion against the violators of democratic rights to satisfy their public's growing dissent. They use the sanctions to "do something" against the autocratic country. For the targeted authoritarian state, however, repression against citizens is crucial for maintaining strict control over the society and limiting the emergence of opposition groups. Simply put, as opposed to the symbolic nature of sanctions for senders, the issue of repression over potential or real opposition movements is an essential element for the survival of the undemocratic state. It is not surprising, then, that the target state will counter sanctions and demonstrate its resolve in the face of external challenges by putting further pressure on prodemocracy groups. This fierce reaction against the threat or imposition of sanctions will allow the authoritarian regime to show its constituency its strength against external challenges. It will also demonstrate to rival groups that the regime has strict command over domestic politics.

Morgan (1995) notes that the U.S. sanctions against China following the Tiananmen Square incident had different meanings for all parties involved. While U.S. leaders saw the issue as a violation of human rights and political liberalization, Chinese authorities perceived the repression an essential tool to oppress antiregime groups that challenged their authority. "Many in the mainland government believe that without the ability to repress opposition their hold on power is lost. . . . American calls for political freedom and civil liberties in mainland China may be heard as calls for political suicide by the mainland government" (Morgan 1995, 36). Emphasizing the existence of an asymmetric issue perception between the United States and China, empirical evidence suggests that the threat of economic coercion against Chinese authorities to promote political liberalization was counterproductive, leading to less Chinese accommodation on improving human rights conditions (Drury & Li 2006). Thus, sanctioning for democracy is serious, regime-threatening tactic when viewed from the perspective of the target state.

EXAMINING THE EVIDENCE

To assess empirically the negative impact that economic coercion has on democratic rights and civil liberties, we turn to two different democracy indicators. We analyze each of these indicators over the length of the sanction episode (i.e., the period of time the sanctions are in effect). Since sanction episodes vary considerably in length (from one to more than fifty years), we focus on the first seven years. We select this period for two reasons. First, slightly more than half of all sanction cases last no more than seven years. This permits us to be more confident that a few extremely long cases, such as North Korea and Cuba, are not driving our results. Second, and just as important, sanctions tend to have an economic impact early in their duration, but after some years the target state adapts its economy to cope with the economic dislocation. Thus, if sanctions are going to have an effect, it is earlier rather than later.

To be sure that we assess the country's level of democracy prior to the onset of the sanctions, we include the five years before the initiation of sanctions. Thus, the measure begins at -5 (or five years prior to initiation) and continues to 7 (or seven years of economic sanctions). We also begin by dividing sanctions into two categories: (1) all sanctions and (2) sanctions aimed at encouraging democracy and/or improving human rights. We make this distinction to determine whether economic coercion with the goal of democratization is counterproductive and worsens rather than enhances democratic liberties.

The first measure of democracy directly taps the civil liberties in the target state. The *Empowerment Rights Index* is an additive index composed of five variables: freedom of movement, freedom of speech, freedom of religion, political participation, and workers' rights. It ranges from 0 (no respect for any of these empowerment rights) to 10 (full respect for all of these rights) (Cingranelli & Richards 2004).[1] In figure 9.1 below, a rather grim picture appears. Following the imposition of economic sanctions, there is a rather steady and very significant decline in the civil liberties of the target country. This negative impact is clearly not a temporary effect: the target state does not repress for a year or two and then begin liberal reforms; instead, the sanctions cause a precipitous, continuous decline in civil liberties past the fifth year of the sanctions. Only then does the effect level off, leaving the citizenry in the target in worse condition than before the sanctions were applied.

Once sanctions are placed against a state, the regime clearly takes steps to limit the public's ability to criticize it. These limitations on civil liberties provide the regime with ammunition to blame the sanctions on the sender state rather than on itself and its policy choices. Further, the sanctions themselves provide the government with the justification for the reduction of such rights: economic coercion is an attack on the state. The targeted state may then claim it must respond, and to do so means an increase of governmental power and a reduction in the people's rights "for their own good" or "for the good of the country."

When sanctions specifically seek to promote democratization, the results are no more encouraging. Figure 9.2 shows that the downward trend is slightly more

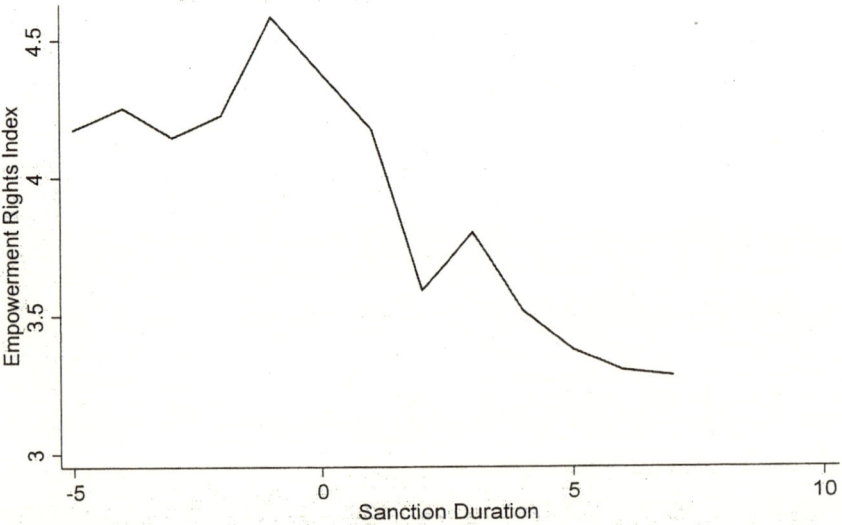

Figure 9.1. Sanctions and Democratic Rights

erratic but to the same end: fewer rights in sanctioned states. The slight increase in the democratic rights after the fifth year of sanctions suggests that the target state may initiate some reforms. Yet this is not evidence that the sanctions are effective. Note that even with the small increase, the civil liberties in the target are considerably lower in year 7 than prior to the sanctions' imposition. The sanctions decrease the rights in the target and do not promote democracy.

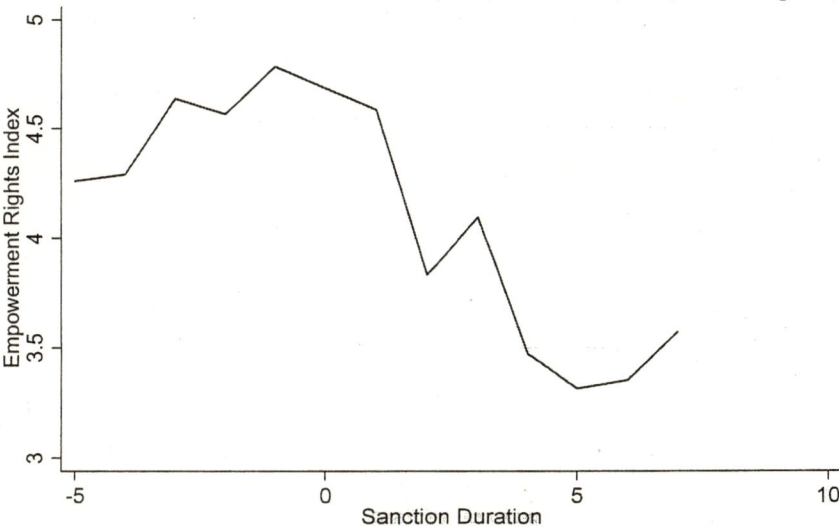

Figure 9.2. Democracy Sanctions and Democratic Rights

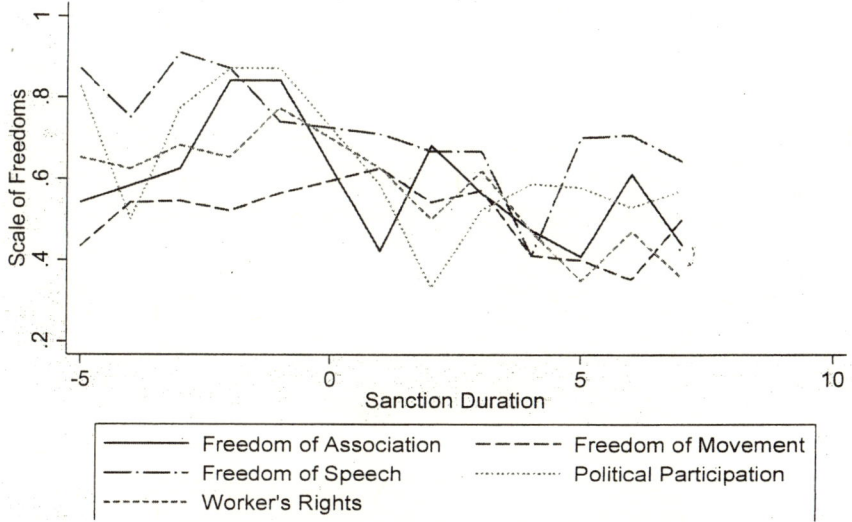

Figure 9.3. Democracy Sanctions and Democratic Rights by Specific Right

The breakdown of the *Empowerment Rights Index* into its components appears in figure 9.3 and shows a similar trend. While respect for each of the rights drops, workers' rights and political participation suffer the most significant declines. The reduction in workers' rights most likely stems from the economic dislocation caused by the sanctions and the regime's attempts to control the worsening economy.

This decrease in political participation validates the argument that the autocratic regime seeks to limit its opposition during a sanction episode. These nondemocratic leaders not only reject the demands to reform, but they also make conditions for their people progressively worse. Thus, two perverse incentives are created by these sanctions. First, government opposition groups in the target may interpret the sanctions as international support for their goals. This situation means that the target country leadership may feel the need to counter any possible opposition, thereby signaling its strength and resolve to the population. As a result, the government increases restrictions on civil liberties.

The second incentive is for the target country leadership to decrease liberties as a future bargaining chip. By placing greater restrictions on the public once the sanctions are initiated, the regime can later offer to lift those restrictions as a show of good faith while negotiating the end of the sanctions. Thus, the initial sanctions become a moral hazard since they become a reason to repress instead of a reason to reform. Ultimately, the sanctions provide the regime with the legitimacy and reason to crack down on political parties and participation. "National unity" rhetoric by the government collapses the political space for any opposition groups, making political participation considerably more difficult.

The same pattern holds for the physical integrity of citizens in the targeted country. As with democratic liberties, we expect that sanctions will decrease the population's physical rights. To assess the relationship between sanctions and physical rights, we use the *Physical Integrity Index*, a measure composed of four variables including extrajudicial killings, disappearances, political imprisonment, and torture. The statistical record reveals an initial, steep drop in those rights, but as the sanctions continue past the first two years, the level of physical repression fluctuates slightly below its presanction level. Similar linkages exist regarding disappearances and extrajudicial killings. Overall, the human rights situation in target countries degrades—quite the opposite of the sanctions' intended outcome.

CONCLUSION

The recent increase in the use of sanctions as a foreign policy tool indicates that economic coercion has become a ubiquitous feature of international politics. Although policymakers frequently use this nonviolent policy tool as an alternative or supplement to diplomacy and military force, our understanding of whether economic coercion causes any negative externalities for targeted countries remains limited. Policymakers are well aware of the low success rate and possible humanitarian consequences of sanctions, but there has not been any comprehensive scholarly research on the possible political consequences of such coercion. We argued that economic sanctions worsen the level of democratic governance and citizen's democratic rights in countries subjected to economic coercion. Our major claim is that sanctions—by inadvertently disrupting the socioeconomic status of average citizens while allowing the targeted elites to escape the burden of coercion—erode respect for civil and political liberties.

The research findings of this chapter have significant implications for the international promotion of democracy. The general understanding of how various international economic and political factors promote political freedoms in nondemocratic societies overlooks the role of economic sanctions. We show that economic coercion leads to lesser political and civil liberties in sanctioned countries. Hence, as economic coercion contributes to the repressiveness of the target regimes, it is unlikely that sanctioned countries will have greater prospects for democratic transition.

This analysis also offers several policy implications. Individual countries and intergovernmental organizations employing sanctions should recognize that applying economic pressure to the target will unintentionally play into the hands of the targeted regimes by reinforcing their repressive capacity and providing powerful incentives to use that capacity on their societies. Therefore, it is evident that the use of "sticks"—at least in the form of economic coercion, but probably extending to military coercion—does not contribute to democratization in the target countries. Because of the collateral damage to democracy promotion efforts caused by sanctions, policymakers should concern themselves less with the question of sanction effectiveness and more with the negative externalities caused by economic coercion. This consideration holds also for those sanctions that are not imposed to promote democracy and that have a reasonable chance at inducing another sort of change in the target's policies. That is, even if a sanction may be successful in fostering some policy change, policymakers must consider the costs to the target's population in terms of the potential loss of civil and physical liberties.

Furthermore, we show that economic sanctions appear to hurt antiregime groups, the very groups that sanctions are intended to help or promote, while causing no major disruption of the coercive capacity of target leadership. A good illustration of this argument is the U.S. sanctions against Cuba. Despite the long history of extensive sanctions against Cuba, Castro's ability to survive sanctions and maintain his authoritarian rule for almost fifty years shows that the political leadership—the major aim of sanctions—in penalized countries is unlikely to be harmed by the coercion.

Sender countries should note that even sanction threats have a symbolic nature that is perceived by the targeted political elites as a serious challenge to their survival. It is likely that threats and/or sanctions with the goal of democracy promotion will not only fail but also have serious repercussions for the relations between sender and target countries and indeed weaken prodemocracy movements within the target. Therefore, alternative policy tools, especially in the form of "carrots," or inducements, such as foreign aid and/or the provision of low-interest economic loans, should be considered more often in the advancement of democratic rights. These engaging policies may have the opposite effect of a sanction. Instead of antagonizing the ties between the sender and target countries, foreign aid and loans may create incentives for the target leaders to take affirmative steps toward the advancement of democratic rights in their countries (Drury & Li 2006).

Engagement is not, of course, always recommended. Sanctions should not always be discouraged. In cases where the target regime is extremely bellicose toward both the international community and its own people, sanctions may be the only answer. The Agreed Framework with North Korea in the 1990s amounted to nothing more than a protection racket where Pyongyang extorted funds (primarily from the United States, South Korea, and Japan) and continued work on its nuclear program. Engagement with such regimes clearly is an ineffective and flawed policy.

Economic sanctions might also become less deleterious for democracy when used prior to or simultaneously with the other external tools, such as foreign aid and economic loans. It is likely that a *mixed strategy*—the mix of stick and carrot diplomacy tools—could be a more successful policymaking strategy in coercive diplomacy (George 1991). Specifically, if sanctioning countries fail to offer some incentives in return for the target leaderships' cooperation, it is unlikely that the target political leadership will concede to foreign demands. Therefore, instead of relying only on punishment or engagement policy tools, a combination of foreign aid and/or loans for future or immediate cooperation and sanctions for punishment might result in more desirable outcomes for sender countries. Detailed research on sanction cases where sender countries also offer incentives might be a starting point in determining to what extent economic coercion combined with other available policy tools contributes to ending political violence and repression by a government.

The United States and other countries imposing sanctions should search for possible ways to improve their effectiveness by inhibiting sanction busting. As suggested above, it is often the case that the targeted leadership continues to enjoy access to the resources made scarce by sanctions through transnational underground actors and black market channels extant in neighboring countries. Sender countries should find ways to obtain cooperation from third-party countries by offering them incentives—for example, foreign aid and loans—in return for their cooperation in severing the ties between third-party countries and the target regimes. Such cooperation would increase the likelihood that the target leadership will feel the pressure of economic coercion.

Finally, the desire of decision makers to spread democracy as a means of spreading peace in the world is problematic when sanctions are involved. Although economic coercion is one of the most commonly used policy tools for democracy promotion, as we have demonstrated, it is counterproductive. If sanctions undermine democracy, they also inhibit the spread of the democratic peace. Put simply, attempts to promote democracy with sanctions as a way of making the world more peaceful has the unintended effect of rolling back the liberal peace. As noted above, leaders should consider engagement policies in place of coercion when the target state is one that may have the capacity for political reform.

NOTE

1. Freedom of movement involves the ability of citizens to travel within their own country and to leave and return to that country. Freedom of speech concerns the extent to which freedoms of speech and press are affected by government censorship. Freedom of religion involves the exercise and practice of religious beliefs without government restrictions. Political participation is the ability of citizens to change the laws and officials that govern them. And workers' rights involves the recognition of international labor standards, including a prohibition on the use of any form of forced or compulsory labor, a minimum age for child labor, and safe working conditions.

10

Washington in the Mideast

A Doctrine, a Dilemma, and Durable Despotism

SEAN L. YOM

From the crucible of the 9/11 terrorist attacks emerged the most ambitious American foreign policy initiative in the young century: the promotion of peaceful democratization in the Middle East and North Africa (MENA).[1] The Bush administration's "forward strategy of freedom" quickly attracted widespread adulation and promised to catalyze democratic transitions in the stubbornly authoritarian regimes of the Arab world. The new doctrine resonated with the ideals of Wilsonian internationalism, bolstering confidence in Washington's post–cold war role as the global beacon of democratic enlightenment. It also reflected hard pragmatism: turning the Arab states into bastions of competitive electoralism could help win the "war on terrorism." By replacing repressive tyrants with moderate liberals and giving voice to hitherto suppressed social forces, democratization would drain the swamp of ideological extremism and reduce violent conflict across the MENA region.

    As this chapter argues, however, the project of encouraging Arab democracy faltered under a devastating self-contradiction. Democratization requires that autocratic incumbents surrender their monopolies over executive authority to legal opposition groups ensconced in parliaments and civic institutions. Yet, in the MENA polities this would likely bring into power Islamist groups that evoke fierce hostility toward Washington's vital strategic interests. An Arab spring of democracy might thus result in a winter of discontent for U.S. policymakers bound by stringent imperatives, such as sponsoring Israeli policies and securing regional oil reserves. Such dissonance has exposed American democracy promotion as an ideological cloak for an unchanged cold war–era policy framework, one that paid lip service to gradual reform while quietly sustaining long-standing support linkages with autocratic allies. The theoretical lesson is stark: observers should expect not the imminent breakdown or even the slow erosion of Arab authoritarianism but, rather, its renewed durability in an era of continuing patron-client ties. Until external powers trade the trusted stability of authoritarian rule for the institutionalized uncertainty of democracy, the impetus for regime change in the MENA will not hail from the international arena.

This chapter is composed of three parts. First, it explains the origins and mechanisms of American democracy promotion in the Arab world, contextualizing this undertaking against the broader backdrop of post–cold war trends. Second, it pinpoints the internal paradox that has haunted advocacy of Arab democratization in U.S. foreign policy: the desire to effectuate regime transition without accepting the possibility of Islamist political advances. Finally, it presents a case study of Jordan's regime trajectory since the mid-1990s to provide empirical evidence that external strategic interests take precedence over demands for democratization. Inside the Hashemite kingdom the government has repeatedly suppressed the Islamist-led opposition through legal manipulation and public crackdowns, authoritarian backsliding that has been rewarded not with rebukes but with material support from the United States and its allies. As the conclusion argues, the righteous mission of democracy promotion does little to dislodge authoritarian incumbents from office. Much like during the cold war, the attainment of geopolitical objectives in the Arab world continues to require the maintenance of client regimes whose autocratic abuses are forgotten in exchange for their cooperation with U.S. foreign policy.

PROMOTING MENA DEMOCRACY: ORIGINS AND MECHANISMS

For comparative political scientists, the MENA is exceptional because it is the only democracy-free geographic zone left in the world. Neither the "third wave" of democratization nor the abrupt demise of the cold war weakened the resilience of Arab authoritarianism, despite the successive collapse of brittle dictatorships in every other region since the 1970s (Posusney & Angrist 2005). Almost no Arab state passes muster against democracy's most basic electoral litmus test—inclusive contestation and public participation in free and competitive elections for political offices of executive authority (Dahl 1971, 4)—much less its more substantive requirement, the protection of civil liberties by legal safeguards immune to raison d'état and other constitutional subversions (Diamond 1999, 10–13). From the kings of dynastic monarchies to the strongman presidents of the single-party republics, Arab autocratic regime incumbents exercise hegemonic authority over their political arenas, brooking few challenges from below and typically forfeiting power only through death or coup.

Academic debates have long contested the underlying reason for the region's entrenched despotism, with several explanations dominating the literature. Traditionally, many scholars blamed Islamic culture and its supposed incompatibility with liberal democratic values (Sharabi 1988). More recently, some analysts have embraced the "rentier state" thesis, which suggests that accumulated revenues from the export of oil and other natural resources have liberated regimes from the need to tax their populations, maximizing their relative autonomy and thus encouraging incumbents to co-opt or repress, rather than bargain with, social forces (Ross 2001). And for those regional governments not blessed with the endowment of black gold, it seems that the expansive capacity of the regime's coercive apparatus—leviathan establishments that include internal security forces, domestic intelligence agencies, and military bureaucracies—is enough to crush, constrict, or co-opt opposition groups (Crystal 1994).

Given these domestic impediments, the end of the cold war excited observers of Arab politics by highlighting the importance of international factors in the struggle for democratization. For four decades the Middle East had been subordinated as a "strategic arena" between two superpowers willing to pour into it vast resources to sustain client regimes and the proxy conflicts they waged (Leitenberg & Sheffer 1979). To many, the sudden collapse of the Soviet Union and the resulting reconfiguration of regional order after the Gulf War meant that the wave of democratization rippling through Central and Eastern Europe might finally expose the illegitimacy of Arab autocracies and elicit Western support for their downfall (Hudson 1991; L. Anderson 1992). This hope gained strength in the early 1990s when economic crises and social unrest forced many local rulers to initiate controlled bursts of political liberalization, which, in polities as diverse as Morocco, Tunisia, Egypt, Jordan, Kuwait, and Yemen, led to the limited empowerment of formal opposition groups, civil society, and elected parliaments (Norton 1995, 1996; Brynen, Korany, & Noble 1995, 1998).

At the time, scholarly advocates of Arab democratization had compelling reason to feel that the global climate for democratic transition was ripe. For the rest of the globe, the collapse of communism had transformed the international environment. The geopolitical alliances and economic linkages that had structured much of the developing world were shattered, thereby shifting the global balance of power toward the West and anointing liberal democracy as the only legitimate type of political rule. Hence, for the United States in the early 1990s, encouraging democratic change abroad not only became a normative priority (McFaul 2004, 155–58) but also provided rationale for a new grand strategy given the missionary gap left by the implosion of the Soviet bloc (Ikenberry 2000, 120–22). Foreign aid agencies poured capital and knowledge into democracy assistance programs like nongovernmental organization–based activism, parliamentary training, and electoral monitoring campaigns (Carothers 1999). The first Bush and Clinton administrations exerted diplomatic pressures and the occasional threat of intervention to deter human rights violations (Schraeder 2002). Interstate organizations like the European Union (EU) used the incentive of institutional membership and the threat of aid withdrawal to prod nearby autocrats toward democratizing reforms (Pevehouse 2005). Western nongovernmental organizations (NGOs) and activist networks, with the support of their governments, pressured dictators to relent on domestic repression while channeling resources and media spotlights to local opposition groups (Keck & Sikkink 1998). These and other international mechanisms, in settings as diverse as Latin America, sub-Saharan Africa, and Eurasia and with varying degrees of effectiveness, helped erode recalcitrant dictatorships by sufficiently raising the cost of repression for authoritarian incumbents such that tolerating liberal opposition groups no longer seemed an unpalatable option (Levitsky & Way 2006).

Yet, by the end of the decade it had become clear that such Western enthusiasm had not penetrated the Middle East. Throughout the 1990s American policymakers rejected democratization as a policy priority in the Arab world. Across the region, what token democracy promotion schemes did emerge through the State Department were organizationally fragmented, sparsely funded, and poorly reinforced at senior levels (Carapico 2002). Arab activists might perhaps excuse European powers for their inaction. Consumed by its revolutionary expansion eastward, the European Union initially viewed its southern Mediterranean neighbors more as security threats than as would-be partners in peace (Xenakis 2000). Yet they remained bitter about Washington's silence, as the refusal of the world's sole remaining superpower to endorse democracy sent a powerful signal to Arab autocrats: domestic repression was still the cheapest option, since no external power was willing to sponsor antiregime opposition groups in their struggles for political change.

Why did advancing Arab democracy elude U.S. foreign policy? With the fall of the Soviet threat, Washington no longer viewed less-developed regions such as sub-Saharan Africa and Central America as battlegrounds for strategic superiority. In turn, this obviated the need to continue supporting authoritarian client states in these areas. Yet the MENA was exceptional. It encompassed certain geopolitical interests that held relevance far beyond the margins of superpower rivalry: first, supporting Israel's security by deterring external aggression, providing massive aid to Tel Aviv, and mediating the Palestinian dilemma; and second, by protecting local oil reserves and extraction facilities (mainly in the Persian Gulf) in order to sustain global hydrocarbon markets (Little 2002, 311–13).

In distant third was containing the specter of enemy ideology, with radical Islamism displacing communism as the reigning evil doctrine (Gerges 1999, 20–35). As in the cold war, preserving patron-client ties with authoritarian incumbents who facilitated these aims and lubricating these relations with generous dollops of diplomatic sponsorship, economic aid, and military arms remained an essential policy tactic. Another was squelching sensitive public talk on democratization. While the Clinton White House did articulate new concerns about human rights under stalwart allies like King Hassan II in Morocco, President Hosni Mubarak in

Egypt, King Hussein in Jordan, and Emir Jabir al-Sabah in Kuwait, it never endorsed transformative reforms that would have threatened the tenure of these incumbents, such as deep reductions in the size of the military or the holding of free elections (Hawthorne 2001). Such an international climate of permissiveness enabled Arab rulers to continue leveraging their coercive resources to defeat antiregime opposition groups while they told Western diplomats that their societies were "not ready" for democracy. Indeed, some countries that began the 1990s with bold political liberalization experiments, such as Ben Ali's Tunisia and Mubarak's Egypt, ended the decade even more closed and repressive than before.

In this milieu, the post-9/11 birth of the American democratizing mission in the Middle East seemed like a paradigm shift away from the stale logic of cold war clientelism. On its coalescence in 2003, the Bush administration's "freedom agenda" threatened to unleash an armada of diplomatic and economic programs to topple Arab autocracies one by one—a "veritable democratic tsunami" (Ottaway et al. 2002). At the most senior echelons of engagement, the White House would pressure Arab governments through public statements and bilateral diplomacy to quicken the pace of political reforms, a burden eased by the promised success of a stable Iraqi democratic model. On the intermediary level, official agencies operated numerous advocacy projects, such as the field-based Middle East Partnership Initiative within the State Department, the multilateral Broader Middle East and North Africa Initiative, and the Middle East Free Trade Area framework. At the quasi-governmental stage, public foundations like the National Endowment for Democracy expanded their grant-making and training programs toward Arab NGOS, journalists, and other local activists.

What bound these disparate elements together was the "gradualist" theory of regime transition. In the MENA context, this assumed that the United States and other external forces could drum up mass mobilization by empowering Arab civil society through, among other things, educating the poor, enriching private-sector business, enfranchising women, encouraging free media, and training political party activists. As international pressures intensified, economic development accelerated, and the restive "Arab street" rallied for change, embattled autocratic incumbents would have little choice but to engage in measured political liberalization, with carefully timed reforms culminating in groundbreaking elections that would enable moderate, secular leaders to take the helm. As dynastic kingdoms melted into constitutional monarchies and single-party dictatorships morphed into multiparty republics, the new pro-Western democracies of the Middle East would finally resolve their interstate conflicts, such as the thorny Palestinian problem, and would reject extremist ideologies, thus eliminating war and terrorism at the same time.

Retrospectively, it is easy to understand why this neoconservative narrative lured soft liberals and hard realists alike. For idealists who identified with the Wilsonian tradition of liberal internationalism, Arab democracy promotion affirmed the widespread view that Washington must serve as a historical agent of positive global change. For them, the American political community was exceptionally endowed with the moral capacity to universalize its experiences by virtue of its democratic traditions, values, and institutions (Monten 2005, 119–29). Modernizing the seemingly despotic Muslim Middle East would cement America's role as a beacon against tyranny, conjuring fond memories of postwar democratization successes in Japan and Germany (Lieven 2006).

For realists, fostering democracy reflected the Bush administration's belief that peace and stability required the assertion of American hegemony over the world, and with it the unilateral freedom to preserve relative security by engaging in aggressive, preemptive action (Jervis 2003). Since democratic regimes neither fought wars nor nurtured terrorism, replacing the Arab world's coercive autocracies with electoral regimes might satisfy national interests. Specifically, a "Middle East pacified, brought into compliance with American ideological norms, and policed by American soldiers could be counted on to produce plentiful supplies of oil and to accept the presence of a Jewish state in its midst" (Bacevich 2005).

From the start, pundits and policymakers shared this sense of urgency regarding Arab democratization. They insisted that "if reform is not insisted upon from outside, even if it is delivered from within, then it will not happen" (Baroud 2004) and drew frequent parallels between their monumental mission and Ronald Reagan's mythologized battle against communism in Eastern Europe. In many Arab countries, Washington's democracy putsch had an instant splash, dictating news coverage, initiating academic conferences, and dominating gossip among nervous political elites (Yacoubian 2005). In early 2005, the project's advocates pointed to the so-called "Arab spring" as proof that local regimes were responding to external pressures and incentives. In January, Palestinians elected Mahmoud Abbas to replace the late Yasser Arafat in the Palestinian Authority's first presidential contest in nearly a decade, and Iraqis voted in their first competitive parliamentary elections since the 1950s. Months later mass demonstrations in Lebanon, triggered by the assassination of Rafiq al-Hariri, compelled the resignation of the government and, later, the expulsion of occupying Syrian forces.

In Egypt, Kifaya (literally, "enough") and other opposition networks celebrated as Hosni Mubarak conceded that the upcoming presidential elections would include opposition candidates, a far cry from the plebiscitary referenda that had previously renewed his mandate. Jordan's King Abdullah II announced sweeping plans for economic reorganization and political pluralization. In April, Saudi Arabia concluded nationwide elections for 178 municipal councils, the first in forty years and a surprise given the monarchy's historical allergy to electoral participation. By that summer of 2005, exuberant editorials trumpeted the rebirth of Middle East history with American ideologues extolling their visionary investment in "people power" (Krauthammer 2005) and Arab intellectuals welcoming the impending *suqut al-anzima al-shumuliya*—the downfall of the dictatorial regimes (Shafiq 2005).

DEMOCRATIZATION VERSUS STRATEGIC INTERESTS

Reports of Arab authoritarianism's demise were greatly exaggerated. In the fall of 2005 Mubarak won his fifth presidential term in a predictably rigged contest, terrorist strikes in Amman sidetracked Jordanian reform promises, and the House of Saud gave no promises of future electoral experiments. By early 2006, Iraq had succumbed to civil war and Lebanon had reverted to sectarian gridlock, while Israeli-Palestinian relations remained tense. Less than a year after the vaunted Arab spring, as the Israeli-Hezbollah miniwar flared and Iran's nuclear ambitions consumed Western attention, jaded commentators began to write off the freedom agenda as a failed project in both American journals (e.g., Kurth 2006) and the pan-Arab press (e.g., Atwan 2006).

Ironically, what shattered neoconservative trust in the Arab street were two democratic electoral exercises. In November 2005, candidates from the Ikhwan Muslimin (Muslim Brotherhood) captured nearly 20 percent of all seats during Egypt's parliamentary elections, far outpacing the handful of victories by secular liberal parties despite the regime's widespread use of coercion and fraud against the Islamist group. In January 2006, the Harakat al-Muqawama al-Islamiyya (Hamas) secured an outright majority of seats in the Palestinian Legislative Council, handing control of the Palestinian Authority over to an Islamist organization that refused to renounce terrorist violence against Israel.

Only after these disconcerting outcomes did Washington temper its rhetorical emphasis on Arab democratization. As the U.S. government and its European allies ceased badgering President Mubarak about his repressive tactics and halted foreign aid flows to the new Hamas-oriented Palestinian government, high-level talk concerning the urgency of regime change began to disappear from official statements by the White House and overseas embassies. Instead, diplomatic chatter now focused on generic issues of "stability," concerned less with fostering democratic transitions and more with defeating "radical" forces such as disarming Iran, isolating Syria, and pacifying Hezbollah. Arab activists sensed the passing of the democratic moment (Fattah 2006). Further, regional pundits had a field day with this about-face. "The Americans were forced to reveal the inherent contradictions between words and actions," one Iranian newspaper declared, while the pan-Arab *al-Hayat* noted that Washington had reaped its own whirlwind by pushing the Egyptian and Palestinian regimes into holding premature electoral contests in which pro-Western candidates had no chance of victory (Badrikhan 2006).

Islamist advances in Egypt and Palestine uncovered the central contradiction in the freedom agenda: Washington's zeal for Arab democratization diminishes when the prospective legitimate successors to current authoritarian incumbents appear antagonistic to U.S. geopolitical interests. To be sure, from the start the democracy promotion doctrine attracted criticism regarding its financial shortcomings and logistical complexities.[2] Yet, far more than these early critiques, the Egyptian and Palestinian elections cast doubts on the doctrine's most basic causal assumption about the nature of political alternation in the neopatrimonial autocracies of the Arab world. The freedom agenda's "gradualist" model of democratization assumed that step-by-step external pressures might empower secular opposition groups to nudge regime incumbents toward piecemeal political liberalization reforms that would institutionalize democracy over time through trust-building compromises.

Since the 1970s, however, the majority of electoral democracies around the world have emerged from the ashes of failed dictatorships through rapid, disorderly drama rather than this plodding pathway. Indeed, after sudden, intense crises exposed authoritarian regimes' lack of legitimacy, mass civic opposition or internal elite defections (or both) caused political systems to collapse, forcefully dislodging incumbents and inaugurating elections for new leaders (Carothers 2005b). At the same time, as the Egyptian and Palestinian experiments demonstrated, in the aftermath of such regime breakdowns in the Arab world, the bread-and-butter constituents of democratization courted by Western donors and diplomats—secular opposition parties, NGO leaders, human rights campaigners, university intellectuals, and other liberal activists—would not be among the top winners in new parliamentary or presidential elections. These forces suffered from leadership fragmentation and a lack of broad-based support, with many citizens regarding them as elitist Western agents out of touch with popular sentiment (Alterman 2004; Ottaway 2005b).

Instead, the balance of power would tilt toward political Islam. As regional observers have long recognized, since the 1970s Islamist movements have flourished by filling the gaps left by the state's economic failings, ideological bankruptcy, and legal repression, promising to revive moribund political life with "authentic" religious values and prescriptions (Rashwan 2005). Powerful groups like the Muslim Brotherhood command sprawling networks of civic mobilization that cut across social classes and cultural spaces, presenting the most attractive opposition choice for ordinary citizens wishing to acquire their first taste of real political participation (Hunter 1988; Wickham 2002). Hence, it is unsurprising that in recent cases where autocratic governments have allowed somewhat free parliamentary elections to proceed, from Algeria in 1991 to the Palestinian territories in 2006, moderate Islamist parties routinely trounce their secular, liberal counterparts (Brown, Hamzawy, & Ottaway 2006).

What disturbs American realists is not the religious nature of these groups. After all, pragmatic policymaking has required close friendships with Saudi Arabia and, most recently, Pakistan; in both countries Islam deeply informs the national constitution, the legal system, and civic institutions. Nor does the potentially illiberal politics of radical Islamists elicit alarm, despite some stereotypical fears that they would harness free elections to gain power only to abolish political rights in favor of theocracy: "one man, one vote, one time" (Zakaria 2004, 2). Mainstream Islamist movements may be ambiguous in their allegiance to democratic principles as defined by Western thinkers, but the Middle East is not a region where U.S. foreign policy has ever required its partners to demonstrate prima facie commitments to Western theories of liberal constitutionalism. Moreover, the most virulent examples of repression under the Islamic banner have unfolded after religious opposition groups launched revolutionary takeovers of decrepit dictatorships, as in Afghanistan and Iran, not after peaceful elections. Islamist regimes treated with the legitimacy accorded to any fairly elected democratic government would be far from extremist and violent.[3]

What chills the nerves of domestic policymakers is the fear that mainstream Islamist groups peacefully winning power in postauthoritarian elections would thereafter promulgate anti-American foreign policies. American officials would face a public relations nightmare in the Muslim world, bound by their post-9/11 oath to champion democratization abroad yet unwilling to condone new leaders who would defy their narrowly defined strategic interests. The fallout in the Arab media after Western powers abruptly cut off aid flows to the elected Hamas government offered a preview of this dilemma (al-Nabulsi 2006). Islamist-oriented governments would condemn the extraordinary depth of U.S. support for Israel's treatment of the Palestinians, even to the point of downgrading relations with the United States and moving instead toward Russia and other would-be hegemons. In the oil-exporting states, they would protest the huge U.S. military footprint in the Persian Gulf and the alleged subordination of regional petroleum reserves to Western ports of call, perhaps favoring more neutral (and equally voracious) Eastern consumers like China. And most of all they would complain about Washington's ingrained fear of any politics couched in the language of Islam, a phobia rooted in the trauma of the 1979 Iranian revolution and intensified by the 1991 Algerian debacle (Gerges 1999, 42–45, 143–70).[4] Further compounding the matter, the standard toolbox for building alliances with authoritarian clients—diplomatic backing, economic aid, and military assistance—might carry little effect given the potency of these ideologically driven policy preferences.

Ironically, listening to Islamist critiques of its foreign policy might actually help American leaders better safeguard the country's long-term interests vis-à-vis energy security and protecting Israel.[5] It might also help reverse endemic anti-Western sentiment across the Middle East: as Arab writers point out, much of the region's public interprets Washington's hostility to Islamist groups as evidence of imperialist hypocrisy (Harb 2007). Unfortunately, the truncated time horizons and domestic lobby pressures that bombard officials between electoral cycles leave little room for such reflective assessments, and policy principals within the diplomatic, intelligence, and defense communities have no appetite for raucous debates that would shine an embarrassing spotlight on America's special relationship with Israel or the pervasive inequities between producers and consumers in global hydrocarbon markets. Thus, the legal ascension of Islamist movements represents a dire threat to U.S. national interests.

Such trepidation explains why the freedom agenda held such "bizarre double standards" in its vision of regime change (G. Robinson 2006).[6] For declared foes like Syria and Iran, whose authoritarian incumbents openly antagonized American interests, fostering democracy meant nothing short of revolution, a comprehensive change of political leadership. For most other Arab states—and particularly for key friends like Egypt, Jordan, and Saudi Arabia—democracy promotion settled on the gradualist model of regime transition, intending only to persuade local rulers to initiate slow, managed liberalization and avoiding abrupt political changes.

The problem, though, is that in the Arab world, managed liberalization never leads to democratization (Brumberg 2002). The trajectories taken by many Arab autocracies in the 1990s demonstrate that short-term political reforms authorized by regime incumbents facing domestic economic or social crises produce immediate expansions of civil liberties but not fundamental redistributions of executive power beyond the ruling elite, much less incumbent turnover through electoral means. As the hype of the Arab spring confirmed, Arab autocrats have grown adept at deploying a stock set of reform tactics to defuse external pressures for democracy while retaining complete authority over the internal levers of state power (i.e., the "trap of liberalized autocracy").

Kings and presidents champion civil society in order to burnish their liberal credentials; while Western think tanks and reporters are paying attention, they favor education for the poor, sponsor women's rights, legalize opposition groups, invest in private-sector capitalism, and encourage independent journalism. When foreign observers lose interest, however, regime leaders solidify their monopoly over core decision-making areas, from military readiness and internal security to foreign policy and economic planning. It is this hegemony over state power that true democratization subjects to public contestation through the ballot box but that American policymakers prefer rest in the hands of rational autocrats. As Takeyh and Gvosdev (2003, 428) observed,

> Ideally, the United States would hope to engender Arab versions of Vladimir Putin—a pragmatic realist capable of cooperating with the United States while effectively managing popular discontent with American policies. An Arab Putin would be a strong chief executive who firmly controls legislative initiatives and the direction of foreign policy while presiding over a regime

that guarantees ample and broad individual liberties yet places controls over organizational freedoms. This would alleviate America's greatest fears in the region: that political and economic reform might undermine America's vital strategic interests.

In the disappointing aftermath of the Arab spring, one commentator announced, "It's *back* to cold war politics in the Middle East" (Ottaway 2007, emphasis added). However, such a statement is misleading: the cold war–style calculus of sustaining authoritarian associates never left America's policy framework in the first place. Since the early 1950s, Washington has preserved its pervasive influence in the Arab world not by winning over the hearts and minds of public audiences but by capturing the personal loyalties of ruling autocratic elites. Central to this framework has been the provision of diplomatic sponsorship, financial grants, and security assistance, mechanisms of bilateral patronage that have historically signaled U.S. gratitude to smaller allies that accommodate its policy imperatives. Indeed, for all the talk of democracy promotion, these networks of international assistance to Arab autocracies with membership in the club of Western allies expanded after 9/11.

Evidence for this rests in U.S. aid transfers to the region, a significant indicator of Washington's eagerness to continue deploying wealth and weapons to woo its client regimes. From 2002 to 2005, the United States spent $44 billion in combined economic and military assistance across the MENA (USAID 2006). Even after deducting the sizeable allocations of funds earmarked for Israeli aid and Iraqi reconstruction efforts, Arab countries received roughly $6.2 billion in economic aid, most of it not in the guise of "development" funds aiming to eradicate poverty but rather in the form of official budgetary grants and other concessional assistance designed to help foreign governments maintain economic stability. The other approximately $7.1 billion manifest as security aid, mostly as loans and subsidies for the purchase of U.S. military hardware, from light arms and radar batteries to combat helicopters and fighter jets. During the same four-year time span, the Middle East Partnership Initiative (MEPI) and other State Department efforts on the frontlines of regional democracy promotion received just $565 million (Wittes & Yerkes 2006, 11).

STABILITY, NOT DEMOCRACY: THE VIEW FROM JORDAN

What happens when the prospects for democratization in an allied Arab autocracy clash with Washington's vital interests? How does external regime support shape the prospects for enduring authoritarianism? The case of Jordan provides disconcerting answers to these questions. The lackadaisical attitudes evoked by U.S. policymakers toward Jordanian democracy after 9/11 trace their origins to 1994, when King Hussein maneuvered his traditionally pro-American kingdom back into the graces of Western patronage by inking a historic peace treaty with Israel. Since then a robust correlation has governed the Hashemite regime's deliberalizing trajectory: (1) an internal retreat from its bold democratic reform program, which had commenced in 1989, quickly propelled an Islamist-dominated opposition to public prominence; and (2) an external arc of escalating aid from the United States and its allies, reflected in ever-expanding levels of diplomatic, economic, and military assistance. Even at the height of the democracy promotion frenzy, as the regime faced economic lethargy and civic mobilization, these conduits of external support reinforced its core financial resources and repressive capacities. They reduced the uncertainty surrounding the monarchy's political future by precluding any international repercussions that might result from its continued autocratic abuses. While State Department officers trumpeted Jordan's "moderate" character as a counterweight to extremism after 9/11, opposition activists confronted empty promises and security crackdowns.

The important role played by Western support in the closure of Jordan's democratic moment is best understood in the context of the 1989 economic crisis that forced the ruling elite to restore parliament and reanimate legal opposition groups. After the 1970 civil war, the Hashemite monarchy had engineered two decades of national stability through a rentier formula of governance. First, it redistributed public economic resources to loyal constituencies in exchange for their political acquiescence. King Hussein guaranteed the collective security of the East Bank community (i.e., Bedouin and tribal elements), his historical bedrock of legitimacy, by engineering their dominance in the civil and military bureaucracies. Thus, by the mid-1980s the bloated public sector was by far the largest component of the statist economy, employing half the labor force (Kanovsky 1989, 381).

Meanwhile, the regime appeased Palestinian private-sector capital by maintaining a low domestic extraction base, with tax revenues never exceeding 15 percent of the GDP (Central Bank of Jordan 1996). As the economy boomed—during 1975–86 per capita in 2000 constant terms doubled to $2,100 (World Bank 2006)—political institutions contracted. With parliament suspended since 1967 and all opposition parties banned since 1957, King Hussein and the royalist elite ruled by decree.[7] The police and the domestic intelligence (*mukhabarat*) muzzled the media and monitored civil society, while the army's brooding guardianship deterred public dissent. The regime spent much of its budget on these coercive organizations, devoting 43 percent of all recurrent expenditures during 1971–89 to army and security payrolls, arms acquisitions, and domestic operations (Central Bank of Jordan 1996).

With no oil and few other exportable resources, the regime required enormous infusions of unrequited foreign capital to sustain this social contract, which swapped economic prosperity for political closure (Khader & Badran 1987; Brand 1994). From 1974 to 1982, Jordan received $11.6 billion in foreign aid and private remittances, most of the former from Gulf allies such as Kuwait, swimming in oil wealth, and most of the latter from the 300,000 expatriates working in these booming economies (World Bank 2006). The oil bust of the mid-1980s, however, dissolved this exogenous revenue flow, leading to years of rising fiscal deficits, structural unemployment, and the exhaustion of the Central Bank's foreign reserves. In early 1989, facing default on its mammoth $8 billion external debt, the regime accepted international financial intervention. To receive an initial $275 million loan package from the International Monetary Fund (IMF) and World Bank, the government was required to lift price subsidies on fuel and other consumer goods. After years of recession, the sudden imposition of fiscal austerity in April sparked mass rioting across the tribal south, and although the army quelled the violence, the royalist elite saw the writing on the wall.

In the ensuing months, King Hussein inaugurated a political liberalization program to both reestablish his ruling legitimacy and soften the bite of structural adjustment (Brynen 1992; Mufti 1999). In November 1989, the monarchy allowed the first national elections for the Majlis al-Nuwaab, the lower house of parliament, in twenty-two years. Candidates from "oppositional" backgrounds—mainly the Jordanian branch of the Muslim Brotherhood but also leftists, Arab nationalists, and independent liberals—obtained more than half of the contested seats despite blatant electoral gerrymandering by the regime that weighted votes more heavily in the conservative tribal districts long regarded as bastions of political loyalty.

The regime's democratic program proceeded apace. In January 1991, Prime Minister Mudar Badran included five Muslim Brotherhood members in a cabinet reshuffle, an unprecedented concession to the Islamist-dominated opposition. In June, a national commission ratified the Mithaq Watani (National Charter), a groundbreaking document that paved the way for the rescinding of martial law in April 1992, the legalization of political parties in September 1992, and the relaxation of press censorship laws in May 1993. An atmosphere of political uncertainty permeated public discourse, as opposition groups emerged from decades of hibernation and new civil society groups pressed for more concessions from the monarchy (Ryan 2002, 15–21). A growing number of Islamists and other activists envisaged an endpoint of constitutional monarchism in which the Hashemite crown would devolve full executive powers to the parliamentary government and assume a symbolic role in the kingdom's political life.

In retrospect, Jordan's political liberalization embodied an institutional response not only to domestic unrest but also to an international environment that could no longer recharge its redistributive capacities. By early 1989, regime elites realized that, unlike previous crises, no foreign patron would provide a quick fix for its woes (Kassay 2002, 51–55). Emergency aid pleas to Saudi Arabia and other Arab allies went unheeded, as these donors struggled with their own economic contractions from the oil bust and the Iran-Iraq War. Also indifferent was Washington, despite its cold war role as Jordan's favored patron. The State Department had long furnished budgetary aid to feed the regime's addiction to public spending. Between 1957 and 1980, it transferred $1.4 billion in economic grant support, equivalent to 14 percent of all the Jordanian government expenditures (USAID 2006). Yet the United States offered just $16 million of aid in 1989. Even worse, the king's refusal to join the U.S.-led coalition against Iraq in late 1990 soured Jordan's relations with the Gulf states and the first Bush administration, with the former retaliating by deporting their several hundred thousand Jordanian expatriates and the latter by cancelling its remaining foreign aid trickle.

As a result, after 1989 the monarchy had scarce breathing room in its decision making. Abandoned by its former patrons and with its rentier lifestyle in tatters, the regime had little choice but to adopt a "survival strategy" of opening up the political arena to greater participation (G. Robinson 1998). Further, no external power rewarded Jordan's budding democratic reforms after the Gulf War, despite its marked contrast to the repression of neighboring Syria, Iraq, and Saudi Arabia. The EU and Washington remained silent, preoccupied with the post-communist transitions unfolding in the former Soviet bloc and devising a comprehensive Arab-Israeli peace process. Of course, the IMF and World Bank did proffer several hundred million dollars in stabilization loans, and the Paris Club of creditors rescheduled over $2.5 billion of Jordan's sovereign debt through 1994. While these measures prevented complete financial collapse, they did not insulate the regime from the existential urgency of systemic reforms, changes that many opposition groups saw as precursors to real democratization.

Economic Decay and Political Retrenchment, 1994–1999

Sensing an opportunity to rebuild ties to the West, King Hussein pursued peace with Israel in the early 1990s, winning accolades from Washington and the EU but raising the ire of the Islamist-dominated parliament. In August 1993, the regime regressed in its democratic commitment by unilaterally amending the electoral law, changing the existing "bloc vote" system to the "one-man, one-vote" model in order to stack the odds against another opposition victory in the upcoming general elections.[8] The manipulation succeeded. In November, tribal and other loyalist candidates trounced the Muslim Brotherhood's Islamic Action Front and other newly minted political parties. Though the newly submissive parliament ratified the October 1994 peace treaty, Islamist leaders spearheaded a resistance movement against normalizing ties with Israel, which included, within the coalition leftist and nationalist parties, student unions, professional associations, and even disenchanted regime veterans (Anderson 1997). The government reacted by clamping down—shutting down public demonstrations, censoring the press, and detaining outspoken activists.

In parallel, the government sternly responded to unrest over deteriorating economic conditions under the structural adjustment program. By 1996, IMF stewardship had restabilized key macroeconomic indicators—the debt-to-GDP ratio dropped to 89 percent, inflation fell to the single digits, and a new general sales tax began raising local revenue (World Bank 2006)—but living standards failed to recover, with the poverty level informally estimated at 25–30 percent. The government continued to follow fiscal austerity and in August 1996 lifted its wheat subsidies, doubling the price of bread. In a small-scale repeat of April 1989, protests spread across the underdeveloped south, where rioters scuffled with police and attacked state offices. Although the army again subdued the strife, the regime framed the incident, unlike the last riots, as a threat to national security rather than a call for political reforms. The king threatened to crush further disorder "with an iron fist" (Andoni & Schwedler 1996).

Such abrasive reactions in the mid-1990s signaled the end of the democratic reform agenda. As the recession worsened, with real per capita incomes declining by 1.5 percent annually in the late 1990s (Siddiqi 2000), the regime continued to ignore grassroots demands to reverse its peace treaty with Israel. Indeed, in the run-up to the November 1997 parliamentary elections, the government imposed new press restrictions that forced the closure of more than a dozen publications, while the *mukhabarat* began to harass civil society groups with threats of suspension and violence. Now on the defensive, the opposition parties boycotted the electoral contest to showcase their dissent against the regime, but the unfazed monarchy refused to delay the vote, resulting in a landslide victory for tribal and other loyalist conservatives.

Divergence between regime elites and popular opinion widened even further over the issue of Iraq in the late 1990s. Despite rife pro-Saddam public sentiment, King Hussein surprisingly turned against his former Arab ally, in part to rebuild relations with the Gulf states and in part to recalibrate Jordanian foreign policy toward Washington (Brand 1999, 63–64). At decade's end, opposition groups languished as a litany of legal restraints and political threats resulted in a more timid press and a loyalist parliament.

Signing the peace treaty with Israel in late 1994 brought immediate material rewards. The Clinton administration wrote off $700 million of Jordan's bilateral debt and increased economic aid from less than $50 million that year to over $220 million in 1999. In 1998, U.S. trade officials also inaugurated the first Qualified Industrial Zones (QIZs), industrial parks from which goods could be exported duty-free to America provided a minimum level of Israeli investment. International financial institutions complied as well—the Paris Club rescheduled more than $1.5 billion of Jordanian debt in 1994 and 1997, while during 1994–98, the IMF and World Bank approved more than $500 million and $200 million, respectively, in new loans.

The United States also bolstered its security ties to the monarchy. After the peace treaty, the Clinton administration delivered light arms, armored vehicles, combat helicopters, and long-coveted F-16 Falcon jets on a grant basis—totaling more than $563 million in military aid during 1994–99, a sum greater than all arms assistance transferred in the preceding decade. U.S. officials later designated Jordan a "major non-NATO ally," a status then accorded to only five other states and which gave its recipients preferential access to future arms grants.

Such patronage nourished the regime's financial health and security apparatus. Paris Club debt relief combined with economic aid (the majority from Washington) averaging nearly $500 million per annum during 1995–99 relieved the balance of payments crunch and alleviated foreign debt burdens. Moreover, the IMF and World Bank treated Jordan with political favoritism, allowing the regime to cheat on its structural adjustment obligations by retaining its chief spending commitments without incurring any penalties on new concessional loans (Harrigan, al-Said, & Wang 2006). For example, in 1999 half the labor force still worked for the public sector, while military and security outlays remained fixed at 33 percent of recurrent spending—figures worthy of technocratic embarrassment in any country after a decade of IMF "adjustment."

For the regime, such measures continued the tried-and-true strategy of redistributing resources to the Palestinian and East Bank tribal communities in return for political acquiescence. Moreover, not only did the regime's coercive agencies continue to operate without sacrificing their operational budgets, but army and air force senior commanders received long-awaited American weaponry to upgrade their aging forces, which had suffered embarrassing equipment shortages since the early 1980s (Bruce 1995). These steps boosted the loyalty of the security sector in the face of multiplying confrontations with angry opposition groups.

As important as the material aid, however, was the diplomatic boost Amman received. By securing Israel's eastern flank through peace, the regime had amplified its geopolitical value in Washington, leading to an implicit guarantee from the mouths of Western diplomats that they would never support a democratic revolution in the Hashemite kingdom. After all, the alternative to the monarchy was an Islamist-led opposition front that threatened to reverse normalization with Israel. Through the late 1990s the United States and its allies thus overlooked the electoral manipulations and civic repression that eviscerated the marginal freedom of democratic activists. Such complicity transformed the logic of political reform for the regime; it signaled the absence of external repercussions for its mounting autocratic backlash. Accordingly, with the cost of domestic repression relatively low, the royalist elite had no incentive to entertain the opposition's dreams for additional political reforms.

Stability Before Democracy: 1999–2006

When Abdullah II ascended to the throne in early 1999 following his father's death, opposition activists hoped that the new, young, cosmopolitan king would revitalize the waning democratic reform agenda. Instead, the regime concentrated on economic modernization, focusing on issues such as foreign investment and technological innovation (Bank & Schlumberger 2004, 40–52). Behind a new generation of technocratic elites, the government trumpeted modest economic successes, such as its accession to the World Trade Organization in January 2000 and the creation of new QIZs. Yet external conflicts soon consumed the regime's attention. The September 2000 outbreak of the Second Intifada in the neighboring West Bank spurred opposition protest rallies against Israel, prompting security forces to launch vigorous crackdowns and a ban on all public demonstrations (Greenwood 2003, 90–92). In August 2001, the regime suspended the upcoming November elections, eventually deciding not to reinstate parliamentary sessions until June 2003. Until then the king ruled by virtual decree through the issuance of "temporary laws," a shrewd tactic that allowed the regime to ignore fiery anti-American public sentiment and to pledge full cooperation with Washington's "war on terrorism" after 9/11. Jordan dispatched peacekeepers to Afghanistan and by early 2003 had allowed the *mukhabarat* to collaborate with the CIA in gathering intelligence on nearby al-Qaeda networks. The country later became a logistical linchpin for the Iraq invasion, providing overflight to American combat jets and hosting thousands of Western military personnel.

At home, the regime subdued passionate opposition resistance to its unpopular alliance with Washington by enacting strict security statutes, codifying barriers against public gatherings, and expanding the scope of press censorship. Further, after the October 2002 assassination of an American diplomat in Amman, public security units launched bloody battles against militants in Ma'an. Terrorist attacks in Aqaba in August 2005 and in Amman later in November precipitated the August 2006 ratification of a draconian antiterrorism law that drastically extended the jurisdiction of the internal security services. Such measures convinced Washington of the regime's resolve to uproot local extremism. But for the Muslim Brotherhood and its civic allies, they encapsulated the state's heightening intolerance with peaceful domestic opposition. In a 2006 poll, 75 percent of all citizens feared criticizing the government in public, a figure that had peaked in 2003 at 83 percent (Center for Strategic Studies 2006). To prove its democratic progress to Western audiences, however, the monarchy began to formulate superficial reform initiatives. An October 2001 cabinet reshuffle abolished the repressive Ministry of Information, but its replacement with a Higher Media Council did nothing to lift existing penal restrictions on press and publications (Economist Intelligence Unit 2001, 16). In

October 2002, the king inaugurated al-Urdun Awalan (Jordan First), a public campaign that called for national unity while propagating several changes, such as a February 2003 amendment that reserved a six-seat quota for women in the lower house of parliament—an autocratic smokescreen that diverted foreign attention away from the Islamists' more basic objections about unfair voting practices and rigged districting laws that allowed tribal and other loyalist candidates to secure a two-thirds majority in the hotly contested June 2003 elections (Ryan & Schwedler 2004, 146–47). In February 2005 the king appointed an elite commission to formulate the National Agenda, which was a far-reaching ten-year plan for economic rejuvenation and political reform, but the November bombings in Amman shelved plans to debate the embryonic framework.

What has sustained King Abdullah's pro-American foreign policy is unprecedented material support from Western patrons. During 1999–2002, Jordan finished its structural adjustment program with another $2 billion of rescheduled debt thanks to the Paris Club and $660 million in IMF and World Bank loans (World Bank 2006). It received more than $730 million in EU grants and loans during 2001–2004 and a staggering $2.5 billion in U.S. economic aid during 2000–2005 (OECD 2006; USAID 2006). In 2003 alone, the Bush administration transferred more than $1 billion in fiscal grants, a budgetary cushion equivalent to 28 percent of the regime's total expenditures that year. Jordan's export sector also enjoyed foreign boosts. As the QIZs successfully attracted foreign investment in October 2000, Jordan became only the fourth country to sign a U.S. Free Trade Agreement. By 2004, the American market accounted for 31 percent of all export earnings. The EU also reinforced trade ties by entering its Association Agreement into force in May 2002 as part of the multilateral Barcelona Process.

On the security front, Washington provided further arms support and force protection. From 2000 through 2006 the Pentagon furnished more than $1.7 billion in military grant assistance, the bulk of which underwrote transfers of heavy weaponry and combat vehicles. In early 2003, it stationed Patriot missile batteries around Amman to improve local air defenses in case of Iraqi attack, and after the invasion it transferred another batch of F-16 fighters to the Royal Jordanian Air Force gratis.

These capital transfers and security guarantees had two effects. First, they toughened the royalist elite's perception that the reversal of political liberalization, so long as they obliged U.S. foreign policy, would engender little criticism in Western capitals. Inside the kingdom, grand talk of the "freedom agenda" after 9/11 resulted in toothless civil society assistance programs, with USAID officials, MEPI officers, and other democracy promotion personnel focusing largely on issues such as educational assistance and women's rights—worthy goals, but a far cry from confronting the backbone institutions of authoritarian control. When a few worried diplomats did raise inquiries on domestic repression and other taboo topics, regime insiders assured them that violent incidents like the November 2005 terrorist bombings would be the potential consequence of allowing Islamic extremism to conquer the Hashemite state. Moreover, seasoned palace veterans knew that the few millions of dollars allocated to Jordan's "democratization" were trivial compared to the vast official aid given to the regime by the State Department and Pentagon. In the context of stabilizing Iraq while protecting Israel, U.S. foreign policy officials realized that the only alternative to the pro-Western King Abdullah was an Islamist-led alternative that, no matter how democratic, would not easily comply with their political wishes (Choucair 2006, 17–20).

Second, anchoring its fiscal and coercive resources to Western largesse enabled the regime to cope with regional instability. The Second Intifada and the Iraq War exposed Jordan's historic vulnerability to external shocks, as colossal collateral damages from these conflicts threatened to rock its fragile economy so soon after its successful "graduation" from IMF structural adjustment. Enhanced quantities of Western aid after 2001, however, protected the balance of payments and enlarged the budgetary resources for economic modernization initiatives, while U.S. and EU free trade arrangements sparked rapid growth in the export sector (Kardoosh 2006, 1–5). All of these foreign additives facilitated a nearly 6 percent annualized GDP growth rate during 2000–2005, an extraordinary figure given the tumult on Jordan's eastern and western flanks (World Bank 2006).

For its part, U.S. security assistance helped preserve the regime's physical capacity to impose domestic calm in the face of passionate opposition hostility toward U.S. cooperation. Generous economic aid transfers helped sustain copious budgetary outlays for the public security and military forces, while the unbroken flow of U.S. arms grants maintained army and air force readiness. Further, high-level interactions with the Pentagon—conducted through formal exchanges with U.S. forces, such as the annual Early Victor joint training exercises—shored up the belief of senior military officials that Washington would remain dutifully hushed as the hunt for "radical" extremists inside the kingdom gutted what little space remained for political activism.

CONCLUSION: DURABLE AUTHORITARIANISM IN THE ARAB WORLD

Jordan presents one context where a retreat to centralized authoritarianism has gone hand-in-hand with a rising pattern of Western support. After the 1989 crisis, external indifference impelled the monarchy to initiate its survival strategy of democratic pluralism. Yet, by tacking the Jordanian flag onto the American mast via the 1994 peace treaty with Israel and, even more firmly, after September 2001 by cooperating with the war on terrorism, the regime extracted political, financial, and military patronage—assistance that played a central role in shaping its increasingly intolerant attitudes toward Islamist-dominated opposition to its foreign policy objectives. After 1994, diplomatic sponsorship from Washington enhanced the ruling confidence of the royalist elite while generous streams of economic and military aid fortified the regime's fiscal health and coercive firepower. A stronger wave of primarily American support after 2001 shielded the regime from the externalities of regional conflict, allowing it to keep its thin democratic veneer while further retarding opposition freedoms. It also curbed the ability of opposition groups to extract policy concessions from the palace through mass rallies, printed criticism, and other acts of public resistance whose earlier fervor had helped spark the initial political liberalization in late 1989. With Jordan now one of Washington's most steadfast regional allies, the prospects of genuine democratization inside the kingdom—which would require the Hashemite monarchy's surrender of its unelected executive power to a parliamentary government determined by competitive and regular elections—remains pure fantasy.

From its perspective, Washington has not merely tolerated but actively encouraged Jordan's steep erosion of civil liberties and political rights since the mid-1990s. Since the institutional uncertainty of democratization would likely bring an Islamist-dominated front to power, U.S. officials regard the stability of the authoritarian monarchy as an irreducible policy interest. Autocratic abuses are "largely overlooked by the caravan of Western leaders who make the pilgrimage to Amman, praise the monarchy for cooperating in the peace process, declare Jordan a modern economic success story, and then move on to those recalcitrants in Cairo" (Glain 2005, 124). Despite American rhetoric about democracy promotion, then, political life inside Jordan after 9/11 was business as usual. The provision of external support to the regime was made implicitly conditional not on concrete benchmarks of democratic progress but on the government's support for U.S. foreign policy, including peace with Israel in 1994 and assistance with the Iraqi invasion after 2003. With international forces tilting the domestic balance of power toward the king and his men, the Islamist-led opposition—manipulated out of parliament, constricted within civil society, and subdued on the streets—stood little chance of reviving the dormant democratic reform agenda.

The theoretical and empirical discussion here provides two lessons for the future study of democracy promotion. First, for the Arab world the relevance of international actors and "great power politics" has not decreased since the end of the cold war. The United States and other Western powers may have failed to advocate democratic transitions outside their hemisphere during the long decades of superpower rivalry, but their overt encouragement of authoritarian rule in the Middle East since the end of the cold war stands in piercing contrast to their more positive attitudes toward democratization articulated elsewhere. For U.S. policymakers, durable despots still represent the surest guarantee for safeguarding long-term geopolitical interests, concerns that dominate all other considerations. For even if dictatorial regimes fail to contain the extremist ideologies that spawned al-Qaeda, they can still be persuaded to make peace with Israel while sustaining petroleum exports.

To be sure, after the supposed paradigmatic shift in U.S. foreign policy in 2001, positive changes did unfold in many Arab countries. Even so, liberalized autocracies change their stripes, not their type. If its hyperbole had ever been taken seriously, then the logical outcome of Arab democracy promotion would have been the institutional transformation of regime *type*, pushing dynastic monarchies and single-party republics into the realm of liberal electoral democracies through turnovers of incumbent leadership. Yet if Jordan is any indicator, the United States has been far more eager to embrace superficial alterations than irrevocable steps toward regime breakdown. For instance, King Abdullah's promulgation of a six-seat quota for women in parliament's lower house in early 2003 was as much celebrated by the State Department as a victory for gender equality in the Middle East as it was despised by seasoned opposition leaders, whose more deep-seated concerns about electoral gerrymandering and police repression went ignored by American diplomats. In essence, Washington's post-9/11 stance merely extended its classic cold war logic of supporting client autocratic regimes while minimizing unpredictable political change, an unspoken dogma that still structures regional policy nearly twenty years after the fall of the Berlin Wall.

Second, the most important variable for future advocates of Arab democratization is not how much *more* the U.S. should give to democracy promotion initiatives but rather how much *less* it must allocate to its traditional policy plank of supporting autocratic clients. As comparative scholars have suggested elsewhere, the durability of authoritarianism in the Arab world has less to do with the "weakness" of opposition forces than with the institutional "strength" of the regime apparatus (Brownlee 2002). Even robust civil societies cannot hope to succeed if they face off against powerful, unified states whose well-protected incumbents have no incentive to commit political suicide by relinquishing power, which is the situation that now characterizes most of the Arab world. As the Jordanian case exemplifies, public mobilization by Islamists and other democratic activists will never compel a crisis-driven regime transition as long as ruling hard-liners possess sufficient political confidence, budgetary health, and coercive forces to crush the most ardent of its opponents and constrict or co-opt the rest. In the MENA experience, a significant determinant of these repressive capacities has been the extent to which external actors, like the United States, have furnished exogenous resources for the sole purpose of bolstering the security of these regimes (Bellin 2004, 148–49). Moreover, as the Jordanian case demonstrates, modest volumes of foreign assistance can exert an enormous impact on the target state.

Why are international forces so critical when considering the future prospects of Arab democratization? The very concept of patron-client relations—defined as mutually beneficial associations between sovereign actors who command unequal wealth and influence but nonetheless engage in reciprocal exchanges of goods and services based on conditional loyalty—is central to the historical development of Arab autocracies. Since the nineteenth century, the Middle East has served as the geopolitical backdrop for great power politics in which generations of would-be hegemons cast their spheres of influence over the region by incorporating local rulers into webs of subordinate strategic relationships (Brown 1984).

External actors were omnipresent in the early formation of most Arab states. For instance, the British installed the Hashemite family as Jordan's monarchy in the early 1920s as a reward for its service in World War I and, until their departure in the 1950s, made little effort to sway the new dynasty toward democracy. Although the United States enjoys influence over much of the region, the diplomatic, economic, and military goods that still connect favored Arab regime incumbents with the foreign policy establishments of Washington and its allies reflect the endurance of patron-client linkages as structural arrangements in the international system, linkages that far predate newer foreign policy fads.

From the perspective of Arab regimes, enlisting the support of foreign actors is particularly important because they rule over what international relations theorists consider "small" states. In small states, domestic weaknesses—e.g., demographic fractures, undersized military, weak resource endowments—make incumbents feel perennially insecure because of threats emanating from foes not only external but also internal (Ayoob 1995). Thus, for Arab authoritarians, foreign policy is not merely an opportunity to project national interests abroad, as it is for large states. Rather, it is the ultimate survival strategy by which they may obtain goods crucial for their survival from constituencies far from their own populations. This, in turn, generates a perverse incentive: political leaders constantly play up local threats of instability in order to preserve their affiliation to external patrons. During the cold war in Jordan, for instance, King Hussein constantly exploited Western fears of Soviet-Communist encroachment in order to needle an unbroken flow of intervention promises, budgetary grants, and combat arms from Washington. The pattern persists today. In the initial post-9/11 years, for example, King Abdullah's regime doggedly warned Washington and the EU that the forces of terrorism were at the doorstep of the Hashemite kingdom and that without substantial international assistance, extremist violence would threaten the stability of not only Jordan but also neighboring Iraq and Israel.

In this climate of durable authoritarianism, paying lip service to political reform while throwing small sums of cash into new democracy promotion schemes only encourages liberalized autocracy at best. At worst, it exposes Western commitments to democratization as vacuous and hypocritical. After all, while the kingdom of Jordan is stable and pro-Western, it is an authoritarian state, not a democracy. If the impetus for change is to come from the international arena, and more specifically from Washington, then U.S. policymakers must transcend their fear of Islamist groups taking political power. They should focus instead on dissolving the international patron-client networks that continue to augment the ruling capacities of local regimes. Western powers might cut off their support linkages to client regimes altogether, forcing incumbents to confront the same unpredictable crises of legitimacy and social upheavals that paved the way for autocratic breakdowns in other regions. More likely, though, senior officials will still surmise that rapid political change would destabilize the Arab world as a whole by threatening the Israeli state, endangering local oil supplies, and generating new strands of terrorism. In addition, authoritarian elites in the region will, as they have for decades, conduct business as usual. If recent history is any indicator, this will be how the project of American democracy promotion in the Arab world ends—not with a bang, but with a whimper.

NOTES

I gratefully acknowledge the generous research support provided by the American Center for Oriental Research, the professional courtesy of overseas State Department personnel, and the personal guidance of Mohammad al-Momany and Marwan Kardoosh in Amman, Jordan. Many thanks as well to Steven Hook and Andrew Barnes, fellow panelists at Kent State University's annual Democracy Symposium, for their advice.

1. Democracy promotion through noncoercive rather than imperial means, as in the example of Iraq, where political change was imposed via foreign military intervention, is a tactic not likely to be replicated on a mass scale.
2. For instance, many analysts carped at the fragmented approach of centerpiece projects such as MEPI, which from its inception suffered from limited funding, thin staffing, and scattershot priorities (Carothers 2005a). Others complained that the United States carried no credibility as a democratizing agent in Arab societies (Khan 2003). Regime elites had no reason to fear external repercussions for their autocratic abuses of previous decades, while public audiences evoked profound suspicions about a superpower advocating democracy overseas while coddling autocratic regimes elsewhere—as in Pakistan and Central Asia—because of their logistical cooperation in the war on terror (Ottaway 2005a). Detractors further attacked the doctrine's structuralist assumption that economic development, driven by free trade and Western capital, might spark private-sector pressures for greater openness. After all, many Arab countries have engaged in market liberalization before but prevented the articulation of political demands by tying the fortunes of the business community to the state apparatus (Cook 2005, 94–95). Finally, critics bemoaned that while highly visible U.S. initiatives asked Arab reformists and grantees to deliver short-term measurable results, meaningful changes would require

long-term commitments to democracy promotion from successive administrations long after the Bush White House (Wittes & Yerkes 2006).
3. After all, mainstream Islamist parties garner far more votes in parliamentary contests than do violent niche groups. Further, substantial research has found that formal political inclusion—as opposed to repressive exclusion—tends to moderate the radical discourse and methods of more extreme Islamist parties by subjecting them to the same centrist pressures placed on all who play by the rules of the electoral game (Hafez 2003; Schwedler 2006).
4. The instructive Algerian example set the tone for current Western attitudes toward Islamist political participation. After the Front Islamique du Salut party swept the first round of Algeria's parliamentary elections in December 1991, the first to allow multiparty competition under the regime's bold program of political liberalization, the military establishment annulled the results, outlawed the Islamist party, and installed a new president. Neither the United States nor its European partners sought to reverse the military's illiberal decision. Such complicity was instrumental in the regime's decision to halt the democratic reform process. The electoral cancellation sparked a decade-long civil war that claimed up to 200,000 lives and derailed its predicted economic development.
5. For instance, most U.S. officials concede the strategic importance of developing alternative energy sources for the national economy. Further, a rising tide of scholars has long argued that sustaining Washington's enormous support for Israel is self-defeating, since it only inflames anti-American and anti-Israeli outrage throughout the Muslim world, delaying resolution of the Palestinian dilemma and providing yet another excuse for Arab regime incumbents to delay promised democratic reforms (Mearsheimer & Walt 2006).
6. Indeed, the lone autocracy whose regime collapsed as a result of U.S. intervention was Iraq, an affirmed enemy of Washington. When the justification of finding weapons of mass destruction evaporated, senior officials reasoned instead that the authoritatrian nature of Saddam Hussein's government warranted unilateral military coercion (i.e., "liberation"). Few policymakers, however, ever explained why other autocratic, repressive states across the region escaped the hand of imperial enlightenment. Hussein may have massacred his countrymen in a manner more brutal than other Arab autocrats, but there was no more "democracy" in Tunisia or Saudi Arabia than in Ba'thist Iraq.
7. In Jordan the central decision-making circle within the regime includes the king, the prime minister, the chief of the Royal Court, the director of the General Intelligence Directorate (or *mukhabarat*), and the ranking commander of the royal military.
8. See Posusney (2005) for more on the political effects of single nontransferable voting (i.e., one-man, one-vote) in Jordan's multimember electoral constituencies.

11
Promoting Democracy by Example

Loch K. Johnson

INTRODUCTION

The democratic peace hypothesis has become central to the study of international affairs. The presumption is that democratic regimes have basic values in common and, as a result, are disinclined to make war against each other. Therefore, a policy of spreading democracy around the world should enhance freedom, human rights, and stability. The empirical evidence for this hypothesis is strong, although not without exceptions. In testing the hypothesis, academic disputes have arisen over the proper definition of democracy. Debate also continues over whether other regime forms might lend themselves to peaceful coexistence with democracies, such as Singapore's model, which emphasizes the rule of law and liberalized trade but with some authoritarian features in its politics (Fukuyama 1992; Zakaria 2004).

Although perhaps best articulated during the Wilson administration, democracy promotion has been a fixture of American foreign policy since the 1800s. Under the George W. Bush administration, that promotion took the form of exporting democracy to Iraq at gunpoint, or what some have referred to as Wilsonianism "on steroids." This chapter accepts democratic peace as a laudable policy objective but rejects the tactics employed by the Bush administration for its advancement. The theme here is that there is a more effective and worthy method for democracy promotion than attempted regime change through military force. In lieu of military intervention (except in the most dire of circumstances, a truly preemptive situation), the United States might set an example for the world through the exercise of a more vibrant democracy at home. The erosion of the rule of law in the United States undermines the potential for the nation to serve as a model democracy.

Studies examining how best to teach children to read uniformly conclude that the most effective method is for children to see their parents reading. Children will witness this activity being enjoyed by their immediate role models and will frequently emulate them. In a similar sense, America's democracy has often served as an example for other nations, since the power of culture and moral suasion combine to make the United States a showcase for those who aspire to modernize and democratize.

"Soft power" is a concept popularized by Joseph S. Nye Jr. In his words, it is the ability to "entice and attract" people abroad toward a favorable opinion of the United States through film, television, music, literature, and popular sports figures (Nye 2002, 9). *Cultural power* may be a more apt term for this phenomenon. Although Nye does not, one may separate out from this cultural mix the appeal of American political ideals—the support for human rights, for instance—and the nation's widely copied constitutional and legal procedures. These features of American society represent the power of moral suasion. Such bedrock political ideals extend far beyond Hollywood to the very core of American ethical beliefs. Supreme Court Justice William O. Douglas spoke movingly about this form of power. America is admired overseas, he observed, not "so much for our B-52 bombers and for our atomic stockpile, but . . . for the First Amendment and the freedom of people to speak and believe and to write, have fair trials." Here, he added, was "the great magnet" that made the United States a respected and worthy world power (Severeid 1980).

Senator Frank Church (D-ID) (1976, 11), who chaired the Senate Foreign Relations Committee in the 1980s, maintained that America's "belief in freedom and popular government once made us a beacon of hope for the downtrodden and oppressed throughout the world." Not everyone abroad, of course, has looked so favorably on the United States. On the contrary, some people—even in Europe, a continent with which this nation has long had close ties—have viewed Americans with ambivalence, antipathy, and even resentment. In some quarters of Europe, this enmity had deep cultural roots, as many Europeans believed that our relatively young nation (although the world's oldest democracy) lacks sophistication in the arts, gravitas in the conduct of diplomacy, and prudence in the use of military force. Despite these concerns, Senator Church was basically correct: public opinion polls during the cold war indicated a generally favorable outlook toward the United States in Europe and in many other parts of the world.

Yet these friendship ties—in Europe a product of America's assistance in liberating the continent from Hitler's grip and of the economic recovery helped immeasurably by the Marshall Plan—dramatically unraveled after September 11, 2001. After the terrorist attacks, Europeans and many others around the world expressed deep sympathy for America's losses. The French newspaper *Le Monde*, which often relishes poking the United States in the eye, famously declared, "We Are All Americans" (Columbani 2001, 15). In Iran, where Americans are regularly derided as Satan personified, tens of thousands rallied spontaneously in the streets of Teheran to demonstrate their solidarity with the people of the United States (Clarke 2004, 285). Indeed, every Islamic nation in the world condemned the attacks.

Support for the United States soon turned to disillusionment, however—even marked hostility. As British historian Sir Michael Howard (2002, 1) noted, "A year after September 11, the United States finds itself more unpopular than perhaps it has ever been in its history." In France a foreign policy expert concluded in October 2002 that "no president since Nixon, and perhaps not even then, has been so unpopular here" as incumbent president George W. Bush (Cohen, Sanger, & Weisman 2004). Hostility toward the Bush administration was hardly isolated to France. Anti-Americanism is pervasive throughout Europe even after the Bush administration's departure. "Animosity toward the United States has migrated from the periphery and become a respectable part of the European mainstream," writes Andrei S. Markovits (2007).

The hostility runs deeper still in the Islamic world. Pollster Daniel Yankelovich reported that in 2004 only 12 percent of Muslims believed Americans respected Islamic values, only 7 percent thought the West understood Muslim culture, and only 11 percent approved of President Bush. Just 13 percent of Egyptians, 6 percent of Jordanians, and 3 percent of Saudi Arabians held a favorable opinion of the United States. In Indonesia an astonishing 74 percent of the public feared a U.S. military attack against them, as did 72 percent in Nigeria, 72 percent in Pakistan, and 71 percent in Turkey. By 2004, a majority of people living in Germany, France, Italy, Greece, the Netherlands, and Pakistan also expressed to pollsters an unfavorable view of the United States (Schorr 2004; Holstein 2005).

Even a majority of the citizens of Great Britain, the main partner of the United States in the war against Iraq initiated in 2003, expressed a belief that typically Americans act solely out of their own interest, without regard for the interests of allies (73 percent) and were a threat to world peace (55 percent). Moreover, even allies such as Australia, whose citizens have had a long-standing positive view of Americans, indicated in 2005 that they had a more favorable opinion of China, France, the United Nations, and seven other countries, regions, or groups than they did of the United States. Indeed, the poll results divided evenly on the question of whether the greatest danger to the world comes from Islamic fundamentalism or American foreign policy (Bonner 2005).

In the aftermath of the terrorist attacks of 2001, why did support for the United States in its time of tragedy rapidly dissolve into widespread expressions of antipathy toward Americans, even among our closest allies? What motivated those who now went out of their way to pillory the United States, almost as if Americans had perpetrated the violence on September 11 rather than been its victims? Why did the world suddenly seem to hate Americans even as they mourned the loss of lives from the cruel kamikaze dive-bombings of the hijacked airplanes?

No doubt the United States has attracted enmity from other countries simply by virtue of envy and resentment over its great wealth and military might—alienation generated by America's power, not just its policies. In addition, basic flaws in the conduct of U.S. foreign policy over the years have led to warranted criticism (see Johnson 2007). The growing antipathy toward the United States in recent years has arisen chiefly as a result of five major grievances: Guantanamo Bay, Abu Ghraib, secret prisons abroad run by the Central Intelligence Agency, extraordinary renditions, and the war in Iraq.

In 2003, at an international conference in Oslo, Eastern European parliamentarians, scholars, and journalists posed troubling questions to me about possible human rights violations of prisoners held by the United States at its Guantanamo Bay naval base in Cuba (Oslo Conference 2003). Captured by American forces during the U.S.-led war in Afghanistan against the al-Qaeda terrorist organization responsible for the 9/11 attacks and their hosts, the Taliban regime, the Guantanamo prisoners were being held indefinitely, without formal charges brought against them or legal counsel. In 2004, the release of photographs by a Pentagon whistle-blower depicting the torture of prisoners by U.S. military intelligence officers at the Abu Ghraib prison in Iraq further inflamed worldwide criticism of the United States. "The photographs shattered our reputation as the world's most admired champion of freedom and justice," concluded Philip Gordon. "That is grave, because without the world's trust, America cannot flourish" (quoted in Cohen, Sanger, & Weisman 2004).

This trust was further eroded by the revelation that the CIA had set up secret prisons overseas to hold suspected terrorists. Moreover, the CIA snatched some suspected terrorists from the streets of European cities and flew them to countries where they were tortured, a practice known as extraordinary rendition. Finally, as the war in Iraq dragged on, people inside and outside the United States increasingly questioned its rationale, since weapons of mass destruction (WMDs), the original casus belli, were not found.

These grievances, though, were only the tip of the iceberg. The United States had allowed its democratic procedures to erode across a much broader front. Consequently, America gave the impression abroad that its devotion to the principles of its own Constitution was weak, not to be relied on, and unworthy of continuing emulation. We had lost our way and therefore why should we be followed by those who had once had confidence in our leadership? The reason for America's disorientation? The answer was fear.

The United States has lost its way in the past as well, from time to time staining its reputation as a champion of democracy and human rights. Early in the nation's history, fear of Native Americans led to their shameful treatment at the hands of federal authorities. Other dark episodes occurred when fear of freedom for blacks produced lynchings and other atrocities; when fear of the Japanese resulted in the corralling of innocent Japanese Americans into guarded camps during the Second World War; and when fear of global communism permitted the excesses of McCarthyism during the cold war. Today the fear of terrorism has had a similarly corrosive effect on American democracy.

The Cold War's Shadow

Civil liberties become malleable in the crucible of fear. This phenomenon is well illustrated by the misuses of the CIA and America's other intelligence agencies during the cold war. In 1975, a Senate investigative panel chaired by Senator Frank Church uncovered a series of shocking improprieties by the nation's secret agencies—all in the name of fighting communism. Among the committee's findings (Church Committee 1976; Johnson 1986; Johnson 2004; Schwarz 2007; Schwarz & Huq 2007) were:

- a CIA program, code-named Operation CHAOS, opened mail to or from selected U.S. citizens and generated 1.5 million names stored in the CIA's computer bank;
- the Federal Bureau of Investigation (FBI) created files on more than 1 million Americans and carried out more than 500,000 investigations of subversives from 1960 to 1974 without a single court conviction;
- the National Security Agency (NSA) monitored every cable sent overseas, or received from overseas, by Americans from 1947 to 1975;
- the Internal Revenue Service (IRS) permitted tax information to be misused by intelligence agencies for political purposes;
- army intelligence units opened investigations against 100,000 U.S. citizens during the Vietnam War era;
- the CIA infiltrated religious, media, and academic organizations;
- the CIA engaged in drug experiments against unsuspecting subjects;
- an FBI counterintelligence program known as COINTELPRO authorized Bureau agents to incite violence among African Americans and attempted to blackmail civil rights leader Martin Luther King Jr., encouraging him to commit suicide; and,
- in this same program the FBI also harassed civil rights activists and Vietnam war dissidents.

Especially troubling among the Church Committee findings were the FBI's COINTELPRO activities. With its spying at home, the CIA violated American laws and values, but COINTELPRO went beyond domestic spying. From 1956 to 1971, the FBI carried out smear campaigns against individuals and groups across the United States simply because they had criticized the slow pace of the civil rights movement, expressed opposition to the war in Vietnam, or belonged to some organization that the Bureau found "un-American." The FBI directed these attacks against people in all walks of life and of various political persuasions. The expansive hatred of the FBI's leaders, notably its director, J. Edgar Hoover, embraced black leaders and white supremacists alike, with opponents of the war in Vietnam thrown in for good measure. As a member of the Church Committee concluded, "no meeting was too small, no group too insignificant" to escape the FBI's attention (author interview with Walter F. Mondale, Minneapolis, February 17, 2000).

Among the thousands of COINTELPRO victims was Dr. Anatol Rapoport, a gifted social scientist at the University of Michigan. He attracted the Bureau's attention because of his criticism of the war in Vietnam and his "suspicious" origins. (He was born in Russia shortly before his parents emigrated to the United States early in the twentieth century.) The FBI's agent in charge for the Ann Arbor area, responding to top-secret directives from FBI headquarters in Washington, D.C., set out to "neutralize"—a term used by the FBI to mean the harassment of an individual as a means of curbing his or her dissent—Professor Rapoport. The Bureau mailed anonymous letters to senior administrators at the university as well as to prominent citizens in Ann Arbor and throughout Michigan, claiming, without evidence, that Rapoport was, if not a Communist, at least an apologist for communism and a troublemaker. The letters were typically signed "a concerned citizen" or "a concerned taxpayer."

The FBI also placed informants in Rapoport's classrooms to report on his "subversive" activities. He was to be embarrassed, discredited, and spied on, in whatever imaginative ways the FBI's special agent could devise. These pressures, whose underlying source Rapoport never knew, eventually led him to resign from the University of Michigan and accept a faculty post at the University of Toronto. The FBI had won. Although he remained a critic of the war in Vietnam, COINTELPRO had damaged Rapoport's career, drained him emotionally, strained his family and professional ties, and driven him from this country (author interview with Anatole Rapoport, Toronto, September 21, 1975).

White supremacists also failed to fit into Hoover's Procrustean bed of conformity. The FBI sent another of its poisonous letters, this time written in southern slang, to a wife of a Ku Klux Klan member, intimating that her husband was having an affair with another woman. The Klan, the women's liberation movement, socialists, the New Left, antiwar and civil rights activists—all became enemies of the Republic whom the Bureau set out secretly to destroy. In the Twin Cities, an FBI agent provocateur encouraged striking taxi drivers to construct a bomb for use in their battle against local teamsters. And in California a Bureau office boasted in a memorandum back to headquarters: "Shootings, beatings, and a high degree of unrest continues to prevail in the ghetto area of southeast San Diego. Although no specific counterintelligence action can be credited with contributing to this overall situation, it is felt that a substantial amount of the unrest is directly attributable to this program" (Church Committee 1976, 2:218).

A member of the Church Committee, Philip Hart (D-MI), recalled in 1975 that he had been skeptical when his own family of political activists had complained about how the FBI was trying to discredit opposition to the war in Vietnam. With his words cracking in emotion, Hart conceded in a dramatic public hearing that they had been right all along. He had been wrong to defend the Bureau. Not a soul stirred in the cavernous and crowded Senate Caucus Room as he continued: "As a result of my superior wisdom in high office, I assured them they are on pot—it just wasn't true. [The FBI] wouldn't do it. What [the FBI witnesses] have described is a series of illegal actions intended to deny certain citizens their first amendment rights, just like my children said" (Church Committee Hearings 1975, 6:41).

The most appalling document uncovered by the Church Committee was an anonymous letter written by the Bureau's special agent in Tampa. It was accompanied by a tape recording. As Dr. Martin Luther King Jr. had traveled around the country pursuing his civil rights activities, FBI agents had followed him and placed listening devices in his hotel rooms, recording compromising romantic liaisons. The bureau then mailed the letter and tape to Dr. King in 1964, thirty-four days before he was to receive the Nobel Prize for peace. In a ploy interpreted by Senate investigators as an attempt by the FBI to push King into taking his own life, the letter read: "King, there is only one thing left for you to do. You know what it is. You have just 34 days in which to do it. (The exact number has been selected for a specific reason.) It has a definite political significance. You are done. There is but one way out for you. You better take it before your filthy, abnormal fraudulent self is bared to the nation" (Church Committee 1976, 2:11, 220–21). A month later the Bureau sent a copy of the tape recordings to Mrs. King, who joined her husband in denouncing the blackmail attempt.

The goal of undermining the civil rights movement stood at the heart of COINTELPRO. The efforts to ruin Reverend King were relentless. All the elements of the bureau's dark side came together as it directed its full surveillance powers against him. In tandem with the blackmail attempt, the bureau initiated whispering campaigns to undermine the moral authority of the civil rights leader and sent anonymous letters to newspapers that questioned his patriotism. The purpose, according to an FBI document, was to knock King "off his pedestal" (Church Committee 1976, 2:11). Like Professor Rapoport, he would be neutralized. Hoover pressured his subordinates to either rewrite their field reports on King, falsely labeling him the pawn of a Soviet agent, or else lose their jobs.

How could the U.S. intelligence agencies stray so far from their rightful duties? Their actions stemmed in large part from the fear and paranoia engendered by the cold war—even though (as acknowledged by William Sullivan, the top FBI agent in charge of COINTELPRO) there were not enough Communists in the United States to carry the smallest precinct in New Hampshire. Sullivan told the Church Committee that the secret agencies had been caught up in an anti-Communist tide that swept aside safeguards against the misuse of power. As he recalled, during the COINTELPRO operations aimed at Reverend King: "No holds were barred. We have used [similar] techniques against Soviet agents. [The same methods were] brought home against any organization against which we were targeted. We did not differentiate." He added that never once had he heard a discussion about the legality or constitutionality of any aspect of the FBI's internal security program. His explanation: "We were just naturally pragmatic" (Church Committee 1976, 2:14, 141).

During the cold war, criticism of the intelligence agencies was widely considered unpatriotic. They had to be given broad discretionary powers if they were to be successful in defeating America's adversaries at home and abroad. Consequently, the secret agencies took on the features of a political police, growing increasingly autonomous, insulated, and aggressive. As William W. Keller (1989, 154) has observed, they became "a state within the state, which would not be bound by the constraints of the constitutional order."

The Church Committee came to the conclusion that during the cold war the overwhelming majority of the men and women in the nation's intelligence agencies had carried out their assignments with devotion to the law and constitutional principles. Some had given their lives in the defense of liberty. America owed its freedom in part to their dedication in the struggle against foreign adversaries. Yet in such instances as CHAOS, SHAMROCK, and the Iran-Contra scandal, the intelligence agencies bore responsibility for undermining the nation's democratic principles by overstepping the boundaries of law and propriety. Driven by the fear of cold war threats, they put the Constitution on hold.

Revived Fears in the War on Terror

This historical record from the cold war era is worth consideration today, for it reminds us of the dangers that may arise when a nation is possessed by fear. In the contemporary world, the fear of terrorism has led some of America's leaders once again to throw aside the nation's constitutional safeguards and misuse the intelligence agencies. The price we have paid is the further erosion of civil liberties at home and the loss of respectability abroad. The American model of democracy no longer shines as brightly as it should.

The list of recent abuses is now well-known to the American public and to the world (Johnson 2007; "The Must-Do List" 2007; Risen 2006; Schwarz & Huq 2007). In addition to the excesses noted earlier, others include:

- the elimination of habeas corpus and legal counsel for suspected terrorists, many of whom were unjustly accused, incarcerated, and mistreated;
- the establishment of CIA secret prisons overseas, where the treatment of "ghost prisoners" could not be scrutinized;
- burgeoning classification rules that threw a wider blanket of secrecy over government activities in the security domain;
- executive branch stonewalling and slow-rolling of legislative efforts at accountability, unmatched in scope since the Watergate era (Johnson 2006b);
- retaliation against intelligence agencies for raising doubts about the administration's use of intelligence, as when the Office of the Vice President attacked the CIA for rejecting the assertion that Iraq had purchased yellow cake uranium from Niger; and
- the use of wiretapping by the NSA, in violation of the 1978 Foreign Intelligence Surveillance Act (FISA), which required warrants for electronic surveillance of perceived security threats in the United States.

The question of wiretap violations warrants closer examination as an example of how the United States is now repeating the abuses of power that plagued it during the cold war. The Bush administration became embroiled in controversy over whether its program of spying by the NSA—a highly classified operation leaked to the public in December 2004—was necessary and lawful in the struggle against global terrorism (Risen & Lichtblau, 2005). The cause of the furor was over the president's authorization of a secret executive order that granted the NSA permission to eavesdrop on Americans without first acquiring a warrant (Johnson 2006a). Critics rightly maintained that the order violated the intent of FISA.

The FISA statute (Public Law 95–511; 92 Stat. 1783 [Oct. 25, 1978]) evolved from the findings of the Church Committee, which revealed that the NSA had taken part in the widespread assaults on freedom and privacy at home. Indeed, Operation SHAMROCK monitored every cable sent overseas or received by Americans from 1947 to 1975, and Operation MINARET swept in the telephone conversations of an additional 1,680 citizens. Illustrative of the messages intercepted by the NSA was a request for a financial contribution scribed by a peaceful antiwar activist to a foreign singer. The effect of such spying, as Senator Mondale noted in public hearings at the time, was to "discourage political dissent in this country" (Church Committee 1976, 2:179). None of these NSA wiretaps underwent judicial review.

In light of these abuses, Congress worked with Presidents Ford and Carter to craft reforms that would protect the civil liberties of Americans against improper uses of the intelligence agencies. The FISA law took aim directly at the problem of warrantless wiretaps by the NSA. No longer could presidents or their aides decide by themselves who in this nation would be subjected to electronic surveillance—a power previously abused by Presidents Johnson and Nixon. Henceforth, an impartial court comprised of experienced judges would decide on the merits of an administration's request for a national security wiretap.

The FISA court has worked well over the years, although some critics have assailed it for too easily approving warrant requests—indeed, all but five of more than 40,000 requests since its inception. But the court is not just a rubber stamp. Administrations have been careful to seek warrants only when the case is strong. If the requests of the Bush administration for wiretaps were as urgent as the president asserted, the court would no doubt have granted approval.

The Bush administration drew on three major arguments to defend bypassing the FISA procedures. First, Justice Department attorneys maintained that the president had an inherent constitutional power to wiretap under the commander in chief authority (Art. II. Sec. 2). Yet, many legal scholars have called into question that argument and often referenced Justice Jackson's famous opinion that a president's power is "at its lowest ebb" when in conflict with the "expressed or implied will of Congress" (see *Youngstown Sheet & Tube Co. v. Sawyer*, 343 U.S. 579, 583 [1952]). The FISA law was an express and specific effort by lawmakers to curtail warrantless wiretaps.

Second, the administration claimed that in the wake of the 9/11 attacks, Congress provided the president with "authorization for use of military force"—a kind of "Gulf of Tonkin Resolution" blank check in the war against global terrorism. That authorization, though, said nothing about electronic surveillance against American citizens. Rather, it gave the president authority to carry out a military campaign against al-Qaeda terrorists in Afghanistan and against their host, the Taliban regime.

Finally, the administration argued that the warrant procedures in the 1978 law were slow and cumbersome as well as outdated in light of new technology; in the struggle against terrorism, the United States must be nimble and fast moving. The FISA law, however, is agile. Warrants may be obtained in hours, or even minutes. Moreover, in times of crisis, the executive branch is permitted leeway to conduct wiretaps immediately for as long as seventy-two hours, applying for a warrant at the end of that period. If the law needs updating, the proper remedy is to hold hearings (in closed session, if necessary) and then amend it, rather than to undermine the rule of law through a secret executive order to waive the FISA statute.[1]

The United States must defeat al-Qaeda and its affiliated terrorist organizations, but at the same time it must maintain civil liberties. Excessive executive branch discretion is a slippery slope, as revealed by the Church Committee investigators in the 1970s. They found that America's secret agencies began by focusing on legitimate national security threats, only to be drawn into political surveillance. Tom Charles Huston (Church Committee 1975, 2:121), the architect of a chilling domestic spy plan promulgated by the Nixon administration to monitor anti–Vietnam War activists, conceded to the Church Committee: "The risk was that you would get people who would be susceptible to political considerations as opposed to national security considerations, or would construe political consideration[s] to be national security considerations—to move from the kid with a bomb to the kid with a picket sign, and from the kid with the picket sign to the kid with the bumper sticker of the opposing candidate. And you just keep going down the line."

What does all of this constitutional and legal trouble at home have to do with democratic peace? The answer may be best posed in the form of another question: How may the United States expect other nations to embrace democratic principles and processes when it fails to live up to those standards itself? As Louise Richardson (2006, 10) has noted, "We are only likely to be successful in the effort [against terrorists] if we can demonstrate that our commitment to liberal ideals and the rule of law is consistently applied and that we hold ourselves and our allies to the same standards as we hold others." The first step in advancing democracy around the world is to put one's own house in order. America's principles are sound, but they must be practiced in order to avoid the corrosive influences of fear. Vital to this goal is the improvement of legislative accountability, especially with respect to the supervision of the nation's intelligence agencies.

STRENGTHENING INTELLIGENCE ACCOUNTABILITY

The public relies on Congress to provide a check on the abuse of power by the executive branch, the sine qua non of America's form of government. Yet intelligence accountability on Capitol Hill—the monitoring by lawmakers of America's secret activities—has been desultory for the most part. The exception is when crises occur. Then members of Congress have performed well, conducting major investigations into intelligence scandals or failures. In between crises, however, lawmakers have performed day-to-day supervisory duties in a manner that falls significantly short of the level of accountability espoused by legislative reformers in 1975, when they uncovered illegal domestic spying.

Eighty-nine lawmakers have served on the Senate Select Committee on Intelligence (SSCI) since it was created in 1976, and 102 lawmakers on its counterpart, the House Permanent Select Committee on Intelligence (HPSCI), created in 1977. Among these individuals, the committee chairs (a total of eleven on the SSCI and ten on the HPSCI) have been particularly influential in determining the vigor of committee oversight. From time to time, though, the ranking minority member, or even a junior member—Democrat or Republican—on one of the oversight committees has made a mark. During the early days of the HPSCI, for example, minority member J. Kenneth Robinson (R-VA) spent more time than any of his colleagues poring over intelligence budget proposals late into the afternoon; as a result, he excelled in closed hearings on funding. He would point to sections in authorization bills that had weak justifications and wielded a scalpel as he proceeded through the mark-ups.[2]

Lawmakers have displayed four general approaches to their supervisory tasks while serving on the intelligence oversight committees and have sometimes oscillated from one approach to another depending on various influences. Stated another way, the four categories are dynamic "centers of gravity," not high-fenced corrals.

The first type of intelligence overseer is the "ostrich," a label for those lawmakers embracing a philosophy of benign neglect toward the intelligence agencies—an approach that characterized almost all members of Congress before the domestic spy scandal of 1975. A classic illustration is Senator Barry Goldwater (R-AZ) when he rose to the chairmanship of the SSCI in 1981. He had also served as a member of the Church Committee. Ironically, in light of his subsequent rise to the position of chair, Goldwater voted against the creation of the SSCI in the first place in 1976. He also opposed most of the other reforms recommended by the Church Committee. Goldwater was content with the system of oversight that existed before 1975—that is, occasional review by a few subcommittees on intelligence housed within the Armed Services and the Appropriations committees in both chambers. These panels were passive for the most part, engaging more in overlook than oversight. They did nothing to halt the rampant domestic spying, the plots carried out by the CIA to assassinate selected foreign heads of state, or the many other horrors uncovered by the Church Committee.

The second type of intelligence overseer is the "cheerleader." Here is the member of Congress who has removed his or her head from the sand only to cheer more loudly for the intelligence agencies. The cheerleader is interested primarily in the advocacy of spies and their activities, the support of intelligence budgets (and the quick granting of supplements when needed), and the advancement of clandestine operations at home and abroad against those who seek to harm the United States. During hearings, the cheerleader specializes in "softball" pitches—easy questions designed to be hit over the center field fence by witnesses from the CIA and the other intelligence agencies. In press conferences, the cheerleader acts as a defense attorney for spies, hinting at their behind-the-scenes, still-secret, "if you only knew" successes; lauding the heroism of intelligence officers and agents in the field, often under conditions of great danger and hardship; castigating journalists for printing leaked secrets that imperil the nation; and warning of threats at home and abroad that may lead to another 9/11 or worse if the intelligence agencies are shackled in any way. Such statements by cheerleaders are often true. Most intelligence officers have served with distinction and sometimes in perilous circumstances; some have given their lives in service to their country. It is the one-sidedness, however, that characterizes the cheerleader type—the absence of a critical eye.

An illustration of the cheerleader is Representative Edward P. Boland (D-MA) when he became the first chair of the HPSCI in 1977. Boland had witnessed firsthand how in 1975 a House investigative committee (led by Otis Pike, D-NY) had prepared a shrill final report widely discredited for its ideological anti-CIA biases. Appalled by its experience with the Pike Committee, the House refused to create an intelligence oversight committee in 1976, when the Senate established the SSCI. It took another year of debate and some cooling down before members of the House voted to establish their own intelligence committee, the HPSCI. As a means of restoring the House to a more balanced perspective on the value of intelligence, Boland bent over backwards from 1977 to 1982 to cooperate with intelligence officials. He often swallowed his own personal skepticism about some covert operations and expressed his full support for the government's secret bureaucracy just to show that the HSPCI could be a partner in the world of espionage, not a reckless reincarnation of the Pike Committee.

A third role type is the "skeptic." This approach is similarly one-sided, only at the opposite extreme from that of the cheerleader. From the skeptic's point of view, nothing the intelligence agencies undertake is likely to be worthy. From this perspective, the secret agencies are inherently immoral, engaged in opening and reading other people's mail, eavesdropping on telephone calls, stealing documents, maybe even assassinating people—unsavory activities one and all. The secret agencies are also incompetent, continues this argument, with the CIA proving unable to dispatch any foreign leader on its hit list, despite its many attempts, or to anticipate the fall of the Soviet Union, the 9/11 attacks, or the absence of WMDs in Iraq.

For the most extreme skeptic, there is but one solution: shut down the secret agencies altogether. In 1996, for example, Senator Daniel Patrick Moynihan (D-NY), a member of the SSCI who was dismayed by the CIA's inability to anticipate the collapse of the Soviet empire, called for the agency's abolition. Representative Robert Torricelli (D-NJ) became such a zealous skeptic of the CIA in 1995 that he did what no other intelligence overseer has ever done: as a member of the HPSCI, he disclosed classified information in a press conference (regarding the CIA's employment of a notably disreputable army colonel in Guatemala). This behavior was a serious breach of the committee's rules, for which Torricelli was swiftly chastised by his colleagues.

The fourth type of overseer is the "guardian." This model conforms best with the hopes of reformers. For instance, in 1975 Church and others favored ongoing congressional action to review the nation's secret operations in order to prevent spy scandals and intelligence failures. Representative Lee H. Hamilton (D-IN), HPSCI chair from 1985 to 1987, argued that the ideal intelligence overseers were members of Congress who were both "partners and critics" of the secret agencies.

Since the American people know little about the activities of the secret side of government, lawmakers have an obligation, within the constraints of protecting sensitive information, to inform the public about the value of these agencies and their programs. The intelligence community spends some $44 billion a year, and those in charge of the purse strings on Capitol Hill must explain this use of the taxpayer's money. Further, when secret agencies legitimately need a friend in court—for instance, when critics charge unreasonably that the CIA should have anticipated some surprise calamity—lawmakers are in a position to provide a defense.

The job description for an effective overseer, though, includes more than just educating the American people on the virtues of having an intelligence capability or coming to the defense of secret agencies when they are maligned. A good overseer must also search for and acknowledge program flaws and seek their correction. This role requires the ability, above all, to be objective. Hamilton has come as close to this ideal as any member of the SSCI or HPSCI. When he was head of the HPSCI, he regularly convened committee meetings, paid close attention to reports from his staff and the intelligence agencies, followed up on media reports alleging intelligence wrongdoing or mistakes, and spent a reasonable amount of time in budget reviews and conversations with intelligence professionals.

Even Hamilton faltered badly, though, during the Iran-Contra scandal. He took at face value the assurance of staffers on the NSC that they were not involved in illegal operations—always a mistake for overseers, who need to cut the cards even when playing poker with their grandmothers. When a Middle East newspaper subsequently revealed the scandal, it was clear that the NSC staff (NSA adviser Robert C. McFarlane and his deputy, Lt. Col. Oliver L. North) had lied to the HPSCI chair about their involvement in Iran-Contra in a face-to-face meeting at the White House.

Members of the SSCI and HPSCI have sometimes exhibited more than one approach to supervision during their tenure on the intelligence committees. Furthermore, even those lawmakers who may generally cluster together in just one of the four centers of gravity may often be some distance apart within a center. For example, some cheerleaders may be mild in their advocacy while others may be zealous. The same logic applies to the skeptics. Or in the case of the ostriches, some may pull their heads out of the sand at least once in a while. As for guardians, some may be better than others at maintaining an even keel between offering praise and finding fault.

Here are some illustrations of these variations. Representative Boland may have felt it necessary to be a strong partner of the intelligence agencies from 1977 to 1982 to offset the bad impression left by the Pike Committee and its savage criticism of the CIA. As the 1980s marched on, however, Boland began to drift away from the posture of cheerleading to assume a more balanced stance as guardian. By 1983, Boland had become increasingly skeptical of William J. Casey, the director of central intelligence (DCI) at the time, and his use of covert action to advance the Contras against the Sandinista Marxist regime in Nicaragua. Boland had reached the conclusion, along with a majority in the Democrat-controlled Congress, that mining Nicaraguan harbors and blowing up power lines, along with other extreme paramilitary operations, were excessive responses to the minimal threat to the United States posed by the Sandinistas. From 1982 to 1985, Boland introduced and guided to passage seven successive amendments bearing his name, each more restrictive with respect to the use of covert action in Nicaragua, until finally the CIA was prohibited from conducting most forms of covert action against the Sandinistas.[3]

By the time his HPSCI tenure came to an end in 1985, Boland's relations with Casey had become highly distrustful, as the chairman had metamorphosed from cheerleader through a stage as guardian and into the role of full-fledged skeptic. In this sense, every member of the SSCI and HPSCI leaves a unique accountability "footprint" for his or her tenure as an overseer. In Boland's case, the stimuli for these changes were twofold: first, the overwrought response of the Reagan administration to events in Central America; and, second, a new, aggressive, and arrogant DCI, William Casey, who did nothing to hide his disdain toward the HPSCI and SSCI. Policy (Nicaragua) and personality (Casey) dramatically transformed Chairman Boland's approach to intelligence oversight from cheerleader to skeptic.

Senator Goldwater went on a similar, though even more extensive, odyssey within the Senate Select Committee on Intelligence. With his head in the sand during the first few years (1981–84) of his SSCI chairmanship, Goldwater initially played the role of ostrich and deferred to Casey and the intelligence agencies at every opportunity, in the style of pre-1975 lawmakers of both parties. The intelligence bureaucrats should be trusted to do a good job under trying circumstances, reasoned Goldwater, just as, during the debate on the War Powers Resolution and efforts by Congress to restore its war powers in 1973, he had opposed the resolution and argued on the floor of the Senate that the president knew best when it came to matters of war making. When Boland began to introduce his restrictive amendments against covert action in Nicaragua, Goldwater claimed that the laws proposed by the HPSCI chair were unconstitutional. Like Vice President Richard Cheney of the Bush administration, in the 1970s and 1980s Goldwater was a leading proponent of the so-called unitary theory of presidential supremacy.

Then the irascible William Casey managed to do the seemingly impossible: he single-handedly yanked Goldwater's head out of the ground and turned the intelligence community's most reliable ostrich into one of its most vocal skeptics. The stimulus for this dramatic transformation was Casey's practice of prevarication, delivering misleading testimony during an appearance before Goldwater's committee. When asked by an SSCI member whether the CIA was mining harbors in Nicaragua, the DCI said no. Only later did it become evident that Casey was relying on a sleight-of-hand technical point: the CIA was not mining harbors, it was mining *piers* within certain harbors. This attempt to fool the SSCI angered Goldwater, as institutional pride trumped feelings of deference toward the intelligence community. He fired off a letter to one of the best venues for venting in the nation's capital, the *Washington Post*. The letter, castigating Casey for his attempts at legerdemain on Capitol Hill, said in part, "It gets down to one, little, simple phrase: I am pissed off!" (Goldwater 1984).

As Goldwater's ire cooled down over Casey's scorn toward the SSCI's hearings on Nicaragua, the chairman drifted into a cheerleading role that better suited his long-standing deference to the executive branch in the conduct of foreign policy. For the reminder of his tenure, through 1985 (the same year Boland left the HPSCI), the arch-conservative Arizonan maintained a unique style of oversight that fluctuated between cheerleader and a more balanced guardianship of the intelligence agencies. Never again on the SSCI, though, unlike before his falling out with Casey, did Barry Goldwater find it prudent to have his head in the sand.

Two more examples of the dynamic nature of oversight roles come from more recent times, just prior to and just after the 9/11 attacks. Before 9/11, Richard C. Shelby (R-AL) led the SSCI (1997–2001). At first he oscillated between the roles of ostrich and cheerleader, apparently seeing in the intelligence community a flawless, creamy complexion—like Alabama, free of whiskers and warts. This rosy outlook would soon change. On April 26, 1999, DCI George J. Tenet (1997–2004) failed to invite the SSCI chairman to the christening of the new George H. W. Bush Center for Intelligence (named after the only DCI to become president). This and other snubs by the DCI, perceived or real, upset Shelby, and he grew more critical of Tenet and the intelligence agencies during the rest of his chairmanship and while remaining on the SSCI for three additional years. Once again, personal affronts had transformed a cheerleader into a skeptic.

The next SSCI chairman (2001–2), Bob Graham (D-FL), likewise moved from cheerleader on the Senate committee to a skeptic as a result of slights from DCI Tenet. In this instance, the pique stemmed from procedural slaps in the face rather than personal affronts. In 2002, Graham became cochair of a special joint committee that temporarily combined the membership of the SSCI and HPSCI to investigate the 9/11 intelligence failure; the other cochair was HPSCI leader (1997–2004) Porter J. Goss (R-FL). Once hearings opened on the events of that tragic day, Graham and Tenet began to butt heads over the committee's authorities and procedures. When Graham asked Tenet to be brief in his introductory remarks before the panel, the DCI instead delivered a lengthy defense of his rule. Tenet also refused to declassify some intelligence documents that Graham thought important for the public record. Moreover, the DCI frequently caused havoc in the proceedings by denying the SSCI access to basic intelligence documents related to the 9/11 attacks, refusing at the last minute to allow scheduled intelligence officers to testify before the committee, and at the eleventh hour even cancelling his own appearance in executive (closed) session.

As the DCI stonewalled and slow-rolled the joint committee, Graham began his transition from cheerleader to skeptic. Tenet had poked Graham and his panel in the eye one too many times, and the senator openly accused the DCI of defying Congress. It was yet one more example of how arrogant behavior by intelligence officials alienated key members of Congress. Another intelligence chief, R. James Woolsey (1993–95), had managed the same feat with the SSCI chair (1993–95) Dennis DeConcini (D-AZ). Through his failure to establish a cordial relationship with DeConcini, Woolsey fanned the fires of estrangement between himself and the SSCI to the detriment of the intelligence agencies.

WANTED: MORE GUARDIANS

The government of the United States is built on a foundation of shared powers among the three branches. Beyond making laws, a primary duty of the legislative branch is to keep watch over the sprawling bureaucracy that lies at the feet of the president. An especially difficult assignment is to maintain vigilance over the hidden side of this terrain: America's secret agencies. Before 1975, lawmakers largely overlooked the responsibility to supervise intelligence operations because the job was time-consuming and daunting in the expertise it required. Moreover, it provided little opportunity to claim credit back home. Plus, being a dedicated intelligence overseer was a job fraught with risk if things went wrong (consider the Bay of Pigs fiasco), and members of Congress might have to share culpability. Better to let the spies go their own way in the back alleys of the world, fighting the justified, if unsavory, war against global communism. The revelation in 1975 that the nation's secret agencies had engaged in espionage against American citizens—the very people they were to protect—challenged the attitude of trust and benign neglect on Capitol Hill. The domestic spy scandal forced lawmakers to take intelligence accountability more seriously.

Since 1975, members of Congress have displayed a range of responses to the call for greater intelligence accountability. Some lawmakers have been throwbacks, "ostriches" content to bury their heads in the sand and continue the earlier era of trust, when lawmakers deferred to the decisions of the executive branch within the domains of intelligence and defense. Others have chosen to become unabashed boosters for intelligence—"cheerleaders" who view their job primarily as one of explaining the value of intelligence to the American people and supporting intelligence missions with strong funding and encouragement. Taking the opposite approach, another group of lawmakers, the "skeptics," have been so critical of intelligence that some have even called for the abolition of the CIA. While not going that far, other skeptics have consistently found fault, and little virtue, in America's attempts to spy on adversaries or overthrow regimes that fail to support U.S. interests. Finally, some members of Congress have been "guardians," striking a balance between serving as partners of the intelligence agencies on Capitol Hill on the one hand, and, through a persistent examination of budgets and operations, demanding competence and law-abiding behavior from these agencies on the other hand.

From among these roles, while lawmakers are scattered along the continuum of possibilities, there has been a particular concentration of cheerleaders in recent years. Members of the congressional oversight committees in the House and Senate have sometimes migrated from one role to another, from adoring cheerleader to dismayed skeptic. One of the main catalysts for this mobility has been a sense of injured institutional pride when lawmakers perceive that intelligence officials have failed to treat Congress with appropriate respect.

Much more research remains to be done in the search for a full understanding of how lawmakers choose their oversight roles and how these roles may change over time. Especially important will be efforts to fathom why more members of Congress have failed to become guardians—the model widely accepted by reformers in 1975 as the ideal because it balances support for intelligence with a determination to avoid (through persistent review) future failures and scandals by the secret agencies. How may lawmakers be urged to spend more time on serious program evaluation? What incentives may be introduced into the culture of Capitol Hill to make accountability a more valued pursuit?

One might think that enough incentives already exist, such as warding off another domestic spy scandal. Another powerful incentive should be the desire to help prevent another 9/11 calamity or avoid false conclusions about weapons of mass destruction abroad of the kind that drew the United States into war with Iraq in 2003.

Most observers agree, however, that lawmakers are performing far below their potential when it comes to intelligence accountability and that, across the policy board and regardless of party affiliation, oversight remains neglected on Capitol Hill. Since the Democratic Party regained control of Congress in 2007, more attention has been paid to intelligence oversight, but it still remains a distant concern for most lawmakers. Correcting this condition is a worthy challenge for educators, journalists, members of Congress, and, indeed, all civic-minded citizens.

The creation of the Office of the Director of National Intelligence was a chance for the U.S. government to establish a leader with full authority over America's top-secret agencies, a spy chief who could coordinate the sixteen intelligence agencies more effectively, thereby overcoming the twin banes of ineffective intelligence: interagency rivalry and parochialism. Ambassador John D. Negroponte served as America's first director of National Intelligence (DNI) beginning in 2005, but he soon fled back to the State Department, serving as DNI for less than two years. His successor, former NSA director Mike McConnell, did not last long either. He stepped down in 2009. His replacement was Admiral Dennis Blair, who has vowed to make sure that the intelligence agencies obey the law, a reaction to criticism over the warrantless wiretaps controversy still boiling in 2009 (Lichtblau & Risen 2009, 1A). Blair got into a spat with the CIA director appointed by the Obama administration, former Congressman Leon Panetta (D-CA), over the question of who would name the chiefs-of-station in U.S. embassies around the world: the head of the CIA (as had been the case since 1947) or the DNI. The argument was a continuation of an earlier round of jousting between the CIA and DNI chiefs.

Negroponte, McConnell, and Blair—all talented, bright individuals—found the DNI job thoroughly frustrating. A last-minute watering down of the reform legislation by Pentagon allies on Capitol Hill in 2004 had left the DNI enfeebled. In its search for greater cohesion in the intelligence community, the U.S. government had instead ended up with an intelligence chief even weaker than the old DCI: a "spymaster" with ambiguous authority, a small staff, and an office far removed from most of the government's intelligence analysts at the CIA in Langley. Just what the nation needed—an isolated director leading the Office of the DNI in what was essentially a hollowed-out seventeenth spy agency.

During the confirmation hearing for McConnell's appointment as DNI, the chairman of the Senate Select Committee on Intelligence, John D. Rockefeller (D-WV), raised thoughtful questions about the weaknesses of the new office. He observed: "We did not pull the technical collection agencies out of the Defense Department [the Scowcroft proposal] and we did not give the DNI direct authority over the main collection or analytic components of the community. We gave the DNI the authority to build the national intelligence budget, but we left the execution of the budget with the agencies. We gave the DNI tremendous responsibilities. The question is: did we give the position enough authority?" (Rockefeller 2007).

For most observers—outside of the Department of Defense, at least—the answer was a clear *no*. Even McConnell, after serving two months on the job, could offer only a euphemistic description of a job he already found unwieldy. The Office of the DNI, in his words, was a "challenging management condition" (Mazzetti 2007a, A10). In particular, he complained about his inability to dismiss incompetent people. "You cannot hire or fire," he told a reporter (*Bloomsberg News* 2007). Early in his tenure, McConnell announced a 100 Day Plan in which he proposed a searching review of the DNI's authority and an ongoing effort to integrate the components of the intelligence "community" (Mazzetti 2007b, A13; see also Best & Cumming 2007).

The next step in intelligence reform, which will require a determined effort by President Obama and his national security team, working together with lawmakers, will be to restore that part of the Intelligence Reform and Terrorism Prevention Act that was omitted in 2004: full budget and appointment powers for the DNI over all the intelligence agencies. Then, at long last, the phrase "intelligence community" will mean something, and the safety of the United States will be significantly strengthened by virtue of a more integrated intelligence system.

CONCLUSION

Worldwide democracy promotion is a worthy goal, but it must be pursued skillfully, not—short of a genuinely imminent threat—with the heavy-handed approach of military intervention. The ongoing war in Iraq has surely underscored that point again for those who had forgotten the Vietnam experience. A subtle and more suitable approach is to encourage the spread of democracy by setting a good example.

To that end, Americans must obey their own laws by rejecting extremist measures like torture and detainment without legal counsel or habeas corpus—in short, by behaving in accordance with constitutional guarantees. At the end of the Second World War, nations turned to the United States for political, economic, and moral leadership. Much of that goodwill has been squandered over the years, in part because of the detention procedures at Guantanamo Bay and Abu Ghraib, the war in Iraq, and revelations of domestic surveillance. The time has come for Americans to live up to their principles, which have won many friends before and may do so again. For this to happen, however, Congress must take more seriously its vital task of ensuring the accountability of the executive branch.

NOTES

1. The president's aides did inform a few lawmakers about the waiver. Those who complained, such as Senator John D. Rockefeller IV (D-WV), were ignored (Jehl 2005). The Intelligence Oversight Act of 1991 requires the executive branch to inform all the members of the Senate and House Intelligence Committees of important intelligence activities (Intelligence Authorization Act, FY1991 [Public Law 102–88, Sec. 502, Aug. 14, 1991]). A

select few members of Congress do not have the authority to permit a presidential bypass of the 1978 law or the 1991 reporting standard.
2. During this same period on the HPSCI, junior members Les Aspin (D-WI) and Roman Mazzoli (D-KY)—though mindful of the importance of the intelligence agencies and willing to praise intelligence witnesses and programs when warranted—became the committee's strongest critics of questionable secret operations. They achieved a commendable balance between expressions of commendation and criticism.
3. The amendments continued to allow the CIA to pursue more benign covert propaganda operations against the Marxist regime.

12
Democracy and Counterterrorism
Multiple Issues, Varied Effects

PAUL R. PILLAR

INTRODUCTION

Theories of democratic peace address classic issues of warfare between nation-states. In recent years, however, public and policy attention has focused at least as much on the threat of violence from nonstate actors—especially terrorists—as on the causes of interstate war. This raises questions about whether the connections between democracy and peace that have been intensively studied at the level of the nation-state have analogues in efforts to counter terrorism. Terrorism, like war, is a form of political violence, and the absence of terrorism is one form of peace.

The core concept of the democratic peace—that democracies do not fight other democracies—does not appear at first glance to have a direct analogue in counterterrorism. Although the internal politics of resistance groups vary, they cannot be analyzed in quite the same terms as the politics of nation-states. Issues involving democracy, however, frequently arise in discussions of counterterrorism, often amid debate over controversial public policies. Some enshrine democracy as the defining characteristic that separates terrorists from their victims; others lament the damage to democracy that some counterterrorist measures allegedly would cause. Like many other points made in the heat of debate over specific policy issues, such references tend to be simplistic, tendentious, and unhelpful to public understanding of the broader subjects involved.

Democracy and democratic values relate to terrorism and counterterrorism in numerous and complex ways. The connections—and the important issues that flow from them—relate both to terrorism itself and to efforts to combat it. They involve the causes of terrorism as well as the consequences of it. They involve principles as well as practice. They include issues that arise abroad and ones that are of more immediate concern at home. Finally, they entail some respects in which democratic values and counterterrorism point in the same direction and other respects in which they pose unavoidable trade-offs and compromises.

This chapter presents a survey of the numerous policy-relevant issues that involve both counterterrorism and democracy. It is intended less to prescribe courses of action than to enhance understanding of the full range of considerations that sometimes make for difficult choices between possible courses of action. To appreciate fully what democracy has to do with fighting terrorism requires review of a complicated range of topics.

DEMOCRATIZATION AND THE ROOTS OF TERRORISM

An appropriate starting point for such a review is the starting point of terrorism itself, which is to say the political, social, and economic milieu from which terrorists and support for their actions and ideologies tend to emerge. There has been no shortage of attention in recent years—and specifically since the terrorist attacks of September 2001—to the issue of how democracy, or rather the lack thereof, may relate to the roots of terrorism. September 11 dealt a severe blow to a belief that had underlain U.S. policy toward much of the Middle East through several administrations. That belief was that the undemocratic and illiberal politics and economics of many Middle Eastern countries, however distasteful they may be to any American who thought about them, did not really require much attention because they did not affect U.S. security or any vital U.S. interest. Based partly on that belief, the United States struck tacit bargains with important Middle Eastern states, especially oil-producing states such as Saudi Arabia. Under those bargains, the United States would receive support on security matters important to it, such as military access rights, as well as reliable access to supplies of energy. In return, the Middle Eastern states received security support that included the right to purchase advanced U.S.-made weapons and—very important to the rulers of those states—no interference in, or even criticism of, their backward and authoritarian internal structures.

September 11 was a dramatic and traumatic demonstration that those structures do matter to U.S. security. It showed that terrorists who came of age in countries such as Saudi Arabia, Egypt, or the United Arab Emirates could cause major harm to U.S. interests and even to the American homeland. The resulting change in thinking among policy elites in Washington was a basis for democratization becoming the dominant theme of the foreign policy of President George W. Bush (2005a), as eloquently expressed in the president's second inaugural address. Cutting the roots of terrorism was not the only motivation for this theme, but it was a major one.

Heated debates over the Bush administration's biggest initiative in the Middle East, the war in Iraq, have clouded subsequent discussions of the political roots of terrorism. Although there have been some thoughtful contributions to that discussion, the preoccupation with the troublesome Iraq expedition has distorted almost every discourse about U.S. policy toward the Middle East, including discourse about democracy and terrorism.

Some have challenged the idea that a paucity of democracy, in the Middle East or anywhere else, can be blamed for the emergence of terrorists. Those making this challenge base their argument primarily on data showing that terrorist attacks occur at least as often in democratic states as in authoritarian ones (Gause 2005). This argument, however, overlooks two important and related distinctions. One is the difference between where terrorism originates and where terrorist attacks are carried out. Statistics refer to the latter, but roots have to do with the former. For example, 9/11's contribution to the statistics is to show a disproportionate number of deaths from international terrorism occurring in a North American democracy, even though the perpetrators of the attack in question, and the group that organized them, came from Middle Eastern autocracies.

The other distinction, related to the first, is between the motivations or drivers of terrorism and operational opportunities for executing terrorist attacks. It is easier to mount a terrorist attack in a free and open society than in a tightly controlled police state. Since democracies tend to exhibit freedom and openness more than autocracies, they also tend to present more operational opportunities for terrorists to exploit. But again, this has nothing to do with the effects that different political structures may have on the likelihood of terrorists and terrorist groups emerging in the first place.

The observation about fewer operational opportunities might suggest a respect in which dictatorships have an advantage over democracies in protecting themselves against terrorism. In this one sense—having to do with the here and now rather than the future, and with defensive security measures rather than with any other aspect of counterterrorism—they do. In this respect, police states work, but not necessarily over the long term. Likewise, although they may control the effects of the threat, they do not reduce the threat.

An instructive case is Egypt, which through harsh internal security measures had quelled by the late 1990s an Islamist terrorist threat that earlier in the decade had become a serious menace to the country's economy and stability. Egypt did not so much eliminate the threat as export it, at least for a time. Some of the same Islamic radicals who had been operating within Egypt—particularly the faction of the Egyptian Islamic Jihad led by Ayman al-Zawahiri—left to join up with Osama bin Laden's al-Qaeda. There they pursued a transnational jihadi agenda aimed primarily against the United States but still retaining the old objective of overthrowing the political order in Egypt.

Although perhaps not reducible to convincing statistics, one empirical pattern that suggests a relationship between a lack of democracy and the roots of terrorism concerns two of the most conspicuous attributes of the Middle East. One is that the Middle East, more than any other region, has been the birthplace of the terrorist groups and individual terrorists most worrisome to the West today. The other is that the Middle East is by most measures the least democratic region of the world. Admittedly, there are other important characteristics of the Middle East that are pertinent to the role terrorism has played in that region, such as the long-running conflict between Israelis and Arabs. But the correlation between terrorism and the paucity of democracy is no accident.

The connection can be understood by reflecting on the most basic principles of political systems and the articulation of political interests. Terrorism is a difficult, dangerous, illegal, and, for most people, immoral business. Few would venture into it if easier and less nasty ways of pursuing the same objectives were available. As a political act, terrorism is used to pursue various interests and express various grievances that more often are pursued and expressed peacefully, when permitted by the political system. Political systems that offer peaceful channels—democracies—are less likely to drive people into terrorism than systems that do not (Pillar 2007).

That is a simple statement of the basic principle involved. In practice, of course, counterexamples abound. Terrorism has many contributing causes, at the level of nations and societies as well as at the level of individuals and their personal situations and psychologies. Any explanation based on one cause, be it a lack of democracy or any other, always will fall short. Yet that does not deny the relevance of the cause or the prospect that addressing that cause could change the magnitude and nature of the terrorist problem.

The principle just offered is consistent with one of the most basic elements of traditional democratic theory. Democracies are good because they are more likely than other political systems to ensure that the interests of the ruled will guide the actions of the rulers. That is because the ruled have more of a role in selecting and removing their rulers. Many causes that terrorist groups pursue involve a population (often defined in terms of religion, ethnicity, or class) that to some degree sees itself as being ruled in a manner contrary to its interests and as not having peaceful means to rectify the situation.

Democratic theory offers other insights pertinent to how more democracy might mean less of a proclivity toward terrorism. Democracy is good not only because it provides a mechanism for the ruled to choose and cashier their rulers but also because of the effects that broad participation in government has on the temperament and habits of the ruled themselves. As one political theorist puts it, a justification for democracy is "as a means to producing certain states or attitudes of mind in the citizens, independence of mind, respect and tolerance for others, interest in public affairs, willingness to think about them and discuss them, and a sense of responsibility for the whole community" (Field 1963). Several of these qualities are the antithesis of the way most terrorists think and operate. Certainly, intolerance and a lack of respect for opposing opinions are central characteristics of the terrorist mindset. Disdain for free discussion—a preference for blowing up negotiating tables rather than sitting at them—is another. Within most terrorist groups there typically is not only a lack of independent thinking but also assiduous efforts by group leaders to quash any hint of it.

A sense of belonging to and responsibility for the community also are important. That means not merely a mythical or longed-for community, such as the *umma*, or community of believers in Islam, that Islamists often invoke as one of their reference points. It means the political system, nation-state, province, and town in which an individual lives. Alienation from one's community is an element in the sources of extremism in much of the Middle East and, to a lesser degree, in other parts of the Muslim world. People see themselves as having little or no stake in the states and political systems in which they live. They are subjects of a political order but do not feel a part of it. Consequently, they may have little compunction about turning violently against that order. To the extent that democracy—by directly, peacefully, and meaningfully involving citizens in the political process—imparts a sense of belonging to the political system, it becomes a disincentive against such violent rejection.

The issue of how democracy, or the lack thereof, is related to the roots of terrorism raises the further question of how terrorists themselves regard democracy. This question came to the fore in the Iraq War, partly because of the Bush administration's need to propound a clear message that the war was a campaign both to fight terrorism and to promote democracy and partly because the most prominent terrorist to emerge during the war, the late Abu Musab al-Zarqawi, presented such outstanding support for that message. In a statement attributed to Zarqawi released prior to elections to the Iraqi constituent assembly in January 2005, he declared a "fierce war" against the "evil principle of democracy and those who follow this wrong ideology" (quoted in Spinner & Sebti 2005, A1). There is no clearer expression of the idea that democracy and terrorism are at opposite poles of a spectrum of political behavior.

Further reflection on Zarqawi's statement, however, raises additional questions about the thesis that an expansion of democracy means a weakening of the roots of terrorism. If Zarqawi and others with his attitude are so strongly opposed to democracy, why should we expect them to avail themselves of peaceful channels of political expression? Would they not be committing terrorism anyway? And if they regard democracy not just as irrelevant to their needs but as evil, might not an expansion of democracy merely stimulate such terrorists to exert even more effort to undermine or defeat it?

Those are valid questions but not directly pertinent to the main ways in which political structures affect the roots of terrorism. Zarqawi and others like him are lost causes. No amount of political change will divert them from their violent path. Again, terrorism has multiple causes, and explanations of Zarqawi's behavior must look at other causes and other personal demons he was chasing.

Two additional distinctions are important. One is the distinction between terrorist groups and leaders who—like Zarqawi and other transnational jihadists in Osama bin Laden's orbit—have goals that are so apocalyptic or extreme that no political reform or restructuring could ever satisfy them and those with more circumscribed goals, such as sharing power in a particular state. The former will not be deterred from terrorism and convinced to lay down their arms in response to democratically based political change; the latter may well be. The outstanding recent example of the latter is the peace process in Northern Ireland, which, after many fits and starts over nearly a decade, has led the Provisional Irish Republican Army (and its political manifestation, Sinn Fein) to move from a terrorist to a democratic path. A different example is Hizballah in Lebanon, which has not given up its terrorist capabilities or the implied threat of using them again in certain circumstances but has drastically reduced its involvement in international terrorism as it has prospered through more peaceful means of competition within the Lebanese political system.

The other distinction is between those who already are terrorists and those who might or might not become terrorists, as well as broader populations that might or might not support what terrorists are doing. Among the Islamic jihadists, most (though not all) who currently are terrorists probably are lost causes. The only appropriate and effective ways of dealing with them are arresting them or otherwise forcibly taking them out of combat. Hence, the prime targets of democratic reform are young men who are not currently terrorists and would be less likely to succumb to the blandishments of extremist recruiters insofar as they see peaceful alternatives for expressing themselves and redressing their grievances. Secondary targets are general populations whose sympathy for, or opposition to, terrorist operations has a major impact on the effectiveness of counterterrorist efforts.

Further questioning of the counterterrorist value of democratization centers on the idea that elections are not a cure-all and that the salutary effects associated with democracy depend at least as much on other elements of a free and mature liberal polity, many of which commonly come under the heading of "civil society." In recent years, some of this line of questioning has really been a criticism of the Bush administration's experiment in forced-draft democratization in Iraq, where much of the trouble encountered since the overthrow of Saddam Hussein has reflected

Iraq's violent and authoritarian political culture and the long time that would be required for it to evolve into something different. However valid the criticism is as applied to Iraq, in a broader sense it is misplaced. Many of the Bush administration's efforts to encourage reform in the Middle East, such as through its Middle East Partnership Initiative, were aimed less at elections than at developing a wider civil society. Moreover, the specifics of the Iraq case should not be allowed to distort broader principles about the effects of democratization.

Nonetheless, the principle underlying this line of questioning is valid and points to a necessary clarification of exactly what is meant by democratization. Democracy indeed does not just mean elections or majority rule. It also means such things as minority rights, a loyal opposition, and the prospect of repeated peaceful transfers of power from one set of rulers to another. The main benefits of democracy—and specifically, as suggested above, the benefits in cutting the roots of terrorism—flow from political rights such as these as well as from a variety of civil rights. In short, what is beneficial is not just democracy but liberal democracy.

A related qualification concerns the *ization* part of democratization: the perils and pitfalls of transition to democracy. Mansfield and Snyder (1995) have shown that although democracies rarely fight other democracies (the concept of the democratic peace), new democracies are among the most warlike states of all. Some of the same attributes of such states that foster external aggression—such as the insecurity of old elites seeking new sources of support—also encourage internal extremism, including terrorism. The implication is that although over the long term a more democratic order in most states is likely to mean less terrorism, the road that must be traveled to that end is likely to be rough. Some of the roughness will come from elements that use terrorism to try to subvert political reform or peace processes.

AFTER DEMOCRATIZATION

Concern about illiberal democracy and about opening elections to groups and leaders who have not always had democratic blood flowing through their veins leads to a further oft-expressed concern: What will the newly elected do with their power? Will they abide by democratic norms, including allowing themselves to be voted out of office in the future, or will they instead use whatever means necessary to hold onto power? And, especially germane to the current topic, will they use the power of the state for terrorist purposes?

This concern frequently is expressed about political reform in the Middle East. Saudi Arabia, with its strategic importance and petroleum-based wealth but medieval, family-ruled political structure, is the textbook case. Most informed observers of the kingdom agree that if free elections for a national legislature and government were held tomorrow, the biggest winners would not be secular, Western-oriented modernizers but instead some type of political Islamists. That prospect, viewed against the backdrop of the type of Islamists who have come out of Saudi Arabia into international attention in the past, gives many Western observers shudders.

In addition to the fact that such elections will *not* be held tomorrow and that whatever political reforms the monarch could persuade the rest of the royal family to accept would be far more limited and gradual than free national elections, this concern overlooks a couple of important considerations. One is that political Islam is not a single ideology but rather an idiom in which a variety of ideologies are expressed. Not only that, but it has become the dominant political idiom in much of the Muslim world, with most real political choices not among the secular and the Islamic but among different varieties of political Islam (Fuller 2004).[1] Electing an Islamist does not mean electing Osama bin Laden or anyone remotely like him. The other consideration is that a Saudi Arabia with an elected government would be so different in so many ways (would it even still be *Saudi* Arabia?) that it is fruitless to try to project the character of a future government based on the character of Islamist opposition to the current government.

Elsewhere in the Middle East, political Islamists in opposition have been permitted a peaceful political role and have given no reason to believe that they would not continue to function peacefully and responsibly if they enjoyed even greater electoral success in the future. In Jordan, the Muslim Brotherhood competes openly as an opposition political party. In Egypt, the Brotherhood is still legally proscribed but is nonetheless tolerated. By running parliamentary candidates as independents or under the labels of other parties, the Muslim Brotherhood has become Egypt's largest and most effective political opposition to the ruling National Democratic Party. In Turkey, the mildly Islamist Justice and Development Party has been in power since 2002 and has given no signs of backing away from Turkey's peaceful foreign policy and commitments as a member of the North Atlantic Treaty Organization.

The Middle Eastern group that most frequently gives rise to concerns about what might ensue from elections is Hamas, which the United States and Israel have shunned and tried to weaken ever since it won a sweeping victory in Palestinian parliamentary elections in January 2006. Previously lacking the sorts of peaceful channels available to similar parties elsewhere in the Middle East, Hamas used terrorism against Israeli targets.[2] Yet, projecting past use of tactics into a very different future (including a Palestinian state with an elected government) ignores several considerations. One is the historical record of resistance groups making the transition from terrorism to peaceful tactics when given the opportunity to compete peacefully for power or a share of it. That record includes the Provisional Irish Republican Army, whose leaders finally came to share power in Northern Ireland through the Good Friday Agreement peace process. The list also includes Irgun and the Stern Gang, which waged terrorist campaigns against British and Arab targets under the British mandate in Palestine but included leaders such as Menachem Begin and Yitzhak Shamir, who later participated in the democratic political process of Israel.

The concern about Hamas also does not take into account how holding office in a Palestinian state would bolster the group's current capability to conduct terrorism, should it choose to do so. Most important, it does not address why, if the long-held dream of a Palestinian state materialized, Hamas would ever so choose. Terrorism has been not an end in itself for Hamas but instead a means for trying to bring a Palestinian state into being. Bearing in mind the likely responses of the far more powerful Israel and other powers, such as the United States, the leaders of Hamas know that any moves toward turning a new Palestinian state into a terrorist state would be suicidal.

Even Iran, the Middle Eastern state that is still appropriately regarded as the foremost state sponsor of terrorism, offers a lesson regarding democracy and terrorism. Iran's terrorist-abetting activities (principally providing aid to Palestinian groups conducting violence against Israel as well as supporting Hizballah in Lebanon and other Shia groups) are the work of the undemocratic, unelected portions of the complicated Iranian political structure—particularly elements of the Revolutionary Guard. The main priorities of most ordinary Iranians lie elsewhere, particularly with domestic economic concerns. During the history of the Islamic republic, the Iranian leader who had the biggest popular, democratic mandate—the former president Mohammad Khatami—openly questioned the advisability of any Iranian involvement with terrorism.

The episode that hangs over discussions of the possible consequences of Islamists coming to power is the cancellation by the Algerian military in 1991 of elections that the Islamic Salvation Front (FIS) seemed poised to win. Those sympathetic to the military's action (including those shaping U.S. policy toward the Middle East at the time) feared that the FIS coming to power would mean "one man, one vote, one time." That would not necessarily have been true. The possibility, rather than the reality, of the Algerian military later intervening in politics probably would have deterred the more wayward actions considered by an FIS-dominated government, similar to how the Turkish military still tacitly imposes limits on governments in Ankara, Islamist or non-Islamist. What is certain is the bloodbath that ensued after the elections were cancelled, with violent offshoots of the FIS waging terrorist campaigns—including brutal massacres in villages—that killed as many as 200,000 Algerians over the next several years.

UNDEMOCRATIC COUNTERTERRORIST PARTNERS

Effective action against transnational terrorist groups requires extensive cooperation with foreign police, security, and intelligence services. The transnational nature of the target means that no one country can tackle by itself all aspects of confronting even a single group. Foreign authorities commonly have major advantages in terms of language, ease of operation on their home turf, and long histories of following particular groups or suspects. This need to rely on foreign partners in counterterrorism commonly raises concerns about cooperating with regimes that do not share many of the same values as the United States, including democratic values. Close cooperation with autocrats can be distasteful.

This issue arises in a case such as Pakistan, whose ruler, Pervez Musharraf, came to be regarded as a major counterterrorist partner of the United States but who took power in a military coup in 1999, banished the principal secular political parties and their leaders from Pakistan, and has done little to put his country back on a more democratic path. Defenders of the U.S. relationship with Musharraf have argued that it may be necessary to hold one's nose and overlook some of the less desirable characteristics of his regime—including its essentially authoritarian nature—to obtain cooperation essential for dealing with the jihadist presence (including al-Qaeda) in the frontier region along the Pakistani-Afghan border. Critics of the relationship, in their turn, have noted its significant costs. These include not only the affront to democratic values but also some long-term costs to counterterrorism itself: the absence of democratic channels may contribute to the breeding of future terrorists for the reasons discussed above.

The relevant overarching point is that trade-offs are inevitable. Cooperation with a state such as Pakistan presents two trade-offs in particular. One is between counterterrorism and other objectives, including the promotion of democracy; the more U.S. leverage used to support one objective, the less leverage there is left to support the other. Not every issue can be number one on the agenda. The other trade-off is between short-term counterterrorism (dealing with existing terrorists and terrorist groups in the Pakistani hinterland) and long-term counterterrorism (influencing social and political development in a direction less likely to nurture future terrorists). These trade-offs are examples of the choices and compromises that are unavoidable whenever a relationship with a foreign country touches on several important U.S. interests.

A related issue is whether effective counterterrorist operations overseas, which are designed to deal with existing terrorists and terrorist groups and not with long-term root causes, are connected in some inherent way to democracy or its absence. Are there, in other words, some counterterrorist tasks that authoritarian partners can perform more effectively because they are authoritarian? This issue has been in the background of considerable attention focused in recent years on the rendition of terrorist suspects. *Rendition* means a quick and usually secret transfer of a suspect from the custody of one state to that of another without going through a formal and lengthy extradition process. Rendition has been widely misunderstood and mistakenly described, usually in associating it with torture or other inhumane treatment of prisoners at the hands of authoritarian regimes. In fact, rendition does not encompass issues of subsequent treatment; it refers only to the transfer of custody. It had been used for many years before becoming controversial. Specifically, it was useful in relocating terrorists to where they were wanted for their crimes and thus removing them from places where, if transfer required formal extradition, they might escape justice by means of assisted jailbreaks, bribed judges, or other measures.

Democracy has nothing to do with rendition, in one direction or the other. Rendition has been employed by both the United States and authoritarian governments. In addition, the United States has not been the only democracy engaged in the clandestine transfer and custody of terrorist suspects, as indicated by the reported involvement of European countries in the "secret prisons" that erupted into controversy in 2006. Even in the still more controversial issues of torture and rough treatment of detainees, there is no clear correlation, either logically or empirically, with democracy or authoritarianism. Dershowitz (2003) has made a serious argument, for example, that torture can be incorporated into the legal structure of a democracy such as the United States. More generally, abusive or counterproductive actions under the banner of the "war on terror" are not the exclusive province of either dictatorships or democracies. Some harsh Russian measures taken under that banner have had less to do with countering terrorism than with suppressing Chechen separatism. The same could be said of some Chinese measures against Uighurs in the Xinjiang Province. Similar things could be said about democratic India's policies regarding Kashmir and about many Israeli actions against Palestinians in the West Bank and Gaza.

So the general answer to the question about a possible inherent connection between the nature of a foreign government's political system and effective counterterrorism is that there is not one. General Musharraf is considered an important counterterrorist partner not because he is authoritarian but rather because of Pakistan's geography and other factors.

One sense in which democracy does make a difference, however, is that it potentially opens up to criticism all aspects of a country's counterterrorist policy—including whatever may be abusive and/or counterproductive—and thereby creates the possibility of policy change. Israelis, for example, often have vigorous debates about treatment of the Palestinians, and Israel's supreme court has weighed in on such issues as torture of terrorist suspects. Nothing comparable is heard in China about treatment of Uighurs. The public row that the "secret prisons" issue raised in

Europe was a reflection of the countries involved being democracies. The main argument that Dershowitz makes in calling for a system of judicial warrants to legalize torture in selected cases is that abuses (meaning in this context torture going beyond the minimum necessary to extract critical information from a terrorist in the event of a "ticking time bomb") would be less likely than if torture were conducted off the books in the way that police states would conduct it. These debates and reviews of counterterrorist policies and practices that take place, or at least could take place, in democracies involve going beyond the issue of what makes for effective counterterrorism. They involve weighing protection from terrorism against other values of free peoples. This balancing characterizes debates about counterterrorism within the United States at least as much as debates in other democracies.

THE DEMOCRATIC PROCESS AT HOME

The balancing of competing values always will be more delicate and more discomforting with counterterrorist policy at home than with policy abroad. What may be at stake abroad are only our sensibilities and empathy for other peoples who experience compromises of their rights and liberties. At home, our own rights and liberties are at stake. The balancing necessary in devising domestic counterterrorist policy may be difficult and sensitive, but democracy is not the main value involved. Other values enjoyed in a free and liberal society are more at issue. Three sets of values in particular are often in tension with counterterrorist measures applied domestically.

One set concerns rights to privacy—limitations on the ability of government to search, investigate, monitor, or otherwise learn details of individual citizens' personal lives. Initiatives taken in the name of counterterrorism that call privacy into question include expanded interception of electronic communications, a variety of investigative tools allowed under the U.S. Patriot Act of 2001 (such as requiring librarians to report what books an individual has checked out), and the collection of other personal data that are the basis for putting names on various watch lists.

A second set concerns personal liberties—each citizen's ability to conduct his or her daily life in accordance with the individual citizen's wishes. A host of security measures erected to foil terrorism impinge on those liberties. We cannot enter certain public spaces that we formerly could enter. We can enter other public spaces only at the cost of emptying pockets and detouring through metal detectors or of obtaining escorts or advance permission. These first two sets of values can affect anyone, and actually do affect most people, even if only in hidden ways.

The third set concerns the rights of those suspected of criminal behavior. These are the values at stake with such issues as the treatment of detained suspects and the rights to judicial review. By its very nature this third set will be of less direct concern to most citizens. Yet the application of new procedures in the name of counterterrorism, including detention of U.S. citizens in stateside facilities, and the fact that rights of the accused are among the basic rights enshrined in the U.S. Constitution make this subject another area of tension between counterterrorist objectives and other values.

One basic point about this tension is that the infringement by counterterrorist measures on values such as personal liberty and privacy is real, material, and often substantial. Fundamental rights are abridged. Nothing is gained by pretending that the contradictions and conflicts do not exist. This does not mean that policy choices that have been made are wrong. It does mean it would be wrong to suggest that such choices are avoidable.

A second point is that there is no optimum balancing point, no perfect solution, for resolving the conflict between counterterrorism and other objectives or values. What is the best compromise is a choice for free peoples, acting collectively, to make. Different peoples may make different choices.

The same sort of choices must be made in the tradeoff between counterterrorism and conserving financial resources. Many aspects of counterterrorism are expensive, and resource constraints almost always are a factor. It is misleading to speak in terms of how much expenditure would be enough to safeguard transit systems, protect ports, or perform some other function related to protecting the public from terrorism. There is no "enough." Rather, it is a question of how much security a society wants to buy, bearing in mind other purposes to which the same financial resources otherwise could be put. Similarly, society has a choice of how much security to "buy" in the form of reduced privacy or liberties.

None of this is unique to counterterrorism. Infringements on values such as personal liberty are regularly made to serve many other purposes, some so regularly that we tend no longer to think of them in terms of restricting liberty. No one questions that the state should restrict my liberty to drive 100 miles per hour on streets and highways and to enforce that restriction in the name of public safety. We are more conscious of infringement of liberty with more controversial matters, such as restrictions placed on speech and expression for such purposes as not inciting violence and preserving order in schools. Restrictions made for counterterrorism are more similar to the latter type of situation than the former. Nevertheless, they are part of a long list of forced collective choices.

Collective choice is where democracy comes in. Democracy is important not as a determinant of any one formula for balancing counterterrorism against the other values; different democracies may choose different formulas, and any one democracy might choose different formulas at different times. It is instead important as the process through which the choice is made. Of all systems of collective choice in large societies, representative democracy is the best at aligning policy choices with the wishes of the governed. Counterterrorist measures may infringe on privacy and liberty. They do not infringe at all on democracy as long as the issues at stake are transparent, political debate is free and thorough, established procedures of representative institutions are observed, and the rules and laws established through those procedures are obeyed.

This is why of all the controversial issues that have surfaced in recent years involving counterterrorist measures within the United States, one of the most important was the Bush administration's interception of electronic communications without the use of court warrants. Critics of the administration's practices on this matter were correct in arguing that the problem was not with the intercept operation itself but with the failure to brief Congress in a form that would permit effective oversight or to conduct the operation under the terms of the Foreign Intelligence Surveillance Act (FISA), which specifies a judicial approval process that the administration circumvented. The critics were also correct in arguing that if the administration believed that existing legislation was cumbersome or ineffective, the solution was to seek new legislation. That is how representative democracies are supposed to operate.

The issue of communications intercepts illustrates one attribute of counterterrorism that tends to make it susceptible to circumvention of democratically established procedures: much of it is secret and must remain so. Counterterrorism is not unique in this regard; the same could be said, for example, about many military operations and most investigations into ordinary crime. Yet secrecy is one respect that distinguishes counterterrorism from many other governmental infringements on personal liberties, ranging from speed limits to bans on obscene speech. The guiding principle in dealing with necessarily secret activities is to distinguish general rules and policies from specific applications of them. The latter may need to be kept secret, but the former do not. General rules and policies, even those governing sensitive security matters, are properly the subject of public attention and debate in democracies.

In the United States, Congress plays a critical role in applying these principles. The main contribution of Congress in this regard is not, as is often supposed, a watchdog function of uncovering poor performance or abuses that have not yet been made public. The attention of Congress is too inveterately episodic for that, with members far more likely to become energized over issues that already have become matters of public scandal or controversy. The actual role of Congress is twofold. First, it establishes through legislation the rules and policies under which counterterrorism operations are to be conducted. Second, it exercises oversight—even before an operation is undertaken—on matters that are specific enough to require secrecy but sensitive and important enough to justify the attention of members of Congress. Such matters include covert action as well as intelligence-collection operations that involve infringements on privacy. Only some members perform such oversight—usually those on the House and Senate intelligence committees. In doing so, they function as surrogates for the American public they represent. The standard they should apply is whether the proposed operation is consistent with the values and priorities of the American people, as the people themselves would judge if they could somehow be let in on the secrets.

PUBLIC SUPPORT AND UNDERSTANDING

A final set of issues involving counterterrorism and democracy is less often discussed but poses some of the most difficult problems within the United States. These issues involve the need for sustained and informed public support for counterterrorism.

A government of and by the people—that is, a representative democracy—brings not only major strengths to national security matters but also important weaknesses. Both the strengths and the weaknesses have been apparent throughout the history of American foreign policy. Scholars such as Walter Russell Mead (2002) have noted some of the most salient patterns, though without specific reference to counterterrorism. The patterns have reflected not merely the democratic character of the American political system but also other aspects of American political culture. It is impossible to separate one from the other. Thus, at least for the American democracy, the implications for counterterrorism are substantial.

The principal strength is that, once aroused, the American public can constitute an immensely formidable opponent against any foreign foe that threatens it. The gigantic national effort that defeated the Axis powers in World War II remains the best demonstration. It was the modern American version of the European *levee en masse* that began with the wars of the French Revolution. It entailed not only the notion of conscription and shared military sacrifice that the original levee involved but also an energized public spirit that was an expression of both democracy itself and a perceived need to defend democracy. This spirit gave the American war effort a strength that no autocracy could match.

Echoes of this democratic arousal were apparent after the terrorist attacks against the United States in September 2001. This time the appropriate reaction was not primarily militaristic in nature, and there was no conscription. Even so, there was a broadly shared sense that the nation needed to devote greater effort and to designate a substantially higher priority to counterterrorism than it had before. This national arousal had specific, beneficial effects in countering international terrorism. At home, for example, it made possible major enhancements in defensive security measures that, although costly and sometimes invasive, help to protect certain types of potential targets and to discourage certain potential types of terrorist attacks. Abroad, the clear and elevated sense of national commitment was instrumental in, among other things, greatly increasing the seizing or freezing of terrorist-related financial assets. Although legal powers to facilitate the use of this financial tool were expanded, the main difference was that U.S. officials could now pound on the desks of their foreign counterparts and insist, more credibly than before, that the American people demanded action.

Offsetting this advantage in how the American democracy responds to security threats from abroad are corresponding disadvantages. One is that it usually takes a shocking, traumatic event to arouse the public. An actual disaster, rather than mere warning of one, is required to elicit the public's attention and concern and thus— being a democracy—stimulate significant change in policy priorities. This means the nation often is slow to respond to dangers until after it sustains major costs. In World War II, the Japanese attack on Pearl Harbor in 1941 provided the necessary shock to pull the country far enough out of its remaining lethargy and isolationism to make the winning war effort possible.

The American response to the 9/11 terrorist attack demonstrated even more clearly the public's tendency to react more to a shocking event than to an underlying reality. America was no more endangered on September 12, 2001, than it had been on September 10. Indeed, the jihadist terrorist threat that manifested itself on 9/11 had been developing for years. Moreover, the elements of the government responsible for national security had been following it and attempting to counter it for years. Those elements, and senior policymakers they served, appreciated the danger and were trying to do something about it well before 9/11. The director of central intelligence was issuing public warnings about a possible attack by al-Qaeda. But because there had not yet been national trauma associated with a terrorist attack, measures that after 9/11 would be implemented without question still faced resistance. This was true, for example, of aviation security. Despite attempts by the Federal Aviation Administration and the intelligence community to direct attention to the vulnerabilities of commercial aviation within the United States to terrorism, the aviation industry resisted, on grounds of cost, significant enhancements to security.

Another disadvantage concerns how the American public tends to perceive foreign dangers and the nature of the campaigns that must be waged against them. Americans tend to perceive threats to their security in terms of known, named, well-defined enemies. They are uncomfortable dealing with more subtle dangers that cannot be identified and personalized in the same way. Americans prefer to regard confrontations with foreign threats in a simple, Manichean way, as contests between a foreign evil and an American good. Indeed, they prefer to think of those contests as discrete struggles or wars that have definite beginnings and clear, definite ends—especially victorious ends.

That perspective was well-suited to the threats the United States faced in World War II. The danger came from specific aggressive regimes. Even just one of those regimes, that of Nazi Germany, embodied enough evil to sustain a dualistic, good-versus-evil way of looking at the war. Hitler fit perfectly the role of a loathsome enemy leader. The campaigns against the Axis were appropriately thought of in the way World War II actually turned out: one big war ending with a complete, clear-cut victory for the American-led side.

The campaign against international terrorism is not at all like that, however, and is ill-suited to the American public's preferred perspective toward national security. Terrorism is not a single enemy or set of enemies but instead a tactic that many different groups and states have used for many different purposes. Even the particular type of terrorism of most concern today—the Sunni transnational jihadist variety, which includes Osama bin Laden and al-Qaeda—is not a single foe but instead a diverse movement with an increasing number of independent centers of action and direction. Countering even this brand of terrorism—let alone terrorism in general—cannot be accomplished in a single war or warlike effort that will have a definite, or even a recognizable, end.

Several weaknesses in the American approach to counterterrorism flow from the influence of this popular perspective. Americans tend not to appreciate differences among terrorist groups and among the different strategies needed to deal with them. They tend, for example, to lump Hamas together with al-Qaeda because they are both Islamist groups that have used terrorism, even though the objectives of the former, having to do with political power in Palestine, are quite different from the transnational jihadist goals of the latter. They tend to see bin Laden as more of a commanding and controlling figure than he really is and therefore will be inclined to declare victory prematurely once he is killed or captured. Most important, they tend to view counterterrorism as a "war on terror" that they will wage for a limited time until victory is achieved. That means their attention and support are likely to flag over time even if the threat does not.[3] That view also confuses issues of how much to compromise values such as liberty and privacy, given that some of the measures that necessitate compromise are misleadingly viewed or justified as temporary "wartime" measures.

None of this is reason to move away from democracy in the interest of achieving more effective counterterrorism. A dictatorship could do better in certain respects but at a fearsome price in terms of other values and interests, including interests related to counterterrorism itself. It may be a cliché, but it also is true that too much compromise of one's own values and way of life in the name of fighting terrorism constitutes a victory of sorts for terrorists. If anything, the United States needs more, not less, rigorous adherence to democratic procedures in establishing counterterrorist policy so that whatever compromises are struck reflect as closely as possible the will and the values of the American people. The weaknesses attributed above to popular American perceptions are a limitation, not a crippling disability, that American leaders need to bear in mind.

In fact, leaders should not merely bear the perceptions in mind but try to channel them in a more constructive direction. Popular American attitudes about counterterrorism, although rooted in U.S. history and culture, are not immutable. Some of the less constructive aspects of those attitudes owe no more to the public's predispositions than to the political leadership's exploitation of those predispositions. This is particularly true of the whole notion of a "war on terror," which not only has the unhelpful effects mentioned above but also has corroded other aspects of Americans' outlook and way of life and has fostered a culture of fear and mistrust (Brzezinski 2007). Leaders in democracies, as in dictatorships, must do exactly that—lead. In this context, leading means avoiding rather than exploiting the less salubrious attitudes of the electorate and educating the public about the real nature of the threats they face.

CONCLUSION

Although terrorist groups are not nation-states, a close examination of the relationship between democracy and terrorism shows that democratic peace theory really does have echoes in counterterrorism. This is particularly true regarding the roots of terrorism and the reasons that individuals do or do not gravitate to that form of violence. Some of the same internal political tensions and dissatisfaction that can increase the chances of external aggression also increase the proclivity to support or engage in terrorism. The entire relationship between democracy and counterterrorism, however, is far broader and more complex.

The best approach to understanding some issues is to simplify them—to cut to the essence of the question under consideration. Not so regarding the relationship between democracy and counterterrorism. There is no single essence to this topic but instead a number of issues that cut in several different ways. On many of these topics, one of the greatest impediments to understanding has been oversimplification (such as the assertion that "democracy does not prevent terrorism"). That is all the more true in considering the entire panoply of issues.

The issues cut across domestic and foreign concerns, leading to this concluding thought. There is much to be learned about the foreign issues by reflecting on the domestic ones, and vice versa. As we evaluate the performance of foreign leaders in balancing counterterrorism against other political interests, for example, we would do well to consider the conflicts of interest that arise as our own democracy makes counterterrorist policy and the difficulties often encountered in trying to resolve those conflicts. The American democracy offers good lessons for foreign governments. Those lessons involve not only the American system's many strengths but also how it handles its own weaknesses.

NOTES

1. The current political order in Saudi Arabia, in which King Abdallah's predecessor assumed the title Custodian of the Two Holy Places and in which the open practice of any religion other than Islam is banned, is highly Islamic.
2. Hamas is in effect the Palestinian branch of the Muslim Brotherhood.
3. This is particularly true if states are fortunate enough to escape more major terrorist attacks over a period of years.

13

Encouraging Democracy or Terrorism?

BARBARA ANN J. RIEFFER-FLANAGAN

More than two centuries ago, a political leader living in unstable times discussed the link between terrorism and democracy. Maximilien M. I. Robespierre sought to achieve the ideals of democratic governance. To achieve this goal, he argued, French revolutionaries needed to use extreme tactics, including the use of terror, against their political enemies. "If virtue be the spring of a popular government in times of peace," he wrote in his 1794 *Report on the Principles of Political Morality,* "the spring of that government during a revolution is virtue combined with terror: virtue, without which terror is destructive; terror, without which virtue is impotent" (quoted in Hoffman 1998, 15).

Robespierre was not alone in suggesting a link between democracy and terrorism. The Bush administration identified this link, but instead of terrorism aiding in the cause of democracy, the latter would limit the former. President George W. Bush argued that promoting liberty and democracy around the world would make the United States more secure. As he stated in a July 2005 speech in Virginia, "Like fascism and communism before, the hateful ideologies that use terror will be defeated by the unstoppable power of freedom and democracy" (Bush 2005b). With these words, Bush expressed a romantic belief in the power of democracy to address one of the most vexing problems of global politics.

Others have suggested that it is no coincidence that the Middle East is both the world's least democratic region and a region that has suffered chronic terrorism. Thus, by encouraging democratic reforms in the region, the United States would foster a decline in terrorism. Morton Halperin, director of policy planning in the State Department during the Clinton administration, believed that al-Qaeda's strength in Middle Eastern countries such as Egypt and Saudi Arabia stemmed from poverty and could only be remedied by the spread of democracy (Halperin, Siegle, & Weinstein 2004). Paul Pillar echoes these sentiments in this volume when he argues that "the correlation between terrorism and the paucity of democracy is no accident." The assumption seems to be that democracy, and by extension democracy promotion, is a potential answer to the threat of global terrorism.

This chapter investigates the claim that democratic political systems and the promotion of democracy around the world will lead to a decrease in terrorism. It argues that both conceptually and empirically democracy promotion is not the magical solution to ending terrorism. Furthermore, some foreign policy decisions that aim to create stable democracies often trigger a backlash and actually exacerbate terrorist threats in the short run. The chapter begins by looking at the conceptual ties between democracy and peace and then offers a general approach to understanding this relationship, beginning with the motivations and aims of those organizations that employ terror against civilians. Democratic reform is only a *potential* answer to decreasing terrorism when dissatisfied groups seek political autonomy and equality. Terrorist organizations with aims of regional domination or global jihad will not be appeased by democracy. Subsequent sections of the chapter examine the goals and tactics of organizations that have used bombings, suicide attacks, and other measures to further their disparate goals.

ASSESSING THE DEMOCRATIC PEACE THEORY

The concept of democracy has been much debated in contemporary history. While there is no universally accepted definition, for the purposes of this chapter *democracy* will refer to a type of political system in which citizenship is inclusive and citizens have the ability to decide who governs. In most Western democracies, this is accomplished by repeated, competitive, free, and fair elections in which adult citizens can express their political preferences. Basic civil and political rights, such as freedom of speech, association, thought, and the press are also required (Dahl 1961; Rieffer & Mercer 2005; Langlois 2003).

But pure majoritarian democracy, even with some limited political rights, is insufficient if it allows the majority to consistently ignore or discriminate against the minority. These "illiberal" democracies are not what politicians refer to when they argue for the promotion of democracy. Such democracies are problematic because elections often usher in repression, discrimination, and violence against minorities (Zakaria 2003; Chua 2004). An alienated minority may turn to violence and terrorism if consistently abused or discriminated against by the majority. Hence, when the West talks about promoting democracy, it means promoting *liberal* democracy that ensures basic rights and freedoms for all citizens.

Makers of U.S. foreign policy have consistently espoused the theory of democratic peace, arguing that democracy promotion programs contribute to U.S. national security because democratic states, at least liberal democratic states, do not threaten or war with each other (Russett & O'Neal 2001; Doyle 1997). Democracies are not less war-prone per se, but rather the wars in which democracies are involved are fought against repressive states. A number of reasons have been offered as to why this may be the case. Immanuel Kant argued that when free citizens are given a voice, they are less inclined than a monarch to go to war. Free citizens would not want to fight in such a war, pay its costs, or suffer its devastation. Thus the choices of citizens in a democratic political system, made out of self-interest, would naturally lead to more peaceful relations among states. Since the leaders of democratic polities are presumed to be responsive to their citizens' wishes, there would be fewer wars.

There are other aspects of liberal democracies that encourage restraint with regard to war. According to John Rawls (1999), citizens in democratic states fight in self-defense, not for economic or territorial gain. Thus, aggressive wars against other liberal democratic societies are improbable. It has also been argued that the separation of powers found in many democratic political systems can slow down and limit the drive to war (Russett 1993, 40). Furthermore, most citizens in liberal democratic societies hold norms of toleration and respect for their fellow citizens.[1] While they may disagree on particular issues, they respect the rights of other citizens to participate and voice their views. If we extend these notions of respect and toleration to liberal democratic peoples in foreign countries, the likelihood of war decreases. Ultimately, the cultural and normative framework that democratic citizens develop results in "peaceful values and expectations" and relations between states (Schafer & Walker 2006).

These norms, as opposed to institutional restraints, are arguably the most relevant to the discussion of terrorism. Democratic dispositions incorporate "a preparedness to work with others different from oneself toward shared ends; a combination of strong convictions with a readiness to compromise in the recognition that one cannot always get everything one wants" (Elshtain 1995, 2). If citizens learn to respect each other at home, even in the midst of profound political differences, then we would not expect them to employ violence to achieve political goals. By extension, such citizens would not resort to terrorism as a means to advance their political agendas.[2]

UNDERSTANDING TERRORISM: CASE STUDIES

To further examine the relationship among democracy, the democratic peace theory, and terrorism, we begin from the standpoint of organizations that use terrorist activities to achieve some predetermined political goals. In investigating the root causes of terrorism, we want to see if the elements of democratic political systems discussed above can limit the resort to violence and terrorism. This section focuses on the potential for democracy promotion to be a successful response to terrorism.

Despite the international community's difficulty in agreeing on a definition of *terrorism*, for the purposes of this chapter the term will refer to political violence that deliberately targets civilians in order to coerce a government to negotiate and compromise (see Juergensmeyer 2000, 5).[3] This chapter distinguishes between state-directed terrorism and that employed by an independent group operating without government support and focuses on the latter. Thus, terrorism is a means to achieve some end and often to force political change.

Employing terrorist tactics can be successful; the creation of an atmosphere of fear can have an enormous psychological impact on a target population. Even when a group fails to achieve its primary objective, it may still be a successful operation because it sends a message to political leaders, strikes fear in the civilian population, or gains supporters (Hoffman 1998). Various groups have used violence against civilians to further political objectives, including al-Qaeda, Hamas, Hizballah, the Tamil Tigers, and the Irish Republican Army (IRA). One study prepared for the U.S. Air Force listed the Revolutionary Armed Forces of Colombia (FARC), Hizballah, and al-Qaeda as the three biggest threats to the United States (Cragin & Daly 2004).

The motives for terrorism vary from group to group. In some instances, the motivation is a complaint about a historic injustice, such as colonization or perceived foreign domination or occupation (see Pape 2005). In other cases, the motivation stems from recent discriminatory government policies and the lack of political rights and freedoms. For some terrorist organizations, including al-Qaeda, regional hegemony may be a long-term goal. For other groups, acts of terrorism advance several objectives at once.

Determining and understanding these various motives is the first step to determining whether the promotion of democracy is likely to have an effect on terrorism. Those groups that seek greater political freedoms and rights within a fixed territory can benefit from democracy promotion programs. Democracy would offer a peaceful means of achieving these political objectives. Organizations that want to achieve a separate independent state may benefit from democracy promotion if the controlling authorities are willing to give up a contested territory, as in the case of the Israeli withdrawal from Gaza. However, groups that seek regional domination, global jihad, or the open-ended spread of religious or ideological beliefs will be dissatisfied with democracy, especially when proposed reforms include constitutional checks on power, the protection of minority rights, and free elections to be held on a permanent basis. In short, when the political objectives of a terrorist organization bear no relationship to democracy, democracy promotion will be ineffective. Therefore, democracy promotion, if effective, will address only some of the grievances of terrorist organizations and hence cannot (without some significant change in group orientation) necessarily lead to a decrease in terrorism.

These lessons regarding the potential utility and actual limitations of democracy promotion as a remedy for terrorism are revealed in historical experience. Specifically, the cases of Northern Ireland, Sri Lanka, and the recent surge in al-Qaeda political violence in several countries offer critical insights into the effectiveness of alternative counterterrorism strategies, including democracy promotion.

Northern Ireland

The Irish Republican Army carried out various violent attacks on civilians and British officials for more than three decades in the late twentieth century. The IRA's grievance with Great Britain originated with the colonization of Ireland. The clans of Ireland, having been converted to Catholicism in the fifth century, were unable to resist the Anglo-Norman invasions of the twelfth century, and this led to the colonization of the island (Cahill 1995). English and later British interference and control of Ireland cemented Irish Catholic identity. Colonial policies included the Penal Laws,[4] Britain's minimal assistance to the Irish during the Potato Famine,[5] discrimination against Catholics (including the prohibition of worship), the barring of Catholics from practicing certain professions (including law), the destruction of Catholic churches, and the slaughter of Irish Catholics at the hands of Protestants. These policies increased Irish loyalty to Catholicism and resistance to British rule (Griffin 2002; Keneally 2000; O'Brien 2002).

Irish Catholics were able to throw off British rule by 1922 with the creation of the Republic of Ireland, but they were forced to concede Northern Ireland (also referred to as Ulster). The IRA then sought to push the British forces out of Ulster and reunite with their brethren in the south. In the late 1960s, a civil rights movement emerged in Northern Ireland. Much like the movement among African Americans in the United States, Catholics in Ulster sought greater equality and freedom from discrimination. The Catholic minority was unable to achieve its political aims. In response to the protests, the British chose to repress the Catholics of Northern Ireland. As Louise Richardson (2006, 67) noted, "the police force in Northern Ireland . . . essentially ran amok in the Catholic neighborhoods in an effort to put the Catholics 'back in their place.'" The Catholic community in Ulster turned to the IRA to defend them since the British government would not.

In response to British policies, including "Bloody Sunday" in January 1972 when twelve Catholic demonstrators were killed, the IRA committed various acts of terrorism, including bombings, kidnappings, beatings, and assassinations (Tanner 2001). For example, on February 9, 1996, a bomb exploded on Canary Wharf in London, killing two people and injuring hundreds (Mitchell 1999). This was done to protest the fact that the organization was not included in political talks with the British government. This was followed by a bombing in Manchester on June 15, 1996. In these and other instances, the IRA took responsibility for violence against civilians and military personnel.

The U.S. government tried in various ways to resolve this conflict in Northern Ireland. President Clinton, having decided to make the region a priority in his foreign policy, sponsored a conference on trade and investment to encourage economic growth and job creation in Northern Ireland (see Mitchell 1999). Clinton also provided diplomatic support by visiting the region while president and by giving Gerry Adams, the leader of Sinn Fein, the IRA's political arm, a visa to enter the United States in 1996. This validated Adams and encouraged the IRA to moderate some of its policies. The United States further encouraged the peace process under the guidance of former senator George Mitchell, whose efforts resulted in the Good Friday accords of April 1998. The agreement, which granted greater political power to the Assembly in Ulster and included a power-sharing arrangement between Catholic and Protestant political parties, marked a significant step forward in ending terrorism in the region.

Since the signing of the Good Friday Agreement, however, all has not gone smoothly in Northern Ireland. After granting autonomy to Stormount, Great Britain was forced to resume authority over the province in the midst of continued unrest. Most significantly, the Unionists, led by David Trimble, refused to continue governing Ulster with Sinn Fein until the IRA had completely decommissioned its weapons, a measure required by the accords. Sinn Fein responded that that the police force in Ulster had not been properly reformed as called for in the agreement. This stalemate continued through the summer of 2005, when the IRA renounced political violence and began pursuing purely democratic and peaceful activities. The British, Irish, and U.S. governments responded positively to this change of position.

The change of approach by the IRA away from terrorism occurred for six reasons. First, there was decreasing support from the United States as American attitudes toward Great Britain grew more skeptical. Second, there was the realization among Catholics in Northern Ireland that time was on their side given the growing Catholic birth rate relative to that of Protestants in the region. Third, especially after the London bombings in July 2005, the IRA did not want to be compared to Islamic extremists, as the media did repeatedly. Fourth, British attitudes changed as well; Northern Ireland became less vital economically to Great Britain and was at times an embarrassment internationally. Finally, since both Ireland and Great Britain were part of the European Union (EU), there was a growing desire on the part of both governments to end the regional dispute. Lastly, in an important shift, the IRA and Sinn Fein saw a viable political alternative to violent struggle as a means to achieve their objectives.

Today the IRA is no longer the terrorist threat that it once was. The IRA, according to the Independent Monitoring Commission, has committed to a political approach to remedy the situation in Northern Ireland. There has been a significant decrease in violence in Northern Ireland. And in 2007 Sinn Fein and the Democratic Unionist Party negotiated a power-sharing agreement to govern the region. Leaders from both parties were sworn in as leaders of the new government (see Cowell & Quinn 2007).

The progress that occurred in this case resulted from the IRA's decision to adopt a peaceful approach to the conflict, a shift that was embraced by the British government. The U.S. government could encourage and cajole, but it could not force the two sides to find common ground. While democratic reforms endorsed by the Clinton administration, particularly those designed to guarantee equal political rights, played an important role in the negotiations, the U.S. mediation effort did not end the violence. A change in British attitudes toward Northern Ireland, as well as compromises by the IRA, was far more instrumental in producing peace in the region.

Sri Lanka

Sri Lanka regained its independence in 1948 after nearly 450 years of foreign domination (Dissanayaka 1984; de Silva 1981). Sinhalese Buddhists, roughly 70 percent of the population, are located in the center, western, and southern parts of the island, while Tamil Hindus constitute roughly 20 percent of the people of Sri Lanka and are largely located in the northeast corner of the island. Sri Lanka was colonized by the Portuguese, the Dutch, and later the British, whose colonization was significant because of London's immigration policy. The British imported Indians to Sri Lanka to work on cinnamon plantations, and by 1891 Indian immigrants numbered 235,000. This significantly altered the national religious makeup of Sri Lanka.

Although the government attempted to promote a pluralistic and secular society in Sri Lanka instead of one based on religious or ethnic identity, this effort did not resonate with the population (de Silva 1993). By 1954, Sinhalese Buddhists became increasingly vocal in national affairs. In 1956, the Freedom Party was elected with the help of political *bhikkhus*.[6] Attempts to "privatize" Buddhism were futile as its followers sought an active public role.

The Freedom Party elevated the status of Sinhalese Buddhists in a number of ways, including a legislative act making Sinhala the official language of the country. The Official Language Act of 1956 replaced English with Sinhala as the official language of the government. Riots broke out shortly after this linguistic change. (Religion, language, and ethnicity are interwoven in Sri Lanka.) One effect of this policy was that jobs that required proficiency in Sinhalese were closed to Tamils, who primarily spoke English. The new policies had economic repercussions and tended to make the Tamils resentful, since they primarily spoke English. Thus the language policy led to economic problems for Tamils, and this in turn led to alienation among Tamils. Despite the alienation felt, many Tamils continued to work within the political system.

This changed in 1983, when Sinhalese Buddhists, using voter registration lists, massacred more than 3,000 Tamils on July 26. Many Tamils, already frustrated with their second-class status in Sri Lanka, were radicalized by this event. As a consequence, after 1983 the Liberation Tigers of Tamil Eelam (LTTE) became engaged in a struggle for political independence with the government in which more than 70,000 people have been killed (Freedom House 2007). By 1986 the LTTE controlled much of the Tamil areas in the northeast part of the island. Support for the LTTE grew because of the government's inability to help or protect Tamils. The LTTE ambushed buses, killed military personnel, and slaughtered Sinhalese Buddhists in villages adjacent to territory they claimed in the northeast. They also used suicide bombers (Black Tigers) and political assassinations. In February 1996, a suicide bomber killed more than 90 people in Colombo, and on October 15, 1997, a bomb blast in Colombo killed more than 100.

In addition to the human rights violations noted above, the status of Sri Lankan democracy has degenerated. Since the beginning of the war in 1983, Sri Lanka has gone from a "free" state, according to the Freedom House (2007) survey, to a "partly free" state. Elections are held regularly and are considered basically free, although they are often accompanied by sporadic violence and intimidation. In December 2001, the conservative United National Party leader, Ranil Wickramasinghe, won parliamentary elections in Sri Lanka and became prime minister. He campaigned on a promise to end the civil war and negotiate a peace agreement with the Tigers. His election and campaign platform initiated a dialogue that occurred throughout 2002 and 2003.[7]

Mediated by the Norwegians, the government and the Tigers tried to negotiate an end to the civil war. Conciliatory actions on the part of the government and the Tigers greatly assisted in this process. In 2002, talks began and provided hope for a more peaceful future. Despite the opposition from Buddhist monks, the government stated that the Tigers should be viewed as equal partners in the development of peace and prosperity in the future of Sri Lanka. A permanent cease-fire accord was signed by the government and the Tigers in February 2002. This cease-fire was declared and supported by the Tigers' leader. In April 2002, Wickramasinghe traveled to the northern Tamil town of Jaffna, marking the first visit by a prime minister in more than twenty years. Four months later, the government lifted the ban on the Tigers.

A significant development in the talks occurred when the Tigers gave up their demand for a separate, independent state and announced that they would be content with greater internal autonomy within a federal system.[8] The Tigers also agreed to refrain from the use of child soldiers and to allow opposition political parties into the north. In response to these changes, the United States had limited contact with the LTTE (U.S. Department of State 2003–4, 15). The Tigers withdrew from the cease-fire in April 2003, however, claiming that the Sri Lankan government had violated its terms.

The limited progress of 2002 and 2003 quickly dissolved into tit-for-tat reprisals. A number of political and natural events hampered the cease-fire's efforts to limit violence and terrorism in Sri Lanka. The tsunami in December 2004 that devastated parts of Indonesia and India also caused significant damage to Sri Lanka. More than 35,000 people were killed and some 500,000 were displaced from their homes (Freedom House 2007). The tsunami resulted in more conflict and less cooperation between the government and the Tigers as they fought over reconstruction efforts and assistance.

Further problems emerged after presidential elections in 2005. Wickramasinghe, with 47 percent of the vote, was defeated by Mahinda Rajapake, who had less political capital and was less willing to compromise or negotiate with the LTTE. He was more interested in strengthening his power via parliament. Instead of negotiating, he increasingly took a hard line by launching air strikes against Tiger strongholds (Freedom House 2007). The Tigers responded to these military moves by initiating suicide attacks and bombings throughout the country. In the latter part of 2005, the Sri Lankan government also reinstated repressive policies to deal with the increased violence. The 1979 Prevention of Terrorism Act, which allowed for "the arrest and detention of subjects indefinitely without court approval," was again invoked (Freedom House 2007).

These harsh responses did not encourage nonviolent accommodation from the LTTE. According to two nongovernmental organizations, Freedom House and the International Committee of the Red Cross, in 2006 more than 3,500 people were killed in a variety of ways, including air strikes and suicide bombings. Another 200,000 people were displaced as violent clashes continued into 2007 (ICRC Annual Report 2007; Freedom House 2007).

Could intervention by the United States on behalf of democracy promotion have prevented the outbreak of terrorist violence in Sri Lanka? As in the case of the IRA, Washington had only limited influence on the parties in the dispute. Demands for a separate state by the LTTE required the Sri Lankan government to relinquish land, a concession that no external power could impose. It was also unlikely that Washington could offer Sri Lanka any military incentives that would moderate its position. Furthermore, giving LTTE control of the northeast would not ensure that the Tigers would develop a democratic political system. Without a change in the position of either the LTTE or the government of Sri Lanka, U.S. democracy promotion was unlikely to succeed.

The United States designated the LTTE as a foreign terrorist organization in 1997 and cut ties to the group as a result. Washington sought to cut all funding from the United States to the group. When the Bush administration came to office, it reiterated its opposition to terrorism and refused to endorse a separate state for the Tamil Tigers. The United States has not taken the lead in seeking an external solution to this conflict; Norway has played the pivotal role in attempting to forge peace between the two groups. The transformation of the Tigers from a terrorist organization to a political party, building on the model of Sinn Fein and the IRA, could advance the peace process significantly. While the devolution of autonomy might bring about lasting peace on the island, it would not be without its difficulties, as minority rights would be inevitably violated if an "illiberal" democracy assumed control.

Al-Qaeda

Al-Qaeda is best understood as a transnational jihadist organization with a primarily regional agenda. Thus it differs from some national insurgent groups, such as Hamas, which has primarily a subnational agenda in the Palestinian territories of Israel. It is opposed to the U.S. presence in the Middle East, especially in Saudi Arabia. It is also opposed to many secular governments in the Middle East, including those of Egypt, Saudi Arabia, Jordan, and most recently Iraq, and explicitly calls for the destruction of Israel. Al-Qaeda targeted the United States for a number of reasons, including Washington's support for Israel and the Mubarak government in Egypt, the stationing of U.S. troops in Saudi Arabia, and the 2003 U.S. invasion of Iraq. As bin Laden asserted in a 1996 fatwa, the United States was guilty of killing thousands of innocent civilians in Iraq in the 1991 Persian Gulf War (Ivie 2006, 137).

Al-Qaeda aims to create an Islamic state, not a democratic one, and ultimately to establish a pan-Islamic caliphate throughout the world. Its members seek to expel non-Muslims from Muslim countries, particularly Saudi Arabia (U.S. Department of State 2003–4, 131). The group has been involved in numerous acts of terrorism in recent years, including the bombings of U.S. embassies in Nairobi and Dar es Salaam that killed more than 300 people. Since 9/11, al-Qaeda has claimed responsibility for the bombing of a housing complex in Saudi Arabia that killed 20 and wounded 39, the attack on the International Committee of the Red Cross in October 2003 in Baghdad, and the November 2003 attack on a housing complex in Riyadh that killed 17 people (U.S. Department of State 2003–4, 89, 132).

It is highly unlikely that promoting democracy in the Middle East will address al-Qaeda's grievances. Their complaint is not about the lack of Western-style democracy in places such as Saudi Arabia or Iraq but about U.S. dominance in the region. Therefore, democratic alternatives will not satisfy al-Qaeda. By 2007, the Bush administration claimed that it had killed or captured much of al-Qaeda's leadership. But these reports mistakenly assumed that al-Qaeda was a well-organized and hierarchical organization, when clearly it was not. Al-Qaeda has mutated and consists today of a diffuse set of actors throughout the world. The organizational structure of various cells is largely unknown and has little direct connection with Osama bin Laden and other group leaders.

Besides the military response, Washington has also made a concentrated effort to limit the funding available to al-Qaeda to carry out attacks. This has been done by freezing bank accounts and cracking down on charities that fund the organization. Still, al-Qaeda retains the ability to strike and produce mass casualties at the time and place of its choosing. This was made clear by the ease in which al-Qaeda cells were able to operate and carry out attacks in Madrid in 2004 and London in 2005. Bin Laden's criticisms of U.S. policies and those of its allies resonate across the Islamic world. It is doubtful that U.S. appeals for democratic reforms in the region would diminish al-Qaeda's appeal, particularly since the group neither desires nor respects Western democratic political institutions.

LESSONS FOR U.S. FOREIGN POLICY

Given this analysis of terrorist organizations, what lessons can be learned for U.S. foreign policy? The first lesson that Washington must learn is the limitations of relying exclusively on democracy to defeat terrorism. Democracy promotion is not a panacea. Programs and foreign policy decisions that aim to promote democracy may lead to a decrease in violence and terrorism when the grievance is a lack of political equality or opportunity. However, terrorist organizations that seek regional or global domination will not be persuaded to renounce violence simply by being offered political opportunities at the ballot box. There are some individuals and organizations that will not compromise on their goals. Simply put, bin Laden and his followers prefer death to a seat at the political table. So U.S. foreign policy must acknowledge the limits of democracy promotion when dealing with some terrorists organizations. Democracy promotion is a limited tool that can be used only in certain circumstances.

Another lesson policymakers must learn is that for democracy to moderate terrorism, the U.S. government needs to have a dialogue with some terrorist organizations. One reason for the progress in Northern Ireland, especially with regard to the decrease in IRA terrorism, involved Washington's and London's willingness to negotiate with Gerry Adams and others associated with the IRA. In order to wean organizations off violence and into the political system, Washington must be willing to engage these dissatisfied groups. Declarations to the effect that "we will never talk to terrorists" preempt any prospect for compromise, let alone reconciliation.

Third, Washington must be patient and allow the democratic process to work. Northern Ireland has seen some success (albeit with some setbacks along the way) because the democratic process was allowed to move forward. Thus, British and American leaders did not refuse to acknowledge Sinn Fein's electoral gains at the ballot box. The United States, when it encourages democracy, must respect the results when the process has been determined to be free and fair. This has not always been the case in U.S. foreign policy.

Throughout the Clinton years, the president asserted that democracy promotion would be one of three main pillars in his foreign policy; however, the reality did not in fact match the rhetoric (Rieffer & Mercer 2005). For example, the U.S. response to Algeria's decision to cancel a second round of elections in 1994 because of a probable victory by the Islamic Salvation Front was silence. Washington feared the consequences of a victory for a party based on Islamic theology. Ultimately, the democratic process was suppressed in Algeria. A question that remains is whether cancelling elections saved Algeria from an even greater danger, or whether the cancellation of democracy led to more violence, including the attacks in April 2007 that killed more than thirty people.

Similar fears were voiced when Hamas won parliamentary elections in the Palestinian territories in 2006. Would Hamas's election result in a cancellation of democratic processes? Having an Islamist group that had employed terrorism repeatedly gain power by democratic means and thus gain political legitimacy was not a pleasant thought for U.S. foreign policy-makers. In such instances, when Washington feared the masses and the choices they could potentially make, the United States turned its back on democratic reform.

The fourth lesson for U.S. foreign policy involves the hazards associated with democracy promotion, which includes assisting in free and fair elections, the construction of government institutions, and the development of civil society. Promoting democracy in countries with little to no history of democracy can lead to violence and instability in the short term (Mansfield & Snyder, 2005). This is especially true when democracy is exported through military intervention.

Evidence of this can be amply found in Iraq and Afghanistan. The results in the latter case have been mixed. The 2004 national elections were unprecedented, resulting in the coming to power of President Hamid Karzai. The rights of women have improved, and other civil rights have been established. However, the country's future remains uncertain despite the presence of a sizeable NATO force. One CIA analyst thought it foolish to pursue democracy in Afghanistan given its fragmented tribal identities, hostile terrain, and the futility of previous great power interventions (Anonymous 2004).

In Iraq, the Bush administration argued that ousting Saddam Hussein in Operation Iraqi Freedom was "an important advance for the global war on terrorism" (U.S. Department of State 2003–4, 58). As in Afghanistan, the White House worked to produce early elections in Iraq. It was argued by some, including Deputy Secretary of Defense Paul Wolfowitz, that democratizing Iraq would effect similar change throughout the region. Nothing of the sort has occurred, however, and it remains to be seen whether Iraq under U.S. influence and protection can move toward power sharing among Shiites, Sunnis, and Kurds. The war has strained the U.S. military, left more than 4,000 Americans dead, and cost its taxpayers hundreds of billions of dollars.

American efforts to promote democracy in these countries may result in an increase, not a decrease, in terrorism for many years to come. This affirms the expectations of many that "the idea of a quick and easy democratic transformation is a fantasy" (Ottaway et al. 2002). Historical evidence suggests that military interventions rarely lead to stable democratic political systems (Germany and Japan being notable exceptions). Jeffrey Pickering and Mark Peceny (2006, 556) argue in their study of liberal military interventions from 1946 to 1996 that "we are left with the uncomfortable truth that most liberal interventions have failed to lead to successful democratization."

The recent U.S. interventions may ultimately produce a setback for U.S. democracy promotion abroad. Conceptually, fighting a war for a democratic peace is puzzling; belligerence for the cause of pacific relations appears to be counterintuitive (Ivie 2006, 6). Thomas Carothers (2006, 56), a leading expert on the subject, concluded that the United States has "weakened the legitimacy of the democracy promotion cause" that many other countries had adopted. Skeptical observers in many countries viewed U.S. democracy promotion as a Trojan horse aimed at regime change only for those current leaders who opposed Bush. Regardless of the White House's motives, the United States lost much credibility during the Bush years that will take many more years to restore (Pew Research Center 2007).

Washington also needs to understand the limits of democracy promotion in stemming mass alienation, a common breeding ground of terrorism. Aside from those in leadership positions, many citizens feel powerless and thus support groups like al-Qaeda because the group gives them a sense of purpose and lends meaning to their lives. To overcome the terrorist threat, U.S. foreign policy–makers must address the roots and consequences of this alienation. As Bruce Hoffman (1998, 128) has argued, "a bridge needs to be found between mainstream society and the extremists so that they do not feel threatened and forced to withdraw into heavily armed, seething compounds or to engage in pre-emptive acts of violence directed against what they regard as a menacing, predatory society."

A more productive way to deal with the alienation felt by many around the world lies in economic development. By connecting these individuals to economic development, they develop a stake in the growth and stability of society. There was an element of this in President Clinton's foreign policy toward Northern Ireland, part of which included job growth and investment in the region, efforts aimed at keeping young people from turning to terrorist groups in desperation. In this respect, it is useful to recall Kant's assertion that people will not choose to fight in wars if their economic self-interest is harmed. So those with economic opportunities may be more reluctant to engage in terrorism if these opportunities are threatened.

Since democracy promotion by itself will not stop terrorism, the question arises as to why the Bush administration argued that democracy was the answer to terrorism. There are a number of reasons for the rhetorical emphasis on democracy. Faced with the absence of weapons of mass destruction in Iraq and the ensuing insurgency across the country, the Bush administration changed its strategic rationale by turning to one of the core aspects of American political culture: democracy (Fallows 2004; Pickering & Peceny 2006). That is the argument that carries the most clout with Congress and public opinion, given the American self-image as a country that advances personal freedom in the world. By arguing that the United States is promoting democracy to defeat terrorism, U.S. leaders appeal to American values and Americans' belief in their inherent virtue. This appeal, however, is lost on many overseas, who have been confronted with the brute force of American power and self-interest.

CONCLUSION

We should be skeptical of claims by Washington that democratization will automatically lead to a decrease in terrorism around the world. Historical experience suggests that this is a more complicated relationship than typically acknowledged. Some terrorist organizations are fundamentally antidemocratic in their attitudes and beliefs. If a majority of voters believes that religious law should govern, or that compromising with nonbelievers is a sin, then democracy will lead to greater repression, not to liberty and human rights.

As we have seen, an end to terrorist violence is possible when terrorist organizations alter their objectives and the tactics used to achieve them. The changes in the IRA and LTTE's desired outcomes came about for a number of complex reasons. In both instances, the desired goals revolved around subnational, not regional, aims. Neither group sought to expand territorial control beyond its homeland, and neither group aspired to spread religious or ideological beliefs throughout the world. Thus, in both cases there was the potential for democracy promotion to have some effect, however limited. The cases of Afghanistan and al-Qaeda are very different. In the former case, an ousted regime (the Taliban) remains bent on a return to power. In the latter case, the actor in question is stateless, theocratic, and determined to transform not only regional but global politics. Iraq, never an al-Qaeda stronghold, is merely the theater of conflict in which Washington chose—unwisely, it appears—to take its stand against Islamist terrorism.

Stable democratic political systems take time to develop. Hence, patience and cultural understanding are necessary for external actors to decrease terrorism through democracy promotion. Compromise is necessary, even if that entails making political compromises with groups that have used terror in the past. Ultimately, the United States needs to recognize the limits of democracy promotion, especially when it is advanced through military intervention. Washington should support democracy promotion in principle, as political reform that empowers mass publics is generally in America's interest. But there is no simple recipe for success, and blind faith in the power of military force to export democracy, and of democracy to transform the world into a pacific utopia, can create more problems than it solves.

NOTES

1. This does not discount the fact that democracies also contain intolerant citizens. However, history shows that few citizens in democratic polities resort to political violence.
2. Citizens in democratic states have occasionally resorted to terrorism. One can look at the Oklahoma City bomber, Timothy McVeigh, to see that some citizens living in a democracy have not been moved by norms of peaceful political change.
3. The State Department employs the following definition of terrorism: "premeditated, politically motivated violence perpetrated against noncombatant targets by subnational groups or clandestine agents, usually intended to influence an audience" (U.S. Department of State 2004, xii).
4. The Penal Laws denied Catholics voting rights, political office, and opportunities in the military and legal professions.
5. Charles Trevelyan, assistant treasury secretary, was philosophically opposed to state interference in the market. His philosophical beliefs resulted in a policy that refused to help the Irish during the famine.
6. It is worth noting that the two most dominant political parties have been the Sri Lanka Freedom Party (liberal) and the United National Party (conservative). Both adopted nationalist policies and supported the elevation of Sinhalese Buddhism.
7. It has been suggested that the move by the prime minister was motivated by economic considerations. The Sri Lankan economy was decimated by the civil war.
8. By creating a homeland with autonomy, or giving the Tamils internal self-determination, the Tamils could have their religious national identity recognized even in the absence of an independent state.

References

Acemoglu, Daron, and James A. Robinson. 2006. *Economic origins of dictatorship and democracy.* Cambridge, UK: Cambridge University Press.

Adedeji, Adebayo. 1999. Comprehending African conflicts. In *Comprehending and mastering African conflict: The search for sustainable peace and good governance,* ed. Adebayo Adedeji, 3–21. London: Zed Books.

Africa Development Bank. 2001. *Annual report 2000.* Abidjan, Cote d'Ivoire: Africa Development Bank.

Ake, Claude. 1989. How politics underdevelops Africa. In *The challenge of African economic recovery and development,* ed. Adebayo Adedeji and P. Bugemba, 316–29. London: Frank Cass.

Ake, Claude. 1993a. The unique case of African democracy. *International Affairs* 69 (2): 239–44.

Ake, Claude. 1993b. Rethinking African democracy. In *The global resurgence of democracy,* ed. Larry Diamond and Marc F. Plattner, 63–75. Baltimore, MD: Johns Hopkins University Press.

Aksu, Esref. 2008. "Perpetual peace": A project by Europeans for Europeans? *Peace and Change* 33 (3): 368–87.

Allawi, Ali. 2007. *The occupation of Iraq: Winning the war, losing the peace.* New Haven, CT: Yale University Press.

Allen, Susan H. 2004. Rallying cry? Economic sanctions and the domestic politics of the target state. Ph.D. diss, Emory University.

al-Nabulsi, Shakir. 2006. Daur arafat fi fauz hamas, *Al-Siyasa.* February 8. [In Arabic.]

Alterman, Jon B. 2004. The false promise of Arab liberals. *Policy Review,* no. 125: 77–85.

Althusser, Louis. 1971. *Lenin and philosophy.* New York, NY: Monthly Review Press.

Anderson, Benedict. 1983. *Imagined communities: Reflections on the origin and spread of nationalism.* New York, NY: Verso.

Anderson, Betty S. 1997. The status of "democracy" in Jordan. *Critique,* no. 10: 55–76.

Anderson, Lisa. 1992. Remaking the Middle East: The prospects for democracy and stability. *Ethics and International Affairs* 6: 163–78.

Andoni, Lamis, and Jillian Schwedler. 1996. Bread riots in Jordan. *Middle East Report,* no. 201: 40–42.

Andreas, Peter. 2005. Criminalizing consequences of sanctions: Embargo busting and its legacy. *International Studies Quarterly* 49 (3): 335–60.

Ang, Adrian, and Dursun Peksen. 2007. When do economic sanctions work? Assymetric perceptions, issue salience, and outcomes. *Political Research Quarterly* 60 (1): 135–45.

Angell, Norman. 1909. *Europe's optical illusion.* London: Norman Angell.

Anonymous. 2004. *Imperial hubris: Why the West is losing the war on terror.* Dulles, VA: Brassey's.

Atwan, 'Abd al-Bari. 2006. Imrika takhdhal al-libraliyeen al-arab. *Al-Quds al-Arabi,* May 18. [In Arabic.]

Ayittey, George B. N. 1993. *Africa betrayed.* New York, NY: Palgrave.

Ayittey, George B. N. 1998. *Africa in chaos.* New York, NY: St. Martin's Press.

Ayittey, George B. N. 2005. *Africa unchained: The blueprint for Africa's future.* New York, NY: Palgrave.

Ayoob, Mohammed. 1995. *The third world security predicament: State making, regional conflict, and the international system.* Boulder, CO: Lynne Rienner.

Ayres, R. William. 2007. Cold war perceptions and the American experience of war. In *America, war, and power: Defining the state, 1775–2005,* ed. Lawrence Sondhaus and A. James Fuller, 182–212. London: Routledge.

Babst, Dean. 1964. Elective governments: A force for peace. *Wisconsin Sociologist* 3 (1): 9–14.

Bacevich, Andrew J. 2005. The real World War IV. *Wilson Quarterly* 29 (1): 36–61.

Badrikhan, Abdel Wahab. 2006. Ifshal Hamas. *Al-Hayat,* February 16. [In Arabic.]

Baer, Michael A., and Dean Jaros. 1974. Participation as an instrument and expression: Some evidence from the States. *American Journal of Political Science* 18 (2): 365–83.

Bakhash, Shaul. 1998. Iran's remarkable election. *Journal of Democracy* 9 (1): 80–94.

Bandy, Joe, and Jackie Smith, eds. 2005. *Coalitions across borders: Transnational protest and the neoliberal order.* Lanham, MD: Rowman and Littlefield.

Bank, André, and Oliver Schlumberger. 2004. Jordan: Between regime survival and economic reform. In *Arab elites: Negotiating the politics of change,* ed. Volker Perthes, 35–60. Boulder, CO: Lynne Rienner.

Baran, Paul A., and Paul M. Sweezy. 1966. *Monopoly capital.* New York, NY: Monthly Review Press.

Barker, Ernest. 1962. *Social contract: Essays by Locke, Hume, and Rousseau.* New York, NY: Oxford University Press.

Baroud, Ramzy. 2004. U.S. initiatives for reform. *Al-Jazeera.net,* December 19. http://english.aljazeera.net/English/archive/archive?ArchiveId=3739.

Baum, Tomas. 2008. A quest for inspiration in the liberal peace paradigm: Back to Bentham? *European Journal of International Relations* 14 (3): 431–53.

Bayart, Jean-François, Stephen Ellis, and Béatrice Hibou. 1999. *The criminalization of the state in Africa.* Oxford, UK: James Currey.

Beck, Nathanial, Jonathan N. Katz, and Richard Tucker. 1998. Taking time seriously: Time-series-cross-section analysis with a binary dependent variable. *American Journal of Political Science* 42 (4): 1260–88.

Bellin, Eva. 2004. The robustness of authoritarianism in the Middle East. *Comparative Politics* 36 (2): 139–57.

Bergman, Lowell, Eric Lichtblau, Scott Shane, and Don Van Natta Jr. 2006. Spy agency data after Sept. 11 led F.B.I. to dead ends. *New York Times,* January 17, A1.

Berman, Bruce. 1998. Ethnicity, patronage, and the African state: The politics of uncivil nationalism. *African Affairs* 97 (July): 305–41.
Best, Richard A. Jr., and Alfred Cumming. 2007. Director of national intelligence statutory authorities: Status and proposals. Report for Congress. Washington, DC: Congressional Research Service.
Betts, Richard K. 1992. Systems for peace or causes of war? Collective security, arms control, and the new Europe. *International Security* 17 (1): 5–43.
Block, Fred. 1987. *Revising state theory.* Philadelphia, PA: Temple University Press.
Bloomsberg News. 2007. Director wants more authority in intelligence. *New York Times*, April 5, A13.
Boduszynski, Monica, and Pierre Englebert. 2008. Poverty and democracy in Africa. In *Democracy and culture: An African perspective*, ed. L. Moshi and A. Osman, 29–50. London: Adonis and Abbey.
Boggs, Carl. 1976. *Gramsci's Marxism.* London: Pluto Press.
Boix, Charles. 2003. *Democracy and redistribution.* Cambridge, UK: Cambridge University Press.
Bonner, Raymond. 2005. U.S. image sags in Australian poll. *New York Times*, March 29, A8.
Booth, John A., and Patricia Bayer Richard. 1998. Civil society, political capital, and democratization in Central America. *The Journal of Politics* 60 (3): 780–800.
Braathen, Einar, Morten Bøås, and Gjermund Sæther. 2000. Ethnicity kills? Social struggles for power, resources, and identities in the neo-patrimonial state. In *Ethnicity kills? The politics of war, peace and ethnicity in sub-Saharan Africa*, ed. Einar Braathen, Morten Bøås, and Gjermund Sæther, 3–22. New York, NY: St. Martin's Press.
Brand, Laurie. 1994. *Jordan's inter-Arab relations: The political economy of alliance-making.* New York, NY: Columbia University Press.
Brand, Laurie. 1999. The effects of the peace process on political liberalization in Jordan. *Journal of Palestine Studies* 28 (2): 52–67.
Brands, H. W. 1998. *What America owes the world: The struggle for the soul of foreign policy.* Cambridge, UK: Cambridge University Press.
Bratton, Michael, and Nicholas Van de Walle. 1997. *Democratic experiments in Africa: Regime transitions in comparative perspective.* Cambridge, UK: Cambridge University Press.
Brown, Carl L. 1984. *International politics and the Middle East: Old rules, dangerous game.* Princeton, NJ: Princeton University Press.
Brown, Michael E., Sean M. Lynn-Jones, and Steven E. Miller, eds. 1996. *Debating the democratic peace.* Cambridge, MA: MIT Press.
Brown, Nathan J., Amr Hamzawy, and Marina Ottaway. 2006. Islamist movements and the democratic process in the Arab world: Exploring the gray zones. Carnegie Paper no. 67. Washington, DC: Carnegie Endowment for International Peace.
Brownlee, Jason. 2002. . . . And yet they persist: Explaining survival and transition in neo-patrimonial regimes. *Studies in Comparative International Development* 37 (3): 35–63.
Bruce, James. 1995. Waiting for helping hands. *Jane's Defense Weekly* 23 (26).
Brumberg, Daniel. 2002. The trap of liberalized autocracy. *Journal of Democracy* 13 (4): 56–68.
Brynen, Rex. 1992. Economic crisis and post-rentier democratization in the Arab world. *Canadian Journal of Political Science* 25 (1): 69–97.
Brynen, Rex, Bahgat Korany, and Paul Noble, eds. 1995, 1998. *Political liberalization and democratization in the Arab world.* 2 vols. Boulder, CO: Lynne Rienner.

Brzezinski, Zbigniew. 2007. Terrorized by "war on terror." *Washington Post*, March 25, B01.
Bueno de Mesquita, Bruce, and George W. Downs. 2005. Development and democracy. *Foreign Affairs* 84 (5): 77–86.
Bueno de Mesquita, Bruce, Alastair Smith, Randolph M. Siverson, and James D. Morrow. 2003. *The logic of political survival*. Cambridge, MA: MIT Press.
Bueno de Mesquita, Bruce. 2002. Domestic politics and international relations. *International Studies Quarterly* 46 (1): 1–9.
Burkhart, Ross E., and Michael S. Lewis-Beck. 1994. Comparative democracy: The economic development thesis. *American Political Science Review* 88: 903–10.
Bush, George W. 2004. Bush speech on American strategy in Iraq. *New York Times*, May 24. http://www.nytimes.com/2004/05/24/politics/25PTEX.FULL.html. Retrieved August 30, 2009.
Bush, George W. 2005a. Second inaugural address. *Washington Post*, January 21, A24.
Bush, George W. 2005b. Speech at FBI Academy, Quantico, VA, July 11. http://www.whitehouse.gov/news/releases/2005/07/20050711-1.html#.
Cahill, Thomas. 1995. *How the Irish saved civilization*. New York, NY: Doubleday.
Callaghy, Thomas M. 1987. *Politics and culture in Zaire*. Ann Arbor, MI: Center for Political Studies, Institute for Social Research, University of Michigan.
Carapico, Sheila. 2002. Foreign aid for promoting democracy in the Arab world. *Middle East Journal* 56 (3): 379–95.
Carnahan, Michael, William Durch, and Scott Gilmore, eds. 2006. *Economic impact of peacekeeping*. Global Policy Forum. http://www.globalpolicy.org/security/peacekpg/general/2006/03impact.pdf.
Carothers, Thomas. 1999. *Aiding democracy abroad: The learning curve*. Washington, DC: Carnegie Endowment for International Peace.
Carothers, Thomas. 2005a. A better way to support Middle East reform. Policy brief no. 33. Washington, DC: Carnegie Endowment for International Peace.
Carothers, Thomas. 2005b. Choosing a strategy. In *Uncharted journey: Promoting democracy in the Middle East*, ed. Thomas Carothers and Marina Ottaway, 193–208. Washington, DC: Carnegie Endowment for International Peace.
Carothers, Thomas. 2006. The backlash against democracy promotion. *Foreign Affairs* 85 (2): 55–68.
Carr, E. H. 1939. *The twenty years' crisis: 1919–1939*. London: Macmillan.
Center for Strategic Studies, Public Opinion Polling Unit. 2006. *Democracy in Jordan—2006*. Amman, Jordan: Center for Strategic Studies.
Central Bank of Jordan. 1996. *Yearly statistical series: 1964–1995*. Amman, Jordan: Department of Research and Studies.
Central Intelligence Agency (CIA). 2007. *World Factbook*. https://www.cia.gov/cia/publications/factbook/geos/us.html.
Chan, Steve. 1993. Democracy and war: Some thoughts on the future research agenda. *International Interactions* 18 (3): 205–13.
Chan, Steve. 1997. In search of democratic peace: Problems and promise. *Mershon International Studies Review* 41 (2): 59–91.
Chazan, Naomi. 1990. Africa's democratic challenge: Strengthening civil society and the state. *World Policy Journal* 9 (2): 279–307.
Chazan, Naomi, Robert Mortimer, John Ravenhill, and Donald Rothchild. 1999. *Politics and society in contemporary Africa*. Boulder, CO: Lynne Rienner.

Choi, Seung-Whan, and Patrick James. 2008. Civil-military structure, political communication, and the democratic peace. *Journal of Peace Research* 45 (1): 37–53.
Choucair, Julia. 2006. Illusive reform: Jordan's stubborn stability. Carnegie Paper no. 76. Washington, DC: Carnegie Endowment for International Peace.
Chua, Amy. 2004. *World on fire: How exporting free market democracy breeds ethnic hatred and global instability.* New York, NY: Anchor Books.
Church, Frank. 1976. Covert action: Swampland of American foreign policy. *Bulletin of the Atomic Scientists* 32 (February): 7–11.
Church Committee. 1975. U.S. Senate, Select Committee to Study Governmental Operations with Respect to Intelligence Activities. *Hearings.* U.S. Senate, 94th Cong., 2nd sess. 6 vols. Washington, DC: Government Printing Office.
Church Committee. 1976. U.S. Senate, Select Committee to Study Governmental Operations with Respect to Intelligence Activities. *Final report.* 94th Cong., 2nd sess. S. Rept. no. 94–755, 6 vols. Washington, DC: Government Printing Office.
Churchill, Winston S. 1950. *Europe unite: Speeches 1947 and 1948,* ed. Randolph S. Churchill. Boston, MA: Houghton Mifflin.
Cingranelli, David L., and David L. Richards. 2004. *The Cingranelli-Richards (CIRI) human rights database.* http://www.humanrightsdata.com.
Clarke, Richard A. 2004. *Against all enemies: Inside America's war on terror.* New York, NY: Free Press.
Cobden, Richard. 1903 [1867]. *Political writings of Richard Cobden,* vol. 1. London: T. Fisher Unwin.
Cohen, Roger, David E. Sanger, and Steven R. Weisman. 2004. Challenging rest of the world with a new order. *New York Times,* October 12, A20.
Collier, Paul, and Jan Willem Gunning. 1999. Why has Africa grown slowly? *Journal of Economic Perspectives* 13 (3): 3–22.
Columbani, Jean-Marie. 2001. We are all Americans. *Le Monde,* September 12, 15.
Congressional Hearings. 1984. Subcommittees on Human Rights and International Organizations and on Asian and Pacific Affairs. *The human rights implications of the Sinhalese-Tamil conflict in Sri Lanka.* 98th Cong., 2nd sess. (2 August), 6–24.
Cook, Steven A. 2005. The right way to promote Arab reform. *Foreign Affairs* 84: 91–102.
Cortright, David, Alistair Millar, and George A. Lopez. 2001. *Smart sanctions: Restructuring UN policy in Iraq.* Goshen, IN: Fourth Freedom Forum.
Cortright, David, and George A. Lopez, eds. 1995. *Economic sanctions: Panacea or peacebuilding in a post–cold war world?* Boulder, CO: Westview Press.
Cortright, David, and George A. Lopez, eds. 2000. Learning from the sanctions decade. *Global Dialogue* 2 (3): 11–24.
Cousens, Elizabeth M., and Chetan Kumar, eds. 2001. *Peacebuilding as politics.* Boulder, CO: Lynne Rienner.
Cowell, Alan, and Eamon Quinn. 2007. Power sharing begins in Northern Ireland. *New York Times,* May 8.
Cox, Robert. 1987. *Production, power, and world order.* New York, NY: Columbia University Press.
Cragin, Kim, and Sara Daly. 2004. *The dynamic terrorist threat.* Santa Monica, CA: Rand.
Craig, Gordon, and Alexander George. 1990. *Force and statecraft: Diplomatic problems of our time.* 2nd ed. Oxford, UK: Oxford University Press.
Crocker, Chester A., Fen Osler Hampson, and Pamela Aall, eds. 2001. *Turbulent peace: The challenges of managing international conflict.* Washington, DC: U.S. Institute of Peace.

Crozier, Michael, Samuel P. Huntington, and Joji Watanuki. 1975. *The crisis of democracy: Report on the governability of democracies to the trilateral commission.* New York, NY: New York University Press.

Crystal, Jill. 1994. Authoritarianism and its adversaries in the Arab world. *World Politics* 46 (2): 262–89.

Dahl, Robert A. 1956. *A preface to democratic theory.* Chicago, IL: University of Chicago Press.

Dahl, Robert A. 1961. *Who governs.* New Haven, CT: Yale University Press.

Dahl, Robert A. 1971. *Polyarchy: Participation and opposition.* New Haven, CT: Yale University Press.

Dahl, Robert A. 1989. *Democracy and its critics.* New Haven, CT: Yale University Press.

Davidson, Basil. 1992. *The black man's burden: Africa and the curse of nation-state.* New York, NY: Times Books.

Dershowitz, Alan M. 2003. *Why terrorism works: Understanding the threat, responding to the challenge.* New Haven, CT: Yale University Press.

De Silva, K. M. 1981. *A history of Sri Lanka.* New Delhi, India: Oxford University Press.

De Silva, K. M. 1993. *Sri Lanka: Problems of governance.* New Delhi, India: Centre for Policy Research.

de Sousa Santos, Boaventura. 2006. *The rise of the global left: The world social forum and beyond.* New York, NY: Zed Books.

Diamond, Larry. 1989. *Beyond autocracy: Prospects for democracy in Africa.* Atlanta, GA: Carter Centre for Emory University.

Diamond, Larry. 1999. *Developing democracy: Toward consolidation.* Baltimore, MD: John Hopkins University Press.

DiLorenzo, Thomas. 2003. *The real Lincoln: A new look at Abraham Lincoln, his agenda, and an unnecessary war.* New York, NY: Three Rivers Press.

Dissanayaka, T. D. 1984. *The agony of Sri Lanka.* Colombo, Sri Lanka: Swastika Press.

Dixon, William. 1993. Democracy and the management of international conflict. *Journal of Conflict Resolution* 37 (1): 42–68.

Domhoff, William G. 2006. *Who rules America? Power and politics and social change.* Boston, MA: McGraw-Hill.

Downing, Brian. 1992. *The military revolution and political change.* Princeton, NJ: Princeton University Press.

Doyle, Michael W. 1983a. Kant, liberal legacies, and foreign affairs. *Philosophy and Public Affairs* 12 (3): 205–35.

Doyle, Michael W. 1983b. Kant, liberal legacies, and foreign affairs, part 2. *Philosophy and Public Affairs* 12 (4): 323–53.

Doyle, Michael W. 1986. Liberalism and world politics. *American Political Science Review* 80 (4): 1151–68.

Doyle, Michael W. 1997. *Ways of war and peace: Realism, liberalism, and socialism.* New York, NY: Norton.

Doyle, Michael W. 2005. Three pillars of the liberal peace. *American Political Science Review* 99 (3): 463–66.

Doyle, Michael W., and Nicholas Sambanis. 2006. *Making war and building peace: United Nations peace operations.* Princeton, NJ: Princeton University Press.

Drew, Elizabeth. 2003. The neocons in power. *New York Review of Books,* June 12, 20–22.

Drury, A. Cooper, and Yitan Li. 2006. U.S. economic sanction threats against China: Failing to leverage better human rights. *Foreign Policy Analysis* 2 (4): 307–24.

Drury, A. Cooper. 2005. *Economic sanctions and presidential decisions: Models of political rationality.* New York, NY: Palgrave.

Economist Intelligence Unit. 2001. *Country report: Jordan.* 4th quarter. London: Economist Intelligence Unit.

Egan, Daniel. 2001. The limits of internationalization: A neo-gramscian analysis of the multilateral agreement on investment. *Critical Sociology* 27 (3): 74–97.

Elman, Miriam Fendius, ed. 1997. *Paths to peace: Is democracy the answer?* Cambridge, MA: MIT Press.

Elshtain, Jean. 1995. *Democracy on trial.* New York, NY: Basic Books.

Emerson, Ralph Waldo. 1979 (1841). Self-reliance. In *Essays: First series.* Cambridge, MA: Belknap Press.

The end of the dream of the greater Middle East. 2006. *E'temad-e Melli,* August 5. [In Farsi, Mideastwire.com translation.]

Englebert, Pierre. 2000. *State legitimacy and development in Africa.* Boulder, CO: Lynne Rienner.

Epstein, David L., Robert Bates, Jack Goldstone, Ida Kristensen, and Sharyn O'Halloran. 2006. Democratic transitions. *American Journal of Political Science* 50 (3): 551–69.

Fallows, James. 2004. Blind into Baghdad. *Atlantic Monthly* 293 (1): 52–77.

Fanon, Frantz. 1961. *The wretched of the earth.* Trans. Constance Farrington. New York, NY: Grove Press.

Fattah, Hassan M. 2006. Democracy in the Arab world, a U.S. goal, falters. *New York Times,* April 10.

Fatton, Robert. 1992. *Predatory rule: State and civil society in Africa.* Boulder, CO: Lynne Rienner.

Fearon, James D., and David D. Laitin. 2003. Ethnicity, insurgency, and civil war. *American Political Science Review* 97 (1): 75–90.

Ferejohn, John, and Frances McCall Rosenbuth. 2008. Warlike democracies. *Journal of Conflict Resolution* 52(1): 3–38.

Fiala, Andrew. 2009. The democratic peace myth: From Hiroshima to Baghdad. *American Journal of Economics and Sociology* 68(1): 77–99.

Field, Guy C. 1963. *Political theory.* London: Methuen.

Finer, Jonathan, and Omar Fekeiki. 2005. Tackling another major challenge in Iraq: Unemployment. *Washington Post,* June 20, A10.

Finer, Samuel. 1999. *The history of government from the earliest time.* New York, NY: Wadsworth.

Fisher, William F., and Thomas Ponniah. 2003. *Another world is possible: Popular alternatives to globalization at the world social forum.* New York, NY: Zed Books.

Fletcher, Laurel E., and Harvey M. Weinstein. 2004. A world unto itself: The application of international justice in the former Yugoslavia. In *My neighbor, my enemy: Justice and community in the aftermath of mass atrocity,* ed. Eric Stover and H. M. Weinstein, 29–48. New York, NY: Cambridge University Press.

Forster, E. M. 1951. *Two cheers for democracy.* New York, NY: Harcourt, Brace and World.

Fortna, Virginia Page. 2004. *Peace time: Cease-fire agreements and the durability of peace.* Princeton, NJ: Princeton University Press.

Freedom House. 2006. *Freedom in the world.* New York, NY: Freedom House.

Freedom House. 2007. *Freedom in the world.* New York, NY: Freedom House.

Freedom House. 2009. *Freedom in the world.* New York, NY: Freedom House.

Friedman, Thomas L. 1999. *The Lexus and the olive tree.* New York, NY: Farrar, Straus and Giroux.

Frum, David, and Richard Perle. 2003. *An end to evil: How to win the war on terror.* New York, NY: Random House.

Fukuyama, Francis. 1992. *The end of history and the last man.* New York, NY: Free Press.

Fukuyama, Francis. 2004a. The neoconservative moment. *National Interest,* Summer: 57–68.

Fukuyama, Francis. 2004b. *State building: Governance and world order in the twenty-first century.* Ithaca, NY: Cornell University Press.

Fukuyama, Francis. 2005. America's parties and their foreign policy masquerade. *Financial Times,* March 8, 21.

Fuller, Graham E. 2004. *The future of political Islam.* New York, NY: Palgrave Macmillan.

Galtung, Johan. 1967. On the effects of international economic sanctions: With examples from the case of Rhodesia. *World Politics* 19 (3): 378–416.

Gartzke, Erik. 1998. Kant we all just get along? Motive, opportunity, and the origins of the democratic peace. *American Journal of Political Science* 42 (1): 1–27.

Gartzke, Erik. 2006. Globalization, economic development, and territorial conflict. In *Territoriality and conflict in an era of globalization,* ed. Miles Kahler and Barbara Walter, 156–86. Cambridge, UK: Cambridge University Press.

Gartzke, Erik. 2007. The capitalist peace. *American Journal of Political Science* 51 (1): 166–91.

Gartzke, Erik, and Quan Li. 2003. War, peace, and the invisible hand: Positive political externalities of economic globalization. *International Studies Quarterly* 47 (4): 561–86.

Gause, F. Gregory III. 2005. Can democracy stop terrorism? *Foreign Affairs* 84 (5): 62–76.

Gause, F. Gregory III. 2006. Beware of what you wish for. *Foreign Affairs* Author Update, February 8. http://www.foreignaffairs.org/20060208faupdate85177/f-gregory-gause-iii/beware-of-what-you-wish-for.html.

George, Alexander. 1980. *Presidential decisionmaking in foreign policy: The effective use of information and advice.* Boulder, CO: Westview Press.

George, Alexander L. 1991. *Forceful persuasion: Coercive diplomacy as an alternative to war.* Washington, DC: U.S. Institute of Peace Press.

Gerges, Fawaz A. 1999. *America and political Islam: Clash of cultures or clash of interests?* Cambridge, UK: Cambridge University Press.

Gettleman, Jeffrey. 2007. After Congo vote, neglect and scandal still reign. *New York Times,* March 28, A11.

Gibbons, Elizabeth D. 1999. *Sanctions in Haiti: Human rights and democracy under assault.* Westport, CT: Praeger.

Gill, Graeme. 2000. *The dynamics of democratization: Elites, civil society and the transition process.* New York, NY: St. Martin's Press.

Gill, Graeme. 2003. *Power and resistance in the new world order.* New York, NY: Palgrave Macmillan.

Gill, Stephen, ed. 1993. *Gramsci, historical materialism and international relations.* New York, NY: Cambridge University Press.

Glain, Stephen. 2005. *Mullahs, merchants, and militants: The economic collapse of the Arab world.* New York, NY: Thomas Dunne.

Gleditsch, Kristian S. 2003. *All politics is local: The diffusion of conflict, integration, and democratization.* Ann Arbor: University of Michigan Press.

Global Witness. 2006. Digging in corruption: Fraud, abuse, and exploitation in Katanga's copper and cobalt mines. http://www.globalpolicy.org/security/issues/congo/2006/07digging.pdf.

Godson, Roy. 2003. Transnational crime, corruption, and security. In *Grave new world: Security challenges in the twenty-first century*, ed. Michael E. Brown, 259–78. Washington, DC: Georgetown University Press.

Goldwater, Barry. 1984. Letter to the editor. *Washington Post*, April 11, A17.

Goodin, Robert, and John Dryzek. 1980. Rational participation: The politics of relative power. *British Journal of Political Science* 10 (3): 273–92.

Gottfried, Paul. 2007. The invincible Wilsonian matrix: Universal human rights once again. *Orbis* 51 (2):239–50.

Gramsci, Antonio. 1971. *Selections from the prison notebooks*. New York, NY: International Publishers.

Green, Donald, Soo Yeon Kim, and David Yoon. 2001. Dirty pool. *International Organization* 55 (2): 441–68.

Greenwood, Scott. 2003. Jordan, the al-Aqsa intifada and America's "war on terror." *Middle East Policy* 10 (3): 90–92.

Griffin, Victor. 2002. *Enough religion to make us hate*. Blackrock, CO: Columba Press.

Guelke, Adrian. 2001. Violence and electoral polarization in divided societies: Three cases in comparative perspective. In *The democratic experience and political violence*, eds. David C. Rapoport and Leonard Weinberg, 78–105. London: Frank Cass.

Gurr, Ted Robert, Monty G. Marshall, and Deepa Khosla. 2000. *Peace and conflict 2001: A global survey of armed conflicts, self-determination movements, and democracy*. College Park, MD: University of Maryland Center for International Development and Conflict.

Habeeb, William Mark. 1988. *Power and tactics in international negotiation: How weak nations bargain with strong nations*. Baltimore, MD: Johns Hopkins University Press.

Hafez, Mohammed M. 2003. *Why Muslims rebel: Repression and resistance in the Islamic world*. Boulder, CO: Lynne Rienner.

Halperin, Morton, Joseph Siegle, and Michael Weinstein. 2004. *The democracy advantage: How democracies promote prosperity and peace*. New York, NY: Routledge.

Hamilton, Alexander. 1787a. General introduction. Federalist Paper no. 1, October 27. http://www.foundingfathers.info/federalistpapers/fed01.htm.

Hamilton, Alexander. 1787b. The same subject continued (the idea of restraining the legislative authority in regard to the common defense considered). Federalist Paper no. 28, December 26. http://www.foundingfathers.info/federalistpapers/fed28.htm.

Hamilton, Alexander. 1788. The structure of the government must furnish the proper checks and balances between the different departments. Federalist Paper no. 51, February 8. http://www.foundingfathers.info/federalistpapers/fed51.htm>.

Harb, Osama al-Ghazali. 2007. Athar tadakhkhul fi attatawur addakhili lil-balad alarabiya. Policy brief, *Arab Reform Initiative*. http://www.arab-reform.net/spip.php?page=article_ar&lang=ar&id_article=769. [In Arabic.]

Hardt, Michael, and Antonio Negri. 2000. *Empire*. Cambridge, MA: Harvard University Press.

Harrigan, Jane, Hamed al-Said, and Chengang Wang. 2006. The IMF and the World Bank in Jordan: A case of overoptimism and elusive growth. *Review of International Organizations* 1 (3): 263–92.

Hartmann, Thom. 2002. Madison's ghost on the intoxicated presidency—and its corporate support group. *Common Dreams*, October 25. http://www.commondreams.org/views02/1025-07.htm. Retrieved August 30, 2009.

Hartz, Louis. 1952. *The liberal tradition in America.* New York, NY: Harcourt Brace.

Hawthorne, Amy. 2001. Do we want democracy in the Middle East? *Foreign Service Journal.* http://www.afsa.org/fsj/feb01/hawthorne01.cfm.

Hayek, Friedrich. 1994. *The road to serfdom.* Chicago, IL: University of Chicago Press.

Hegre, Haavard. 2000. Development and the liberal peace: What does it take to be a trading state. *Journal of Peace Research* 37 (1): 5–30.

Held, David. 1987. *Models of democracy.* Stanford, CA: Stanford University Press.

Hellmann, Gunther, and Benjamin Herborth. 2008. Fishing in the mild west: Democratic peace and militarized interstate disputes in the transatlantic community. *Review of International Studies* 34: 481–506.

Henderson, Errol A. 2000. *States and power in Africa: Comparative lessons in authority and control.* Princeton, NJ: Princeton University Press.

Henderson, Errol A. 2002. Democracy and war: The end of an illusion? In *Hemmed in: Responses to Africa's economic decline,* ed. Thomas M. Callaghy and John Ravenhill, 280–332. New York, NY: Columbia University Press.

Henderson, Errol A. 2008. Disturbing the peace: African warfare, political inversion, and the universality of the democratic peace thesis. *British Journal of Political Science* 39:25–58.

Herbst, Jeffrey. 1993. The politics of sustained agricultural reform. In *Hemmed in: Responses to Africa's economic decline,* ed. Thomas M. Callaghy and John Ravenhill. New York, NY: Columbia University Press.

Hess, Stephen. 1987. Why great men are not chosen presidents: Lord Bryce revisited. In *Elections American style,* ed. A. James Reichley, 75–94. Washington, DC: Brookings Institution.

Higley, John, and Richard Gunther, eds. 1992. *Elites and democratic consolidation in Latin America and southern Europe.* Cambridge, UK: Cambridge University Press.

Hirst, Paul, and Grahame Thompson. 2001. *Globalization in question.* 2nd ed. Cambridge, UK: Polity Press.

Hoffman, Bruce. 1998. *Inside terrorism.* New York, NY: Columbia University Press.

Holstein, William J. 2005. Erasing the image of the ugly American. *New York Times,* October 23, E10.

Holsti, Ole, and James Rosenau. 1988. A leadership divided: The foreign policy beliefs of American leaders, 1976–1984. In *The domestic sources of American foreign policy: Insights and evidence,* ed. Charles Kegley and Eugene Wittkopf, 30–44. New York, NY: St. Martin's Press.

Hook, Steven. 2005. *U.S. foreign policy: The paradox of world power.* Washington, DC: CQ Press.

Howard, Michael. 2002. Smoke on the horizon. *London Financial Times,* September 7, 1.

Hudson, Michael. 1991. After the Gulf War: Prospects for democratization in the Arab world. *Middle East Journal* 45 (3): 407–27.

Hunter, Shireen T., ed. 1988. *The politics of Islamic revivalism: Diversity and unity.* Bloomington, IN: Indiana University Press.

Huntington, Samuel. 1981. *American politics: The promise of disharmony.* Cambridge, MA: Belknap Press.

Huntington, Samuel. 1982. American ideals versus American institutions. *Political Science Quarterly* 97 (1): 1–37.

Huntington, Samuel. 1984. Will more countries become democratic? *Political Science Quarterly* 99 (2): 193–218.

Huntington, Samuel. 1991. *The third wave: Democratization in the late twentieth century.* Norman, OK: University of Oklahoma Press.

Ikenberry, G. John. 2000. America's liberal grand strategy: Democracy and national security in the post-war era. In *American democracy promotion: Impulses, strategies, and impacts,* ed. Michael Cox, G. John Ikenberry, and Takashi Inoguchi, 103–26. Oxford, UK: Oxford University Press.

Ikenberry, G. John. 2001. *After victory: Institutions, strategic restraint, and the rebuilding of order after major wars.* Princeton, NJ: Princeton University Press.

Inge, William Ralph. 1919. *Outspoken essays.* London: Longmans, Green.

Institute for War and Peace Reporting (IWPR). 2006. Afghan opium: A failed jihad? http://www.iwpr.net.

International Committee of the Red Cross (ICRC). 2007. *Annual report.* Geneva, Switzerland.

International Crisis Group (ICG). 2001. Bosnia's precarious economy: Still not open for business. *Europe Report* 115 (August).

International Crisis Group (ICG). 2004. Liberia and Sierra Leone, rebuilding failed states. *Africa Report* 87 (December).

International Crisis Group (ICG). 2005. Afghanistan elections: Endgame or new beginning? *Asia Report* 101 (July).

International Crisis Group (ICG). 2006a. Countering Afghanistan's insurgency: No quick fixes. *Asia Report* 123 (November).

International Crisis Group (ICG). 2006b. Escaping the conflict trap: Promoting good governance in the Congo. *Africa Report* 114 (July).

International Crisis Group (ICG). 2006c. The next Iraqi war? Sectarianism and civil conflict. *Middle East Report* 52 (February).

IRIN News. 2005. Blue helmets quit, but "peace elusive." December 14. http://www.irinnews.org/report.aspx?reportid=57569.

Ish-Shalom, Piki. 2008. The rhetorical capital of theories: The democratic peace and the road to the roadmap. *International Political Science Review* 29 (3): 281–301.

Ivie, Robert, 2006. *Democracy and America's war on terrorism.* Tuscaloosa, AL: University of Alabama Press.

Jackson, Robert H. 1992. Juridical statehood in sub-Saharan Africa. *Journal of International Affairs* 46 (1): 1–16.

James, Patrick, Eric Solberg, and Murray Wolfson. 1999. An identified systemic model of the democracy-peace nexus. *Defense and Peace Economics* 10 (1): 1–37.

James, Patrick, Eric Solberg, and Murray Wolfson. 2000. Democracy and peace: A reply to Oneal and Russett. *Defense and Peace Economics* 11 (2): 215–29.

Jefferson, Thomas. 1786. Letter to George Wythe, written August 13 from Paris. http://odur.let.rug.nl/~usa/P/tj3/writings/brf/jefl47.htm.

Jefferson, Thomas. 1787. Letter to James Madison, written January 30 from Paris. http://odur.let.rug.nl/~usa/P/tj3/writings/brf/jefl53.htm.

Jehl, Douglas. 1997. Persian Gulf's young Turk: Sheik Hamad, emir of Qatar. *New York Times,* July 10, A1.

Jehl, Douglas. 2005. Among those told of program, few objected. *New York Times,* December 12, A23.

Jentleson, Bruce. 1992. The pretty prudent public: Post post-Vietnam American opinion on the use of military force. *International Studies Quarterly* 36 (1): 49–74.

Jervis, Robert. 1976. *Perception and misperception in international politics.* Princeton, NJ: Princeton University Press.

Jervis, Robert. 2003. Understanding the Bush Doctrine. *Political Science Quarterly* 118 (3): 365–88.

Johnson, Loch. 1986. *A season of inquiry: The Senate intelligence investigation.* Lexington, KY: University Press of Kentucky.

Johnson, Loch. 2004. Congressional supervision of America's secret agencies: The experience and legacy of the Church Committee. *Public Administration Review* 64 (January–February): 3–14.

Johnson, Loch. 2006a. Spy law works: Don't bypass it. *Atlanta Journal-Constitution,* January 30, A14.

Johnson, Loch. 2006b. Supervising America's secret foreign policy: A shock theory of congressional oversight for intelligence. In *American foreign policy in a globalized world,* ed. David P. Forsythe, Patrice C. McMahon, and Andrew Wedeman, 173–92. New York, NY: Routledge.

Johnson, Loch. 2007. *Seven sins of American foreign policy.* New York, NY: Longman.

Juergensmeyer, Mark. 2000. *Terror in the mind of God: The global rise of religious violence.* Berkeley, CA: University of California Press.

Kanovsky, Eliyahu. 1989. Jordan's economy: From prosperity to crisis. In *Middle East contemporary survey.* Vol. 12, *1988,* ed. Colin Legum. New York, NY: Holmes and Meier.

Kant, Immanuel. 1932 [1795]. *Perpetual peace.* Los Angeles, CA: U.S. Library Association.

Kaplan, Lawrence F., and William Kristol. 2003. *The war over Iraq: Saddam's tyranny and America's mission.* San Francisco, CA: Encounter Books.

Kardoosh, Marwan. 2006. *The Jordanian economy into the third millennium: In the eye of the regional storm; Developments in 2003–2005, outlook for 2006–2007.* Amman, Jordan: Jordan Center for Public Policy Research and Dialogue.

Karl, Terry Lynn. 1990. Dilemmas of democratization in Latin America. *Comparative Politics* 23 (1): 1–21.

Kassay, Ali. 2002. The effects of external forces on Jordan's process of democratization. In *Jordan in transition: 1990–2000,* ed. George Joffé, 45–65. London: Hurst.

Kaufman, Chaim. 2004. Threat inflation and the failure of the marketplace of ideas: The selling of the Iraq War. *International Security* 29 (1): 5–48.

Keck, Margaret E., and Kathryn Sikkink. 1998. *Activists beyond borders: Advocacy networks in international politics.* Ithaca, NY: Cornell University Press.

Keller, William W. 1989. *Liberals and J. Edgar Hoover: Rise and fall of a domestic intelligence state.* Princeton, NJ: Princeton University Press.

Keneally, Thomas. 2000. *The great shame.* New York, NY: Anchor Books.

Khader, Bichara, and Adnan Badran, eds. 1987. *The economic development of Jordan.* London: Croom Helm.

Khan, Muqtedar. 2003. Prospects for Muslim democracy: The role of U.S. policy. *Middle East Policy* 10 (3): 79–89.

Kloby, Jerry. 2003. *Inequality, power, and development: Issues in political sociology.* Amherst, NY: Prometheus Books.

Krauthammer, Charles. 2004. In defense of democratic realism. *National Interest,* Fall: 15–25.

Krauthammer, Charles. 2005. Three cheers for the Bush Doctrine. *Time Magazine,* March 7. http://www.time.com/time/columnist/krauthammer/article/0,9565,1035052,00.html.

Kurth, James. 2006. America's democratization projects abroad. *American Spectator* 39 (8): 40–47.
Langlois, Anthony. 2003. Human rights without democracy? A critique of the separatist thesis. *Human Rights Quarterly* 25 (4): 990–1019.
Larson, Eric V., and Godgan Savych. 2005. *American public support for U.S. military operations from Mogadishu to Baghdad.* Santa Monica, CA: RAND.
Layne, Christopher. 1994. Kant or cant? The myth of the democratic peace. *International Security* 19 (2): 5–49.
Leeson, Peter T., and Andrea Dean. 2009. The democratic domino theory: An empirical investigation. *American Journal of Political Science* 55 (3): 533–51.
Leita, Jose Correa. 2005. *The world social forum: Strategies for resistance.* Chicago, IL: Haymarket Books.
Leitenberg, Milton, and Gabriel Sheffer, eds. 1979. *Great powers in the Middle East.* New York, NY: Pergamon Press.
Lektzian, David, and Mark Souva. 2009. A comparative theory test of democratic peace arguments, 1946–2000. *Journal of Peace Research* 46 (1): 17–37.
Levitsky, Steven, and Lucan Way. 2006. Linkage versus leverage: Rethinking the international dimension of regime change. *Comparative Politics* 38 (4): 379–400.
Levy, Jack S. 1988. Domestic politics and war. In *The origin and prevention of major wars,* ed. Robert I. Rotberg and Theodore K. Rabb, 79–99. Cambridge, UK: Cambridge University Press.
Levy, Jack S. 1994. The democratic peace hypothesis: From description to explanation. *Mershon International Studies Review* 38: 352–54.
Li, Quan, and David Sacko. 2002. The (ir)relevance of militarized interstate disputes for international trade. *International Studies Quarterly* 46 (1): 11–34.
Lichtblau, Eric, and James Risen. 2009. U.S. wiretapping of limited value, officials report. *New York Times,* July 10, 1A.
Lieven, Anatol. 2006. Wolfish Wilsonians: Existential dilemmas of the liberal internationalists. *Orbis* 50 (2): 243–57.
Lindsay, James M. 1986. Trade sanctions as policy instruments: A reexamination. *International Studies Quarterly* 30 (2): 153–73.
Linz, Juan J., and Alfred Stepan. 1996. *Problems of democratic transition and consolidation: Southern Europe, South America, and post-Communist Europe.* Baltimore, MD: Johns Hopkins University Press.
Lipset, Seymour M. 1959. Some social requisites of democracy: Economic development and political development. *American Political Science Review* 53: 69–105.
Lipset, Seymour M. 1963. *The first new nation: The United States in historical and comparative perspective.* New York, NY: Basic Books.
Little, Douglas. 2002. *American orientalism: The United States and the Middle East since 1945.* Chapel Hill, NC: University of North Carolina Press.
Looney, Robert. 2006. Economic consequences of conflict: The rise of Iraq's formal economy. *Journal of Economic Issues* 40 (4): 1–17.
Lowi, Theodore. 1969. *The end of liberalism.* New York, NY: Norton.
Luxemburg, Rosa. 1968. *The accumulation of capital.* New York, NY: Monthly Review Press.
Lyons, Terence. 2002. The role of postsettlement elections. In *Ending civil wars: The implementation of peace agreements,* ed. Stephen Stedman, Donald Rothchild, and Elizabeth Cousens, 215–36. Boulder, CO: Lynne Rienner.

Madison, James. 1787. The same subject continued (the Union as a safeguard against domestic faction and insurrection). Federalist Paper no. 10, November 23. http://www.foundingfathers.info/federalistpapers/fed10.htm.

Madison, James. 1788a. The same subject continued (the powers conferred by the Constitution further considered). Federalist Paper no. 43, January. http://www.foundingfathers.info/federalistpapers/fed43.htm.

Madison, James. 1788b. The particular structure of the new government and the distribution of power among its different parts. Federalist Paper no. 47, February 1. http://www.foundingfathers.info/federalistpapers/fed47.htm.

Madison, James. 1788c. These departments should not be so far separated as to have no constitutional control over each other. Federalist Paper no. 48, February 1. http://www.foundingfathers.info/federalistpapers/fed48.htm.

Madison, James. 1865 [1795]. Political observations (April 20). In vol. 4 of *Letters and other writings of James Madison*, ed. Philip R. Fendall. Philadelphia, PA: Lippincott.

Maliniak, Daniel, Amy Oakes, Susan Peterson, and Michael J. Tierney. 2007. Inside the ivory tower. *Foreign Policy*, March–April: 62–68.

Mamdani, Mahmood. 1996. *Citizen and subject: 1960 contemporary Africa and the legacy of late colonialism*. Princeton NJ: Princeton University Press.

Mani, Rama. 2002. *Beyond retribution: Seeking justice in the shadows of war*. Malden, MA: Polity Press.

Mann, James. 2004. *Rise of the Vulcans: The history of Bush's war cabinet*. New York, NY: Viking.

Mansfield, Edward, and Jack Synder. 1995. Democratization and the danger of war. *International Security* 20 (1): 5–38.

Mansfield, Edward, and Jack Snyder. 2007. *Electing to fight: Why democracies go to war*. Cambridge, UK: MIT Press.

Maoz, Zeev. 1997. The controversy over the democratic peace. *International Security* 22 (1): 162–98.

Markovits, Andrei S. 2007. Western Europe's American problem. *Chronicle of Higher Education*, January 19, B6–B9.

Martin, Edward J., and Rodolfo D. Torres. 2004. *Savage state: Welfare capitalism and inequality*. Lanham, MD: Rowman and Littlefield.

Mazzetti, Mark. 2007a. Intelligence chief finds that challenges abound. *New York Times*, April 7, A10.

Mazzetti, Mark. 2007b. Intelligence director announces renewed plan for overhaul. *New York Times*, April 12, A13.

McFaul, Michael. 2004. Democracy promotion as a world value. *Washington Quarterly* 28 (1): 147–63.

McMichael, Philip. 2003. *Development and social change*. Thousand Oaks, CA: Sage.

McNally, David. 2006. *Another world is possible: Globalization and anti-capitalism*. Winnipeg, Canada: Arbeiter Ring.

Mead, Walter Russell. 2002. *Special providence: American foreign policy and how it changed the world*. New York, NY: Routledge.

Mearsheimer, John J. 2001. *The tragedy of great power politics*. New York, NY: W. W. Norton.

Mearsheimer, John J., and Stephen Walt. 2002. "Realists" are not alone in opposing war with Iraq. *Chronicle of Higher Education*, November 15.

Mearsheimer, John J., and Stephen Walt. 2006. The Israel lobby. *London Review of Books*, March 23.
Melman, Seymour. 2001. *After capitalism: From managerialism to workplace democracy.* New York, NY: Knopf.
Migdal, Joel S. 1988. *Strong states and weak societies: State-society relations and state capabilities in the third world.* Princeton, NJ: Princeton University Press.
Miliband, Ralph. 1969. *The state in capitalist society.* New York, NY: Basic Books.
Mill, John Stuart. 1859. *On liberty.* Repr., New York, NY: Macmillan, 1985.
Mill, John Stuart. 1998. *On liberty and other essays.* New York, NY: Oxford University Press.
Mitchell, George. 1999. *Making peace.* Berkeley, CA: University of California Press.
Miyagawa, Makio. 1992. *Do economic sanctions work?* New York, NY: St. Martin's Press.
Monroe, James. 1823. The Monroe doctrine. Avalon Project. http://Avalon.law.yale.edu/19th_century/monroe.asp.
Monten, Jonathan. 2005. The roots of the Bush Doctrine: Power, nationalism, and democracy promotion in U.S. strategy. *International Security* 29 (4): 112–56.
Montesquieu, Baron de. 1989 [1748]. *Spirit of the laws.* Cambridge, UK: Cambridge University Press.
Moore, Barrington. 1966. *Social origins of dictatorship and democracy.* New York, NY: Beacon,
Morgan, T. Clifton. 1993. Democracies and war: Reflections on the literature. *International Interactions* 18 (3): 197–203.
Morgan, T. Clifton. 1995. Clinton's Chinese puzzle: Domestic politics and the effectiveness of economic sanctions. *Issues and Studies* 31 (August): 19–45.
Morgenthau, Hans J. 1985 [1948]. *Politics among nations: The struggle for power and peace.* New York, NY: Knopf.
Mousseau, Michael. 2000. Market prosperity, democratic consolidation, and democratic peace. *Journal of Conflict Resolution* 44 (4): 472–507.
Mousseau, Michael. 2009. The social market roots of democratic peace. *International Security* 33 (4): 52–86.
Mousseau, Michael, Haavard Hegre, and John R. Oneal. 2003. How the wealth of nations conditions the liberal peace. *European Journal of International Relations* 9 (2): 277–314.
Mueller, John. 1989. *Retreat from Doomsday: The obsolescence of major war.* New York, NY: Basic Books.
Mueller, John. 1995. *Quiet cataclysm: Reflections on the recent transformation of world politics.* New York, NY: HarperCollins.
Mueller, John. 1999. *Capitalism, democracy, and Ralph's pretty good grocery.* Princeton, NJ: Princeton University Press.
Mueller, John. 2004. *The remnants of war.* Ithaca, NY: Cornell University Press.
Mueller, John. 2005. The Iraq syndrome. *Foreign Affairs* 84 (6): 44–54.
Mueller, John. 2007. The demise of war and of speculations about the causes thereof. Paper presented at the annual convention of the International Studies Association, March 1, Chicago, IL.
Mufti, Malik. 1999. Elite bargains and the onset of political liberalization in Jordan. *Comparative Political Studies* 32 (1): 100–129.
"The must-do list." 2007. *New York Times*, March 4, WK11.
Nadelmann, Ethan A. 1990. Global prohibition regimes: The evolution of norms in international society. *International Organization* 44 (4): 479–526.

Nafziger, Wayne E. 1993. *The debt crisis in Africa.* Baltimore, MD: Johns Hopkins University Press.

Ndulu, Benno J., and Stephen A. O'Connell. 1999. Governance and growth in sub-Saharan Africa. *Journal of Economic Perspectives* 13 (3): 41–66.

Norton, Augustus Richard, ed. 1995, 1996. *Civil society in the Middle East.* 2 vols. Leiden, Netherlands: Brill.

Nozick, Robert. 1977. *Anarchy, state, and utopia.* New York, NY: Basic Books.

Nye, Joseph. 2002. *The paradox of American power: Why the world's only superpower can't go it alone.* Oxford, UK: Oxford University Press.

O'Brien, Conor Cruise. 2002. *Edmund Burke.* London: Vintage.

O'Donnell, Guillermo, and Philippe C. Schmitter. 1986. *Transitions from authoritarian rule: Tentative conclusions about uncertain democracies.* Baltimore, MD: Johns Hopkins University Press.

Offe, Claus. 1984. *Contradictions of the welfare state.* Cambridge, MA: MIT Press.

O'Hanlon, Michael, and Jason Campbell. 2007. Iraq index. Brookings Institution. April 17. http://www.brookings.edu/iraqindex.

Ollapally, Deepa. 2003. Unfinished business in Afghanistan: Warlordism, reconstruction, and ethnic harmony. Special Report no. 105 (April). Washington, DC: U.S. Institute of Peace Press.

Olson, Mancur. 1982. *The rise and decline of nations: Economic growth, stagflation, and social rigidities.* New Haven, CT: Yale University Press.

Olson, Mancur. 1993. Dictatorship, democracy, and development. *American Political Science Review* 87 (3): 567–76.

Olson, Richard Stuart. 1979. Economic coercion in world politics: With a focus on north-south relations. *World Politics* 31: 471–94.

Oneal, John R., and Bruce Russett. 1997. The classical liberals were right: Democracy, interdependence, and conflict, 1950–1985. *International Studies Quarterly* 41 (2): 267–93.

Oneal, John R., and Bruce Russett. 1999a. Assessing the liberal peace with alternative specifications: Trade still reduces conflict. *Journal of Peace Research* 36 (4): 423–42.

Oneal, John R., and Bruce Russett. 1999b. Is the liberal peace just an artifact of cold war interests? Assessing recent critiques. *International Interactions* 25 (3): 213–41.

Oneal, John R., and Bruce Russett. 1999c. The Kantian peace: The pacific benefits of democracy, interdependence, and international organizations. *World Politics* 52 (1): 1–37.

Oneal, John R., and Bruce Russett. 2000. Comment: Why "an identified systemic model of the democracy-peace nexus" does not persuade. *Defense and Peace Economics* 11 (2): 197–214.

Oneal, John R., and Bruce Russett. 2001. Clear and clean: The fixed effects of the liberal peace. *International Organization* 55 (2): 469–85.

Oneal, John R., Bruce Russett, and Michael L. Berbaum. 2003. Causes of peace: Democracy, interdependence, and international organizations. *International Studies Quarterly* 47 (3): 371–93.

Oneal, John R., Frances H. Oneal, Zeev Maoz, and Bruce Russett. 1996. The liberal peace: Interdependence, democracy, and international conflict, 1950–1985. *Journal of Peace Research* 33 (1): 11–28.

Oren, Ido. 1996. The subjectivity of the democratic peace. In *Debating the democratic peace,* ed. Michael E. Brown, Sean M. Lynn-Jones, and Steven E. Miller. Cambridge, MA: MIT Press.

Organisation for Economic Cooperation and Development (OECD). 2006. *Geographical Distribution of Financial Flows to Aid Recipients. Part I: Developing Countries.* International Development Statistical Database Online.

Oslo Conference. 2003. Making intelligence accountable: Executive and legislative oversight of intelligence services. September 18–20, Oslo, Norway. http://www.cmr-net.ch/legal_wg/ev_oslo_030919_prog.pdf.

Osman, Abdulahi A. 2007. *Governance and internal wars in sub-Saharan Africa: Exploring the relationship.* London: Adonis and Abbey.

Ottaway, Marina. 2005a. The problem of credibility. In *Uncharted journey: Promoting democracy in the Middle East,* ed. Thomas Carothers and Marina Ottaway, 173–92. Washington, DC: Carnegie Endowment for International Peace.

Ottaway, Marina. 2005b. The missing constituency for democratic reform. In *Uncharted journey: Promoting democracy in the Middle East,* ed. Thomas Carothers and Marina Ottaway, 151–70. Washington, DC: Carnegie Endowment for International Peace.

Ottaway, Marina. 2007. Who wins in Iraq? Six Arab dictators. *Foreign Policy* 159. http://www.foreignpolicy.com/story/cms.php?story_id=3710.

Ottaway, Marina, Thomas Carothers, Amy Hawthorne, and Daniel Brumberg. 2002. Democratic mirage in the Middle East. Policy brief no. 20. Washington, DC: Carnegie Endowment for International Peace.

Owen, John M. 1994. How liberalism produces democratic peace. *International Security* 19 (2): 87–125.

Owen, John M. 2005. Iraq and the democratic peace. *Foreign Affairs* 84 (6): 122–27.

Paine, Thomas. 1986 [1776]. *Common sense.* New York, NY: Penguin.

Panitch, Leo. 1996. Rethinking the role of the state. *Globalization: Critical reflections,* ed. James H. Mittleman, 83–113. Boulder, CO: Lynne Rienner.

Pape, Robert. 2005. *Dying to win: The strategic logic of suicide terrorism.* New York, NY: Random House.

Parenti, Christian. 2004. *The soft cage: Surveillance in America from slavery to the war on terror.* New York, NY: Perseus.

Parenti, Christian. 2008. *Lockdown America: Police and prisons in an age of conflict.* Rev. ed. New York, NY: Verso.

Parenti, Michael. 2007. *Democracy for the few.* 8th ed. Belmont, CA: Wadsworth.

Parsons, Talcott. 1966. On the concept of political power. In *Class, status, and power: Social stratification in comparative perspective,* eds. Reinhard Bendix and Seymour Martin Lipset, 240–65. New York, NY: Free Press.

Pateman, Carole. 1970. *Participation and democratic theory.* London: Cambridge University Press.

Payne, James L. 2006. Election fraud: Democracy is an effect, not a cause, of nonviolence. *American Conservative,* March 13, 11–12.

Peceny, Mark. 1999. Forcing them to be free. *Political Research Quarterly* 52 (3): 549–82.

Peceny, Mark, and Jeffrey Pickering. 2006. Can liberal intervention build liberal democracy? In *Conflict prevention and peacebuilding in post-war societies: Sustaining the peace,* ed. T. David Mason and James D. Meernik, 130–48. London: Routledge.

Perkins, John. 2004. *Confessions of an economic hit man.* New York, NY: Berrett-Koehler.

Pevehouse, Jon C. 2005. *Democracy from above: Regional organizations and democratization.* Cambridge, UK: Cambridge University Press.

Pew Research Center. 2007. Global unease with major world powers. http://www.pewglobal.org/reports/display.php?ReportID=256.

Pickering, Jeffrey, and Peceny, Mark. 2006. Forging democracy at gunpoint. *International Studies Quarterly* 50 (3): 539–59.

Pietrzyk, Mark E. 2002. *International order and individual liberty: Effects of war and peace on the development of governments.* Lanham, MD: University Press of America.

Pillar, Paul R. 2007. The democracy deficit: The need for liberal democratization. In vol. 2 of *Countering terrorism in the 21st century,* ed. James J. F. Forest, 42–55. Westport, CT: Praeger.

Piven, Frances Fox, and Richard A. Cloward. 1997. Breaking the social compact: The globalization hoax. In *The breaking of the American social compact,* ed. Frances Fox Piven and Richard Cloward, 3–16. New York, NY: New Press.

Podhoretz, Norman. 2002. In praise of the Bush Doctrine. *Commentary* 114 (2): 19–28.

Pollins, Brian. 1989a. Conflict, cooperation, and commerce: The effect of international political interactions on bilateral trade flows. *American Journal of Political Science* 33 (3): 737–61.

Pollins, Brian. 1989b. Does trade still follow the flag? *American Political Science Review* 83 (2): 465–80.

Posusney, Marsha Pripstein. 2005. Multiparty elections in the Arab world: Election rules and opposition responses. In *Authoritarianism in the Middle East,* ed. Marsha Pripstein Posusney and Michele Penner Angrist, 91–118. Boulder, CO: Lynne Rienner.

Posusney, Marsha Pripstein, and Michele Penner Angrist, eds. 2005. *Authoritarianism in the Middle East: Regimes and resistance.* Boulder, CO: Lynne Rienner.

Poulantzas, Nicos. 1974. *Political power and social classes.* London: New Left Books.

Pressman, Steven. 2006. *Alternative theories of the state.* New York, NY: Palgrave.

Prestowitz, Clyde. 2003. *Rogue nation: American unilateralism and the failure of good intentions.* New York, NY: Basic Books.

Priest, Dana. 2005. CIA holds terror suspects in secret prisons. *Washington Post,* November 2, A1.

Przeworski, Adam, Michael E. Alvarez, José Antonio Cheibub, and Fernando Limongi. 2000. *Democracy and development: Political institutions and well-being in the world, 1950–1990.* Cambridge, UK: Cambridge University Press.

Putnam, Robert. 2000. *Bowling alone: The collapse and revival of American community.* New York, NY: Simon and Schuster.

Pye, L. W. 1990. Political science and the crisis of authoritarianism. *American Political Science Review* 84 (March): 3–19.

Raghavan, Sudarsan. 2007. Four years after Hussein's fall, regret in Iraq: Harley fan who helped topple statue wants old order back. *Washington Post,* April 9, A8.

Rapoport, David C., and Leonard Weinberg. 2001. Elections and violence. In *The democratic experience and political violence,* ed. David C. Rapoport and Leonard Weinberg. Portland, OR: Frank Cass.

Rappard, William E. 1940. *The quest for peace since the World War.* Cambridge, MA: Harvard University Press.

Rashwan, Dhia. 2005. *Dalil al-harakat al-islamiya fi al-alam.* Cairo, Egypt: Al-Ahram Center for Political and Strategic Studies. [In Arabic.]

Rasler, Karen, and William R. Thompson. 2004. Democratic peace and a sequential, reciprocal, causal arrow hypothesis. *Comparative Political Studies* 37 (8): 879–908.

Rasler, Karen, and William R. Thompson. 2005. *Puzzles of the democratic peace: Theory, geopolitics, and the transformation of world politics.* London: Palgrave.
Rawls, John. 1999. *The laws of peoples.* Cambridge, MA: Harvard University Press.
Ray, James Lee. 1993. Wars between democracies: Rare or nonexistent? *International Interactions* 18 (3): 251–76.
Ray, James Lee. 1996. *Democracy and international conflict: An evaluation of the democratic peace proposition.* Columbia, SC: University of South Carolina Press.
Ray, James Lee. 1998. Does democracy cause peace? *Annual Review of Political Science* 1: 27–46.
Reiman, Jeffrey. 2007. *The rich get richer and the poor get prison: Ideology, class, and criminal justice.* 8th ed. Boston, MA: Allyn and Bacon.
Richardson, Louise. 2006. The roots of terrorism: An overview. In *The roots of terrorism,* ed. Louise Richardson, 1–16. New York, NY: Routledge.
Richmond, Oliver. 2006. The linkage between devious objectives and spoiling behavior in peace processes. In *Challenges to peacebuilding: Managing spoilers during conflict resolution,* ed. Edward Newman and Oliver Richmond, 59–77. Tokyo, Japan: United Nations University Press.
Ricks, Thomas E. 2006. *Fiasco: The American military adventure in Iraq.* New York, NY: Penguin.
Rieffer, Barbara Ann, and Kristan Mercer. 2005. U.S. democracy promotion: The Clinton and Bush administrations. *Global Society* 19 (4): 385–408.
Riker, William H. 1982. *Liberalism against populism.* San Francisco, CA: Freeman.
Risen, James. 2006. *State of war: The secret history of the CIA and the Bush administration.* New York, NY: Free Press.
Risen, James, and Eric Lichtblau. 2005. Bush lets U.S. spy on callers without courts. *New York Times,* December 16, A1.
Robinson, Glenn E. 1998. Defensive democratization in Jordan. *International Journal of Middle East Studies* 30 (3): 387–410.
Robinson, Glenn E. 2006. Imperial democratization: Rhetoric and reality. *Arab Studies Quarterly* 28 (3–4): 55–87.
Robinson, William. 1996. *Promoting polyarchy: Globalization, U.S. intervention, and hegemony.* New York, NY: Cambridge University Press.
Robinson, William. 2004. *A theory of global capitalism.* Baltimore, MD: Johns Hopkins University Press.
Rockefeller, John D. 2007. Opening statement. Confirmation hearings of John M. McConnell to be DNI, Select Committee on Intelligence, U.S. Senate, 110th Cong., 1st sess. (February 1).
Rosati, Jerel, and James Scott. 2007. *The politics of United States foreign policy.* 4th ed. New York, NY: Thompson Wadsworth.
Rosato, Sebastian. 2003. The flawed logic of democratic peace theory. *American Political Science Review* 97 (4): 585–602.
Rose, Richard. 2001. A diverging Europe. *Journal of Democracy* 12 (1): 93–106.
Ross, Michael. 2001. Does oil hinder democracy? *World Politics* 53 (3): 325–61.
Rotberg, Robert, ed. 2003. *State failure and state weakness in a time of terror.* Washington, DC: Brookings Institution Press.
Rothchild, Donald. 2000. The African state and state system in flux. In *Africa in world politics: The African state system in flux.* 3rd ed., ed. John W. Harbeson and Donald Rothchild, 3–20. Boulder, CO: Westview Press.

Roulier, Scott M. 2004. *Kantian virtue at the intersection of politics and nature.* Rochester, NY: University of Rochester Press.

Rousseau, Jean-Jacques. 1968. *The social contract.* New York, NY: Penguin Classics.

Roy, Olivier. 2003. Europe won't be fooled again. *New York Times,* May 13, A31.

Russett, Bruce. 1990. *Controlling the sword: The democratic governance of national security.* Cambridge, MA: Harvard University Press.

Russett, Bruce. 1993. *Grasping the democratic peace: Principles for a post–cold war world.* Princeton, NJ: Princeton University Press.

Russett, Bruce. 1995. The democratic peace: And yet it moves. *International Security* 19 (4): 164–75.

Russett, Bruce. 2005. Bushwhacking the democratic peace. *International Studies Perspectives* 6 (4): 395–408.

Russett, Bruce, Christopher Layne, David E. Spiro, and Michael W. Doyle. 1995. Correspondence: The democratic peace. *International Security* 19 (4): 164–84.

Russett, Bruce, and John Oneal. 2001. *Triangulating peace: Democracy, interdependence, and international organizations.* New York, NY: Norton.

Russett, Bruce, John R. Oneal, and David Davis. 1998. The third leg of the Kantian tripod for peace: International organizations and militarized disputes, 1950–1985. *International Organization* 52 (3): 441–67.

Ryan, Curtis. 2002. *Jordan in transition: From Hussein to Abdullah.* Boulder, CO: Lynne Rienner.

Ryan, Curtis, and Jillian Schwedler. 2004. Return to democratization or new hybrid regime? The 2003 elections in Jordan. *Middle East Policy* 11 (2): 138–51.

Sandbrook, Richard. 1993. *The politics of Africa's stagnation.* New York, NY: Cambridge University Press.

Sartori, Giovanni. 1976. *Parties and party systems: A framework for analysis.* Cambridge, UK: Cambridge University Press.

Sassen, Saskia. 1996. *Losing control? Sovereignty in an age of globalization.* New York, NY: Columbia University Press.

Scarff, Lawrence A. 1975. Two concepts of political participation. *Western Political Quarterly* 28 (3): 447–62.

Schafer, Mark, and Stephen Walker. 2006. Democratic leaders and the democratic peace: The operational codes of Tony Blair and Bill Clinton. *International Studies Quarterly* 50 (3): 561–83.

Schmitter, Philippe, and Terry Lynn Karl. 1991. What democracy is . . . and is not. *Journal of Democracy* 2 (3): 75–88.

Schorr, Daniel. 2004. Washington notebook. *The New Leader* 81 (September–October): 5.

Schraeder, Peter J. 2000. *African politics and society: A mosaic in transformation.* Boston, MA: Bedford/St. Martin's.

Schraeder, Peter J., ed. 2002. *Exporting democracy: Rhetoric vs. reality.* Boulder, CO: Lynne Rienner.

Schumpeter, Joseph. 1976. *Capitalism, socialism and democracy.* London: Allen and Unwin.

Schwarz, Frederick A. O., Jr. 2007. Intelligence oversight: The Church Committee. In vol. 5 of *Strategic intelligence: Intelligence and accountability, safeguards against the abuse of secret power,* ed. Loch K. Johnson, 19–46. Westport, CT: Praeger.

Schwarz, Frederick A. O., Jr., and Aziz Z. Huq. 2007. *Unchecked and unbalanced: Presidential power in a time of terror.* New York, NY: Free Press.

Schwedler, Jillian. 2006. *Faith in moderation: Islamist parties in Jordan and Yemen.* Cambridge, UK: Cambridge University Press.

Schweller, Randall L. 2001. The problem of international order revisited: A review essay. *International Security* 26 (1): 161–86.

Schweller, Randall L. 2002. Correspondence. *International Security* 27 (1): 181–85.

Severeid, Eric. 1980. Interview with William O. Douglas. *CBS Evening News,* January 19.

Shafiq, Munir. 2005. Al-Inqilab al-thaqafiyah wa al-siyasiyah. *Al-Adab* 53 (6–7): 13–15. [In Arabic.]

Shapiro, Ian. 2003. *The state of democratic theory.* Princeton, NJ: Princeton University Press.

Sharabi, Hisham. 1988. *Neopatriarchy: A theory of distorted change in Arab society.* New York, NY: Oxford University Press.

Shaw, Martin. 1988. *Dialectics of war: An essay in the social theory of total war and peace.* London: Pluto Press.

Showstack, Anne Sassoon. 1987. *Gramsci's politics.* London: Hutchinson.

Siddiqi, Moin. 2000. Economic report: Jordan. *The Middle East* 304: 38.

Singer, Max, and Aaron Wildavsky. 1993. *The real world order: Zones of peace, zones of conflict.* Chatham, NJ: Chatham House.

Sisk, Timothy D. 2001. Democratization and peacebuilding: Perils and promises. In *Turbulent peace: The challenges of managing international conflict,* ed. Chester A. Crocker, Fen Osler Hampson, and Pamela R. Aall, 785–800. Washington, DC: U.S. Institute of Peace Press.

Sissener, Tone K., and Linda Kartawitch. 2005. *Afghanistan: Parliamentary and provincial elections September.* Norwegian Centre for Human Rights/NORDEM Report 14. September. http://www.humanrights.uio.no/forskning/publ/publikasjonsliste.html.

Sklair, Leslie. 2001. *The transnational capitalist class.* Oxford, UK: Blackwell Publishers.

Sklair, Leslie. 2002. *Globalization: Capitalism and its alternatives.* New York, NY: Oxford University Press.

Small, Melvin, and J. David Singer. 1976. The war-proneness of democratic regimes. *Jerusalem Journal of International Relations* 1: 50–69.

Smith, Tony. 1994. *America's mission: The United States and the worldwide struggle for democracy in the twentieth century.* Princeton, NJ: Princeton University Press.

Spanier, John, and Eric Uslaner. 1994. *American foreign policy making and the democratic dilemmas.* 6th ed. New York, NY: Macmillan.

Spinner, Jackie, and Bessam Sebti. 2005. Militant declares war on evil principle. *Washington Post,* January 24, A1.

Spiro, David E. 1994. The insignificance of the democratic peace. *International Security* 19 (4): 50–86.

Starr, Harvey. 1997. Democracy and integration: Why democracies don't fight each other. *Journal of Peace Research* 34 (2): 153–62

Stedman, Stephan. 1997. Spoiler problems in peace processes. *International Security* 22 (2): 5–53.

Stedman, Stephan John, Donald Rothchild, and Elizabeth M. Cousens, eds. 2002. *Ending civil wars: The implementation of peace agreements.* Boulder, CO: Lynne Rienner.

Steger, Manfred B. 2002. *Globalism: The new market ideology.* Lanham, MD: Rowman and Littlefield.

Stuart, Douglas. 2008. *Creating the national security state.* Princeton, NJ: Princeton University Press.

Tabb, William K. 2001. *The amoral elephant: Globalization and the struggle for social justice in the twenty-first century.* New York, NY: Monthly Review Press.

Takeyh, Ray, and Nikolas K. Gvosdev. 2003. Democratic impulses versus imperial interests: America's new Mideast conundrum. *Orbis* 47 (3): 415–31.

Talentino, Andrea Kathryn. 2005. *Military intervention after the cold war: The evolution of theory and practice.* Athens, OH: Ohio University Press.

Talentino, Andrea Kathryn. 2007. Perceptions of peacebuilding: The dynamic of imposer and imposed upon. *International Studies Perspectives* 8 (2): 152–71.

Tanner, Marcus. 2001. *Ireland's holy wars: The struggle for a nation's soul, 1500–2000.* New Haven, CT: Yale University Press.

Teeple, Gary. 2000. *Globalization and the decline of social reform: Into the twenty-first century.* Amherst, NY: Humanity Books.

Thomas, Clive Y. 1984. *The rise of the authoritarian state in peripheral societies.* New York, NY: Monthly Review Press.

Thompson, William R. 1996. Democracy and peace: Putting the cart before the horse? *International Organization* 50 (1): 141–74.

Tilly, Charles. 1985. War making and state making as organized crime. In *Bringing the state back in,* ed. Peter Evans, Dietrich Rueschemeyer, and Theda Skocpol, 169–87. Cambridge, UK: Cambridge University Press.

Tilly, Charles. 1992. *Coercion, capital, and European states.* Cambridge, MA: Blackwell.

Tocqueville, Alexis de. 1990 [1835]. *Democracy in America.* Trans. Henry Reeve. New York, NY: Vintage.

Tocqueville, Alexis de. 2001 [1835]. *Democracy in America.* New York, NY: Signet Classics.

United Nations Department of Peacekeeping Operations (UNDPKO). 2005. *Peacekeeping operations in the Democratic Republic of the Congo: The perception of the population.* New York, NY: United Nations.

United Nations Development Program (UNDP). 2001. *Human development report.* New York, NY: United Nations.

United Nations Development Program (UNDP). 2004. *Human development report.* New York, NY: United Nations.

United Nations Industrial Development Organization (UNIDO). 1989. *Industry and development global report.* Vienna, Austria: UNIDO.

United States Agency for International Development (USAID). 2004. *Global terrorism report.*

United States Agency for International Development (USAID). 2006. US overseas loans and grants: Obligations and loan authorizations online database. http://qesdb.cdie.org/gbk/home.html.

United States Department of State. 2003–4. Supporting human rights and democracy: The U.S. record. http://www.state.gov/g/drl/rls/shrd/2003.

United States Department of State. 2004. *Patterns of global terrorism.* Washington, DC: Department of State.

van der Pijl, Kees. 1998. *Transnational classes and international relations.* New York, NY: Routledge.

Verba, Sidney, and Norman H. Nie. 1998. *Participation in America.* New York, NY: Addison-Wesley.

von Hippel, Karin. 2000. *Democracy by force: U.S. military intervention in the post–cold war world.* New York, NY: Cambridge University Press.

Walter, Barbara F. 1997. The critical barrier to civil war settlement. *International Organization* 51 (3): 335–64.
Walter, Barbara F. 1999. Designing transitions from Civil War. In *Civil wars, insecurity, and intervention*, ed. Barbara Walter and Jack Snyder, 39–72. New York, NY: Columbia University Press.
Waltz, Kenneth N. 1959. *Man, the state, and war.* New York, NY: Columbia University Press.
Waltz, Kenneth N. 1979. *Theory of international politics.* Reading, MA: Addison-Wesley.
Waltz, Kenneth N. 2002. Structural realism after the cold war. In *America unrivaled: The future of the balance of power*, ed. G. John Ikenberry, 29–67. Ithaca, NY: Cornell University Press.
Weber, Max. 1964. *The theory of social and economic organization.* New York, NY: Free Press.
Weiner, Myron, and Joseph LaPalombara. 1966. The impact of parties on political development. In *Political parties and political development*, ed. Joseph LaPalombara and Myron Weiner, Princeton, NJ: Princeton University Press.
Weiss, Thomas G. 1999. Sanctions as a foreign policy tool: Weighing humanitarian impulses. *Journal of Peace Research* 36 (5): 499–510.
Weiss, Thomas G., David Cortright, George A. Lopez, and Larry Minear, eds. 1997. *Political gain and civilian pain: Humanitarian impacts of economic sanctions.* Lanham, MD: Rowman and Littlefield.
Welsh, David. 1996. Ethnicity in sub-Saharan Africa. *International Affairs* 72 (3): 477–91.
Whitehead, Laurence. 1986. International aspects of democratization. In *Transitions from authoritarian rule: Comparative perspectives*, ed. Guillermo O'Donnell, Philippe C. Schmitter, and Laurence Whitehead, 3–46. Baltimore, MD: Johns Hopkins University Press.
White House. 2002. National security strategy of the United States of America. http://www.whitehouse.gov/nsc/nss.html.
Wickham, Carrie Rosefsky. 2002. *Mobilizing Islam: Religion, activism, and political change in Egypt.* New York, NY: Columbia University Press.
Wilson, Woodrow. 1918. Bases of a general peace: Fourteen points; Address to a joint session of the United States Congress, January 8. *Congressional Record*, vol. 56.
Wittes, Tamara Cofman, and Sarah E. Yerkes. 2006. What price freedom? Assessing the Bush administration's freedom agenda. Analysis paper no. 10. Saban Center for Middle East Policy. Washington, DC: Brookings Institution.
Wittkopf, Eugene, Charles Kegley Jr., and James M. Scott. 2003. *American foreign policy: Pattern and process.* 6th ed. New York, NY: Thompson and Wadsworth.
Woodward, Bob. 2006. *State of denial.* New York, NY: Simon and Schuster.
Woodward, Bob. 2004. *Plan of attack.* New York, NY: Simon and Schuster.
World Bank. 1981. *Accelerated development in sub-Saharan Africa.* Washington, DC: World Bank.
World Bank. 1982. *Accelerated development in sub-Saharan Africa.* Washington, DC: World Bank.
World Bank. 1989. *Sub-Saharan Africa: From crisis to sustainable growth.* Washington, DC: World Bank.
World Bank. 1993. *World development report, 1992.* Washington, DC: World Bank.
World Bank. 1995. *Ghana: Is growth sustainable?* Operations Evaluations Department. Report no. 99. Washington, DC: World Bank Publications.
World Bank. 2001. Diagnostic surveys of corruption. http://www1.worldbank.org/publicsector/anticorrupt/Bosnianticorruption.pdf.

World Bank. 2005a. Bosnia and Herzegovina: Country economic memorandum. Report no. 29500-BA. http://siteresources.worldbank.org/INTBOSNIAHERZ/Resources/BHCEM.pdf.

World Bank. 2005b. Bosnia and Herzegovina: Labor market update; The role of industrial relations. Report no. 32650-BA. http://siteresources.worldbank.org/INTBOSNIAHERZ/Resources/LaborMarket Update.pdf.

World Bank. 2006. World development indicators online database. http://devdata.worldbank.org/wdi2006.

Wright, Quincy. 1942. *A study of war.* Chicago, IL: University of Chicago Press.

Xenakis, Dimitris K. 2000. Order and change in the Euro-Mediterranean system. *Mediterranean Quarterly* 11 (1): 75–90.

Yacoubian, Mona. 2005. Promoting Middle East democracy II: Arab initiatives. Special report no. 136. Washington, DC: U.S. Institute of Peace.

Young, Crawford. 1994. *The African colonial state in comparative perspective.* New Haven, CT: Yale University Press.

Zahar, Marie-Joëlle. 2006. Understanding the violence of insiders: Loyalty, custodians of the peace, and the sustainability of conflict settlement. In *Challenges to peacebuilding: Managing spoilers during conflict resolution,* ed. Edward Newman and Oliver Richmond, 40–58. Tokyo, Japan: United Nations University Press.

Zakaria, Fareed. 2003. *The future of freedom: Illiberal democracy at home and abroad.* New York, NY: W. W. Norton.

Zakaria, Fareed. 2004. Islam, democracy, and constitutional liberalism. *Political Science Quarterly* 119 (1): 1–20.

Zinn, Howard. 2005. *A people's history of the United States: 1492–present.* New York, NY: HarperCollins.

Contributors

R. WILLIAM AYRES is an associate professor of international relations in the Department of Political Science and director of the Center for Global Citizenship at Elizabethtown College, Pennsylvania. His current work includes the Violent Intrastate Nationalist Conflicts (VINC) project and a project on irredentist foreign policy in Russia and Eastern Europe.

A. COOPER DRURY is an associate professor of political science at the University of Missouri. His research interests include foreign policy analysis, the international political economy, and economic sanctions. He is the author of *Economic Sanctions and Presidential Decisions: Models of Political Rationality* (2005), along with numerous articles in journals such as the *Journal of Peace Research, Foreign Policy Analysis,* and *International Political Science Review*.

DANIEL EGAN is professor and chair of the Department of Sociology at the University of Massachusetts, Lowell. He is also the director of the peace and conflict studies minor and codirector of the Peace and Conflict Studies Institute. His areas of expertise include social theory, social stratification, political sociology, war and peace, and globalization. He is coeditor with Levon Chorbajian of *Power: A Critical Reader* (2005).

ERIK GARTZKE is an associate professor of political science at the University of California, San Diego. His research interests include the impact of information on war, peace, and international institutions. His research has appeared in many journals, including the *American Journal of Political Science, International Organization, International Studies Quarterly, Journal of Conflict Resolution,* and *Journal of Politics*.

STEVEN W. HOOK is professor and chair of the Department of Political Science at Kent State University. In addition to writing numerous articles and book chapters, he is the author of *National Interest and Foreign Aid* (1995) and *U.S. Foreign Policy: The Paradox of World Power* (2nd ed. 2008) and the co-author (with John Spanier) of *American Foreign Policy since World War II* (18th ed. 2010). He is also the editor of *Foreign Aid Toward the Millennium* (1996) and *Comparative Foreign Policy: Adaptation Strategies of the Great and Emerging Powers* (2002).

LOCH K. JOHNSON is Regents Professor and Josia Meigs Distinguished Teaching Professor in the Department of Political Science at the University of Georgia. His research interests include the president, Congress, and national security policy. He is the author of numerous publications, among them *Seven Sins of American Foreign Policy* (2007).

JOHN MUELLER is professor of political science and the Woody Hayes Chair of National Security Studies, Mershon Center, at The Ohio State University. His research interests include international politics, foreign policy, defense policy, public opinion, democratization, economic history, postcommunism, and terrorism. He is the author of numerous texts and articles, including *The Remnants of War* (2004) and *Overblown: How Politicians and the Terrorism Industry Inflate National Security Threats and Why We Believe Them* (2006).

TODD H. NELSON is a doctoral candidate in political science at Kent State University. His research interests include human rights, transitional justice, and the impact of state control of media and education as methods of controlling historical discourse. He is currently coauthoring a manuscript on U.S. torture policy and the democratic peace.

ABDULAHI A. OSMAN is an assistant professor and the coordinator of the minor in African studies at the University of Georgia. His research interests involve governance, African political systems, conflict studies, internal security and wars, and comparative governments. His previous research has appeared in the *Journal of Ethno-Development* and in the anthology *Ethnic Identity Groups and U.S. Foreign Policy* (2002), edited by Fran Scott.

DURSUN PEKSEN is an assistant professor of political science at East Carolina University. His research interests include economic statecraft, coercive diplomacy, and civil wars. One of his recent articles is "Better or Worse? The Effect of Economic Sanctions on Human Rights," which appeared in the *Journal of Peace Research* (2009).

PAUL R. PILLAR is a professor and director of graduate studies at the Center for Peace and Security Studies at Georgetown University. He retired in 2005 after twenty-eight years in the U.S. intelligence community, in which his last position was national intelligence officer for the Near East and South Asia. He is the author of numerous chapters and articles as well as the books *Terrorism and U.S. Foreign Policy* (2001) and *Negotiating Peace: War Termination as a Bargaining Process* (1983).

BARBARA ANN J. RIEFFER-FLANAGAN is an assistant professor of political science at Central Washington University. Her current research interests include human rights, religion and politics, and democracy promotion. She is the coauthor of *The International Committee of the Red Cross: A Neutral Humanitarian Actor* (2007).

ANDREA KATHRYN TALENTINO is an associate professor of political science at Drew University. Her research focuses on international security, specifically military intervention, civil conflict, peacemaking and peacekeeping, and the links between nation building and political violence. She has authored numerous articles on military intervention and postconflict rebuilding as well as the monograph *Military Intervention after the cold war: The Evolution of Theory and Practice* (2005).

SEAN L. YOM is a Hewlett Post-Doctoral Fellow at the Center for Democracy, Development, and Rule of Law at Stanford University. Beginning in the fall of 2010, he will be an assistant professor of political science at Temple University. His research focuses on authoritarian politics, state formation, and late development in the Middle East.

Index

Abbas, Mahmoud, 203
Abdullah II, King (Jordan), 214–15, 219
Abu Ghraib prison, 9, 225
Accountability, 166; effects of, 160, 176–77; electoral, 95; as goal of government, 148; in supervision of intelligence agencies, 230, 232–41; war and, 95, 154
Acemoglu, Daron, 63
Adams, Gerry, 267, 272
Adams, John Quincy, 151
Afghanistan, 175, 177, 214; forced democratization in, 4, 8, 53, 142–43, 152–53, 273; lawlessness and corruption in, 1, 273; nation building in, 173, 180; outside intervention as imposition on, 170–71; terrorism and, 225, 275
Africa, 51. *See also* Middle East and North Africa (MENA); colonial legacy in, 101–2; democracies in, 97–98, 107–9; democratic peace theory and, 4, 7; democratic values of, 28, 100; democratization in, 11, 95–96, 98, 103; economic development lacking in, 106–7; effects of slave trade, 120; instability in, 97, 110; lack of development in, 107; leaders in, 102–3, 108; nation building in, 101–2, 104; political parties in, 99; poverty in, 103–6; sub-Saharan, 97, 105–7, 201
Agency, citizenship and, 164
Al-Qaeda, 9, 245–46; democracy and, 217, 271; efforts against, 214, 225, 252, 258, 271–72, 275; goals of, 259, 271; targeting U.S., 265, 271–72

Al-Sabah, Emir Jabir (Kuwait), 202
Algeria, democratization and reversal of, 47, 57, 206, 221n4, 251, 273
Ali, Ben (Tunisia), 202
Allende, Salvador, 121
Anarchy, 43n34, 59n1, 60n17, 64, 67; international, 26–27; prevention of, 35, 76
Angola, 109
Angolan War, 123
Arab world, 206, 210, 224. *See also* Islamic countries; Middle East and North Africa (MENA); specific countries
Arafat, Yasser, 203
Arbenz, Jacobo, 121
Argentina, 51
Aristide, Jean-Baptiste, 188
Aristotle, 42n28
Arms: control, 117, 129–30; nuclear weapons, 7, 132–33; in "security dilemma," 26–29; weapons of mass destruction, 9, 55
Aron, Raymond, 29–30
Asocial sociability, 32–34
Aspin, Les, 242n2
Assets, freezing, 184, 186
Athens, democracy in, 99
Australia, 53, 90, 121, 224
Austria, 23–24, 39n8, 48
Authoritarian regimes. *See also* Military regimes: democracies compared to, 71, 259–60; democracies' relations with, 2,

Authoritarian regimes (cont.)
50, 51, 121–22, 129, 196, 219; democratization of, 207, 208–16, 219–20; effects of, 63, 70, 205; effects of economic sanctions on, 189–91, 195; influence of oil on U.S. relations with, 12–13, 244; in Middle East, 1, 198–99, 207, 219, 262; new African states as, 101; power struggles within, 49–50, 70, 205; reforms as suicide for, 189–91, 218; repressing criticism of, 192, 194; responses to economic sanctions, 189–92, 194; retreat to, 189–92, 216; terrorism and, 245, 252–53, 259–60; U.S. support for, 198–99, 201–2, 206, 216–18

Authoritarianism, 59n1; in Imperial Germany, 39n8; persistence in Middle East and North Africa, 199–204; to preserve order, 38n4; in semidemocratic governments, 180; transition to democracy from, 166; working class, 85

"Axis of evil," proposal to expand, 54, 59n15

Ayres, R. William, 11

Babst, Dean, 2
Badran, Mudar, 210
Balance of power, 7–9, 17, 28, 119
Bandy, Joe, 93
Baran, Paul A., 82
Barry, Brian, 125–26, 140n72
Begin, Menachem, 251
Bentham, Jeremy, 13n2
Bethmann-Hollweg, Chancellor, 39n8
Bilateral trade ties, in countries' relations, 7
Bin Laden, Osama, 271, 272
Bismarck, Chancellor, 39n8
Blair, Dennis, 240
Block, Fred, 82–83
Boix, Charles, 65–66
Boland, Edward P., 234–36
Bosnia, 179, 181, 183n4; democratization of, 53, 56, 162, 170–71; nation building in, 162, 171–72, 180
Botswana, 95, 108
Brands, H. W., 147
Britain: Argentina vs., 51; coercive democratization by, 53; colonialism of, 100–101; France and, 23; Germany and, 117–18; Ireland and, 121, 266–68; Sri Lanka and, 268; U.S. and, 23, 25, 37, 224

Bryce, James, 46
Bureaucracies, African leaders building, 102–3
Burundi, 177, 180
Bush, George H. W., 53, 57, 155, 200
Bush, George W., 3, 10; democratic peace theory under, 9, 54; democratization mission of, 4, 52, 198, 202, 222, 244, 248–49, 262, 274–75; European animosity to U.S. under, 224; foreign policy of, 9, 55, 203; National Security Agency spying under, 230–31; war on terror under, 1, 231, 275

Canada, 75, 90
Cape Verde, 108
Capital: accountability of, 88–91; intellectual, 66, 71–73; mobility of, 65–66, 71, 87, 90
Capitalism: class relations under, 84; democracy's relation to, 79–80, 84, 86; global, 86–88; under liberalism, 19, 31; nation-states' role in, 79, 81–83, 87–88; relation to state, 80–81, 83
Capitalist globalization, 92
Caribbean, U.S. imperialism in, 121
Carothers, Thomas, 274
Carter, Jimmy, 37, 103, 122, 231
Casey, William J., 236–37
Castro, Fidel, 189, 195
Central African Republic, 1
Central America, 201, 236. See also Latin America
Cheney, Dick, 53, 236
Chile, 6, 121, 185–86
China, People's Republic of, 1, 139n63; human rights in, 10, 13n1, 105, 253; U.S. and, 9, 130, 191
Chinese Civil War, U.S. intervention in, 123
Choi, Seung-Whan, 7
Church, Frank, 223
Church Committee, investigating abuses of civil liberties, 12, 226–33
Churchill, Winston, 59n3
CIA, 6, 242n3; abuses during cold war, 226–29; congressional oversight of, 233–41; secret prisons of, 225, 230
Citizen participation: effects of, 180–81, 246–47, 276n1, 276n2; inhibition of, 163, 194; methods for increasing, 172–75, 181–82; nation building and, 163, 179–82; needed for democracy, 162–68

Citizens, 160; alienation of, 167, 172–75, 180, 274; bearing burden of economic sanctions, 188–91, 195; interaction with government, 155–57; nation building and, 168–72, 180; preferences in democracy, 164, 166–67; resistance to war, 31, 264; violence against, 194
Citizenship, 38n3, 86
Civil liberties. *See also* Freedom; Human rights: abuses of, 12, 225–32; counterterrorism *vs.*, 229–32, 254–57, 270; in definitions of democracy, 263; and political rights, 249; protecting, 231–41; suppression of, 1, 13; in U.S. definition of human rights, 10
Civil-military structures, 7
Civil rights movement, Ulster, 266
Civil rights movement, U.S., 226–29
Civil society, 175; effects of, 2, 210, 218, 248–49; expansion of, 200, 202; global, 92–93; influence of, 99, 165–68, 200, 207; repression of, 171, 209, 212
Civil wars, 276n7; in Algeria, 221n4; as breakdown of democracies' mode of conflict resolution, 49–50; in Sri Lanka, 269–71
Civilians, attacks on, 1. *See also* Terrorism
Class, social: democracy seen as threat to elites, 84–86, 94; middle class associated with democracy, 72; relations among, 81–84; in "third wave" democratization, 166
Client regimes, U.S. support for, 198–99, 201–2
Clinton, Bill: concern about human rights violations, 200–202; democratic peace theory used to justify military interventions under, 7, 9, 53, 273; on Jordan's peace treaty with Israel, 212–13; trying to mediate conflict in Northern Ireland, 267, 274
Coercion, power based on, 91
COINTELPRO, loss of civil liberties in, 226–29
Cold war, 3, 8; arenas for competition in, 200–201; democratic peace theory and, 2, 4; democratization and, 103, 110; economics of, 63, 185; effects on Africa, 103, 107, 109; loss of civil liberties during, 226–29; Third World countries exploiting, 103, 219; West supporting dictators during, 50, 104, 217–18
Colonialism, 23, 82, 137n51, 268; in Africa, 95, 97–98, 100–102, 108–9; effects of, 13n2, 50, 120–21, 137n52

Common good, 146, 163, 165
Communism: battle against, 129, 151, 203, 226–29; collapse of, 139n63, 200; Islam fundamentalism replacing as evil ideology, 201; perceived aggressiveness of, 118–19; as threat to human rights, 10, 121; U.S. not distinguishing Soviets from, 122–23
Communist states, 27, 122
Community, 247, 274
Conflict resolution, and democratic habit, 160
Congo (DRC), 109, 181; effects of corruption in, 177, 179; nation building in, 171–72
Congo-Brazzaville, 103
Congress, U.S.: control over matters of war, 154; oversight of intelligence agencies by, 231–39, 241n1, 242n2, 256–57; presidents' power *vs.*, 232–39; presidents' powers *vs.*, 231
Consent, 85, 91, 116
Constitutional world order, 3
Constitutions, 31, 170
Constructivist studies, 6
Consumer protection laws, as nontariff barriers to trade, 88
Consumerism, dominance in value system, 87
Cooperation: experience of, 34–35; in "Prisoner's Dilemma" game, 43n34; states' disincentive for, 26–27
Corporations, transnational, 87
Correlates of War Project, 41n22
Corruption, 182; in Afghanistan, 1; in Africa, 99, 101, 104; culture of impunity for, 176–79; in democracy *vs.* autocracy, 71; in illiberal democracies, 104; in Iraq, 175
Cosmopolitan law, 32, 35
Council on Foreign Relations, 88
Covert actions, nonmilitarized, 6
The Crisis of Democracy (Trilateral Commission), 85
Crowe, Eyre, 117–18
Cuba. *See also* Guantanamo Bay: economic sanctions against, 90, 186, 189, 191, 195
Cult of personality, of African leaders, 102
Cultural rights, in definitions of human rights, 10
Culture. *See also* Democratic culture: influence on multilateral negotiations, 89–90; power of U.S., 223
Culture of impunity, economic, 176–79
Czechoslovakia, 36

Index 305

Dahl, Robert A., 99
Darfur, genocide in, 1
Davidson, Basil, 101
De Tocqueville, Alexis, 59n3, 137n52, 163
Dean, Andrea, 4
Debt: in economic sanctions, 184–86; in Jordan, 210–13; in sub-Saharan Africa, 106–7
DeConcini, Dennis, 238
Democracy, U.S., 157; effects of coerced democratization on, 153–57; Enlightenment influence on, 149–50; erosion of, 158, 225–26, 232; as experiment, 74; as model, 222–23, 232, 241; moral superiority of, 149–50, 202–3; secrecy in, 256; security vs., 144–48, 157, 232–41; universalism of, 202–3; values of, 144–48, 157–58
Democracy/democracies, 145–46. *See also* Democratic peace theory; ability to export, 76–77; benefits of, 47–48, 65–66, 71, 160; breakdown of conflict resolution in, 49–50; capitalism and, 79–80, 84, 86; choice in, 162, 255–56; citizen participation in, 85, 156, 162–68, 180–81; citizen preferences for, 11, 164, 166–67; compared to other forms of government, 60n17; counterterrorism efforts in, 255–56, 257–60; criticisms of, 47–48, 85, 88, 247–48, 271; as cure for terrorism, 262–63, 265–66, 271, 275; definitions of, 5–7, 57, 67–68, 95, 98–99, 263; development of, 65, 99; as device for aggregating policy preferences, 11, 45, 51–52; economics and, 63–64, 75–77, 104; effects of coerced democratization on domestic, 143–45; expansion of, 61, 75; factors facilitating, 60n17, 71, 74, 107–8; foreign policy and, 55–56, 59n3, 196; illiberal, 104, 108, 249–50, 263; individualism vs. communalism in, 108–9; leadership of, 34, 46; limitations of, 46–47, 54, 56, 85; lobbying in, 46, 55; measures of, 192; models of, 11, 84, 97, 99, 108–9; mystique surrounding, 51–52, 56–57; neoliberalism on, 85, 88; new vs. established, 4, 7; obstacles to, 99, 103–5, 273; outside interventions by, 6, 50, 121; peace and, 49, 61–63; rarity of wars by, 2, 7, 51, 264; relations with authoritarian regimes, 2, 51; representative vs. direct, 77n3, 84, 145–46; republic vs., 145–46, 148–49; resistance to, 84–86, 102, 105; seen as solution to problems, 97, 104, 110, 262; social class and, 72, 94; success of, 9, 74, 107–8, 164; terrorism and, 203, 245–46, 247–48, 269–70, 271; threats to, 58, 85, 153; use of torture in, 253–54; war aversion and, 41n23, 49–54; wars by, 7, 50–51; in Westernization, 49, 202

Democratic culture: development of, 175–76, 180, 248–49; habits of, 160, 165–68
Democratic domino effect, 4, 53–54
Democratic imperialism, by U.S., 4
Democratic peace theory, 63; application to foreign policy, 4, 6, 8–10, 144; applied to terrorism, 243, 246–47, 260; causation in, 7, 11, 57–58; definitive articles of, 2; effects of, 62; influence on U.S. foreign policy, 7, 9, 203, 263–64; limited to one conception of democracy, 94–95; misapplications of, 54; theoretical validity of, 4–7; universality of, 3–4
Democratic realism, 53–54
Democratic values, 53, 264; in Africa, 99, 100, 107; citizens less likely to use violence, 276n1, 276n2; development of, 13, 174; terrorists and, 247; U.S., 144–48
Democratization. *See also* Liberalization: in Africa, 11, 95–96, 98, 103, 110; in Arab world, 199–204; bandits and peasants parable about, 64–65; to counter terrorism, 160, 248–49, 265–66, 272; dangers of forcing, 8, 11–12; domestic effects of forced, 143–45, 153–57; domino effects in, 273; economic issues in, 109–10, 196–97, 200, 220n2; economic sanctions in forced, 185–86, 190–91, 195; effectiveness of forced, 142–43, 158, 203; effects of, 11, 273–74, 276; EU pressure for, 200–201; exemptions from pressure in Middle East and North Africa, 213, 217–18, 244; factors leading to, 65–67; forced, 52–53, 104, 155–56, 159n6 (*See also* War); forced in Iraq, 9, 248–49; forcing, as moral obligation, 5, 153; gradualist theory of regime transition, 202, 205, 207; hypocrisy in U.S. pressure for, 198–99, 204–8, 219–20; ineffectiveness of forced, 48, 222, 274; in Jordan, 213–17; Latin America moving toward, 48; in Middle East and North Africa, 200–201, 203–4, 207, 219; Muslim

306 INDEX

countries moving toward, 47–48; in nation building, 161–62; NGOs pressure for, 201; noncoercive methods of, 110, 196, 220n1, 241; obstacles to, 76–77, 109; resistance to, 1, 109, 207, 219–20; reversals of, 221n4, 273; "second wave" of, 11; terrorism and, 244–49, 274; "third wave" of, 97, 166; time needed for, 1, 275–76; U.S. drive to spread, 148–51; U.S. geopolitical interests and, 198, 202, 204–8, 218; U.S. pressure for, 4, 9, 144, 152–53, 205, 208–16; in U.S. foreign policy, 142–43, 150–51, 213, 262–64, 273

Dershowitz, Alan M., 253–54
Deterrence, prestige *vs.* arms in, 27
Deutsch, Karl, 40n20
Developed countries, military interventions by, 63, 73–74
Developing countries, 1. *See also* Third World; democracy pushed as remedy for, 97, 104; developed countries' interventions in, 73–74
Diamond, Larry, 165–67, 175–76
Dictatorships, 127. *See also* Authoritarian regimes; redistributing wealth, 125; West supporting, 104, 110, 138n57
Diplomacy, 116–17, 119
Dissent. *See* Civil liberties
Domhoff, William G., 82
Dominican Republic, 48, 121–22
Douglas, William O., 223
Downing, Brian, 77n1
Doyle, Michael, 2, 4, 6–8, 11, 13n3
Drury, A. Cooper, 11

East Asia, foreign aid in, 106
East Bank, Jordan's resources to, 213
East Timor, 53
Eastern Europe, 3, 50, 203
Economic aid. *See* Foreign aid
Economic development, 65; democracy and, 63–64, 103–5; in democratization, 202, 220n2; disappointments in, 97; effects of, 7, 11, 63, 274; sustainable *vs.* market-driven, 93
Economic rights, in definitions of human rights, 10
Economic sanctions: costs of, 186; effectiveness of, 186, 196; effects of, 186–96; functioning of, 185–86, 191; ineffectiveness in democratization, 186, 190, 197; length of, 191; methods of increasing cooperation with, 196–97; responses to, 189–91, 196–97; uses of, 11, 184, 191, 194–96
Economy, 31, 194; Africa's, 109; benefits of peace to, 35, 70, 95, 276n7; China's, 1; culture of impunity in, 176; democracy and, 75–77; democratization and, 196, 202; effects on evolution of world politics, 133; growth in, 105–8, 216; illegal and informal, 177–78, 180, 187–88, 196–97; Jordan's, 212, 214, 216; legal system strengthening, 178–79; under liberalism, 19, 36; officials judged by state of, 82–83; political uses of, 184–85, 196, 209; Soviet collapse and, 63; state control and regulation of, 79, 131, 182; transnational practices in, 87; as weapon, 184–85
Ecuador, 39n7
Education, effects of, 181–82, 202
Egalitarianism, in U.S. politics, 149
Egan, Daniel, 11
Egypt: election results in, 57, 203–4; influence of Islam in, 56–57, 204; liberalization in, 200, 202; nationalism of, 120–21; opposition parties in, 203–4; terrorism and, 245–46, 262; U.S. and, 54, 201–2, 204; U.S. pushing for democratization in, 103, 207; U.S. relations as double standard, 9, 204, 244
El Salvador, 122
Elections: demand for, 162, 170; in democratization, 170, 248–49; effects of, 123, 182; in Egypt, 57, 203–4; as element in democracy, 99, 263; ill-effects of, 172–75, 179, 249–50, 269; in illiberal democracies, 99, 104, 249–50; Islamic victories in, 221n3, 221n4; in Jordan, 210, 211, 214–15, 218; lack of, 101, 199; need to allow democratization to work through, 182, 272–73; in peace building, 160–61; political Islamists in, 205, 250; in Saudi Arabia, 203–4; West's fear of results of, 205, 250–51, 273
Electoral accountability, as obstacle to war, 95
Elites: average citizens and, 166, 169–72, 175–76; effects of economic sanctions on, 187–89, 195–97; nation building focused on, 169–72; U.S. relations with Arab, 207–8
Elman, Miriam Fendius, 51

Empire, 29–30, 75. *See also* Colonialism
Employment, 176, 188
Empowerment Rights Index, 192, 194
England, 30
Englebert, Pierre, 108
The Enlightenment, 2, 149, 155, 157
Environmental protection laws, as nontariff barriers to trade, 88–91
Equality, 10, 38n4, 46, 93, 146, 147; economic, 11; social *vs.* political, 86
Equilibrium, as interstate peace, 29–30. *See also* Balance of power
Ethnic divisions, 101; elections polarizing, 173–74; in Sri Lanka, 268, 276n8
Ethnic identity, in Africa, 99–101
Eurasia, pressure for democratization in, 201
Europe, 37, 190; relations with U.S., 223–24; "secret prisons" in, 253–54
European Union (EU), 89, 200–201, 267; Jordan and, 211, 215–16
Evolution: natural, 32–33; political, 32–33
Experience, influencing peace, 28
Extraordinary rendition, human rights abuses after, 225

Falkland Islands, 51
Fanon, Frantz, 101
Fascist states, 27, 116–18
Fashoda crisis, 23
FBI, abuses of civil liberties during cold war, 226–29
Federalists, U.S., 74, 153–54
Feudal states, relations among, 27
Fiala, Andrew, 6
Finland, 6
Fisher, William F., 93
Ford, Gerald, 231
Foreign aid: in economic sanctions, 184, 186; as incentive for democratization, 196, 200; to Israel, 201; to Jordan, 209–13, 215–16; to Middle East, 208; to sub-Saharan Africa, 106–7
Foreign policy: application of democratic peace theory to, 4–5; changing purposes of, 73–74; democratization in, 150–51, 153; effects of authoritarianism on, 39n8; influence of democracy on, 59n3; liberal, 38n1, 132; liberalism in, 19, 23, 127, 139n63; liberalism's failures in, 115–16, 119–24, 135n39;

obligations of liberal, 128–29; protection of pacific union through, 131, 139n63; use of economic sanctions and incentives in, 184–85, 194–96
Foreign policy, U.S.: under Bush, 9; changing, 3; in cold war, 8; democratic peace theory in, 4, 263–64; democratization in, 8, 11, 142–43, 148–51, 198, 204, 272; domestic effects of, 143–45; as "exceptional," 8; goals of, 55–56, 142, 198, 204, 220; importance of power in, 150–51; influence of assuring access to oil on, 12–13; Jordan's compliance with, 208–18; in Middle East, 54–55, 198, 201, 204, 220, 244–49; under Obama, 9–10; Realism in, 128, 146–47; relations with autocrats in, 201, 220n2; restrained intervention as harmful, 139n63; toward nonliberal world, 128; unilateralism in, 9; values in, 144–45, 146–47, 157–58; vindicationist *vs.* exemplarist, 147
Forster, E. M., 46
France, 23, 28, 58, 90, 103; colonialism of, 50, 100–101; monarchy *vs.* republic in, 149–50, 159n3; revolution in, 99, 262
Freedom, 18, 31, 52, 105. *See also* Civil liberties; Rights; in democracies, 99, 108, 192
Frontier, 74–75
Frum, David, 54
Fukuyama, Francis, 54–55

Gabon, 103
Game theory, 26–29
Gartzke, Erik, 11
Geography: as factor in democratization, 66; as factor influencing peace, 28–29
Germany, 13n3, 36, 58, 117; Imperial, 6, 39n8; successful democratization of, 8, 48, 121, 203; wars of, 6, 23–24, 28
Gibbons, 188
Gill, Graeme, 166
Gladstone, William, 120–21, 137n53, 138n57
Global systems theory, as break from state-centrism, 87
Globalization, 88; capitalism and democracy in, 79–80, 91–94; effects of, 11, 63, 94; inevitability of, 79–80, 95; institutional failures in, 89, 92
Goldwater, Barry, 233, 236–37
Gordon, Philip, 225

Goss, Porter J., 237
Government, 183n4. *See also* Nation-states; States; capacity of, 182; central, 177–78, 185; changing systems of, 167, 170; citizens' perceptions of, 160, 169, 172, 173; coercion by, 71–75, 81–82; factors influencing types of, 66–67, 71; formation, in bandits and peasants parable, 64–65; instability of semidemocratic, 180, 182; limiting power of, 147–48, 254–57; monarchies *vs.* republics, 149–50, 159n3; negotiations in, 83, 170; privatization of, 175; public goods provided by, 69, 71; response to economic sanctions, 189–91; in retention *vs.* redistribution of wealth, 65–66, 68–69, 71; secrecy in, 256; secular, 271; separation of powers in, 33, 148, 256–57, 264; social group leadership in, 83; support for, 174–76, 178–79; types of, 59n1
Government, local, 175, 181, 182
Government, U.S., 230; citizen interaction with, 153, 155–57, 166; exceptionalism of, 149–51; goals of founders, 145–48; presidential powers in, 236, 241n1; separation of powers in, 154–55, 232–39, 238, 241n1
Government officials, in illegal and informal economy, 177–79, 180. *See also* Corruption
Graham, Bob, 237–38
Gramsci, Antonio, 82–84
Great power politics, in Middle East, 217–19
Gregory, Ross, 43n38
Grenada, 48, 53
Guantanamo Bay, abuse of prisoners at, 9, 225
Guatemala, 6, 121
Gulf War, effects of, 200, 211

Haas, Michael, 41n22
Hadrian's Wall, 73
Haiti, 172; elections in, 57, 170; U.S. efforts to impose democracy in, 48, 53, 188
Halperin, Morton, 262
Hamas (Harakat al-Muqawama al-Islamiyya), 204, 206, 261n2; election victories of, 250–51, 273; goals of, 259, 271
Hamilton, Alexander, 149–50, 159n1, 184
Hamilton, Lee H., 235
Hardt, Michael, 88
Hariri, Rafiq al-, 203
Hart, Philip, 228

Hartz, Louis, 147, 157, 159n4
Hassan II, King (Morocco), 201–2
Hayek, Friedrich, 85
Hegemony, 36; transitions among, 37, 41n21, 43n38; as type of interstate peace, 29–30
Hegre, Haavard, 63
Held, David, 84–85
Hellmann, Gunther, 7
Helms-Burton Act, 90
Henderson, Errol A., 4, 7
Herborth, Benjamin, 7
Hezbollah, 204
History, efforts to change, 5
HIV/AIDS epidemic, in sub-Saharan Africa, 97
Hizballah, 248, 265
Hobbes, Thomas, 26–28, 38n4, 40n11, 159n1
Hoffman, Bruce, 274
Hoover, J. Edgar, 118, 227
Hospitality, 32, 35
Houphouet-Boigny, Felix, 102
Howard, Michael, 224
Hull, Cordell, 116
Human rights, 2, 10, 127, 223. *See also* Civil liberties; declining under economic sanctions, 194–95; liberal interventions in Third World not promoting, 122–23; protection of, 143, 160, 184–85, 191
Human rights abuses, 97; as erosion of U.S. democracy, 225–26; responses to, 110, 119–20, 200–202
Humanitarian aid, responsibility for, 125, 130
Hume, David, 115, 135n39
Huntington, Samuel, 47, 85, 166–67
Hussein, King (Jordan), 209, 219; human rights violations by, 202, 212; liberalization under, 210
Hussein, Saddam, 55, 73–74; belief in WMD of, 9, 55; effects of removing, 58, 221n6, 273
Huston, Tom Charles, 232

Income tax, federal, 151. *See also* Taxes
India, 50–51, 253
Individualism, as value in American politics, 11, 147
Individuals. *See also* Citizens: in nation building, 168–69
Industrialization, and democracy, 99, 104
Inequality, and responsibility for humanitarian aid, 125

Index 309

Information, open flows of, 4
Inge, William Ralph, 59n3
Institutionalists, on failure of development, 107
Institutions, 74, 92, 156, 174; capitalism and, 79, 82; in conservative *vs.* liberal liberalism, 19; democratic, 79, 93, 163; in nation building, 162, 168–69; transnational, 79, 89, 92–93
Intellectual property rights, 87, 89
Intelligence agencies. *See* Security sector
Intelligence Reform and Terrorism Prevention Act, 241
Interdependence, transnational, 2
Interim Governing Council (IGC) (Iraq), 173–74
International law, 34–35
International Monetary Fund (IMF), 79, 87–88, 211–13
International relations: "games" in, 26–29; liberal, 63; pacific union as "treaty" in, 31–32; war and, 67, 70
Internationalism, 148, 159n2, 198, 202–3
Internment camps, as erosion of U.S. democracy, 226
Investments, 89–91, 130. *See also* Capital
Iran, 47, 54; revolution in, 206; as terrorism sponsor, 251; U.S. foreign policy goals in, 204, 207; U.S. interventions in, 6, 121, 186
Iran-Contra scandal, 235
Iraq, 275; and belief in democratic domino effect, 53–54; as democracy, 57, 60n17, 202; economy of, 176, 178; effects of regime change in, 58, 221n6, 273; effects of U.S. war against, 9, 225, 245, 273–74; forced democratization of, 4, 8–9, 142–43, 152–53, 220n1, 248–49, 273; influence of Islam in, 56; Jordan and, 211–12, 214–15; nation building in, 171–75; U.S. war against, 55–56, 147, 214–16, 271
Ireland, 121. *See also* Northern Ireland
Irgun, moving to democratic path, 251
Irish Republican Army (IRA): moving to democratic path, 275; Provisional, 248, 250–51; terrorism by, 266–68
Ish-Shalom, Piki, 6
Islam, 47, 224, 247; resistance to Jordan's peace treaty with Israel, 211–13; U.S. fear of, 206–7, 216, 220
Islam, political, 250; in Algeria, 221n4, 251; as anti-American, 206; in Egypt, 245–46;

increased influence as danger of elections, 205, 213, 216–17, 249–51; influence of, 56, 205, 261n1; in Iraq, 56; in Jordan, 213, 216–17; mainstream *vs.* extreme, 216, 221n3; in Saudi Arabia, 261n1; terrorism and, 216, 245–46
Islamic culture, blamed for authoritarianism, 199–200
Islamic fundamentalism, 198, 201
Islamic jihadists, 245–48, 252, 259, 267, 275
Islamic states: democracy and, 9, 12, 47–48; terrorism and, 224, 271
Isolationism, of liberal states, 131, 148, 159n2
Israel, 39n7, 251, 271; election results not always desirable to, 56–57; Jordan's peace treaty with, 209, 211–12, 216; Palestinians and, 206, 214, 253; U.S. support for, 54–55, 198, 201, 206–7, 218, 221n5
Italy, 23–24, 48, 121

James, Patrick, 7
Japan, 8, 37; successful democratization of, 48, 121, 203
Jefferson, Thomas, 149, 159n1, 159n3
Jervis, Robert, 29
Johnson, Loch, 11
Johnson, Lyndon, 231
Jordan, 50, 219, 221n7, 250; human rights violations in, 202, 211–13; Iraq and, 211–12, 214–15; peace treaty with Israel, 209, 211–12, 216; remaining autocracy, 209, 213, 220; superficial reforms in, 200, 204, 214–15; U.S. and, 202, 214; U.S. democracy promotion in, 207, 208–16; U.S. support for, 199, 210–11
Juridicial freedom, 31
Justice, and redistribution of wealth, 125–27

Kamuzu Banda, 104
Kant, Immanuel, 5, 42n24, 42n32, 116, 164; on citizens' resistance to war, 264; democratic peace theory originating with, 2, 63; on development of pacific union, 42n25, 42n26, 141n82; on global sovereignty, 125–26; on liberal values, 18–19, 120, 128; *Perpetual Peace* by, 31, 80; on political evolution, 32–33, 132–35; on sources of peace, 42n28, 133–35; on three definitive articles of peace, 31–32

310 INDEX

Kaplan, Lawrence, 53–54
Karzai, Hamid, 273
Keller, William W., 229
Kennan, George, 117, 147
Kennedy, John, 122
Kenyatta, Jomo, 101
Khatami, Mohammad, 251
King, Martin Luther, Jr., 228–29
Kissinger, Henry, 147
Korean War, U.S. intervention in, 123
Kosovo, 170, 183n2
Krauthammer, Charles, 53–54
Kristol, William, 53–54
Kuwait, 200, 202
Kwame Nkrumah, 102

Labor, 74–75, 82, 86–87
Labor laws, 88–91, 194
Latin America, 51. *See also* Central America; democratization in, 48, 201; U.S. interventions in, 147, 151
Layne, Christopher, 5–7
Lebanon, 39n7, 54, 203, 248
Leeson, Peter T., 4
Left parties, opposition to liberalization in, 89
Legal system, strengthening economy, 178–79
Lektzian, David, 4
Lektzian and Souva, 4
Lesotho, 108
Less developed countries, Westernization of, 49
Leviathan (Hobbes), 38n4
Liberal globalism, Wilson's, 151
Liberal imperialism, 8, 120–23, 135n40, 137n51
Liberal international theory, 23
Liberal internationalism, among liberal states, 36
Liberal-patriotic view, Reagan's, 38n1
Liberal states: alliances among, 35, 37; attitudes of, 23, 63, 116–17, 138n54; chronological listing of, 20–22; conflicts of interests among, 30; cooperation among, 36, 115–16; in Eastern Europe, 3; economic influences on, 36, 139n63; exceptionalism of, 31, 37; foreign policies of, 122–24, 128–29, 131; foreign policy failures of, 115–16, 119, 135n39; libertarian states *vs.*, 135n40; peace among, 3–4, 23, 25–27, 31–32, 131; problems of, 20; relations with nonliberal states, 116–21, 136n46, 138n57,

139n63; right to nonintervention and, 23, 116; size of, 125–26; trade and, 127, 131, 139n63; values of, 17, 36, 116, 127–28, 131; wars between, 34, 39n7
The Liberal Tradition in America (Hartz), 147
Liberal values, 3, 11, 120, 128, 131. *See also* Democratic values
Liberalism, 85; colonialism suppressing, 120–21; conservative, 121–22, 124; definitions of, 39n8; in foreign affairs, 23, 34, 63, 121–22, 127, 160; hegemonic, 127–28; ideology of, 17, 19, 131–32; increase of, 19–20; influence on peace, 17–18, 28, 31; successfulness of, 19–20, 121; types of, 19, 38n4, 122, 124, 129
Liberalization, 91. *See also* Democratization; in Jordan, 210, 215; in Middle East, 200, 202, 207; opposition to, 89; through MAI, 89–91; use of economic sanctions in, 185, 187, 191
Liberation Tigers of Tamil Eelam (LTTE), 269–71, 275
Liberia, 170–71, 176
Libertarian states, *vs.* liberal states, 135n40
Liberties. *See* Civil liberties; Freedom
Liberty, 199; definitions of, 197n1; effects of economic sanctions on, 186–95; in goals of U.S. government, 146–48; protection of, 147–48, 155–57; tension with power, 143, 146; threats to, 154–55, 157–58, 159n1, 217
Libya, 1, 54
Lincoln, Abraham, 151
Lipset, Seymour M., 85, 147, 149
Liska, George, 43n38
Living standards, declining in sub-Saharan Africa, 106
Lloyd George, David, 52
Loans: to Jordan, 211–13; in mixed strategy of sanctions and incentives, 196
Locke, John, 85, 164
Lucretius, 41n21
Luxemburg, 82
Lyons, Terrence, 172

Madison, James, 74, 85, 148–49, 158, 159n1
Mali, 47–48
Maliki, Nouri al-, 174, 183n3
Mani, Rama, 170
Manifest destiny, in U.S. foreign policy, 8

Mansfield, Edward, 4, 180
Maoz, Zeev, 13n4
Markets, 35, 86, 88; accommodation of Third World through, 130–31; influence of, 36, 48; liberalization of, 19, 86
Markovits, Andrei S., 224
Mauritius, 95, 108
Mazzoli, Roman, 242n2
McConnell, Mike, 240–41
McFarlane, Robert C., 235
Mead, Walter Russell, 257
Mearsheimer, John, 55
Medvedev, Dmitry, 1
Mexico, 75
Middle East and North Africa (MENA), 200, 251. *See also* specific countries; as anti-American, 206; authoritarianism in, 1, 12–13, 199–204, 216, 219, 221n6, 244, 246; democratic peace theory applied to, 9; democratization in, 12, 47–48, 53–54, 198, 203–8, 220n2; effects of regimes on U.S. security, 244–49; election results in, 56–57, 250; foreign aid to Jordan from, 209–10; great power politics in, 200, 217–19; influence of Islam in, 56–57, 250; oil and U.S. relations with authoritarian regimes, 12–13, 244; pressure for democratization in, 200–203, 205, 217–18; secular governments in, 271; small states in, 219; terrorism and, 246, 262, 271; U.S. foreign policy in, 12–13, 204, 217–18, 220; U.S. in, 207–8, 271; U.S. support for Israel in, 54–55, 221n5
Miliband, Ralph, 82
Militarism, restraining, 4
Military, 33, 50, 77n1, 251; cost of, 36, 73, 74, 187; economic sanctions and, 184, 187, 189; forced democratization through, 53, 94, 153; purposes of interventions, 7, 9, 73–74; standing armies, 13n2, 153–54, 157
Military aid, U.S.: to Jordan, 213, 215, 216; to Middle East, 208
Military intellectuals, 14n8
Military regimes. *See* Authoritarian regimes
Mill, John Stuart, 5, 120, 128, 137n51, 163
Mitchell, George, 267
Mobutu Sese Seko, 102, 104
Modernization, democratization as, 203
Monarchies, 19, 47; aggressiveness of, 31, 33; sharing power, 1, 33, 70

Mondale, Walter, 230–31
Monroe, James, 151
Monroe Doctrine, 8, 151
Montesquieu, Charles, 31
Moore, Barrington, 104
Moral freedom, liberalism's commitment to, 18
Morgan, T. Clifton, 191
Morgenthau, Hans J., 27, 146
Morocco, 200–201
Mossadegh, intervention against, 121
Mousseau, Michael, 63
Moynihan, Daniel Patrick, 234
Mubarak, Hosni, 54; human rights violations by, 201–2, 204; opposition parties to, 203–4; U.S. and, 201–2, 271
Mueller, John, 11
Multilateral Agreement on Investment (MAI), 89–92
Musharraf, Pervez, 252–53
Muslim Brotherhood (Ikhwan Muslimin), 261n2; election victories of, 56–57, 204–5, 210; in Jordan, 210–11, 214, 250
Myanmar, 1

Nation building, 8–9, 11, 102; citizen participation and, 163, 179–82; citizens and, 168–72; corruption and, 176–79; democratization in, 160–62; ill-effects of, 163, 176–82; liberal models for, 160; other interventions *vs.*, 162
Nation-states. *See also* Government; States: capitalism and, 80–82, 87, 94–95; democratization of, 91, 94; effects of global capitalism on, 87–88; globalization and, 91, 94–95; terrorist groups compared to, 243; transnational states *vs.*, 91–92
National Security Act of 1947 (U.S.), 14n8
National Security Agency (NSA), U.S., 226, 230–31
National Security Council (NSC), U.S., 235
National Security Strategy, Bush's, 4
Nationalism, 101, 215; liberals and, 17, 120–21; in response to economic sanctions, 189, 194
Nationality, as national-state rights, 140n72
Native Americans, U.S. treatment of, 75, 226
Natural law, Kant on, 116
Negri, Antonio, 88
Negroponte, John D., 240
Neoclassical economic theory, 80–81

312 INDEX

Neocolonialism, 107, 109
Neoconservatives, 9, 53–54, 204
Neoliberalism, 85–88, 94
Neorealists, 8, 146
Nepotism, by African leaders, 101
"New world order," Bush's, 3
New Zealand, 121
Nicaragua, 48, 121, 236–37, 242n3
Nigeria, 97–98
9/11 attacks: causes of, 237–38, 244; responses to, 9, 208–9, 223–25, 257–60
Nixon, Richard, 231
Nongovernmental organizations (NGOs), 90, 171, 201, 202
Nonliberal states. *See also* Authoritarian regimes: accommodation of Third World, 130–31; liberal states' relations with, 116–20, 128
Noriega, Manuel, 48
North, Oliver, 235
North Africa, 9. *See also* Middle East and North Africa (MENA)
North Korea, 1, 54, 196; economic sanctions on, 186–87, 191
Northern Ireland, 276n4; preventing terrorism in, 272, 274; Provisional Irish Republican Army in, 248, 250–51; terrorism in, 266–68
Norway, 269, 271
Nozick, Robert, 85
Nuclear weapons, 7, 132–33
Nye, Joseph S., Jr., 40n20, 223
Nyerere, Julius, 102

Obama, Barack, 9–10, 241
Offe, Claus, 82–83
Office of the Director of National Intelligence (DNI), U.S., 240–41
Official Development Assistance (ODA), 106
Oil, 207, 221n5; influence on U.S. policies in Middle East, 12–13, 198, 201, 218, 244; political uses of, 206; wealth from, 200, 209–10
Olson, Mancur, 63–65, 69
Oneal, John R., 2–3, 63
Oren, Ido, 5–6
Organization fro Economic Cooperation and Development (OECD), 89–91, 90
Organizations, international, 3. *See also* Nongovernmental organizations (NGOs)
Osman, Obdulahi, 11

Pacific union, 31–32, 40n20, 42n25, 42n26, 127; expansion of, 132, 134, 141n82; threats to, 36–37, 131
Paine, Thomas, 41n23
Pakistan, 9; efforts against terrorism, 252–53; India *vs.*, 50–51; moving toward democracy, 47–48
Palestinian Authority, 54, 56–57, 203–4
Palestinians, 39n7, 202, 213–14; electing Hamas officials, 250–51; Israel's treatment of, 206, 253
Panama, 48, 53, 147, 152, 155
Panetta, Leon, 240
Paris Club, rescheduling debt for Jordan, 211–13
Patriot Act (2001), 254
Peace. *See also* Democratic peace theory: among liberal states, 4, 23, 25–27, 31–32 (*See also* Pacific union); attitudes toward, 28, 34; building, 2, 160–61, 164–65; definitions of, 67–68, 243; economy and, 63, 75–77, 80, 142, 197; explanations for link with democracy, 49, 57–59, 61–63; factors influencing, 2–3, 7, 28–29, 34–35, 74; interstate, 29–30, 67–68; liberal, 27–28, 30; paths toward, 17–18, 28, 30, 33, 133–35; sources of, 42n28; sovereigns' obligation to seek, 27; terrorist groups moving to democratic paths, 267–68; trade and, 31, 58
Peace building, citizen participation in, 170
Peceny, Mark, 274
Peksen, Dursun, 11
Periphery, subordination of, 87, 91
Perle, Richard, 54, 59n15
Perpetual Peace (Kant), 3, 31–32, 80, 134–35
Peru, 39n7, 121
Philippines, 75
Physical Integrity Index, 194
Pickering, Jeffrey, 274
Pike, Otis, 234
Pike Committee, 234–35
Pillar, Paul, 12–13, 262–63
Pluralistic security community, 40n20. *See also* Pacific union
Podhoretz, Norman, 54, 56
Political parties, 99; in Africa, 101–2; in Jordan, 210; in Sri Lanka, 276n6; terrorist groups changing to, 271; U.S., 140n73
Political rights, 1–2; in democracy, 249, 263; in human rights, 10

Index 313

Politics, 62, 86, 251; acceptance of defeat in, 71, 76; centrist pressures in, 221n3; coercion's costliness, 70, 72, 74; divisiveness of, 173, 179–80; domestic *vs.* international, 67–68, 70–72, 76, 78n4; evolution of world, 132–35; participation in, 166; redistributive, 68, 78n6; self-enforcing bargains in, 64–65

Politics, U.S.: exceptionalism of, 149–51; as ideological, 147, 149

Ponniah, Thomas, 93

Poverty, 188; democracy as remedy for, 103–5, 110; effects of, 109, 212, 262; in sub-Saharan Africa, 95–96, 105–6

Powell, Colin, 97

Power, 176; centralized, 159n1, 185; economic, 184–85; elites', 187–88; envy of U.S. for, 225; of government, 148, 151, 159n6; importance of, 150–51; informal economy giving, 177, 179; sovereigns' uses of, 69; struggles for within states, 1, 27, 69–70; tension with liberty, 143, 146

Preemptive attacks, motives for, 27, 29

Prestige *vs.* arms, in deterrence, 27

"Prisoner's Dilemma" game, 43n34

Prisons: abuse in, 1, 9; secret CIA, 225, 230, 253–54

Private property. *See* Property rights

Privatization, in neoliberal program, 86

Productivity: under authoritarian regimes, 63, 70; in bandits and peasants parable, 64; of creative people, 71–72; government's ability to coerce, 71–72; intellectual capital in increasing, 66

Property rights, 19, 140n72; protection of, 81, 120–21; redistribution *vs.*, 122; valued above social welfare, 88

Prosperity, as U.S. foreign policy goal, 142

Protectionism, liberal states avoiding, 131

Provisional Irish Republican Army, 248, 250–51. *See also* Irish Republican Army

Prussian Model, 42n29

Przeworski, Adam, 104

Putin, Vladimir, 1, 58

Qatar, 47–48

Rajapake, Mahinda, 270

Rapoport, Anatol, 227

Rationalism, pacifism as, 31

Rawls, John, 264

Ray, James Lee, 6

Reagan, Ronald, 9, 37, 38n1, 203, 236

Realism, 43n34, 129, 159n1; democratic peace theory and, 26–28, 30, 42n24, 62; on liberals, 37, 124; on power, 119, 150–51; U.S. foreign policy and, 3–4, 8, 128, 147

Reason: in American character, 159n4; truth discovered through, 150, 155, 157

Reform movements, 1, 49

Reforms, 3, 11, 104. *See also* Democratization; Liberalization

Religion: in Irish oppression, 266–68, 276n4; in Sri Lanka, 268, 276n8

Rendition, 225, 253

Report on the Principles of Political Morality (Robespierre), 262

Representation, 2, 18, 31, 33, 39n8

Republican constitutions, of states, 31–32

Republics: democracies *vs.*, 145–46, 148–49; evolution of, 32–33; liberal, 19; peacefulness of, 33–34, 63

Resources, 70; availability to government, 71–72, 74; conflict over, 32–33; effects of economic sanctions on control of, 187–88; natural, 82

Revolutionary Armed Forces of Colombia (FARC), 265

Rhodesia, 186, 189

Richardson, Louise, 232, 266

Rieffer-Flanagan, Barbara Ann, 13

Rights, 38n3. *See also* Civil liberties; Human rights; citizen participation in protecting, 165–66; in international law, 34; liberal, 18–19; of nations, 23, 119–20, 137n53; political, 1–2, 10, 249, 263; repression of, 99, 101

Riker, William, 47

Robinson, J. Kenneth, 233

Robinson, James A., 63

Rockefeller, John D., IV, 240, 241n1

Rogue states, 4, 9

Roosevelt, Franklin, 8, 14n7

Rousseau, Jean-Jacques, 26–27, 164

Russett, Bruce: on democracy, 5–8; on democratic peace theory, 2–3, 52–53, 55

Russia, 1, 58, 105, 186, 253

Sandbrook, Richard, 102

Sanderson, Lord, 117–18

Sandinistas, U.S. interventions against, 121, 236–37
Sarajevo Crisis, 39n8
Saudi Arabia, 210, 262; elections in, 203–4, 249–50; Islam in, 249–50, 261n1; U.S. relations with, 9, 54, 207, 244, 271
Scarff, Lawrence, 165
Schumpeter, Joseph, 85
Second Intifada, 214, 216
"Second wave" of democratization, 97
Security, 43n34, 177; counterterrorism efforts and, 254–55, 257–60; democratization increasing, 55, 144, 160, 263–64; effects of, 35, 245–46; effects of Middle East regimes on U.S., 244–49; as foreign policy goal, 55, 129, 155, 208; liberty *vs.*, 12, 33, 157, 226–29; sovereigns' obligation to seek, 27–28; states' cooperation in, 36
"Security dilemma," 26–29, 35, 69–70
Security sector: abuses of civil liberties by U.S. intelligence agencies, 12, 226–29; counterterrorism efforts by, 254–55; extensive structure for, 103, 200; increased repression by, 214–16; supervision of U.S. intelligence agencies, 213, 232–41, 241n1, 242n2
Senegal, democracy in, 95
Serbia, forced democratization in, 53
Seretse Khama, 108
Settlement, right of, 120
Seychelles, 108
Shamir, Yitzhak, 251
Shapiro, Ian, 164–65
Shelby, Richard C., 237
Siad Barre, West supporting, 104
Sierra Leone, 180–81; democratization of, 53, 170; economic problems in, 176–77
Singapore, 105
Singer, J. David, 41n22
Singer, Peter, 125
Sino-Soviet split, West's delay in recognizing, 119
Sklair, Leslie, 87
Slavery, 74–75, 100
Small, Melvin, 41n22
Small states, insecurity of, 219
Smith, Humphrey, 138n54
Smith, Jackie, 93
Snyder, Jack, 4, 7, 180
Social democratic welfare states, 88
Social groups, *vs.* corporations, 90–91
Social movements, 62, 85, 92–94
Social rights, in human rights, 10
Social strife, in sub-Saharan Africa, 96
Social welfare, state spending on, 19, 81, 94, 95
Socialism, under liberalism, 19
"Soft power," 223
Somalia, 1, 100
South Africa, economic sanctions on, 186
South America, U.S. hegemony over, 30
South Korea, 105, 121
Souva, Mark, 4
Sovereigns, 28; in bandits and peasants parable, 64–65; functions of, 27, 76; leadership of democracies *vs.* other governments, 34, 46; power of, 69–70
Sovereignty, 26, 125
Soviet Union, 6, 136n46; collapse of, 7–9, 50, 63, 104, 139n63, 200, 234; liberal interventions in Third World to limit, 122–23; U.S. and, 8–10, 103, 118–19, 123, 129–30; U.S. not distinguishing communism from, 122–23
Spain, 36
Spiro, David E., 5
Sri Lanka, 268–71, 276n6
"Stag dilemma," 26
State building. *See* Nation building
State deregulation, in neoliberal program, 86
States, 19, 34. *See also* Government; Nation-states; African, 101, 108; alienation from, 247; capitalism and, 35, 83, 88–89; legitimacy of, 108, 180; power of, 69, 74, 249–51; power struggles within, 69–70, 88; redistribution of income and, 69, 126; rent seeking *vs.* plundering by, 64, 74; republican constitutions of, 31–32; resources of, 27, 153; with similar structures and values, 27
Stern Gang, moving to democratic path, 251
Structural adjustment policies, 87, 92, 212, 215
Structuralists, on failure of African development, 107
Stuart, Douglas T., 14n8
Sudan, 1
Suffrage: as element in democracy, 38n3, 99; expansion of, 77n1, 78n5, 202
Sullivan, William, 229
Sun Tzu, on economic sanctions, 184
Swaziland, 108

Index 315

Sweezy, Paul M., 82
Syria: Lebanon and, 39n7, 203; U.S. and, 54, 204, 207

Takeyh and Gvosdev, 207–8
Talentino, Andrea, 11
Taliban, 9, 225
Taxes, 154, 200
Teeple, 87
Tenet, George J., 237–38
Terrorism: 9/11 attacks, 9, 224; absence as peace, 243; al-Qaeda's, 271–72; American public perceptions of war on, 258–60; causes of, 176, 244–49, 264–66, 274; civil liberty abuses in war on, 225, 229–32, 253; cost of efforts against, 255, 258; definition of, 265, 276n3; democracies not nurturing, 203, 245–47, 262, 264; democracy as cure for, 198, 262–63, 275; democratic peace theory applied to, 246–47, 260; democratization to counter, 103, 160, 202, 248–49, 272, 274; effectiveness of, 265; effectiveness of efforts against, 13, 245–46; efforts against, 1, 252–53, 271–72, 274; efforts against by democracies *vs.* autocracies, 220n2, 252–54, 259–60; fear of state power used for, 249–51; in French revolution, 262; in Jordan, 214–16; Jordan in war on, 214, 216; need for public support of efforts against, 257–60; in Northern Ireland, 266–68; responses to fear of, 9, 219, 229–32, 250–51; sponsors of, 55, 251; in Sri Lanka, 269–71; values in efforts against, 13, 254–57
Terrorist groups, 247, 265; American perceptions of, 259, 271; goals of, 248, 264–66, 269, 271–72, 275, 276n8; moving to democratic paths, 13, 247–48, 250–51, 267–68, 271, 273, 275; need for dialogue with, 270–72
"Third wave" of democratization, 97
Third World. *See also* Developing countries; specific countries: accommodation of nonliberal states in, 121–22, 130–31; communism's perceived aggressiveness in, 118–19, 121; interventions in, 122–23, 140n75; liberal foreign policy in, 119–21
Thucydides, 27, 40n11, 184
Timor-Leste, nation building in, 180

Torricelli, Robert, 234
Totalitarianism, 59n1
Trade, 2, 32, 35, 79, 124, 133. *See also* Economic sanctions; Economy, use of incentives; free, 127, 131; intervention to protect, 120–21; Jordan, 215–16; between liberal and nonliberal states, 117, 129–30, 136n48; nontariff barriers to, 88–89; preferred to conquest, 63, 73; relation to peace, 31, 58
Transnational historical materialists, 87–88
Transnational practices, in global systems theory, 87
Transnationalization, 87–94
Transparency: lack of, 104, 179; limited in war on terror, 230; needed to limit corruption, 176–77
Trevelyan, Charles, 276n5
Trilateral Commission, 85
Trimble, David, 267
Triple Alliance, 23–24
Trujillo, Rafael, 122
Truman, Harry, 136n48
Trust, lacking between liberal and nonliberal states, 116–18
Tunisia, liberalization in, 200, 202
Turkey, 47–48, 250
Turkmenistan, dictatorship in, 1

Uighurs, China *vs.*, 253
UN, 3, 8, 10
Unilateralism, in U.S. foreign policy, 9
United Arab Emirates, authoritarian regime, 244
United States. *See also* Democratization; Foreign policy, U.S.: accused of hypocrisy in democratization, 9, 57, 215, 219–20, 220n2; in cold war, 7, 103, 201, 203, 226–29; democracy in, 11–12, 74, 99, 144–48; economy of, 36, 95; fear of communism, 122–23, 203; hegemony of, 30, 36, 127–28; imperialism by, 4, 75, 121; Islam and, 201–2, 206–7, 271; oil dependency of, 12–13, 198, 221n5; power of, 8–9, 184, 223, 257; prestige of, 9–10, 53; reputation of, 1, 9, 223–25, 229–30, 241, 274; Soviets and, 8–9, 118–19; terrorism and, 1, 270–72; as terrorist target, 245–46, 265, 271–72; in WWI, 25
Unity, republican governments bringing, 33
Universal Declaration of Human Rights, UN, 10

Universal hospitality, right of, 120
Uzbekistan, Russian sanctions against, 186

Venezuela, resistance to structural adjustment policies in, 92
Vietnam War: effects of, 123, 147; opposition to, 12, 226–29, 232
Violence, 93, 194, 269; citizens of democracies less likely to use, 276n1, 276n2; in democratization, 162, 273; from economic sanctions, 188–89; militarized, 96–97; semi-democracies prone to, 180, 182

Walt, Stephen, 55
Waltz, Kenneth N., 5, 78n4
War: causes of, 41n22, 76; chronological listing of international, 24–25; cost of preparedness for, 70; declining incidence of, 58, 61, 72–73; definitions of, 5, 6; by democracies, 50–51; economic sanctions as attack, 189; effects of democracy on, 41n23, 202; effects on democracy, 61; Latin America and Africa's lack of involvement in international, 51; liberal, 23, 34, 39n7; likelihood of, 26, 58, 67; motives for, 27, 29, 42n32, 180, 264, 274; near-misses, 6–7; by new *vs.* established democracies, 4; obstacles to, 95, 264; preemptive, against rogue states, 4; separation of powers and, 154–55, 264
War aversion, 33–34, 180–81; citizens', 3, 264; democracy linked to, 11, 49–54
"War Message" (Wilson), 25, 43n38
War of 1812, 5–6
War on terror. *See* Terrorism
The War over Iraq (Kaplan and Kristol), 53–54
Washington, George, 8
Wealth, 91, 109, 225; in Africa, 101–3; government in retention *vs.* redistribution of, 68–69, 71; leaders' control of, 1, 102–3; redistribution of, 92–93, 125–27; requirements for retention of, 65–66; temptation to conflict over, 70–71
Weapons of mass destruction (WMD), 9, 55
West, 206. *See also* specific countries
West Bank, Second Intifada in, 214
Westernization, 49
White supremacist movements, 227
Wickramasinghe, Ranil, 269–70
Wilhelm II, 39n8
Wilson, Woodrow, 8, 48, 52, 142, 151; "War Message" of, 25, 43n38
Wolfowitz, Paul, 53–54, 273
Woodward, Bob, 53
Woolsey, R. James, 238
Workers' rights, 88–91, 194
World Bank, 88, 92, 211–13
World government, restriction of anarchy by, 67
World Social Forum (WSF), 92–93
World Trade Organization (WTO), 79, 87–89, 92
World War I, 6, 8, 63; liberal *vs.* illiberal states in, 23–25; war aversion's growth following, 49–50
World War II, 6, 36, 63, 88; American public arousal in, 257–59; forced democratization after, 48, 121; Roosevelt's "four freedoms" to follow, 8, 14n7

Yankelovich, Daniel, 224
Yemen, liberalization in, 200
Yom, Sean, 12
Yugoslavia, 50, 119, 136n48

Zahar, Marie-Joelle, 164–65
Zarqawi, Abu Musab al-, 247
Zawahiri, Ayman al-, 245–46
Zolberg, Aristide, 38n4

Index 317